W9-DHS-248

"One of the saddest lines in the world is, 'Oh come now—be realistic.' The best parts of this world were not fashioned by those who were realistic. They were fashioned by those who dared to look hard at their wishes and gave them horses to ride. *Wishcraft* has become one of the most popular books among those who want their lives to count for something. Barbara Sher is to be commended, for making hope practical."

Richard N. Bolles,
author of What Color Is Your Parachute?

"A sprightly, sensible book brimming with advice, suggestions, and examples."

Pittsburgh Press

"The most irreverent and refreshing self-help manual now on the market ...Feisty, funny, and down-to-earth, this book is bound to benefit all those who sense they may have temporarily lost track of their true goals."

New Age Magazine

"What makes Sher's philosophy strikingly different from other authors is her compelling belief that 'There is no strategic problem that cannot be solved'...Comprehensive and inviting....Eminently practical."

San Francisco Examiner and Chronicle

"Wise, compassionate, and pragmatic. Written by an expert for people of all ages who seriously want *that something* in life."

Theodore Isaac Rubin, M.D.

"Can really be of help....A most useful and enlightening book."

The Houston Post

Wishcraft

How to Get What You Really Want

BARBARA SHER

with Annie Gottlieb

BALLANTINE BOOKS · NEW YORK

Copyright © Barbara Sher 1979.

All rights reserved. Published in the United States by Ballantine Books, a division of Random House, Inc., New York, and simultaneously in Canada by Random House of Canada Limited, Toronto.

Library of Congress Catalog Card Number: 79-11711
ISBN 0-345-31100-0
This edition published by arrangement with Viking Press, New York.

Manufactured in the United States of America
First Ballantine Books Trade Edition: May 1983

10   9

To my mother,
who has always believed in me.

Acknowledgments

Because I tried to be a good person, fate dropped into my life just the people I needed to get my notions into a book: Rhoda Weyr, my agent; Annie Gottlieb, my collaborator; Amanda Vaill, my editor; and Paulette Lundquist, who did both her job and mine at the office. They are the best team anyone could ever wish for. Without them there would have been no book.

Five men belong here as well: John, who kept me going when the going got rough; Danny, Matthew, Freddy, who were always proud of me (and kept house—such as it was—for ten years); and my Dad, who showed me how to be a person who trusted herself and didn't quit. Without them, there would have been no Barbara.

—BARBARA SHER

Special thanks to my grandmothers, for the gift of words: Anne Preaskil Stern, who taught me the alphabet; the late Dorothy Kuh Gottlieb, who shared with me her passion for books.

And to Jacques Sandulescu, Margaret Webb, Gita, Harry and Jean Gottlieb, and J. Barnes and Mina Creech.

—ANNIE GOTTLIEB

Contents

Four

CRAFTING II: MOVING AND SHAKING

Introduction

This book is designed to make you a winner.

Not the Vince Lombardi, get-out-there-and-stomp-'em kind—unless that's really your heart's desire. But I don't believe it. I don't think most of us get real pleasure out of stomping the competition and ending up all alone on top of some mythical heap. That's just a booby prize we go after because nobody ever told us what winning *is*. I have my own definition, and it's a very simple, very radical one.

Winning to me means getting what you want. Not what your father and mother wanted for you, not what you think you can realistically get in this world, but what *you want*—your wish, your fantasy, your dream. You're a winner when you have a life you love, so that you wake up every morning excited about the day ahead and delighted to be doing what you're doing, even if you're sometimes a little nervous and scared.

Is that you? If it isn't, what would make it that way for you? What's your fondest dream? It might be to live in peace on your own five-acre farm, or to step out of a huge Rolls-Royce with flashbulbs popping; to take pictures of rhinoceroses in Africa, or become a vice president of the company where you now type and file; to adopt a child or make a movie . . . start your own accounting business or learn to play the piano . . . open a dinner theater or get your pilot's license. Your dream will be as individual as you are. But whatever it is—and whether it's grand or modest, fantastic or practical, far away as the moon or just around the corner—as of right now I want you to start taking it very, very seriously.

Contrary to what you may have been taught, there is nothing frivolous or superficial about what you want. It isn't a luxury that can wait until you've taken care of all the "serious" business of life. It's a necessity. *What you want is what you need.* Your dearest wish comes straight from your core, loaded with vital information about who you are and who you can become. You've got to cherish it. You've got to respect it. Above all, you've got to *have* it.

And you can.

Wait a minute. You've heard that before. If you're at all like me, the very words "You can do it!" are enough to set off a little alarm bell in your head. "The last time I fell for *that,* I broke every bone in my body. It's a tough world out there, and I'm not in such great shape in here. I don't think I'm up for any more of that positive-thinking stuff. Maybe *you* can do it. I happen to know from hard personal experience that I can't."

As the bruised veteran of every success book and program that ever promised me ten easy steps to self-esteem, self-discipline, will power, or a positive attitude, I know what I'm talking about when I say this book is different. I wrote it for people like me—people who were born without any of the virtues that made Horatio Alger great and who have given up all hope of ever developing them. Can you persevere? I can't. There is no diet of any kind, physical, emotional, or financial, that I haven't fallen off by Wednesday if I started it on Monday. Self-discipline? I jogged once—I think it was about four years ago. Self-confidence? I've walked out of success seminars bursting with it. It lasted three days. I'm an ace procrastinator; I love nothing better than to watch old movies on the Late Show when I'm supposed to be doing something important. My positive attitudes are invariably followed by gloomy slumps. As a well-meaning but tactless friend once said to me, "Barbara, if you can make it, anyone can."

And I did.

I landed in New York City eleven years ago, divorced and penniless, with two small children to support and a B.A. in anthropology. (I hope you're chuckling, because it means you know exactly what that's worth.) We had to go on welfare until I found a job. But luckily, I found one I loved, working with people, not with paper. Over the next ten years I started and ran two very successful businesses of my own, wrote two books and the training manual for my seminars, and raised those two boys up healthy and sweet. (I lost twenty pounds, too. And I even quit smoking. Twice.) And all this without the slightest noticeable self-improvement. I still can't stick to things. I still have a rotten attitude a lot of the time. But I made it—on my own terms—and I love my life even on the days when I hate myself. By my own definition, I am a winner. And that means you can be, too.

How?

I have the kind of unholy respect for that little three-letter word that someone who's been starving has for bread. If, ten years ago, some kind soul had given me hard information on how to turn my dreams into realities, instead of just assuring me blandly that it could be done, it would have saved me an incredible amount of time and anguish. As long as I kept trying to believe in myself and reform all my bad habits, I kept crashing—and blaming myself. It wasn't until I gave up on ever fixing *me* and tried to improvise a set of aids that would work for me anyway (because I wasn't going to go to my grave without getting what I wanted, whether I deserved it or not) that I stumbled on the real secret behind the scenes of all successful people's lives. It's not superhero genes and a jaw of steel, like the myths say. It's something much simpler. It's know-how and support.

To start creating the life you want, you don't need mantras, self-hypnosis, a character-building program, or a new toothpaste. You do need practical techniques for problem-solving, planning, and getting your hands on materials, skills, information, and contacts. (See Chapters 6, 7, and 8 on "Plotting the Path to Your Goal.") You need commonsense strategies for coping with human feelings and foibles that aren't going to go away, like fear, depression, and laziness. (See Chapter 5, "Hard Times, or The Power of Negative Thinking," and Chapter 9, "Winning Through Timidation.") And you need ways of riding out the temporary emotional storms your life changes can cause in your closest relationships—while still getting the extra emotional support you need for risk-taking. (See Chapter 10, "Don't-Do-It-Yourself.")

That's the "craft" part of *Wishcraft*. It is based on the needs and potentialities of human beings as we are, not as we ought to be. I had to figure it all out for myself, by trial and error. I don't think you should have to do it the hard way. So I'm giving you the results of my experiment: techniques already tested by thousands of women and men who have used them in Success Teams to bring their dreams to life—from horse ranches to hand bookbinding, from choral singing to city planning, from writing children's books to selling blue-chip stocks. The whole second half of this book is a detailed answer to the question, "How?" All I'm going to tell you right now is that you won't have to change yourself because, one, it can't be done, and two, you're fine the way you are. With nothing more than pencil and paper, your imagination, your family and your friends, you're going to create a life-support system that will do much of the hard work for you and free you to function at your best.

But first, of course, you have to know what you want.

The first half of this book is all about wishing. Unlike the skills for bringing dreams into actuality, which are nuts-and-bolts skills like engineering or carpentry, wishing doesn't have to be learned. It's inborn in human beings the way flying is in birds. For your desirous imagination to take wing, nothing—no knowledge—has to be added to you. But it's very likely that something *does* have to be taken away: the spellbinding cultural curse that says, "It can't be done," and the heavy weight of discouragement you may be carrying if you've tried for your dreams before and failed. Because so many of us never were told how to make our dreams happen, after a few tries we assumed it was impossible or horribly difficult. So we adjusted our sights downward and settled for what we thought we could get. But it's a funny thing: the craft of WISHCRAFT won't really work for you unless you bring your highest hopes and deepest dreams to it. Because while technique and strategy are the "how" of winning, wishing is the all-important "why"—the power source that makes all that machinery run.

Our language is full of phrases that tell us wishing is unrealistic and impotent: "Wishing won't make it so." "She wants the moon." "Idle fantasy." "He's an incurable dreamer." That's nonsense. Wishing and dreaming are the beginning of all human endeavor. Look—mankind wanted the moon for thousands of years, and in the twentieth century we got there. That's what *wishing plus technique* can do: it can change reality. It's true that wishing *alone* won't make it so. Like steam without an engine, it just dissipates. But technique without desire is like a cold and empty engine: it won't go. If you've ever found it difficult to do things, stop and consider what you've been finding it difficult to do: typing? digging ditches? mopping floors? You can do them if you have to, but it's awfully hard to get your heart into any of them as a lifetime goal.

There are plenty of hard-working, responsible men and women in our society who do know *how* to get things done but have never felt free to explore themselves and find out *what* they want to do. If you are one of them, the first half of this book will be a revelation. It will show you how and why you may have lost touch with your dreams, and it will give you simple, enjoyable exercises for rediscovering them. And then it will help you shape a real-world goal out of what you love. So far from being "impractical" or "irresponsible," doing what's closest to your heart is like striking oil: you tap into a surge of energy that will propel you to the heights of success.

If, on the other hand, you've picked up this book already knowing what you want and just looking for clear instructions on how to get it, you may be tempted to skip to the "craft" part. Take the time to read "wish" anyway. It will help you define your goals more clearly than you ever have before—which is half the battle toward getting them—and I promise that it will greatly enrich your sense of what's possible in one human lifetime.

The well-known psychotherapist Rollo May once wrote a book called *Love and Will.* This book is about *love and skill*—the two vital ingredients of real success. Here's to yours.

One

The Care and Feeding of Human Genius

–1–
Who Do You Think You Are?

Who do you think you are?

That's a very interesting question. Or it would be, if the people who asked it when we were young had really wanted a thoughtful answer. Unfortunately, they weren't looking for an answer at all. They already had the answers. This is what they were saying:

"Who do you think you are, Sarah Bernhardt? Take that shawl off this minute and finish the dishes." *Or:*

"Who do you think you are, Charles Darwin? Get that disgusting turtle off my dining room table and do your arithmetic." *Or:*

"You—an astronaut? A scientist like Madame Curie? A movie star? Who do you think you are?"

Does that sound familiar? Most of us heard that question at some time during our growing up—usually at the vulnerable moment when we ventured some dream, ambition, or opinion close to our hearts. But imagine those words being spoken in a curious, open, wondering tone of voice, for once—not in that scalding tone of scorn we've all had burned into our brains.

I'd like to invite you to try a simple experiment. I'm going to ask you that question again, only this time *try hearing it as a real question.* Who do you think you are?

EXERCISE 1: Who Do You Think You Are?

Take a blank sheet of paper (we're going to be using a lot of blank paper in this book—it's the staff of life) and, in a few sentences to half a page, answer the question: "Who do you think you are?" I am genuinely interested in the answer. What do you consider the four or five most important characteristics that define your identity? There are no right or wrong answers, and there's only one rule: don't think too long or hard. Put down the first and surest things that come to mind: "This is me."

Now take a look at your answer. There's a better than 50 percent chance that you said something like this:

"I'm 28, Catholic, single, a secretary in an electronics firm, live in Buffalo." *Or:*

"I'm 5'10", 175 pounds, black hair, brown eyes, Italian, former running back, vote Democratic, Vietnam veteran, appliance salesman." *Or:*

"I'm a former teacher, married to a man I love, an M.D. in internal medicine, and I'm the mother of three terrific kids: Marty, 13, Jimmy, 8, and Elise, 5 1/2." *Or:*

"I'm black, born in Detroit, oldest of five kids. My father worked for GM. B.A. from Wayne State. Computer programmer. Marrying my high school sweetheart next summer."

All variants of "This is what I do for a living, here's where I live, I'm married, not married, I make money, I don't, I'm so-and-so's mother, I'm Episcopalian, I'm in school"—the kinds of things we usually tell each other when we meet. When we've exchanged these vital statistics, geographical and occupational details, we feel we've declared our identities and begun to get to know each other.

Well, we're wrong.

There's no question that these things have been important in our lives. In fact, they have usually shaped our lives. They are experience, history, role, relationship, livelihood, skill, survival. Some of them are choices. Some, including many we'd call choices, are compromises. Some are accidents.

None of them is your identity.

This may surprise you, but if I were sitting down with you to help you choose a goal and design a life individually tailored for you, I would not ask you for any of this information. I would not want to know what you do for a living, unless you were really excited by your job. I would not want to know any of the things you put in a resume—your background, your experience, your skills. All too often we are skilled in things we never really chose, things we have had to do—like typing or scrubbing floors (those were my skills)—not things we love.

When it comes to picking out what you'll do with energy and joy, what you can be a smashing success at, your skills are not only unimportant—they can get in the way, unless you assign them to a strictly secondary role. For the moment, I'd like you just to forget about them.

What?

That's right. And just for now, I'd like you to forget your job (unless you love it), your family (even though you love them), your responsibilities, your education, all the things that make up your "reality" and your "identity." Don't worry. They won't go away. I know they are important to you. Some of them are necessary and dear to you. But they are not you. And right now the focus is on *you.*

What I'm interested in is *what you love.*

You may or may not be able to say what that is. If you can, it may be your work, or a hobby, or a sport, or a pastime like going to the movies, or something you've always loved reading about, or a subject you wish you had studied in school, or just something that gives off a special whiff of fascination for you whenever it goes by, even though you know very little about it.

There may very well be several things you feel that way about. Whatever they are—guitar music, bridges, bird-watching, sewing, the stock market, the history of India—there is a very, very good reason why you love them. Each one is a clue to something inside you: *a talent, an ability, a way of seeing the world that is uniquely yours.* You may not know you have it. You may have a case of amnesia about it. That amnesia can be so total that you're not even sure any more what you love. And yet, *that is you!*

That is your identity, your core.

It is something more. Because "who you are" isn't passive or static or unchanging. It is a vital design, as one philosopher put it, that needs to unfold and express itself through the medium of your whole life. And so that unique pattern of talents and gifts that lies hidden in the things you love is also the map to your own life path.

Did you ever go on a treasure hunt when you were a child, or read Poe's "The Gold Bug"? Then you know that the first thing you have to do before you can find the treasure is find the map. It may be hidden, it may be torn in half, or in a million pieces, but your first job is to find it and put the fragments back together, like a jigsaw puzzle. That's what we're going to be doing for you in the first section of this book.

The clues to your life path are not lost. They are just scattered and hidden—some of them right under your nose, in plain sight. They need to be gathered together and carefully examined before you can begin to know how to design a life that truly fits *you*, a life that will make you feel like jumping out of bed in the morning to meet the world, a little scared at times, maybe, but fully alive.

If you are low on energy, if you need a lot of sleep and feel like you're always dragging yourself around at half throttle, it may not be because you need vitamins or have low blood sugar. It may be because you have not found your purpose in life. You will recognize your own path when you come upon it, because you will suddenly have all the energy and imagination you will ever need.

This is part of the secret of all genuinely successful people: they have found their paths. They also happen to have some very special skills for making their visions come true in reality. That is very important, and it's the purpose of the second part of this book to teach you those skills. But first you must liberate your own ingenuity and drive, and the only way to do that is to discover your own path. It is the only path that will ever truly absorb you. And the treasure at the end is success.

Right now I'd like you to do something symbolic. Take that piece of paper on which you answered the question, "Who do you think you are?" Glance through it one more time. Now *crumple it up and throw it in the wastebasket.*

This is the only piece of paper I'm going to ask you to do that with, and as I said, you'll have occasion to write on quite a few sheets of paper as we go along. Alternatively, you might want to save this one as a souvenir. It will serve nicely as the first in a pair of "Before and After" pictures. Call it the souvenir of a misconception. Because if you're like most of us, you are not who you think you are.

Who are you really?

You've forgotten—but you knew once—when you were a very small child. So that's the place to start our search for the lost treasure map of your talents: in the first five precious and mysterious years of your life—the greatest learning period you ever had.

I'll tell you one thing about who you were then.

You were a genius.

YOUR ORIGINAL GENIUS

Now you're probably laughing, but I'm serious. I don't care what you've accomplished in your life or what your I.Q. is—you were born with your own unique kind of genius. And I mean that in the fullest sense of the word. Not genius with a small 'g' as opposed to Albert Einstein. Big "G" genius, *like* Albert Einstein.

We confer the honorific title "genius" only on those very rare people who we believe were born with a mysterious something extra: great brilliance, original vision, incredible determination. And we believe that "something extra" cannot help but express itself with such force that it overpowers the most difficult circumstances. Look at Mozart. Born overflowing with music. Look at Picasso—another genius, the sculptor Louise Nevelson, says Picasso was "drawing like an angel in the crib." Those are geniuses, not you and I. Or so the standard reasoning goes.

OK, let's take the three characteristics I named as defining genius—great brilliance, original vision, incredible determination—and see whether you had them when you were 2 years old.

"Great brilliance" is a little hard to define. We've found out now that we can't test I.Q. very reliably after all. But even if we could, it only measures one very narrow range of knowing and doing. So we'd better call "great brilliance" a special case of "original vision": intellectual vision, as opposed to the artistic or musical kind, or a dozen other kinds of vision we have or haven't discovered yet: political, emotional, athletic, humanitarian . . . you name it.

You had original vision when you were 2 years old. You may not remember, but that's because it's always difficult to remember things we don't have words for. The fact is, in those early years you were seeing the world in such an original way that no one around you could give you the words for it. And if you found the words for it, usually no one could understand them!

If you've ever listened to a very small child—if you're a mother, for instance—you know that they say some pretty strange and amazing things. That is because they are trying to tell us what the world looks like, seen for the first time, from a point of view that has never existed before! Great poets are people who have held on to that ability to see things new and say what they see, but we all had it once. You had it, when you were 2. You were very busy when you were 2. You were not only reinventing the English language for your own purposes, you were, as a physicist friend of mine told me, doing original research into the nature of the universe.

So you had that: original vision. A new way of seeing the world that was all your own.

You also had "incredible determination."

You knew perfectly well what you loved and what you wanted. And you went after it without the slightest hesitation or self-doubt. If you saw a cookie on the table, you didn't think "Can I get it? Do I deserve it? Will I make a fool of myself? Am I procrastinating again?" You thought, *Cookie.* And you cried, you wheedled, you crawled, you climbed, you piled boxes up on the floor, you did everything you could think of to get that cookie. If you didn't get it, you made a fuss, took a nap, and changed the subject. And it didn't stop you in the least from going right for the next wonderful thing you saw.

Notice that you don't need "self-confidence" when you're like that. The word has no meaning. You're not even aware of yourself. You're completely focused on the thing you're after.

Those "rare" and "special" qualities we think distinguish geniuses from all the rest of us? You had them. I had them.

Where did they go?

As long as you were too young to listen to reason or to be trained to do anything "useful," you had a marvelous freedom to be who you were. By the time you were 5 or 6, if not even sooner, the precious right to make choices based on your own wishes began to be taken away. As soon as you were old enough to control yourself and sit still in school, the honeymoon was over.

You have probably forgotten what it was like to walk into the first grade. You'd just had five years of solid experiences—seeing things; knowing things; feeling, hating, and loving things. But schools are not designed to learn from you; they are designed to teach you. Inadvertently, they probably gave the impression that your knowledge, tastes, opinions were of zero value.

Just by ignoring who you were, they cancelled the whole rich inner world you had brought in with you. All they saw was a blank board that they were going to fill up with everything worth knowing. If it was important to you to talk to your best friend, or daydream, or draw, and they were doing multiplication tables, you got punished. If you happened to know how to talk to plants and plants talked back to you, they didn't ask you, "Do you want to learn how to spell, or did you have something else in mind?" They said, "Get away from the plants and let's see how fast you can learn the alphabet."

If you talked to plants, or if you talked to dogs, or if you made sculptures out of mud, or if you were going to be a movie star or ice skate to Eskimo land, you understood very quickly that that didn't count for much. And so, little by little, you forgot it. You developed amnesia about it. *Now* if you walked out into the world and somebody asked, "What are you good at?" you could easily say, "Nothing," meaning "Nothing that anyone would consider important." Or you might say, "Well, I'm good at math," or "I can type." It would never occur to you to say, "I love plants. I can remember all their names, and I think I understand what makes them happy."

All the people we call "geniuses" are men and women who somehow escaped having to put that curious, wondering child in themselves to sleep. Instead, they devoted their lives to equipping that child with the tools and skills it needed to do its playing on an adult level. Albert Einstein was playing, you know. He was able to make great discoveries precisely because he kept alive the originality and delight of a small child exploring its universe for the first time.

The first thing you will need to do is reawaken those child qualities in yourself. So let's go back and try to get a look at the genius you were. That is the first important clue to your life design—to the discovery of what you'll be happiest doing and what you'll be best at.

It's true that original achievements, great works of art, and the kinds of lives that are works of art almost always have their roots in childhood. Ask any famous woman or man, and you will probably find that they remember having a very clear sense of what they were meant to do at a very early age. A *Redbook* magazine article about singer Linda

Ronstadt says that "Her first memory is of saying to her parents, 'Play me some music.' . . . She was four years old and singing with them one evening when she began to harmonize. Her father said, 'You aren't singing the melody.' She said, 'I know.' "* And the sculptor Louise Nevelson, in her memoir *Dawns & Dusks,* remembers, "From earliest, earliest childhood I knew I was going to be an artist. I *felt* like an artist. . . . I drew in childhood, and went on painting daily. . . . As a young child I could go into a room and remember everything I saw. I'd take one glance and know everything I saw. That's a visual mind."†

The only real difference between these people and you is that there is an unbroken continuity between the children they were and the adults they have become. We're going to go to work to reestablish that continuity for you. But first we need to know: who was that child? What did she or he love? The design of your life path is right there in miniature, like the genes in a seed that say it's going to become a tomato plant, a palm tree, or a rose. So I'd like you to think back to your childhood, and see how much you can remember that might point to your own special kind of genius.

Or, since that word still sounds presumptuous to our ears, I've got an even better name for it. Let's call it your *original self.* And I mean that in both senses of the word "original": "there from the beginning" and "unique, new, never seen in the world before."

EXERCISE 2: Your Original Self

Let your mind wander back through your childhood memories—especially the private, special times when you were allowed to play or daydream or do whatever you wanted to do. Now, on a fresh sheet of paper, try to answer these questions:

What especially attracted and fascinated you when you were a child?

What sense—sight, hearing, touch—did you live most through, or did you enjoy them all equally?

What did you love to do, or to daydream about, no matter how "silly" or unimportant it may seem to you now? What were the secret

---

*Elizabeth Kaye, "Linda Ronstadt: Why Is She the Queen of Lonely?" *Redbook* 152 (February 1979): 130.

†Louise Nevelson, *Dawns & Dusks.* Taped conversations with Diana MacKown. (New York: Charles Scribner's Sons, 1976), pp. 1, 13, 14.

fantasies and games that you never told anybody about?

Does it feel like there's still a part of you that loves those things?

What talents or abilities might those early interests and dreams point to?

Marcia, 32, answered this question very poignantly:

"I actually went back to what I'd experienced in the first five years of my life. Since then it's been downhill. This exercise was very emotional for me. I've had a lot of therapy, but I never realized my first five years were so good."

Here are some other answers:

Ellen, 54: "I remember I had this thing about trees. I used to stand and stare up at them and put my arms around their trunks. I think I knew what it felt like to be one."

John, 35: "I was nutty about rhythm. I was always patting out private little riffs on the dinner table. Nobody could eat their dinner."

Bill, 44: "I loved color. I know I was drawing from the time I was old enough to clutch a crayon. I covered sheets of paper, the pages of books, and the wall next to my bed with brightly-colored scribbles."

Anna, 29: "This will sound ridiculous, but there was a commercial on TV in the Midwest for a beer called Hamms that was made in Minnesota. They had this little song—I can still remember the words and the tune: 'From the land of sky-blue waters / From the land of pines, lofty balsams / Comes the beer refreshing / Hamms, the beer refreshing.' It had a haunting sound and Indian tomtoms and they showed a lake sparkling in the moonlight. Well . . . at night in bed I used to put my head under the covers and pretend I was an Indian princess in the Land of Sky-Blue Waters."

If you didn't have a goal when you started this book, congratulations. You may not believe it, but you have just taken your first step toward choosing one.

Ellen's youngest daughter just left for college, and Ellen is looking for a career. She could have been—and still could be—a botanist, a forester, a gardener, a poet or a painter, or even a psychotherapist.

John is a skilled machinist. He doesn't know much about music, but he could have been—and still could be—a fine jazz drummer or dancer.

Bill is a lawyer, like his father. He makes a good living and he likes his work OK—but he has a gifted artist or interior decorator hiding inside just waiting to be discovered.

Anna is an editorial secretary in a publishing house. She had, and still has, the kind of imagination it takes to be a writer or film director or an editor-in-chief.

What was your answer? What does it tell you about what you want and what you could be good at?

Now comes the real question.

How was Albert Einstein able to become Albert Einstein, while Marcia, Ellen, John, Bill, and Anna—and maybe you—have not made the fullest use of your talents?

If we really did all come into the world with full-sized helpings of originality and drive, how do you explain Albert Einstein? Mary Cassatt? Luther Burbank? Margaret Mead? They had to make it through the first grade. They had to grow up and pay the rent. How did they manage to keep their treasure maps intact? They must have had some mysterious quality—strength of character, perseverance, self-confidence, self-discipline, belief in themselves, even an instability verging on madness—something that puts those "special" people in a separate category from you and me.

It's true. The "geniuses," the truly successful, the self-fulfilled, did have something we did not. But there is nothing the least bit mysterious about it. It's not something you have to be born with, nor is it a character virtue you must develop over years of lonely struggle. I'll tell you exactly what Albert Einstein got.

Soil and air and water and sun.

ENVIRONMENT

If a seed is given good soil and plenty of water and sun, it doesn't have to try to unfold. It doesn't need self-confidence or self-discipline or perseverance. It just unfolds. As a matter of fact, it can't help unfolding.

If a seed has to grow with a rock on top of it, or in deep shade, or without enough water, it won't unfold into a healthy full-sized plant. It will try—hard—because the drive to become what you are meant to be is incredibly powerful. But at best it will become a sort of ghost of what it could be: pale, undersized, drooping.

In a way, that's what most of us are.

I am talking about nurture, nourishment, care. I am saying that the difference between a genius and you and me is in our environment—and that means our first environment, our childhood family.

In essence, what Albert Einstein got was this:

Somebody—I don't know who, his mother, his father, his grandfather, his uncle—somebody told him it was fine for him to do whatever he wanted to do. They saw something in him, something stubborn, shy, special, and they respected and cherished it. And I wouldn't be at all surprised to learn that somebody gave him a compass, a gyroscope, some books, and a conspiratorial grin, and then let him alone.

It's that simple. And that rare.

It's hard for us to believe in ourselves if no one has ever believed in us, and it is almost impossible for us to stick to our own vision in the face of overwhelming discouragement. And we cannot so much as build a bookshelf if no one ever told us we could do it, gave us the materials, and showed us how. That's our nature. That's how we are.

In the age of ecology, we ourselves are the only creatures we would ever expect to flourish in an environment that does not give us what we need! We wouldn't order a spider to spin an exquisite web in empty space, or a seed to sprout on a bare desk top. And yet that is exactly what we have been demanding of ourselves.

As a result, most of us are not aware that we didn't grow up in an environment that nurtured genius. We just think *we* aren't geniuses, and blame heredity or our own lack of character for the spot we're in. Whatever was amiss with the environment we grew up in, we figure "geniuses" had it just as bad or worse. *They* just had the mysterious fortitude to overcome it. We don't see that grandmother or special teacher who was there with the right kind of love and help at the right moment. We wouldn't recognize the key features of a nurturing environment if we fell over them.

In the next chapter, I'm going to show you what that environment really is, and just how it differs from the one most of us grew up in. And then I am going to demonstrate to you that all genuinely successful people—the ones who love their lives—have had that environment . . . or some parts of it . . . or they've figured out how to create it for themselves.

And then we are going to start creating it for you.

– 2 –
The Environment That Creates Winners

I am going to ask you some questions now about the family you grew up in.

If your answer to all or most of these questions is "Yes," congratulations. I'm jealous. You are one of the rare and lucky ones. You had the great good fortune to be raised in *the environment that creates winners* —the optimum environment for the growth and flourishing of human beings.

The fact is that very few of us were lucky enough to grow up in such an environment. I certainly wasn't. It wasn't our parents' fault. They weren't raised in that kind of environment either, and they couldn't have had any idea how to create one. Given their own upbringing, it's moving that most of them still managed to provide us with at least one or two features of that environment—because they loved us.

Every "Yes" you can answer to one of these questions is something inside you that you can build on—the beginning of a bridge between your child genius and its full adult expression. For every "No," I'll invite you to give a little thought to how your life could have been different if you'd been able to answer "Yes." Even if you answer every one of these questions "No," don't despair. With the help of this book, you will be able to build that bridge now.

Here goes.

In your family, when you were growing up:

1. Were you treated as though you had a unique kind of genius that was loved and respected?

I hope you are lucky enough to be able to answer "Yes" to this one. Unfortunately, if you are like many of us, you not only weren't treated as if you were precious and special, but if you let it slip that *you* thought you were pretty hot stuff, you probably got cooled down fast.

The sad thing is, our parents sometimes did this because they loved us, and they wanted to protect us from the kinds of disappointment and humiliation they had suffered. A lot of them went out there with nothing on their side but their own frail, brave conviction of specialness, and they got clobbered. And they figured maybe if they cut our expectations down to size for us—nipped them in the bud, so to speak—we could avoid that pain. Sort of a bitter way of saying, "Don't try that, honey, you'll only get hurt. Believe me. I've been out there. I've tried."

Of course, sometimes there was a darker motive. Jealousy. Your parents may never have felt that they had the right, much less the opportunity, to get what they wanted out of life. Let's face it. How many of our mothers really had a chance to do anything but keep house, raise babies, and maybe work to supplement the family income? How many of our fathers really got the chance to explore their own talents and interests? Most of them had to start earning a living and supporting a family when their own lives had hardly begun. My parents were like that. If yours were, how do you imagine they felt when you came along? Proud. Delighted. Hopeful. But then you began to grow . . . and demand . . . and suddenly they saw blooming in you all the qualities they'd had to squelch in themselves: open, shameless wanting; free fantasy; originality; ambition; pride. They saw you grabbing the limelight when they had never gotten enough of it. They had learned at great inner cost to be modest and self-sacrificing and resigned—often for your sake—and they said, "*I* learned that lesson. You'll learn it too."

As very small children, we sense that message. We'd rather forget our destiny than risk hurting or angering the person whose love is life itself to us.

So perhaps, whenever that stubborn "special" feeling does raise its head, it may be immediately followed by a wave of shame and an automatic little tape recording that says "Who do I think I am?" If that happens to you, it's a sure sign that your answer to Question Number 1 was "No."

Think about it: how might you and your life have been different if you had been treated differently? Where might you be today?

2. *Were you told that you could do and be anything you wanted—and that you'd be loved and admired no matter what it was?*

This is nothing more than love and respect in action. To truly cherish someone's genius is to give it complete freedom to choose its own mode of expression—and then to support and honor that choice.

This means that when you came home from school and said, "I've decided I'm going to be a doctor when I grow up," or "I'd sure like to be a movie star," or "I want to be a clown in the circus," your parents said with real enthusiasm, "That sounds great! I think you'd be really good at it."

Instead, what most of us heard was something like this:

"A doctor? Well, dear, you could become a nurse." Or:

"If it was so easy to be a movie star, everybody would be doing it. Stop daydreaming and start thinking about the kind of grades you'll need to get into college." Or:

"Ugh, what a disgusting idea. The circus is so dirty."

And so on.

This is where both our present behavior and our future ambitions began to be shaped to fit our parents' ideas about what it was possible and proper for us to be, even if that was very different from what we really were and yearned to become. A steelworker's son born to be a brilliant scholar may be in trouble. So may a lawyer's daughter who dreams of being a jockey. Many families believe that certain occupations are either "beyond us" or "beneath us," and they pass these preconceptions on to the child, so that the range of available possibilities is restricted from the start.

Of course, one of the most powerful sets of shaping preconceptions is, "What is a boy?" and "What is a girl?"

If you're a man, when you were growing up I'll bet there was one pair of words you never heard set up against each other with regard to you and your life, and that is *selfless* and *selfish.* These words are for women. Oh, from time to time your mother may have told you you were selfish, but she didn't really mean it. After all, you were different from her. You were supposed to be so absorbed in your own activities that you were more or less oblivious to the state of order or disorder in your room and the subtle mood changes of the people around you. You got love for being precisely that way—active and self-absorbed and good at things. (Good at *what* things is the rub, but I'll get back to that in a moment.)

If you were a little girl, you probably weren't told you were selfish unless you tried to do something you wanted to do that wasn't for anybody but you. And then—especially if you got so wrapped up in it that you forgot to be nice to your baby brother or to set the table—it was made swiftly clear to you that you lacked the quality that makes for lovable people and you'd better shape up.

Women are raised for love. That is, we have been raised to give it in order to get it. Our upbringing trained us to nurture other people. We're supposed to be good to our children so that they can grow up and realize themselves. We're supposed to back up our husbands so that they feel free to go out and realize themselves. In other words, the flowers are to grow, and guess what that makes us? Fertilizer—to put it politely. That's how most of us were taught we would get love—not by being flowers ourselves. If we dared to flower—to be active and self-absorbed and good at things—nobody would feed our roots, and we would die. At least, that's how it felt.

The psychologist Abraham Maslow has written that all human beings have a *hierarchy of needs.* Our more basic needs have to be fulfilled before we can even start thinking about the higher ones. First come food and shelter—the physical, survival needs. Then come the emotional needs—love for ourselves as we really are and a sense of belonging. Only when all those needs are fulfilled do we really feel secure enough to seek self-realization. Love is such a fundamental need that people go where the love goes just the way the roots of a plant turn toward water and the leaves turn toward light. Our culture trains us to take certain roles by putting the love in that direction—and we just grow that way! And the fact is that in our culture, until very recently, most men have gotten love for realizing themselves; most women have gotten it for helping other people realize themselves.

That means a man can—if he's lucky—fulfill his whole hierarchy of needs with the same actions. Did you ever hear of a little boy who thought he was going to have to make a choice between a career and a wife?! On the contrary, the better he is in his career, the better the wife he's able to get! If you were a little girl, however, somewhere in the back of your mind you probably knew that that was one of the choices you were going to have to make. You could go ahead and be a success, sure, but you'd be loved just about as much as Joan Crawford was in all those movies, which is not at all. No wonder so many women feel divided about success if not downright terrified of it! We're being forced to choose between two of our own human needs—a higher one, self-realization, and a more basic one, love. And that's an impossible choice.

Little girls are being brought up differently these days. But if you were born before, say, 1968—and it's safe to say that covers almost every reader of this book—chances are you bear at least some of these marks of a nice old-fashioned girlhood:

1. You find it difficult to think in terms of what *you* want—to be, to do, to have, to see—because you've never been encouraged to think that way.
2. Even if you've managed to keep your dreams alive, you may have trouble taking them seriously, because you've never been taken seriously. Your talents and interests were considered, at best, qualities that would make you more attractive to a man, provided you didn't develop them seriously enough to threaten him!
3. You don't know how to ask for help in getting what you want, because you feel you're supposed to give help, not get it.
4. Even if you can ask for help, you don't know how to put human resources to work for you in an effective, task-oriented way. Most women are personality-oriented. We are hypersensitive to personalities and feelings, and we tend to get bogged down in them.
5. By far the most devastating: you are afraid that if you dare to go after what you want, you'll be all alone, because that's selfish—and selfish means alone.

Take heart. We'll be talking about all these problems—and finding real solutions for them—as this book goes along.

Men have other problems.

If you are a man, the odds are that you were taken seriously—maybe too seriously. You knew very early that you were going to be expected to earn your living when you grew up . . . but your parents may have had some very definite ideas about just how you should earn that living.

They wanted you to be a success, all right—their kind of success. You had to get into a good college or make the Law Review, or take over the family business. You certainly had to do something "masculine." Whether your family's idea of a man was a professor, a company president, or a longshoreman, it's likely to have been rather clearly defined, if not rigid. And your childhood play and daydreams were expected to conform to that idea. If you were a boy who happened to like to read a lot, or play the piano, or play with dolls (dolls are toy humans and little boys, being human, are often interested in them), what did you do if your dad got a sick look in his eyes? You put down your book or doll and picked up your baseball glove and went out and threw a few with him. As a result, as early as the age of five you may already have had a full-blown case of amnesia about what *your* unique talents and interests were. I suspect that there are a lot of poets and chefs and dancers walking around out there disguised as lawyers, even from themselves.

Whether you're a man or a woman, if your answer to question No. 2 was "No," think about it: how might you and your life have been different if you had been lovingly told that the whole world of human possibilities was open to you to take your pick? Where might you be today?

3. Were you given real help and encouragement in finding out what *you wanted to do—and* how *to do it?*

This one is terribly important. Because without it, even if you *did* get No. 1 and No. 2, they may not have been much use to you. In fact, they may have done you more harm than good. Ask those of us who were told we could be whatever we wanted—and then weren't told how.

What this means is that if you said, "You know, I'd really love to be a scientist," or if you spent your free time drawing or taking things apart to see how they worked, your parents noticed your interest, gently encouraged it, and helped you feed it by putting all kinds of resources at your disposal: books, materials, people. They helped you get a library card and showed you where the science shelf was. They helped you set up a terrarium, or they gave you a microscope or a good set of pastels for your birthday. They introduced you to a scientist or an art teacher or an inventor or a mechanic who was actually doing something that clicked with your interests and was happy to let you watch—and teach you how.

In other words, they used their adult knowledge of the world to show you some of the wonderful things that could be done—and were being done—by people like you.

Many parents, with the best will in the world, didn't do this because they thought it would be "pushing" you. Or it may have been a sneaky Puritan test of your motivation: if you really cared, you'd have the ingenuity and the guts to go find out for yourself. But when you're 5 years old, or 8 years old, how are you going to know that there are pastel chalks in all the colors of the earth and sky unless somebody shows them to you? When you're 10, or 12, you take a look at the awesome competence of a grown-up dancer or doctor or carpenter, and you're just not going to see how you'll ever make it—unless someone takes the trouble to tell you that she or he started at the beginning, like you, with nothing but curiosity and love. Talent is inborn. Know-how is acquired. And you don't acquire it out of the air; you acquire it from the people who've got it. If your family was confident and aware enough to help you get in touch with even a small part of the big and thrilling world of grown-up play—the world of skills and activities and ideas— you're in luck.

Relatively few women have gotten this kind of help, and most of them come from wealthy or accomplished families, like Marya Mannes and Margaret Mead. More men got it because it's considered important for a boy to develop skills and interests. But on the other hand, he may also be expected to do it all by himself. Now here's a very interesting question:

If you did get No. 1 and No. 2, but not No. 3, did you blame yourself for not becoming all they said you could become?

I'll bet at least once, and probably eleven times, you've pulled yourself together, decided you could really make it, walked out the front door, and then not had the slightest idea where to go next. Of course not! *Nobody ever told you.* But instead of walking up to somebody and saying, "Excuse me, but where do I go next?" you said to yourself, "Here I've been secretly thinking I was something special. It's not true. I'd better be content with just typing 80 words per minute and being a good person." And you went back in the house and sat down, glad that nobody had seen you. That lasted maybe a year or two, until the dream-hunger rose up again and you tried again and wound up standing on that same sidewalk, thinking, "That's twice. That proves I'm a dummy." And all because nobody ever told you that you're supposed to walk out that door ignorant, and that you are then entitled to get all the information, instruction, help, and advice you need!

If your answer to No. 3 was "No," think about it: how might you and your life be different if you had been helped to decide *what* you wanted to do—and then helped to learn *how* to do it? Where might you be today?

4. Were you encouraged to explore all your own talents and interests, even if they changed from day to day?

That means when you came in at the age of 7 and said, "Mama, I am going to be a movie star," she said, "You know, you might be good at that." Then she got out the Super-8, let you put on her makeup, took a movie of you, let you see it, and showed you and your best friend how to use the camera. And two days or two months later, when you announced, "I've given up my career as an actress. I've decided to be a fireman and rescue people," she said, "Sounds good to me. Want to go over to the firehouse and look at the engines?"

The key word is *explore.* Childhood is a great time for trying out all the myriad possibilities of your being. (Adulthood isn't a bad time for doing that, either, as you'll find out as we go along.) And taking a child's talents and interests "seriously" does not mean expecting a 7-year-old to choose her lifetime career.

If your answer to No. 4 is "No," how do you think your life might be different today if you'd been encouraged to explore *all* your talents and interests? Because most of us do have more than one, you know.

5. Were you allowed to complain when the going got rough, and given sympathy instead of being told to quit?

This one breaks down into two parts:

5a. Were you allowed to complain when the going got rough?

That means it was OK to come in and say, "It's too hard. I can't. I won't. I'm going to flunk. I don't know how. They yelled at me. I hate it. I've changed my mind. I'm never going to do anything again." And . . . they listened. They didn't get hysterical and say, "I knew it—she can't make it. I was afraid of this." And they didn't get furious and say, "Stop that! Pull yourself together!" They really listened, so that you felt that they cared about you, and that doubt, fear and discouragement were normal, acceptable feelings—not shameful or frightening ones.

5b. Were you given sympathy instead of being told to quit?

A lot of us—especially women—were given sympathy as a *part* of being told to quit. "Welcome home, poor darling. You're right, it is too hard. Of course you should give up. Go to bed and relax. It doesn't matter. We still love you. We'll take care of you."

I know a woman, very unsure of her capacities as a student, who started medical school at 27. She was overwhelmed by the masses of material she had to learn, but she was struggling bravely through it all when her father called her up one night and said, "You know, we'll still love you if you fail." Of course he was trying to be kind, to take the pressure off. She could have killed him.

What we really needed, and what practically none of us got, was to be told, "Yeah, it sounds awful. Really rough. I remember when I was in school—it's murder." And then, when you'd griped and moaned your heart out for fifteen minutes and were feeling lighter: "Finished? All right, come on. Time to get out there and try again. Yes, it *is* hard. And you can do it." And maybe even: "I'll help."

If your answer to one or both parts of No. 5 was "No," how do you think your life might have been different if you had been given that kind of tender toughness?

6. Were you bailed out when you got in over your head—without reproach?

This one really breaks down into two parts, too.

6a. Were you bailed out? If you got into trouble and called Mama and Daddy, did you get help? A lot of us did.

6b. But without reproach? Not likely. Most of us vividly remember the scoldings on the way home in the car when we'd done something a little too adventurous or impulsive and had to be hauled out of the drink by the scruff of the neck. A lot of that anger was just the anxiety and pain of parents who would have liked to spare us the uncomfortable but priceless experience of making mistakes. Some of it may have been embarrassment at the way our conduct reflected on them. But trying something and messing it up is a complete and self-contained learning experience. Just about all a parent or teacher can do is point that out. Throwing anger or blame at somebody who's already smarting from a mistake only damages the learner's feeling of self-worth and his or her eagerness to try things again. Yet how rare it was to be told, "Mistakes don't mean you're bad. They're how you learn."

If your answer to No. 6 was "No," how might your life be different if you had been told just that?

Now comes the toughest and most important one of all:

7. *Were you surrounded by winners who were pleased when you won?*

That is: were the people in your family people who had really gotten what they wanted out of life—who had gotten their chance, and taken it—so that when *you* won, they felt great about it?

They didn't have mixed emotions. They cheered: "Terrific! Another one on board! We are some bunch of talented people."

That sounds like Heaven to almost all of us. We live in a society that has made it heartbreakingly, unnecessarily difficult for people to get what they want, or even to believe that they should or can get it. So most of us grew up surrounded by people who'd either never had a chance, or who'd had a chance but no support or encouragement. They had *not* gotten what they wanted—and they either blamed circumstances ("hard reality"), or they blamed themselves. Either way, they could not be anything but ambivalent about the prospect of our success . . . afraid for us if we tried, helpless to help us, jealous and lonely if we made it across the line into the winners' world.

Have you caught on to the secret? This one single quality of the ideal family is the key to them all. *The environment that creates winners is almost always made up of winners.* That doesn't necessarily mean famous people, hot shots, or superachievers. It does mean people who are contented and curious, open and vital, who trust life and respect themselves—so that they can allow and encourage you to make your own unique experiment.

People who are happily absorbed in what they are doing are real, reachable "role models" for their children. Their kids can observe, close up, *how things really get done*—not by magic, but step by possible step —whether it's practicing the piano or building a bookshelf. What's more, parents who are "winners," so far from "not having time" for their children's interests, are the most likely to encourage them, too, to experience the satisfaction of doing things they love. And they will know, because they've done it themselves, how to help their children get in touch with the skills, information, and resources they need. People who have tried, failed without blame, tried again in a different way, and succeeded—and all winners, without exception, have done this countless times—will be able to help their children overcome discouragement and learn from their mistakes.

Because information about what it really takes to win has not been made freely available in our society, there has been almost no way to learn it except by being lucky enough to get close to people who are doing it. If you didn't grow up in a family of winners, there was really only one other way to learn the secrets of winning. And that's the long, hard way I did it—by trial and error, against tough inner and outer odds: fear, loneliness, and ignorance.

I want to change all that. I don't think anybody should have to do it the long, hard way. Life is too short, and the unique human potential of each one of us is too precious to waste. The purpose of this book is to give you the inside dope on what it really takes to win. But first, I'd like you to ask yourself a question that may be a little painful. Daring to answer it, in spite of that pain, is an important first step on the road to success.

Suppose you had grown up in a family of winners—people who had gotten what they wanted out of life, who knew how to help you get what *you* wanted, and who were nothing but delighted when you got it.

How do you think you and your life might have been different? Where might you be today?

I'm going to run through the list of qualities of that ideal family once more, and as I do, you'll have an opportunity to pull together all the thoughts you've had in the course of this chapter.

EXERCISE 3: What You Might Have Been

Remember what you learned in the last chapter about "your original self"? Now imagine that that gifted child—you—had grown up in a family in which you were:

• treated as though you had a unique kind of genius that was loved and respected . . .

• told that you could do and be anything you wanted—and that you'd be loved and admired no matter what it was . . .

• given real help and encouragement in finding out *what* you wanted to do and *how* to do it . . .

• encouraged to explore *all* your own talents and interests, even if they changed from day to day . . .

• allowed to complain when the going got rough, and given sympathy instead of being told to quit . . .

- bailed out when you got in over your head—without reproach . . .
- surrounded by winners who were pleased when you won.

What do you think you would be doing now? What would you already have done? What kind of person would you be?

Think BIG. Be as extravagant and far-fetched as you like. What I want to hear is the big one, the dream you think you would have gone for if everything had been on your side. If you really think you might have been President of the United States, say the President of the United States. After all, we're only talking "what if." All the rules of "reality" and "possibility" and "modesty"—even the law of gravity, if it cramps your style—are hereby suspended for the duration of this exercise. We'll deal with them later. Right now, I want your imagination free to fly just as far as it can in whatever direction it chooses.

The pain can come in as it dawns on you how much you might really have done if your circumstances had been different. But uncomfortable as it is, that is a *good sign*. It means you are beginning to cherish and respect yourself—and without that, you'll never know how much you still can do. So just let any anger or pain lend your imagination defiant wings. Your capacity to do will depend on your capacity to dream, so prove that *that* capacity, at least, has survived intact.

What might you have been?

I'd have been a famous movie star and gotten bored with it and given it up already!

Here are some answers given by a roomful of perfectly "ordinary" people:

"I'd either be Judy Collins or the president of a corporation."

"I'd be a whole lot richer."

"A great surgeon."

"The Sarah Bernhardt of the 1970s."

"I'd have my own company."

"A traveling news correspondent."

"A top administrator in the school district."

"I'd be an architect."

"A world-famous organist."

"An anchorwoman."

"This is very immodest, but I'd be the president of General Mills."

Stop right there! I asked you to throw out modesty, but this woman —it *was* a woman—said, "very immodest." That's an important thing to notice about women: whenever we confess to having big dreams or ambitions, we get embarrassed and apologetic. Show me a man who feels that it's "immodest" to head for the top of any business or profession! You don't have to dream of being Barbara Walters or the president of a corporation—to open a plant store or learn to play the guitar is every bit as fine an ambition—but if that *is* the kind of thing you yearn for, don't apologize!

"I'd have made a movie, traveled all over the world, and had several hit records."

"I would have given Mme. Curie a run for her money."

"I'd have three Olympic gold medals."

"I'd be the female counterpart of Johnny Carson."

"I'd have published a novel, and I'd play folk guitar, and I'd be studying mime, sign language, drums, Spanish, and Japanese!!"

"I'd be a multilingual interpreter at the UN."

"I'd be the originator and head of a very unusual kind of textile center—a design and manufacturing center for fabrics and a learning institution. Or I'd be a painter. Or an anthropologist. And a folksinger in twenty languages on the side."

Yes. There's evidence that we are all, at least potentially, "Renaissance people"—that a single human brain contains many more capacities than we realize.

Now look at your answer. Were you as daring as the people quoted above?

Examine your answer carefully. Make sure you're not pulling your punches, settling for the "possible" or the "realistic." If you are, stop and readjust your sights upward. Remember, this is fantasy. We're talking about you as you would have responded to a loving, encouraging, instructive environment expressly designed to cultivate your genius.

I'll bet you would have done some pretty fantastic things.

Would you still like to do them? Or a lot of other things that are just as fun and grand?

You still can.

I don't care how old you are, or what your past history has been, or what your present circumstances are: you can still do and have and be anything in the world you really want. And the way you do it is by creating the environment that creates winners around you *now*.

BEYOND "FREUDIAN FATALISM"

"But isn't it too late?" you may be asking. "The damage is done. OK, I can see how growing up in that kind of family would have made me creative and strong and unafraid. But I didn't. So I've already lost my best years for learning skills, and I don't have any of those fabulous inner strengths that are built by good early nutrition—self-confidence and self-esteem and the courage to take risks. I'm going to have to limp along through life without them—unless I can undo some of the damage in therapy, and that's a long, slow process."

I believe in therapy. But if I'd waited for it to fix me up, I'd have been 90 before I walked out the door. It's not only that untying all those emotional knots takes time. (After all, it took years to tie them, and deeply impressionable years at that.) It's that *understanding is one thing and action is another.* You can spend years understanding your fear of water and still never walk to the edge of the pool and jump in.

But you don't have to be doomed to a half-life by the environment you grew up in. Put us in a nourishing environment, even late in a hard life, and we burst into bloom. The misconception I call "Freudian fatalism" has had its day. Now many therapists themselves are rejecting the idea that character is almost irreversibly stamped by the early years of life. They have discovered that we never lose the capacity for growth —or for new learning.

But we never lose our basic needs, either—for food and shelter, acceptance and love. And if you know somebody who's winning and *loving* it (and that's the only definition of winning I'll accept), you can bet that there's a source of support and nourishment in that person's life. And I don't mean only in the past. I mean right now.

You know that "self-reliant" entrepreneur who made it to the top by lonely struggle? He's got . . . a wife. A woman who cheered him up when he was low, listened to his gripes, told him he could do it, typed his proposals, and fed him his dinner. In Chapters 5 and 10, you'll learn to create that kind of support for yourself without taking over anyone else's life—whether you're a man or a woman.

He has something else, too. A little black book full of phone numbers he knows he can call—classmates, cronies, colleagues, friends—whenever he needs information, advice, an introduction, a loan, or an expert's services. That's called *the old-boy network,* and you will learn to create one for yourself in Chapter 7, even if you're not old-boy yourself, or if you're a girl.

And how about that ever so "self-disciplined" novelist who turns out a complete first draft in nine months, when you can't get past page one? She has a structure. A deadline. An expectant editor waiting for her work. A place to sit down undisturbed. A certain number of hours a day. A regular daily output of words or pages. Someone to give her a cup of coffee and a sendoff like Odysseus in the morning, and then meet her at three and say, "How'd it go?" and maybe even read what she's written. Virginia Woolf had Leonard. George Eliot had George Henry Lewes. Gertrude Stein had Alice B. Toklas. Soil and air and water and sun.

You know how hard it is to get anything done entirely on your own. You look for any reason to stop, or you forget, or your pencil breaks, or your finger gets stuck in the typewriter. You don't do it. *And nobody notices.* The times in your life when you have gotten things done, it was probably in a situation where somebody set tasks for you and would have noticed and minded if you didn't do them—like when you worked in an office, or when you got assignments and papers in school. That isn't a terrible weakness. It's human nature. A structure is to us what a loom is to a weaver, or a doorframe to a spider. That's why the first thing all "self-motivated" people do is to set up a structure that will not only help them but *make* them do what they want to do! You will learn to create that kind of structure for yourself in Chapters 6 through 11: a plan that breaks down your goal into manageable tasks and assigns them to you one by one, and a *report-in system* that puts your boss and conscience outside yourself.

To succeed in our thin and chilly atmosphere, you need a Portable Life Support System, like the backpacks the astronauts wore on the moon to give them oxygen, comfortable pressure, and communication. The rest of this book is going to be your Portable Success Support System. It will provide all the features of the environment that create winners. Since you are a unique individual, you will adapt this support system to your own needs. Which parts of it you find most useful will depend on which features were missing in your past:

- *If you were never treated as if you had a special kind of genius that was worthy of love and respect,* you will find that genius alive and well in Chapter 3, "Stylesearch."
- *If you weren't told that it was fine to do and be anything you wanted,* Chapter 4, "Goalsearch," will help you find what's exactly right for you out of all the possibilities in the world.
- *If you weren't helped to figure out what you wanted to do—and HOW to do it,* Chapter 4 will take care of the "what"; the whole "craft" section of the book will show you HOW.
- *If you weren't encouraged to explore ALL your own talents and interests,* Chapters 3 and 4 (and especially "Five Lives," p. 83) will introduce you to some you didn't even remember you had—and show you how they can all be active in your life.
- *If you weren't allowed to complain and given sympathy instead of being told to quit,* you'll have a ball in Chapter 5, "Hard Times, or The Power of Negative Thinking."
- *If you weren't bailed out of trouble without reproach,* you'll find ample permission to goof up in Chapter 9, "First Aid for Fear."
- *If you weren't surrounded by winners who were delighted when you won,* Chapter 7 ("Barn-Raising"), Chapter 10 ("Don't-Do-It-Yourself"), and the Epilogue ("Learning to Live With Success") will show you how you can encourage your friends and family to win with you. But this whole book was written in the hope that we can gradually change the desert around us—with its rare, lush oases of celebrity—into a worldwide garden of winners who are delighted with and for each other.

Two

Wishing

– 3 –

Stylesearch

I'd like you to begin making your life come true by taking a loving look at your own style: how you dress, how you decorate your apartment or house, what colors and foods and movies and music and books you like, all the thousand little details of choice and preference by which you please yourself.

We ordinarily think of personal style as something that "doesn't matter"—fun, but rather trivial and optional; a private game we play in our leisure time after we've dealt with the serious business of life. Style seems like the last place you'd be likely to find the key to success. And yet, after your memories of what you loved best as a child and your fantasies about what you'd have loved to be, your style is your most precious clue to your genius.

Just because it isn't considered "important," style is the biggest field of free play and free choice left to you. Your deepest resources—your talent, your imagination, your identity—cannot be completely suppressed. They *must* declare themselves. And they do—in the one "safe" area society has left free from expectations or consequences. Your style only needs to be noticed and taken seriously to start furnishing rich clues for the direction and design of your life.

If this sounds a little exaggerated, you can demonstrate its truth for yourself. Here's a simple exercise that will reveal the unsuspected importance of your style. It was originated by Jack Canfield, Director of the Institute for Wholistic Studies in Amherst, Massachusetts, and it's one of my favorites.

EXERCISE 4: Pick a Color ("I am blue")

Choose a color that appeals to you. It doesn't have to be your all-time favorite, or a color you especially like to wear—though it may be. The best way to pick one is to look at a selection of colors, and I'd also like you to have your color in front of you while you do this exercise. So you might glance through a brightly colored magazine . . . or look around for a color that catches your eye in a painting or print, a chair or a rug, in the room where you're sitting right now . . . or if you have a child's box of crayons, or a set of chalks or paints, that will give you an excellent range to choose from. (Remember the delicious feeling of choice you got when you opened a brand-new box of forty-eight sharp-pointed crayons and decided which one to draw with first: silver? flesh? forest green?)

Now I would like you to role-play that color. That means you are going to pretend you *are* that color and speak for it, since it cannot speak for itself. It can't tell us what it's like to be royal purple, or buttercup, or black. You will have to tell what it's like to be your color.

Take a sheet of paper, and start by writing, "I am red" . . . or "I am yellow" . . . or "I am cerulean blue"—whatever color you've chosen. Do *not* say "I like blue because . . ." or "I think blue is . . ." From this moment on you *are* that color.

Now, in a few words to a few sentences, tell what qualities you have *as that color*—not as yourself. For instance, "I am dark blue. I'm quiet and deep like the ocean." Or, "I am yellow. I'm cheerful, intelligent, efficient but warm." (Don't let these responses influence *your* response. There are no right answers to this exercise. If you happen to find black a cozy color, or you think white is depressing and blue is cheerful, great!)

This is a deceptively simple little exercise, and it has so much to tell that I'm going to break its revelations down into three parts, each of which will lead to questions and exercises of its own—choice and identity, uniqueness *vs.* competition, and assets and "objectivity."

I. CHOICE AND IDENTITY

The first thing you may have noticed is that it took you a while to pick your favorite color. You found yourself being very particular and choosy, and it was hard to make up your mind. That happens to a lot of people, and there's a very good reason for it: you didn't want to pick a color that wasn't right.

Somewhere down deep, not much is left to you on which to take a stand—so you'll take it on preferences. You'll fight for your tastes. When it comes to color, or whether you want to eat Chinese or fried chicken, or how you want your house to look, or how you wear your hair, or whether you prefer Elvis Presley or opera, you will take a life and death stand—because that's where your integrity is.

You choose your color so carefully because subconsciously, half-consciously, you know that style is anything but trivial. When you pick your color, or your records, or your necktie, or the print for your curtains, you are doing far more than just pleasing or indulging yourself. You are declaring yourself. You are saying, "This is who I am." That's why those "little" choices are so important to you.

With this in mind, let's take a closer look at your style.

EXERCISE 5: The Private-Eye Game

Play detective. Snoop around your own house or room as if you were a private-eye trying to find out who lived here just from the style revealed in the house. After all, in a way you *are* learning about a stranger. You are following the tracks and examining the fingerprints of a unique individual you do not know who happens to be you.

Look in the clothes closets, the kitchen cabinets, the book and record shelves. Look at the furniture, the rugs, the curtains, the pictures on the walls, the food in the refrigerator, the colors, the state of clutter or order, the arrangement of space. Make an inventory of as many characteristics and interests as you can find.

For instance, would you say that the person who lives here is organized or scatterbrained? Sociable or solitary? Sensual or intellectual? Or some of both? Would she rather read fiction or history? Does he prefer Bach or Eric Clapton? Or both? Do the furnishings this person chose show a preference for rough, natural materials or for finished, classy ones? Does the house or apartment have a striking central feature, or a favorite lived-in place: the kitchen, a writing desk, a fireplace, the stereo? What are the clothes in the closet saying about the person who chose them? (I have never met a person who wasn't carefully costumed!) And so on.

When you've gathered all the clues you can, sit down and read through the detective's profile you've compiled. It is a portrait of yourself.

Are you surprised?

Ruth, a 38-year-old English teacher, was. She had never thought of herself as a visual person. If you'd asked her, she would have said she was primarily interested in literature and music, and didn't know anything about painting. And yet she had covered one whole wall of her apartment with cork board, and pinned up an arrangement of postcards that revealed an instinctive sense of color and design. She'd done it simply because she liked them—because they looked pretty and made her feel good! She'd never given it a second thought. Only when she played the Private-Eye Game did it dawn on her that she was, in fact, a highly visual person who needed to—and knew how to—please her own eye.

Margaret, 26, works as a computer programmer in an office that requires her to dress neatly and conservatively. She thinks of herself as efficient and tidy. When she goes out on weekends, she likes to wear splashy, glamorous clothes—big hats, plunging necklines, capes, and spangles. When she looked at all her evening dresses hanging together in her closet, she felt like Clark Kent looking at Superman's cape. Those clothes added up to a second secret identity: an actress or adventuress, reckless and dramatic, with a love of costume and gesture.

Bill, an accountant who does a lot of his work at home, had devised his own color-coded, fast-access filing system, which he thought of as nothing more than a convenience. When he looked at it with the eye of a detective, he realized that it showed real logic and ingenuity—a talent for organization and design.

Jacob, a 45-year-old bachelor poet-in-residence at a small New England college, recorded the fact that his house had not one center, but two: the library and the kitchen! His spice racks were as carefully stocked as his bookshelves, his copper pots were as lovingly polished as his sonnets, and he had to admit that the man who lived here was considerably more sociable and sensual than the melancholy recluse he'd thought he was.

The Private-Eye Game may give that kind of pleasant shock to *your* self-image. In any case, it is bound to enrich it. Your tastes and choices often reveal aspects of you that you aren't very conscious of, or have never taken seriously. If you've been thinking of yourself as an indistinct person with no special talents or interests, this exercise will lay that idea to rest! You may be puzzled at how you can parlay the discoveries you've made into a goal, activity, or profession, but don't worry about that now. In the next chapter I'll be showing you how to shape a goal—one that is possible in the real world—out of all these characteristics of yourself. Right now, your job is just to have fun discovering them. You're getting to know your multitalented self.

The same goes for you if—at the other extreme—you are already a very goal-directed, even single-minded person. Your style may serve as a safety-deposit box for all the other talents you're not using right now —like Ruth's visual ability. You need to be aware that those talents are there. You don't have to become a dilettante or "spread yourself thin," but you should know that your life will be richer, your energy more abundant, the more of your inborn gifts you can bring into play. In the pages ahead you'll find out how to make room in your life for all of them.

Your style is the place where you still exercise the creative power to shape your world and design yourself. *It is proof that you haven't lost that power at all.* All you need is permission, encouragement, and guidance to expand it into a wider domain: your whole life.

II. UNIQUENESS VS. COMPETITION

Now I'm going to go back to the color exercise and show you another very interesting facet of it. Just take a look at some of the responses other people gave.

"I am red. I am intense, hungry, and angry, like fire."

"I am red. I'm lively and giving."

"I am red. I am a firelit living room with a red velvet couch—I am fiery and passionate, but also cozy and warm."

"I am red like blood—very deep and very vital."

"I am blue. I'm cold, distant, but intelligent."

"I am blue. I'm soothing and serene."

"I am blue—electric blue—crackling with energy."

"I am yellow. I am a new kitchen with lots of sun and flower pots. I am cheerful and like company, order, and comfort."

"I am yellow. I'm quiet, simple, straightforward, sincere."

"I am yellow. I'm heavy, rich and valuable, like gold, like cream."

One thing you can't help noticing right away is the striking variety of answers. But even more important, look how completely different the same color appears through different people's eyes! This can be true right down to the physical level. I have seen two people look at the same color and heard one say "I am rust" and the other say "I am rose."

Do you remember when we were talking about early childhood, and I said that each one of us sees a different world? There it is—in this simple-minded little exercise on color. Your style is a style of perception, a way of seeing and feeling the world, that is unique—as unique as your fingerprints. You are born with it, and it develops as you grow, and it is not like anyone else's in the world. It is literally incomparable.

There is only one way you can compare people with each other, and that is to select one single feature that can be measured quantitatively. Take height. Obviously, some people are taller and some shorter. That doesn't tell you much about them as individuals, but as far as it goes, it is a valid basis for comparison. Unfortunately, in our society comparison, in turn, often becomes the basis for *ranking*. We have an obsessive need to know who is "better," so we take a single quantitative yardstick —like grades in school, or income—and we evaluate a whole individual by his or her performance on that one scale. When you really think about it, this is as absurd as declaring that tall people are superior to short people, or that an orange is better than a rose because it weighs more! And yet we've all been trained to think this way, to compare ourselves to others and worry about whether we "measure up."

Think about it. When you walk into a room full of strangers, don't you immediately, half-consciously "case" it according to your own favorite standard—smart/dumb, rich/poor, pretty/ugly, accomplished/not accomplished, or whatever—and then rank yourself? For instance, if pretty/ugly is your private yardstick, you may think, "Let's see . . . I've got more taste than she does, but that one over there has prettier eyes than I do, and . . ." It's embarrassing to admit, but very few of us are completely immune to this game.

But what would happen to this ranking system if you met people—

and they met you—in terms of individual style? Suppose, for instance, you were going to meet the people who "spoke for their color" in the examples above. How would you rank their answers? Where would you rank your own? Which one do you think is "best"?

Of course. You couldn't even compare them, much less rank them. Because the truth is that human beings are not comparable. You can't compare us any more than you can compare roses and oranges, or mountains and the sea, or France and England. You might prefer living by the sea to living in the mountains. You might rather take your vacation in England than in France. And you certainly like some people better than you like others. Preferences are perfectly valid . . . they're just your style asserting itself again. But you'd feel pretty silly saying, "England is a better country than France," or "The sea is better than the mountains." And it's every bit as silly to go around saying, "I'm better than Mary, but Joe is better than me."

The notion of competition—the idea that there is someone out there just like you, only better—is untrue. What's more, it keeps your attention focused away from yourself, on the struggle to meet the ill-fitting standards of other people, instead of looking inside and discovering your own. The things that are unique and incomparable about you are the only basis on which you can design a life that will truly satisfy *you*. And it is you who must be satisfied. There is no authority outside you who can tell you what's right for you.

When you become aware of your own uniqueness, that's when you really begin to cherish and respect yourself—and to respect others! If you met people on the basis of their style, you would respect each one instinctively, and they would respect you. And there would be genuine mutual interest and curiosity. If we're not in competition with each other—if we're not threatened by our differences or busy trying to rank them—then our differences become resources. I'm not like you, and I don't want to be like you, because then I wouldn't have anyone around me who could tell me anything I didn't know, show me anything I couldn't see. I'd only have me. I want you, too, because you're different.

III. ASSETS AND "OBJECTIVITY"

When you were speaking for your color, did it strike you that you felt free to say *anything?* "I am red; I'm intense and angry. Well, of course it's OK to say I'm angry! I'm red, aren't I?"

Or did you find that you had some difficulty saying things like "I am intelligent, I am passionate, I am sad, I am giving"? Did you feel at all shy about it?

That was a pretty thinly veiled exercise, wasn't it? I'm sure you realized rather quickly that you were talking about yourself—or at least a facet of yourself. If you had been asked to pick your favorite color on a different day, it might have been a different color. But certainly this color represented a part of you . . . and it revealed some pretty intimate things about you, too. That's why it may have been hard for you to talk about it. You were breaking a rule of our culture, the rule against saying, "I am the kind of person who . . ."

How many of us walk through life saying to ourselves and everyone else within earshot, "I'm a passionate person! I may not be organized, but I've got fire and drive"? No, we say, "Lord, I'm fat." That's because we learned very early that to speak honestly about ourselves—and especially to say anything good about ourselves—was taboo. If you're like me, more than once in your life you've walked up to a prospective lover or employer and, convinced that you were being honest and "objective," said, "I want to know everything that's wrong with me in advance!"

Luckily, there are a few loopholes in the taboo—a few places where you *are* allowed, just as a game, to say "I am the kind of person who." Magazine quizzes are one such place. Astrology is another. That's why magazine quizzes and astrology are so popular! Notice that your sign of the zodiac doesn't say you're perfect. It says you're good at this, you're bad at that, these are your wonderful qualities, these are your awful qualities. And you love them all. I'm a Leo. That gives me an excuse to say, "I'm a showoff, I'm a ham, I'm an amateur at everything, I need a lot of affection"—and all without the slightest bit of embarrassment.

That's real objectivity—the kind of loving objectivity that says you're fine and fascinating just the way you are. But take off the mask of your astrological sign, and all of a sudden you're not allowed to say those things any more. *A direct statement about yourself is considered objective only if it is negative.* If it's positive, it is considered *subjective.* And "objective" means it is accurate, and "subjective" means it is conceited self-delusion.

We all have negative tapes running constantly in our heads, reciting our shortcomings, until we know what's wrong with us backwards, forwards, and upside down. Very few of us have positive tapes to tell us all the things that are right with us! And yet, *only when you have a clear, unembarrassed view of your own assets do you have a truly objective picture of yourself*—one you can draw on to design a creative and satisfying life. And so you sorely need some positive tapes that you can play whenever the negative ones get too insistent.

Positive information about yourself isn't as hard to come by as you may think. If you were asked to sit down and give a thoughtful, accurate inventory of your best friend's good qualities, could you do it? Sure—in about two minutes. Well, your best friend can do the same for you. The truth is, you're not hiding your good qualities from anybody except yourself. They're as plain as the nose on your face to anybody who knows you—or even just meets you. You would be surprised and delighted if you could really see yourself through other people's eyes. And so that's exactly what I'm going to invite you to do in this exercise.

Exercise 6: Seeing Yourself as Others See You

This exercise comes in two versions—one for extroverts and one for introverts (there's another fun classification for you). If you've got even a little nerve, try Version No. 1. If you're shy but imaginative, you may feel more comfortable with Version No. 2.

VERSION NO. 1: PRAISE BE!

Pick somebody you love and trust—a good friend, or your mate, lover, or child. Sit down with a pen and a piece of paper (no erasing!) and ask him or her to spend about three minutes telling you precisely what's good about you. And you write it down, word for word. This is going to be your positive tape, so get it right.

Don't let your partner get away with saying something vague, like "You're nice," or even "You're wonderful." That's the only kind of praise most of us have ever gotten, and it doesn't help. You need to hear things like: "You have a delightful imagination, you're articulate, your energy is contagious, and you help everyone around you to see the world in fresh, new ways." Or: "Do you know that you move beautifully? You're really graceful—and really giving and kind. You touch people a lot, and you mean it. Anybody in trouble can come to you and feel soothed." This isn't flattery, it's information.

Accurate, perceptive praise is a rarity in our society. It shouldn't be. We all need it, and we'd all love to give it—it's just that nobody ever told us it was OK. Well, I'm telling you now. Everybody needs practice at being both the praiser and the praisee, so after your partner has told you what's right about you, switch roles. There are just a couple of simple rules to follow.

For the praiser: Don't let any criticism sneak in, even if it's "constructive" or compassionate. (This rule is especially important for husbands, wives, and lovers; friends are less likely to want to improve each other.) That means you may not say, "If you just took your glasses off and let your hair down, you'd be really beautiful," or "Some people might say you're opinionated and stubborn, but I think you're definite and strong." The person being praised already knows all that negative stuff by heart and doesn't need to hear it again. Be honestly positive. You'll be amazed how it enhances your appreciation of someone you love to put your perceptions of him or her into words.

For the praisee: As difficult—and delicious—as you will find it, for three minutes you are allowed to do nothing but sit and listen and take dictation like a very conscientious secretary. Don't interrupt. Don't argue. And don't inwardly discount every word your partner says. You're always ready and waiting for criticism, but praise will sneak right up and sock you in your tummy. If you just sit and take it, it can give you gooseflesh, it can even make you cry. So you may try to wiggle out of it. If your partner says, "You're very sensitive," you'll think, "Ah hah. Weepy, weak, hysterical." If s/he says "Sensuous," you'll go, "Fat." Don't do that. Take your partner at his or her word—and get those words down on paper, so you can't revise, edit, and qualify them in memory.

There are a couple of variations on this theme if you find it hard to take your praise right between the eyes. One is to have your partner put it in writing. Another, even better, is to get together with two friends, turn your back on them, and listen while they discuss your good qualities with each other. Then switch around and put somebody else in the "warm seat."

But if you'd really rather not have to ask someone else to tell you the good news, there's a way that you can find out for yourself.

VERSION NO. 2: CREATING YOUR CHEERING SECTION

The truth is, you already know what your own assets are. Whenever you get the chance to talk about yourself in a safe disguise—like astrology—that knowledge pops out. It's there. The color exercise was one of those disguises. When you spoke for your color, I'll bet you declared all its powerful and beautiful and tender qualities. You didn't choose that color in the first place for being ugly or drab, did you? And that color is *you*—a vital part of you.

It's time to come out of all the disguises and start admitting that your positive qualities really do belong to you. But that's hard to do without help. Like every human being, you need *positive feedback* from someone who's on your side before it becomes safe to feel openly good about yourself. Your own family may not have known how to give you that kind of feedback when you were growing up, but now that you are grown up, you can get it for yourself. You can create an imaginary ideal family to be your private cheering section. They will tell you all the good things about you that you really know—but aren't allowed to tell yourself!

The imagination is a very powerful tool, and we'll be using it a lot in this book. We think that only novelists and storytellers have the ability to create characters and give them life. It's not true. That's a human power, and everybody has it—we use it in our dreams! I'm going to show you how to use it consciously, to help you realize your life dreams.

The imaginative technique we're going to use in this exercise is called role-playing. If you pretend that you're someone else—your mother, your father, a famous baseball player, an Eskimo, a beagle—you tap into a deeper source of knowledge, and you'll discover that you know all kinds of things you didn't know you knew. In this case, you're going to pretend you are some very special people who are taking a loving look at you and saying what they see.

Take a few minutes now to think of the four or five people you would choose if you could have anyone in the world—anyone in all history and literature—as your family. I mean your *ideal* family, the kind I described as "the environment that creates winners": a group of people who cherish what's special about you, encourage you to explore all your own talents, and help you keep going when you're down. Give this some thought and care, because you will be meeting these people again as we go along. When you start working toward an actual goal they'll be there to help you feel that you're not alone—that you have the best and most select company in the world.

Choose people you feel a special kinship with: people whose ideas or activities strongly appeal to you, people whose life experience or temperament would make them sympathetic to you (Katharine Hepburn might say, "I know how it is to have a hot temper"), people whose faces you love. Choosing your "family" is like choosing your color: you're asserting your style to select and shape the world around you. You will pick each of your "family" members for a very good reason.

I chose Albert Einstein because he looked as kind as my grandfather, and because he had done badly in math and had a trivial job as a patent clerk, but was so wrapped up in his interests that it never stopped him. And I chose Bette Davis because she is both tough and vulnerable, self-sufficient, witty and smart, and I'd like to have her on my side in a fight! Other favorites of mine are Margaret Mead and Alice's waitress friend in the movie, "Alice Doesn't Live Here Any More."

A writer I know chose the great Austrian poet Rainer Maria Rilke because he'd traveled disconsolately all over Europe bumming off his aristocratic friends, worrying about money, waiting for inspiration, and deploring his own lack of self-discipline. The other members of her family are John Keats, Glenda Jackson, Colette, and Pelé—because she likes his smile!

Write the names of your "family" members down on one or two sheets of paper, with a good paragraph's worth of space under each one. Now close your eyes and imagine that you are one of those people, *and you are watching yourself come through the door.* From the point of view of your "family" member, notice how you move, how you talk to people, the way you use words, the expressions on your face. Watch kindly, with curiosity, interest, and fondness, as if you were watching your favorite child. Write down all the *positive* qualities you see. *Only the positive ones! (Same rule as in Version No. 1, and for the same reason: you don't need to hear all the negative stuff for the umpteenth time.)*

For example:

Einstein: "I can see that Barbara has a good mind—quick, eager, varied. She has a lot of original ideas, and she knows how to make herself understood. She speaks clearly and chooses words well. She's warm and interested in other people. I like the way she responds to everything that is going on around her. She's involved. And she has a lot of energy."

When your first family member has said all she or he has to say, move on and become the next. Each one has a very different point of view and will notice different positive qualities about you. Like this:

Bette Davis: "She's tough, she's got a sense of humor and a great belly laugh. She's not afraid of life. And she sings well, too, with a wistful quality that contradicts the toughness." (Describing myself as myself, I'd be likely to say, "I'm disorganized, impulsive, and probably talk too much." It was a shock to me the first time I saw myself through others' eyes!)

I've told you about my past record, so if *I* can do this, believe me, *you* can.

When you have role-played each member of your "family" in turn, go back and read through their answers. You will have a comprehensive portrait of what's right with you.

Surprised?

There's just one more exercise in your Stylesearch proper—one more useful thing to know about yourself before you take the next step: designing a whole life for yourself in imagination.

YOUR PERSONAL STYLE IN ACTION

Remember that one of the things I asked you to have your "family" members notice about you was *how you move?* Your style is not only a way of seeing the world, but also a unique way of moving through it. If the colors and belongings you surround yourself with reveal your style of *vision,* the activities you enjoy reveal your style of *action.* Sid Simon, author of *Values Clarification* (Hart Publishers) has developed a way of classifying your favorite activities to come up with a *life quality profile:* a concise portrait of *how you like to live.* Fast or slow-paced? More physical or mental activity? With constant company or more by yourself? With what unique balance of these and other factors?

If someone asked you these questions directly, you might be able to give an approximate answer. But after doing this exercise you'll even be able to put it into percentages if you're mathematically inclined

("60–40 in favor of physical"). And again, you may find some surprises, because you'll be looking at your actual preference pattern rather than the often inaccurate image of yourself you've been carrying around in your head.

EXERCISE 7: Twenty Things You Like to Do

Twenty?? Yes. You have to come up with twenty. That's the only rule. I don't care how trivial some of them seem to you—like "eating ice cream"—and I don't care why you like to do them. If you get down to nineteen and you're really desperate and can't think of one more, put "Scratching when it itches." Anything.

Make a simple chart. In the "down" column on the left-hand side, write the things you like to do, one through twenty, in whatever order they come into your head. Don't bother trying to rank them in order of preference, because that's impossible—it's roses and oranges again.

In the "across" column along the top, write the following questions (if you turn the paper sideways and write them vertically, you'll have room):

How long since last done?
Costs money or free?
Alone or with someone?
Planned or spontaneous?
Job related?
Physical risk?
Fast or slow-paced?
Mind, body or spiritual?

You can add any other intriguing categories that occur to you. (For instance: On my list five years ago? Mother/father likes also? City or country? At home/out in the world?) Everything we've done in this section has been to show you that you have the power and the right to reshape the world to fit you. And that includes the exercises in this book! If you can improve on them, or tailor them to your own needs and insights, do it!

When you have filled out your chart, see what patterns you can find.

What did you learn about yourself . . . the kind of life you're living now . . . and the kind of life you'd love to live?

Here's how some other people answered:

Marianne, 32, wife and mother: "I was surprised to find out that there really are easily twenty things I like to do!"

Doris, 45, nurse: "First I got depressed. I said, 'There's no way I could ever do them all.' And then I thought, 'Why not?' "

Ellen, 28, medical student: "I was surprised by the variety. My life has become so single-minded . . . there are a lot of dimensions of me that aren't getting much expression right now."

Jim, 43, lawyer: "It's been altogether too long since I've felt I had time to do about 90 percent of the things I enjoy!"

Lucille, 25, secretary: "It's more important to me than I realized to be physically active and spontaneous. I really shouldn't be spending eight hours a day at a desk."

Allen, 19, student: "Most of the activities I love best really require very little money. This was a revelation to me, because my father had convinced me that I should go into a profession or business where I could earn a six-figure salary. After doing this exercise, I thought, 'What for?' "

Judy, 35, writer: "I'm going to need to earn more to live the kind of life I really want. Travel, skiing, going to concerts and theater and restaurants are all important to me, and they all cost money. Maybe I'd better give some serious thought to trying for a bestseller."

Maurice, 68, retired restaurateur: "I like to be surrounded by lots of busy, noisy people! What am I doing in this goddamned Golden Age condominium?"

Dolores, 24, bookstore cashier: "I'm happiest when I can spend most of my time by myself or with the person I love."

A good look at your own style can tell you many things you never realized about who you really are and what you want. And it can give you a new confidence in yourself. Once you see that every move and choice you make puts your unique stamp on the world, you realize that *you already have the power to shape your life.* Now you're ready for some fantasy practice at expanding that power into wider realms.

LIFE DESIGN REHEARSAL

Using the information you've gained about yourself through your Stylesearch, you're going to play at shaping space and time to fit your needs. First you're going to design an environment so perfectly tailored to *you* that in it all your best qualities would emerge. And then you are going to imagine your ideal day.

Your total environment is often shaped less by your needs and preferences than by whom you live with and what you can afford. How you spend your days is largely determined by your responsibilities. We assume that these factors are pretty much unchangeable—"hard realities." Sure, we could live exactly as we pleased—if we won the lottery, or deserted our families! And the first is improbable and the second is unthinkable. So we may sometimes daydream about a life cut and measured to our desires, but we know those dreams are "self-indulgent" and "unrealistic." Life's just not like that.

And yet that kind of daydreaming is extremely important. You should be doing more of it—and taking it seriously—because it's trying to tell you something. It's your genius itching to get its hands on some of that big-time, space-time clay and start making worlds. All right, let's turn it loose and find out what kind of world it wants to make!

There's only one rule for the kind of imagining you'll be doing in these next two exercises, and that is *no reality considerations!* In the world of play, like the world of dreams, there is no law of gravity, no death or taxes—and no irreconcilable conflicts. So if you want two things that seem to contradict each other, don't worry about it. Put them both in. If you love two people, you get to have two lovers. If you want to be in the country *and* in the city, or you need to be alone *and* live with people, or you want to have two beautiful children *and* a full-time career, say so. In these fantasies you don't have to do what you were told to do at age 5: "Make up your mind." You get everything.

EXERCISE 8: Your Ideal Environment

In one paragraph—or more, if you like—answer this question:
In what imaginary environment would your best self emerge?
Most of us have never asked ourselves that question because it's not

considered askable. What we've been trained to ask is, "How can I fit into some preexisting environment? How can I change myself to fit the world?" When we go to the store, we hope we'll fit into the clothes on the racks. If the jeans are too long or too narrow, it's we who are too short or too fat. If we happened to have three arms, we'd cut one off rather than politely but firmly insist on a jacket with three sleeves!

Just in fantasy, I'd like you to try shaping the world to your needs for a change. Imagine an environment that is perfect for someone with all your present characteristics—a world so tailored to your nature that you'd be at your best in it without changing yourself one bit. Let the environment do all the work for you.

I'm going to stop right here and define my terms a little bit. By "environment," I don't just mean your physical surroundings. Sure, it would be nice to have a house with a patio and a swimming pool and a huge fireplace, and it might be even nicer to be in the Bahamas under a palm tree. But I don't want you to spend too much time on the color of your walls or the climate and the vegetation, unless that is vital to your best state of mind. It may be. But "environment" is also, very importantly, your *human* environment: the kinds of people you'd like to be surrounded by; how much privacy you need, and how much interaction; what kinds of help you'd like; what kinds of responses you'd want to your ideas.

You might need to be challenged . . . or just really listened to. (You will certainly need to be respected.) You might want to be a teacher, with the opportunity to inspire your students; or you might like to be a learner, surrounded by people who could teach you all kinds of fascinating things. You might want to be in charge of a large operation staffed by totally cooperative, efficient, loyal people who are dying to do whatever you tell them to. Or you might prefer to be a member of an egalitarian group effort. It's entirely up to you.

And "Let the environment do the work for you" means *don't change yourself* in this fantasy. Above all, don't improve yourself. Improve the world, so that your characteristics stop being problems. If you hate doing the housework, don't imagine *you* being more self-disciplined or patient. Imagine eight little gremlins following you around cleaning up after you! (Be as whimsical as you like—this is fantasy, so anything goes.) If you're disorganized, or you need a lot of love, or you're shy, or you tend to procrastinate, don't think of those characteristics as "weaknesses" that need changing. Think of them as *design problems*—challenges to your ingenuity as a world-maker. Create an environment that fits and supports you as you are, so that you are comfortable, secure, and free to turn in your best performance.

Gerry, a 38-year-old accountant, said, "One feature of my ideal environment is that everyone around me would be clumsy—because I'm clumsy, and I'm sick of being noticed for it!" Soft-spoken Miriam said, "No one can ever hear me. I'm always struggling to speak up. In my ideal environment, I'd live in a big, spacious house in the middle of a forest with my family and my best friends, and no one would speak above a whisper. I'd be the loudest one there!" Personally, as an old pro at procrastination, I'd like my ideal environment to include a total boss who knew exactly what I wanted to do and would make me do it! A real tyrant who would make me toe the line of my own path.

After you've imagined your ideal environment, I'd like you to do one more thing: list a few adjectives telling what *positive* qualities in you—intellectual, emotional, creative—would emerge if you were in that environment. ("Loving," "assertive," "playful," "productive," "serene," "independent," "sexy," etc.) In EXERCISE 6: *Seeing Yourself as Others See You,* you discovered the good qualities you have right now. This time I'm inviting you to do something a little different, and even more daring: *imagine yourself in full bloom.* (If you still catch yourself feeling naughty or spoiled, or saying "Who do I think I am," just give a Bronx cheer for the incredible tenacity of those negative tapes. Give them a big hand for trying. And then go ahead and dream.)

Here's how some other people described their ideal environments—and their blossoming selves. Notice especially how specific they've been in describing the kind of *human* environment they'd flourish in.

Julia, a 32-year-old free-lance writer: "I'd like to live by myself, in the country, and near a wide variety of friends who are doing all different kinds of things. And I'd like to have a terrific lover who has work of his own he loves, and who lets me know that he loves me, but leaves me alone to work all day without making me feel either guilty or anxious. And I'd like never to quite know when he's coming over, but I'd like to be able to call him if I'm lonely, too. In short, secure, but not too secure—a little drama and suspense. The qualities that would emerge in me would be independence, lovingness, intensity, energy, sensuality, and creativity. I'd get a lot done."

Betsy, 38, mother of three: "I'd like a combination of Mary Poppins, Misterogers, Phil Donahue, and Marlo Thomas to take care of my children; a housekeeper to do that mundane pain-in-the-ass cleaning and cooking and shopping; a secretary to take care of the bills and the phone; and I'd go out and work! Qualities that would emerge: delight in being with people, sense of humor, creativity."

Tom, 55, divorced and job-hunting: "The single thing that stood out for me was how much I need love and emotional support—more than anything else. I also need an uncluttered environment where things are well-organized, because I get distracted easily. Qualities that would emerge: I'd be resourceful, kind, serene, playful, warm, and wise."

George, 43: "A cabin by a lake in the High Sierras, a small, excellent library, several good trout rods, a kerosene lantern, a bar, no telephone, the Wall Street Journal delivered to my doorstep, and my best fishing buddy on weekends. Qualities that would emerge: I'd write and think a lot. I might be the next Thoreau, instead of an investment counselor. But maybe every third month or so I'd come down into the city and work, and see a lot of movies, and be persuasive, witty, and urbane— and then go back to the mountains."

I knew George was married, and yet in his fantasy he didn't mention his wife. When I asked him about her, he said, "Of course she'd be there! I took that so for granted, I just assumed . . ." On further questioning, I learned that she'd also obligingly *not* be there on the occasions when he needed to be alone, or with his friends. George liked to cook, but he "just sort of assumed" that his wife would keep the cabin tidy for him, just as she takes responsibility for keeping their city apartment clean.

In other words, George already has—and takes for granted—a kind of emotional and practical support many of us can only write into our wildest fantasies! Another human being, a woman, provides it for him —at what cost to herself and for what real rewards, I can only guess, because I didn't meet George's wife. The changes that are taking place between men and women right now are painful and creative precisely because men like George are being forced to become conscious of how much their comfort, freedom, and productivity depend on a human support base. That there might also be a genuine pleasure in nurturing —in providing some aspects of a support base—is a discovery the

Georges of this world are just beginning to make.

Arthur, a 28-year-old educational-test designer: "I have to punch in and punch out at work, and that really goes against my nature. I like being creative, but not on order. I'd like to have a fluid situation with no fixed schedule at all—a balance of discipline and freedom. I need the support and acceptance of people who really like my work and say so; I also need occasional solitude. In that environment I'd be self-confident, abundant, creative, happy, electric, fun. I'd be good at what I do; my ideas would never end."

Vickie, 48, a novice theatrical agent: "I need energetic, supportive people around me who love and are excited about the theater. I was really surprised when I realized that I had written 'I need to be *allowed* to create and develop my own ideas.' Evidently I'm still waiting for permission! Anyway, the qualities that would emerge are: high creativity (I'm blushing!), enthusiasm, energy, drive, tenacity, leadership, communications skills, ability to organize and implement my own ideas."

Jo Ann, 36, single mother and graduate student: "Constant stimulation—learning, conversation, working on projects with other people, all kinds of physical audible tangible input and excitement. In that kind of environment my mind would be very active and alive. I'd shoot off sparks."

I think I could characterize most women accurately by saying that they are understimulated and underchallenged. Their emotions may be overused, but their minds and talents are underused. Notice that most of the environments described here include challenge and stimulation as well as comfort and support. Note also that among the qualities that would emerge, almost everyone listed "creativity." Placed in a lively, nourishing environment, the human animal is creative.

Bill, 39, artist and draftsman: "The most important thing I need in my environment is CONTINUITY—everything I'm doing relating to everything else, so that it all ties together. Right now I've got a few pieces of what I want, but they have nothing to do with anything else I'm doing. I also need ECONOMY—my life pared down to the most essential activities, not cluttered with a lot of options and distractions. Qualities that would emerge: originality, productivity, and steadiness."

What did you learn about yourself and what you would need to become all you could be?

This exercise is an important rehearsal for real-world life design. Because even at its most playful and fantastic, it is very revealing of what you really do need to function at your best. The optimum environment for you will be one that provides real equivalents for all the major features of your fantasy. *And this book is going to help you create that environment*—because you have a right to it.

Of course the actual process of creating that environment will be a little different from just shutting your eyes and dreaming. It's going to involve dealing with stubborn, resistant substances like time and money, habit and fear—and stubbornest of all, other people! But believe it or not, all these inner and outer obstacles can be overcome. That's purely a matter of strategy. And *fantasy comes before strategy.*

Unless you can dream, how do you know where you want to go? And until you know where you want to go, how can you sit down and plan how to get there? I'm going to show you how to get there; the whole second half of this book is packed with practical strategies for tackling "hard reality." But *you* have to imagine the "where."

SHAPING TIME

Suppose you lived in a real-life version of your ideal environment, and all your best qualities were in full bloom. How would you spend your time? What activities and people would fill your day? (EXERCISE 7: *Twenty Things You Like to Do* should give you plenty of material!)

In this next exercise, you're going to do a very special kind of imagining. I call it *real daydreaming.* It is one of the most important techniques you'll be using in this book.

If someone asked you what it would be like if you had a million dollars, you'd probably answer something like, "It would be terrific. I'd have a house by the sea, and a sailboat, and an airplane, and I would . . ."

Stop right there! *Any response with the word "would" in it is not real daydreaming.*

When you have a dream at night, do you lie there thinking in your sleep, "Wouldn't it be interesting if this were really happening?" No. It *is* happening. It's *real.* You are experiencing it. When you were a child, your daydreams were just as vivid and present as your night dreams, simply because you hadn't been taught to label them "unreal." What you're going to do now is deliberately revive that power of visualization and belief.

"Real daydreaming" is *present-tense, first-person, visual,* and *sequential.* In other words, it's *happening.* You see, feel, and experience everything that's going on around you; time passes just as it does in real life, only faster. Like this: "This is fantastic! I'm sitting here with a million dollars. Let's see. What shall I do first? . . . OK. I'm in a mansion on a hill above the sea in Maine. My airplane is in a little hangar behind the house. I can see my sailboat rocking down at the dock. It's a cool, sunny morning, and the whole day stretches ahead of me. . . ."

EXERCISE 9: Your Ideal Day

With pen in hand and as much paper as you need (or a tape recorder if you prefer to dream out loud), take a leisurely walk through a day that would be perfect if it represented your usual days—not a vacation day, not a compromise day, but the very substance of your life as you'd love it to be. Live through that day *in the present tense* and *in detail,* from getting up in the morning to going to sleep at night. What's the first thing you do when you wake up? What do you have for breakfast? Do you make it yourself—or is it brought to you in bed, with a single rose and the morning paper? Do you take a long, hot bath? a bracing cold shower? What kinds of clothes do you put on? How do you spend the morning? the afternoon? At each time of day, are you indoors or outdoors, quiet or active, alone or with people?

As you go through the hours of your fantasy day, there are three helpful categories to keep in mind: *what, where,* and *who.*

What are you doing—what kind of work, what kind of play? Imagine yourself at the full stretch of your capacities. If you'd like to sing or sail, and you don't know how, in this fantasy you do know how.

Where—in what kind of place, space, situation? A London flat, an Oregon farm, a fully equipped workshop, an elegant hotel room, a houseboat?

Who do you work with, eat with, laugh and talk with, sleep with? You will undoubtedly want to write some of your favorite real people into your fantasy; you might also want to include some types of people you'd like to be surrounded by—writers, musicians, children, people your own age, people of all different ages, athletes, Frenchmen, financiers, simple country people, celebrities.

Just as you did with your ideal environment, turn your imagination loose. Don't put down what you think is possible—put down the kind of day you'd live if you had absolute freedom, unlimited means, and all the powers and skills you've ever wished for.

Most people put a lot of loving care into this exercise. It's one of my favorites, and I enjoy finding out about other people's ideal days almost as much as I like making up my own. As you read the following responses, notice the kinds of details each of these very different people has found important in each of the three categories: what, where, and who.

Julia, 32, the free-lance writer we've already heard about: "I wake up at 6 A.M. I'm living in a cool, spacious adobe house in New Mexico, with Navajo rugs on the floor and red peppers strung from the rafters. I get out of bed without disturbing my husband or the three cats who are still asleep on and around him. I go out to the stable, with the two beautiful salukis bounding beside me, feed the Arabian mare, and let her out to pasture. Then I do a little jogging in the cool morning air.

"I go back in and have coffee and a light breakfast with my husband. By 7 A.M. I go into my study, which has a big window looking out over the mesas and a big wooden desk with a broad top and lots of drawers. I write at least until noon, and two or three hours longer if I feel like it. I write whatever I please—no deadlines, no space limits, no editors' requirements. That's all over for me. I've made my reputation—and a very modest fortune that's producing interest in the bank. I've got land and a vegetable garden. I can write for myself and my friends, and if somebody wants to publish it too, fine.

"It's very important that I get lots of mail from friends all over the country and even the world!

"I meet a friend for a late lunch in town, and browse for an hour in the bookstore. In the afternoon I practice guitar and write songs; or I set type on my old hand press for a friend's book, while bread bakes in the oven and Bach plays on the stereo. Before sunset I go for a ride on the mare—gently, because I'm pregnant!

"Friends—writers, carpenters, teachers, potters, farmers, and their kids—come over for dinner, which my husband cooks. After dinner, I play guitar, and we sing, laugh, and talk around the fire. When the guests have left, we read for an hour or two, take a walk with the dogs in the starlight, and then go to bed."

Aline, 45, executive secretary to a Chicago magazine publisher and mother of three teen-agers: "I wake up, slowly, at about 7:30. That's important. I don't have to worry about getting everybody's breakfast, because John and the kids not only make their own—they bring me mine on a tray. After all, I am an important executive with weightier matters on my mind than who likes his or her eggs over easy!

"The kids wash the dishes and get ready for school while I put on my makeup and dress in the gray Chanel suit I selected the night before. (I'm twenty pounds thinner, of course.) We live in a high-rise coop with a picture window overlooking Lake Michigan, and there's time for us all to have a cup of coffee by the window and discuss what each of us is going to do today.

"Unless the weather's really miserable, I walk the ten blocks to work. It clears my head and gives me a chance to organize my thoughts for the day. When I walk into my big corner office, with the blue rug that matches the lake, I'm greeted by my secretary, who hands me a sheaf of urgent memos and letters awaiting my signature. The working day is a lot like my present boss's—phone calls to both coasts, difficult decisions, lunch with Muhammad Ali and his agent to negotiate for his memoirs, a boardroom meeting on a possible merger, the private screening of a film by our production affiliate—except that *I'm* the boss. I'm the general. And it taxes every bit of my intelligence, courage, and charm!

"I take a taxi home at 7:30. Whoever's had time has made dinner—or if the kids were all too involved in their own activities, they've ordered a pizza! I take off stockings, earrings, all the lady-executive trappings, and get into jeans. After dinner, I sit on the rug and play a ferocious game of Scrabble with my son, or help the twins with their homework. Before bed, I look over the next day's schedule in the office and decide what I'm going to wear. And then John and I share a precious half hour of jazz and brandy."

Peter, 25, a truck driver for an oil company: "I wake up late—around 9—because I've been up all night helping one of my cows deliver a calf.

It's OK because I have a staff that got the milking machines out at 6 this morning. They've gone away and won't be back until this evening. I walk downstairs into the kitchen. It's a big room with a table in the middle, and my wife is sitting there feeding our baby. The coffee is on and smells great. They both give me a big smile, and the baby stops eating and insists I pick him up. I have him on one arm, the coffee in my hand, and my wife is standing beside me with her arm around my waist, and we're all looking out the window at the beautiful farm we own, with a three-story red barn and the cows grazing up on the hills. It's a sunny, beautiful day.

"I have to go out to the other building and work on one of our trucks. They're big trucks, for transporting cattle, but they're in beautiful condition and I keep the motors in perfect shape. I'm so good at that that the neighbors are often coming over to have me help them with their engine work, and we sit around and drink beer, and work on the trucks sometimes. I arrange with my wife that I'll come down and get her and the baby at lunchtime and we'll go up to the pond and have lunch there.

"All morning I check the trucks out, tuning up a little here, adjusting there. I have a perfectly equipped garage, which is clean and organized, and every tool is in place. I do a little painting on one of the trucks— bright red—and neaten things up, and then I go outside.

"I go for a walk up on the hill to cut down a stand of briar that's getting into the coats of my cattle, and into their mouths too. Oh yes, I have a dog running after me. A nice big one, who likes to play, but can be very quiet too, when I feel like being quiet. We get to the briar patch and hack it down. It's good, hard work. Then we burn it while he keeps the cows away.

"The whole day is great. The work is steady and sometimes hard, but it's outdoors and I love it. I go to the barn when it starts to get dark, and pull the hay down for the cows, and the staff gets the milkers hooked up. The baby's asleep or something, because my wife is up in the loft with me, helping me throw the hay down. She's small, but she's strong, and funny. Makes me laugh all the time, because I can get too serious. Finally she starts tripping me so I fall down in the hay and she gives me a big hug and we're laughing a lot.

"Dinner is good and big, and some friends come over to eat. After- wards we sit around and talk for a couple of hours, and then they go home. I go around, tighten things up. Check out the doors, and the boiler, and the barn. Listen to everything, and everything is quiet and all right. We go up to bed early—maybe 10 or 11 o'clock because we're getting up early tomorrow and going into town to do some shopping. We fall asleep with our arms around each other."

Now let's take a closer look at your ideal day. By asking seven simple questions about it, you can learn a great deal about what you really need to be happy . . . how much of it you've already got . . . and what's preventing you from getting the rest of it.

FANTASY ANALYSIS: GETTING DOWN TO BASICS

I invited you to embellish your fantasy day with everything you could think of that would make that day perfect for you. But some of the things you put in may be much more important to you than others. Let's find out what they are.

Question No. 1: In each of the three categories—what, where, who —*what elements of your ideal day are absolutely indispensable to your happiness?* That is, if you never had them, you'd always be dissatisfied and long for them?

Question No. 2: What elements are *optional, but still very desirable?*

Question No. 3: What elements are *pure frills*—they'd be nice, but you could do without them and never really be unhappy?

You may find it helpful to make a little chart, like Julia did:

INDISPENSABLE

What:　　writing
　　　　　music to listen to
　　　　　physical exercise
　　　　　animals

Where:　a private study with a big desk
　　　　　a fairly spacious place to live

Who:　　my husband
　　　　　lots of friends near and far

OPTIONAL BUT DESIRABLE

What: learn to play guitar

Where: live in beautiful country near a culturally lively town

Who: a baby (strange as it may sound, I *could* be content without having a child—but I'd rather have one!)

FRILLS

What: the horse
the printing press

Where: my own adobe house in New Mexico
(I'd be thrilled if I had these things, but I wouldn't pine away if I didn't.)

That doesn't mean you shouldn't get them! I don't want you to think for a minute that this breakdown to basics is the first step toward a craven compromise with "reality." It is not. I firmly believe that you are entitled to *everything* you want—including all the frills. All we're doing here is zeroing in on your *priorities:* the things you really can't live without, the things you must therefore concentrate on getting into your life first and soonest, so that you will have the abundant energy to go for the rest.

Julia, for instance, has identified writing as the center of her life. If she doesn't have adequate space and time to write, learning to play the guitar won't be much of a consolation. In fact, she won't feel like doing it. But if her writing and living are in order, her energy and confidence will overflow naturally into the "optional but desirable" category. Her horizons will expand outward in widening circles from a happy center. And so will yours.

Not every fantasy day can be broken down as neatly as Julia's. Aline said her only indispensable element (apart from her family in the "who" category) was a "what": the executive job. And yet the high-rise apartment and designer clothes, which could be classified as "optional but desirable," would follow naturally from the kind of position and salary she wanted. Peter insisted that virtually all the elements of his fantasy day—having a dairy farm—were indispensable. Nothing less than the full scenario would satisfy him. Fine—more power to him! However your fantasy breaks down, our next task is to *measure the distance* between your life as you now live it and the minimum ideal day that would make you happy.

Question No. 4: What happens when you walk through an adjusted fantasy day with only the indispensable elements in it?

Obviously if you feel the way Peter does, your adjusted ideal day isn't going to look much different from your full-fledged fantasy. Julia, on the other hand, was able to describe a day like this:

"I'm living in New York City, where I live now—but in a bigger apartment. I get up early, have coffee with my husband, feed the cats, and walk to my study a few blocks away. It's a top floor room I've rented in a brownstone that overlooks a pretty courtyard. I write until noon, or longer if I feel like it. Then I pick up the mail, go to a health club, work out and swim.

"The rest of the day is basically the same: lunch with a friend . . . browsing in a bookstore . . . baking bread . . . listening to music . . . dinner with friends. Just take out the house, the horse, the printing press, and the guitar—for now."

Once you've got your adjusted ideal day clearly in your sights, there are three more important questions to ask about it.

Question No. 5: What—if any—elements of that day *do you already have?*

Very few of us are totally discontented with the status quo. Some of our wishes and choices have managed to find their way into reality. This question shows you what's *right* with your life; it makes you aware of the sources of satisfaction you already have. Those will be your base and your energy source as you start moving and adding more of what you want to your life. Knowing what you've got also helps you to localize and focus your discontent—the subject of the next question.

Question No. 6: What elements of the adjusted ideal day are conspicuously absent from your life right now? Use the three categories—what, where, who—to help you pinpoint what's missing.

These two questions really work together—and the results may surprise you. Julia realized that her adjusted ideal day really isn't all that different from the way she's living now. She has all the "what" and "who" elements—her work, four cats, a husband and friends, music and exercise. The big hole in her life is "where." Her apartment is small and cramped, and she hasn't got proper space to work. Aline already has the basic pattern of the life she wants—a family she loves, a responsible paying job—but she wants them on a grander scale, in brighter, bolder colors. She wants to be an executive, not an executive secretary. She wants to go all the way. And at home, she'd like more cooperation from her family.

Peter, on the other hand, said, "I really don't have any of the elements of my ideal day—what, where, or who. I'm driving a truck and living in a damn small apartment. But wait a minute, I am a good mechanic, and I keep the trucks in top shape, when I can. If I had some money, or could save some, I could probably buy one of the trucks from my boss. But it's not for cattle, really. Anyway, the farm is the point. How could I ever get my hands on a farm? I am lucky, though. I know that lady already, and I know she'd like living on a farm."

Now you've got fantasy and reality matched up so you can compare them. You may have learned that your present life isn't as far off the mark as you thought it was; or, like Peter, you may have confirmed that you really are light years from where you want to be. But in either case, you now know more precisely what's missing . . . and you know what you've got to work with. Dream and reality are in focus. *Now let's try focusing in on the gap—or the barrier—between them.* For the first time since we began, I'm going to ask you to take a good look at "hard reality."

Question No. 7: What stands between you and having your adjusted ideal day tomorrow? That is, what would it take to get all the missing elements? What problems or obstacles are presently stopping you from getting them?

For Julia, it's money. A bigger apartment would cost her twice the rent she's paying now, and she'd have to pay at least $100 a month more for a separate study.

Aline realized that all she's really lacking is self-confidence, or a belief in herself. She said, "I think I have the experience and the knowledge for an executive job in magazine publishing. In fact, I know I do! But I'm scared to stand up and make my move. Same thing with my family. I could ask for—or demand—more help, but I don't want them to be mad at me!"

Peter said he needed so many things—a farm, money, some experience with cows and the business of running a dairy farm—that he tended to get overwhelmed and give up before he started. He was able to sum up his feelings of futility in two major obstacles. "One: I don't really believe it's possible to save the money to buy a farm from a workingman's salary. Two: even if it is possible, I wouldn't know where to start with all the details."

What stands between you and your modified dream day—the minimum "what," "where," and "who" that would make you happy?

I want you to know that you are certainly going to need what Aline needs. Not courage . . . not self-confidence . . . but *support.* You'll find it in the last section of this book. And you are certainly going to need what Peter needs. Not a pep talk (You can do it, kid!) . . . not an inheritance from an obscure rich uncle . . . but a *game plan* that tells you what to do first, and then what to do next after that, and so on, all the way to the goal. You'll find that in Section III. As you saw in Chapter 2, everybody needs structure, and everybody needs support. The ones who don't need 'em have already got 'em! So those are universal problems.

But then come all the specific, personal, circumstantial obstacles that keep us from having what we want. For you, it may be money . . . or a school degree that's required to do the kind of work you want to do . . . or a new job . . . or the contacts to get one . . . or a skill you don't have . . . or the time to learn it . . . or twenty extra pounds that are cramping your style with the opposite sex . . . or several of the above . . . or something else I haven't even mentioned.

I'd like you to do a very simple thing—so simple that you won't believe it's the first step to overcoming those obstacles. But it is. Take a sheet of paper. Write the word "Problems" across the top. And then just list them—all the real-world reasons why you can't have your dream.

You have now begun to see "hard reality" for what it really is: not an all-pervasive nerve gas that poisons hope and paralyzes will, just a couple of concrete and clearly-defined problems. At this point, I know those barriers to your dream may look insurmountable. Don't worry about it. Just write them down. As we work on clearly defining your goals in the next chapter, more problems, obstacles, and objections will probably occur to you. Add them to the list. I want you to keep that Problems List with care—because a little later on it's going to turn out to be a gold mine.

When you're choosing a concrete goal to go for—and that's going to be your next task—it's more important than ever to get reality considerations out of the way, so that they don't dim or diminish your vision. I want your goal to be larger than life (our lives are too small!) and in living color, so that it's worthy of the real you—and something you can fall totally in love with. But that doesn't mean we're not going to come back and deal with reality. On the contrary! We're going to tackle it with relish—and technique. When I show you how to convert insurmountable obstacles into solvable problems, and how to liberate the inborn problem-solving capacity of your mind, your Problems List will yield all the raw materials you need to build a good, solid road to your goal. But first, let's get a good sharp fix on where you're going.

You've discovered that you know how you want your days to be, just as clearly as you know what clothes you want in your closet. Now it's time to start shaping fantasy and style into something you can actually get your hands on.

– 4 –

Goalsearch

What is a goal?

A goal is the basic unit of life design. It's easy to dream; with just a little encouragement you can close your eyes and conjure up a whole new life for yourself. But if you want to make that life come true, you will have to start by choosing one piece of it and deciding that that's the one you're going to go for first. Then you may still have to do a little work on that piece to turn it into something that's really reachable— not a mirage that keeps on receding ahead of you. A true goal—the kind that will hold still and let you catch it—lives up to two basic rules.

Rule No. 1: A goal is *concrete.* It is a matter of facts, not feelings. You will know beyond a doubt when you've arrived, because you will have something in your hands that you can look at, touch, and show off to other people. I'll give you an example.

Suppose you think your goal is "to be a doctor." In fact, that's still a dream. Your *actual* goal is, "To get my M.D. degree." Why? Because on the day when they hand you that piece of paper, you and society will agree that you are now a doctor. You may not feel much like a doctor. Or you may feel like a doctor one day and a terrified fake in a white coat the next. The process of growing into the healer's role is gradual, complex, and uncertain; you cannot predict the exact date when you will at last feel unshakably sure that "I am a doctor." But there's nothing uncertain about an M.D. Either you've got it or you haven't —and you can take concrete steps to get it by a specific date.

That's a key point. Your true goal, or *target,* has to be a *concrete*

64

action or event, not only so you'll know for sure when you get there, but so that you can make that date with success in advance! Setting a *target date* is the beginning of all effective planning—the antidote to both procrastination ("Oh, I'll get there someday") and despair ("I'll *never* get there"). If you know you've committed yourself to write three short stories by April, or to get your M.D. degree by June, 1985, then *time* suddenly becomes a quantity you can work with—and had better start working with right now if you don't want to miss that deadline. I'll have more to say about target dates later on. Right now it's enough simply to recognize that you won't be able to set a target date unless you have a target. Nobody has ever succeeded in designing and building a bridge to a cloud.

Becoming a doctor is an easy example, because the target—getting an M.D.—is ready-made. But suppose your goal—like the goal of two young actresses I worked with—is something like "To be a movie star"? That's still a dream, of course, because how are you going to know when you're a movie star? The answer is, *only you can decide.* You can make your target any concrete, specific action or event that will satisfy you that you've arrived—but you must choose one, or you'll never get on the road at all.

What would have to happen for you to be able to say, "Now I am a movie star" (or the best literary agent in New York, or a successful racing yacht designer, or famous, or rich)? Your answer won't be the same as anybody else's answer, because the "same" goal can mean completely different things to different people. (Remember how two people could look at the same color and call it "rust" and "rose"?) I know I'll be rich when I have $100,000 free and clear—and I know millionaires who aren't there yet! For Carol, a Minneapolis secretary and part-time model, being a movie star means glamour and publicity —her name in all the gossip columns, her face in all the poster stores, furs, limousines, flashbulbs. June, an undergraduate student of theater, sees stardom as getting the best parts and the highest accolades for her acting. So when Carol and June both sit down to make a *target* out of "being a movie star," Carol might say, "A poster of me in every poster store," and June might say "Getting my first Oscar." And they'd both be right. *The only person you have to satisfy is yourself.*

There are two guidelines you can use in the actual process of goal choice that will help you zero in on the right target for you. I call them your *touchstone* and your *role model.*

Your *touchstone* is *the emotional core of your goal*—what you want and need from it, what you love best about it. It's the sweet center of that goal for you. Creative fulfillment . . . fame . . . money . . . the chance to help people . . . closeness to nature . . . love—if you can put *your* touchstone into one or a few words, it will not only help you pick a target that's loaded with the kind of sweets that nourish *you,* it will also show you how to design the shortest, most direct and gratifying route to that goal, and it will get you to the essence of any goal that looks impossible.

A *role model* is someone you'd like to be, someone who's actually done what you want to do—or the closest thing to it. You probably already have at least one role model. Whom do you particularly admire? Whose life and achievements do you covet? Role models are not only good for goal definition, but for inspiration, encouragement —and practical guidance. If anyone anywhere on Planet Earth has done what you want to do, it means that you can do it too. Put that person's picture up on your wall. Go to the library, read about his or her life, and find out how s/he did it! You might get some ideas. Remember Peter, who wanted to be a dairy farmer, starting from scratch, but didn't believe it was possible? I suggested he pick up local newspapers from the towns he drove through in dairy country, until he got to know something about the local people and saw how a lot of them made it through the yearly business of farming on sheer determination—not because they had a lot of money. He found an interesting role model. A young man from a nearby city who had never been on a farm, and moved into the area—onto a dairy farm which also served as an inn or hotel for hunters in hunting season—and who ran a snowmobile and "all-terrain vehicle" dealership from his garage.

Here's how touchstone and role model can help you draw a bead on your target:

Carol	Dream:	movie or TV star
	Touchstone:	glamour and publicity

Role Model:	Farrah Fawcett-Majors
Target:	my face in every poster store

June	Dream:	movie star
	Touchstone:	acclaim for fine acting
	Role Model:	Anne Bancroft
	Target:	Get an Oscar

This process should give you a target that passes the second test for goals:

Rule No. 2: When you say "This is what I want," *you're not fooling.* If I could wave a magic wand and POOF! you'd have that goal right now, you honestly think you'd be delighted.

The purpose of this rule is to distinguish real, gut dreams from passing fancies. Many of us have daydreamed at one time or another of being a movie star, or a mountain climber, or even President of the United States. But if I waved my magic wand and POOF! you were halfway up Everest, would you be in your element—or would you long desperately to be home in your nice warm armchair daydreaming about it? There's an easy way to find out. Use your own built-in magic wand —"real daydreaming"! Remember? First person, present tense, visual, and sequential. Like this:

"POOF! I am the President of the United States. I am sitting at my desk in the Oval Office. It is 9:30 in the morning. On my left is a stack of paper about two feet high, urgently requiring my decision on such matters as the energy crisis, the Middle East peace negotiations, the SALT talks, and the diplomatic status of the People's Republic of China. On my right is a red telephone, ominously silent. I . . . I . . . Agghh!! Let me out of here!"

That, my friend, is the acid test for any goal. Try living it in imagination. How does it feel? Love it? Great. Hate it? Change the target. Not just whims, but also "shoulds"—the things you think you ought to want because your father, grandmother, wife, husband, or favorite teacher wanted them for you—will be unmasked by this "magic wand" test. When I say that you must have what you want, it's equally important for you to know that *you must not work hard to get what you don't want.* It will only give you indigestion—and you won't be any good at it anyway. So try to rule it out from the start.

"But what if I'm not sure?" you may be saying. "I've come up with something I think I'd love, but supposing I get there—or even halfway there—and discover that I've made a terrible mistake and it's not what I want after all?"

Simple. You will take the piece of paper on which you wrote down that goal, tear it up into little pieces, and throw it out the window. And then you will take another piece of paper and write down another one. *No goal is written in blood.*

One of the most harmful misconceptions in our society is that you've got to figure out what you want and then you've got to *stick* to it. This attitude is one of the things that makes it so hard to get into action. We hesitate to commit ourselves to our choices because we're afraid they will be life sentences! That's nonsense. Goals exist only to serve you and make you happy. You don't exist to serve *them.* If a goal isn't serving you, you are free to change it. It's just that sometimes there's no way to find out whether or not a particular goal really suits you except by trying it. If it doesn't suit you, you will still have gained something priceless: *the experience of making real progress toward a goal—and the practical skills for doing it.* Those skills can be applied to any goal— just as your hands, once they've actually built a bookcase, can easily craft a kitchen cabinet.

CHOOSING A TARGET

The way you go about actually choosing your target will depend on what kind of dreams you cherish—and that in turn depends on who you are and where you are in your life right now. You may be a single-minded achiever with one burning ambition, or you may be an "artist of living" to whom the total quality of life is all-important. You may be basically happy with your life as it is, yet have one or more long-dormant interests you'd like to work into it for your own pleasure. You may be in one of the adolescences of life (I think there are at least two), when everything is up in the air and you aren't really sure what you want. You may be a "Renaissance person" who isn't happy unless you have two or three irons in the fire at a time. And *you may be any or all of the above at different times in your life.*

Wherever you start, you'll have a different set of design problems to grapple with. Your goal may seem too vague, too distant, or too broad to fit neatly into target form; you may feel you have no goal at all— or too many goals altogether. But in each case you can arrive at a target that is *carefully tailored to you* and *realizable in time.* Here's how some real people have done it.

The Naked Touchstone: Andrea

It took quite a bit of coaxing before Andrea, a 26-year-old New York secretary, admitted with embarrassment that what she really wanted was *to be famous*—she wasn't even sure what for. "I think it's really kind of sick that I feel this way," she said. "It keeps me from being able to just do things and enjoy doing them."

The first thing I did was give Andrea a friendly little lecture to get her off the hook of her own guilt. I'll give it to you too, because this kind of apologetic attitude is so common and so crippling. *What you want is what you need—and you must have it.* I don't care what it is —short of blatantly destructive or self-destructive acts—and "Why do you want it?" is one question I never ask. If what you want is to marry a millionaire, fine! I've actually helped someone do that. If it's fame, great! Andrea doesn't have a guilty secret, she has *a touchstone in search of a goal.* Before it can find one, though, it needs to be more clearly defined.

I asked Andrea whether any kind of fame at all would satisfy her. What if she designed a new kind of shoelace, made five million dollars, and got written up in *Time* as one of "The New Millionaires"? Would that do it? She said, "No, money isn't that important to me." Well, then how about going over Niagara Falls in a barrel? Another decisive "No." So we were *not* simply talking about fame. I asked Andrea whether she could name some of the things she thought she might enjoy being famous for.

"Well . . . movie star or director, singer, photographer, fashion designer. It's fame for performance, for a kind of continual performance —not a one-shot deal. The trouble is, I don't know whether I'd really like to do those things, or whether I'd just like to be famous for them!"

I asked her whether she would like to be *respected* for what she did —for the quality of her work. She said yes, that would be important. So Andrea's touchstone could now be defined: "Fame for continual, quality performance."

Now we had to figure out how she could get some of that flavor of fame into her life as quickly as possible.

That's a point I'm going to be driving home for the rest of this chapter—and the rest of this book. *The sooner you start getting some of what you really want, the more energy you'll have to go for the rest of it!* You'll also be happier, healthier, and nicer to be around. That's why it's so important to identify your touchstone—and to pick a target that gets at least a shining chip of it into your hands right away. I'm not a believer in "delayed gratification." Never take the long way around if you can get the essence of your goal by a shorter route.

Since fame itself was more important to Andrea than the field she got famous in, it would speed things along if she picked a field where she didn't have to start from scratch. So I asked her if she already had skills and experience in any of the things she thought she'd like to be famous for—filmmaking, photography, fashion design. She said she'd done some photography, and had even gotten so involved that she'd stayed up all night developing prints in a friend's darkroom! So photography it was. Now we needed to find out what kind of photography would bring Andrea the celebrity she wanted by the speediest route.

Fine art photography was out. Andrea would undoubtedly find the artist's route to fame far too slow, hard, and chancy; she'd give up in frustration long before she got her first taste. That's what I mean by not going the long way around. Both fashion photography and photojournalism looked more promising, but Andrea thought fashion was too technical and competitive and news photography too anonymous and dull. At this point, I told her to try naming a *role model;* it might jell the process of goalsearch for her.

Andrea chose two: Richard Avedon, the controversial portrait artist who started out as a fashion photographer, and Annie Leibowitz, the young *Rolling Stone* photojournalist whose pictures of rock stars have been collected in two books. Her choices were inspired—because *celeb-*

rity is contagious! Celebrities are vain. They *love* to have their pictures taken. And some of their stardust is bound to rub off on anyone who makes it her business to take their pictures. Andrea's quickest route to fame with quality might very well be taking good pictures of famous people.

From there it was a short step to defining Andrea's *target:* "To have one or more photographs of celebrities published in a quality national magazine." It was beautifully tailored to Andrea's needs, it could be planned for a target date—and she knew she'd love it. Of course, she came up with all kinds of problems. I told her to put them down on her Problems List:

"I can't afford to quit my job—too little time to work on this

"Big magazines won't take unknown photographers

"I'm afraid I'm not good enough

"I'm too shy to approach famous people."

Don't forget to compile a Problems List of your own as you define *your* target.

The Long Haul: June

What had always stopped Andrea from thinking clearly about her goals before was the feeling, "I know what I want, but I think I shouldn't want it!" For June, the theater student whose target was "Getting my first Oscar," the problem was different: "I know exactly what I want, but it's so far away—how will I ever get there?"

June was a senior at a large state university who had fallen in love with acting in student productions and had gotten rave reviews in the school paper. She was bravely aiming high, but she didn't even know whether to move to New York or Los Angeles after graduation, much less how to put her new ambition on the shortest road to success.

When you have a long-range target like June's, it's still, in a way, a dream. You can and should set a date to it—that will help to make it real—but it isn't a goal you can plot your path to, reach out and grab . . . at least not soon enough to give you joy and hope. So you will need to set yourself a *first target:* a smaller goal that's both a step on the road to your ultimate destination and a little triumph in its own right. And once again, the most important factor to keep in mind is your touchstone. Since June's touchstone was "recognition for fine acting," it would make little sense for her to move to L.A. and try to get her first TV commercial—a first target that might be perfect for Carol, the other aspiring star I knew whose touchstone was "glamour and publicity." June will get more of her kind of satisfaction sooner if she makes her first target something like, "To star in my first Off-Off-Broadway workshop." Once she's reached that, she might make it her next target to land a major part in a low-budget or student movie.

Touchstone planning is high-energy planning. By designing her path so that she gets the kind of experience and recognition she wants right up front, June may find that she reaches her goal—that Oscar—much sooner than she ever dreamt possible. On the other hand, she'll also have plenty of chances to decide on the basis of *experience, not fantasy,* that yes, this flavor of success really is for her . . . or it really isn't . . . or it was, but she's had enough now and is ready for something else —like teaching or painting or a year in Spain.

Remember: long-term goals especially are never written in blood. Because we change. And one of the things that changes us most is getting what we want. Sometimes your touchstone is like a stone in the middle of the road: until you get it, you can't get past it. When you do get it, it may whet your appetite for more of the same . . . or a part of you may be at peace for the first time, so that you can suddenly hear the voices of your other loves. So if you think you have a long-range goal, a first target is a handy *unit of commitment*—a sort of trial marriage! It's also just the right size for learning and practicing the planning techniques in the second half of this book.

The Ideal Day: Peter, Aline, and Julia

You may have another kind of trouble arriving at a first target if the goal you want is a broad one—a vision of a total lifestyle. Suppose you're a city mouse with a tidy little apartment and a tidy little salary, and what you really long to be is a country squire living on a vast estate? Or suppose that like Peter, the would-be dairy-farmer, you've made your actual target "To live my ideal day in every detail"? (That, by the way, is something you *can* put a date on.) When you look at the gap between where you are and where you want to be and the thousand things that have to be done to cross it, your question is going to be, "Where on earth do I start?"

Again, setting a first target—one that both makes you happy *now* and leads toward the rest of your dream—is the key to action and the antidote to despair. But in this case the process of choosing that first target is a little different. Instead of using your touchstone, you'll use the breakdown of your ideal day.

In each of the three categories—*what, where,* and *who*—you decided which elements of your fantasy day you've really got to have, which are optional but desirable, and which ones are just the sugar roses on the cake. The most important question you can ask yourself now is: *What is the highest-priority item that is missing from my life right now?* If you can give a single resounding answer to this question, you've got your first target.

For example, if you live in the city and you've just got to be down on the farm, your first target is a "where": to get yourself into a house with at least a few acres and a few chickens around it. (If you think that's impossible, just write down all the reasons why it's impossible on your Problems List and put them aside for later.) If you're like Aline, the executive secretary who wanted to be an executive, then a "what" —a promotion or change of job—will be your first target. Or you may be like my 32-year-old lawyer friend Miriam, who has "everything but" —she has a good job with an insurance law firm, a beautiful apartment, nice clothes, friends she loves—and has calmly decided to find the one piece that's missing for her: a husband.

But what if more than one crucial piece of your dream is missing? You may remember that Peter had almost none of the elements of his ideal day—and he wanted all of them! If you're in that bind, there's a second question that will help you get out of it: *Of the essential elements that are missing, which one can I get most quickly, cheaply, and easily?* That's where you'll start—because my objective is to get you on your path without more delay. That first target will lead you toward the next element of your dream . . . and the next . . . and the next.

Julia, the free-lance writer, needed *space:* living space and working space. If she had both, she'd already be living her stripped-down ideal day—and making progress toward the full scenario. But she didn't think she could afford both. Which should she make her first target? To move to a bigger apartment with an extra room to write in could solve the problem in one stroke, but it would more than double the rent of Julia's little rent-controlled studio, and moving would take at least two months away from her work. She realized that the quickest, cheapest, and easiest alternative was to keep her apartment and rent a separate work space for about $100 a month. With a good place to work in, she'd get more done, earn more money—and be better able to afford an apartment she really loved.

One thing Peter could do right away, at no expense, was to pull his fiancée into the project and spend some time researching the whole project. That would get him on his path by providing two of the pleasures of his ideal day: working on solving problems that had to do with being a farmer, and doing it with someone he loved. Once the two of them find some likely locations and start visiting some of the farms, they'll be ready to think about the money details. In fact, it may very well be that some of the situations they want could be available without huge down payments or the need for Peter to give up his present job right away. Peter might even find a job as driver and mechanic in a farm-equipment dealership in the area of his choice. He could repair tractors and combines and get to know the local farmers and their farms, so although he won't be living on a farm, he'll be doing what he loves—and surrounding himself with country life, country thinking, and learning actual facts about the requirements of his dream. (By the way, if there's a lot of "who" missing from *your* life, I'll tell you a secret: *there's nothing like doing what you love to attract the people you need.* Get your show on the road, and you'll find that a lot of people want parts in it.)

Impossible Dreams: Adele

It happens at least once in every Success Teams seminar, when I make the outrageous statement that everyone—regardless of age, sex, income, or education—can get what she or he really wants. Somebody always raises a hand and says, "Oh, yeah? Not me." Adele, a handsome woman in her early 50s, said, "What *I* want is to be prima diva in the Metropolitan Opera. And I've never sung a note in my life. Let's face it . . . there's no way."

Some people say things like that just to prove that I'm wrong, that you *can't* get what you want in life. Those people usually flunk the magic-wand test. They don't really want to be President of the United States or the next Beverly Sills; they just want to protect their real dreams against hope and the pain of disappointment. But sometimes we're dealing with something much more serious: an old childhood dream that's refused to die. Remember the exercise where you thought about "What You Might Have Been" if your childhood environment had been different? Well, what if you still secretly long to be that concert pianist, ballerina, heart surgeon, Chairman of the Board, astronaut, or famous novelist—and you're 30, 40, 50 or 60 years old?

I stick by my statement. If you really, really want that dream, *you can still have it*—unless it's a dream like Adele's. She really does have a problem, because she has chosen the pinnacle of one of the few professions—there are only a few—in which it's truly impossible to make it to the top from a late start. These are the physically demanding arts and sports in which the youthful capacities of the body, plus early training, are a must. A 45-year-old insurance salesman, however physically fit he is, cannot make it his goal to become a major-league ballplayer, a professional boxer, a principal tenor at the Met, or Rudolf Nureyev. (That's not to say he couldn't take up dance or singing or boxing or baseball and achieve considerable skill and pleasure.) And Adele cannot be Beverly Sills. She's right about that. But that doesn't mean she should give up her dream. She should take it very, very seriously, because it's telling her what she needs to be happy. And that is something she can and must get—*her touchstone.*

If you're deeply in love with a goal you're sure is impossible, don't become bitter about "what might have been" and consider your life wasted. Ask yourself, *what is the touchstone?* Why do I want this goal? If you came to me with Adele's dream, I'd try to find out what it is about being Beverly Sills that you'd love so much. Is it stardom—being rich, famous, adored? Or do you just love to sing and long to be able to make those wonderful sounds? Is it opera in particular that you love to sing? Have you always wanted to get on stage and sing in an operatic production? Or are you so crazy about professional opera that you'd do anything just to be around a top-flight opera company, even if you can't sing a note?

Now take that touchstone and design a goal around it!

If what you want is to be a star and get interviewed on every talk show from coast to coast, you can do it. I promise you, there is something unique in your style or your experience that you can parlay into stardom. People have achieved celebrity for everything from bridge to gardening, from a love of cats to the experience of motherhood. And everybody knows that once you are a star, you get the chance to do all kinds of things—even get up in front of people and sing!

If what you love is to sing . . . sing! In the shower, in the morning, at the top of your lungs, at the drop of a hat. I love to sing. I do it in my kitchen all the time. I don't need good reviews, and I can wear whatever I want! Seriously, take voice lessons. Why not? You can get good enough to please yourself, good enough to sing *Lieder* with the accompanist from your local music society, even good enough, if opera is your passion, to star in an amateur production . . . and if you can't find one, start one. You might just wake up one day and find yourself the local Beverly Sills.

If you want to get next to a professional opera company, there are a dozen ways to do that. You can march straight to the production office and tell them they need a crack secretary who knows opera from A to Z. (It's OK to use your skills to get through a door.) You can start an Introduction to Opera course for adults or children, and arrange to take them backstage after performances. You can organize charity benefits. You can write program notes. You can interview company members on public-access cable TV. The list could go on and on—and it should include *every idea that comes into your head,* no matter how silly, far-fetched, or half-baked it seems. "Take off all my clothes and streak across the stage during Act I of *Aïda*" would be a perfectly legitimate item on your list.

This is *basic brainstorming*—the simplest form of a proven technique for liberating the ingenuity to solve problems. It's a way of casting your net as wide as possible before you haul it in and examine your catch. If you're afraid to let your thoughts go beyond the limits of "reality" and "good sense," you may never catch that one fugitive idea shining on the margins of possibility that holds the answer for you.

When you've put down all the ideas you can think of, you go down the list and look at each one. No matter how absurd or impractical that idea is, *you must find something useful in it.* Then note problems; *what I learned about myself* (the goofiest idea that pops into your head can give you clues to your own talents and needs); and finally, *suggestions and lessons.* That way, even if you throw that idea out, you're only throwing out the shell; you've saved the meat, and you can get new ideas from it.

For example:

Idea: Streaking

Useful: It gets lots of attention *fast*

Problems: Wrong kind of attention—too anonymous, short-lived, embarrassing, and you wind up in jail

What I learned about myself: There's a little voice in me saying "Look at me —see me"

Suggestions and lessons: A more dignified kind of publicity stunt? Street theater? Singing in the park? Speechmaking?

Then you go on from there. And sooner or later you're going to find a target that will get you the core satisfactions of your "impossible" dream in eminently possible form.

But I want you to know that most dreams are not impossible. We've just been brainwashed into thinking they are. A few limits to possibility are in the human body. A few. *The rest are in the mind, and those can be changed.* Look how drastically the rules about what women can and can't do have changed in the last ten years! We've got female executives, astronauts, truck drivers, West Point cadets, and jockeys. It's about time for another cruel set of myths to get their comeuppance—the myths of ageism, the ones that say "It's too late." Those myths don't only hurt "senior citizens" facing forced retirement. They do violence to our whole life cycle, lopping off another set of possibilities at each decade. If you're not studying ballet at 10, if you're not a concert pianist by 20, a promising scientist or novelist by 30, an up-and-coming young executive by 35, and at the top of your field by 45 . . . forget it!

It's just not true—not a word of it. A former concert pianist in her 60s has told me that some of her best and most serious pupils are people in their 40s. What they may have lost in agility, they more than make up in drive and concentration. Unlike so many young people, they know what they want, they know how to work, and they know the value of time. And the same is true of older people in pursuit of any goal. There are examples all around us of people who've started a whole new activity or career in the second half of life and been resoundingly successful—like English professor Norman MacLean, who published his first book to rave reviews at the age of 72. Or like Grace Bloom, who got her Master's degree at the age of 86. Or like Catherine Zirpolo, who "always wanted to be in the theater. 'When I was about nine, I wanted to be like Theda Bara or someone like that. I would practice in front of the mirror.' Although Zirpolo's family discouraged her theatrical ambitions, and marriage at eighteen and children soon after further postponed her plans, she never lost her love for the theater. . . . 'And at the age of seventy-five I began!' she marvels." She is a featured player with the New Wrinkle Theater of Greater Boston, a performing troupe made up entirely of players over 60.* So it's hardly "too late" for a 28-year-old to take up the cello, or a 54-year-old to get into politics!

Short of total impossibility, there's only one question to ask yourself about an ambitious goal like "What You Might Have Been." And that is: *Am I willing to work for it?* Are you willing to spend the ten or fifteen years building a political career that it would take to run for the Senate? Do you have the competitive passion for the corporate climb? Are you willing to be the only 40-year-old woman in your medical school class, and to be 45 before you start your practice?

I don't mean, "Are you too scared to do it?" If your goal is worthy of you, if it really challenges you, you're bound to be scared. That fear is natural, and it's no reason to give up on a dream you crave. The real question here is, *How badly do I want it?* If the answer is, "Badly enough to go all the way," then more power to you, and I'll show you how to deal with the fear. But what if you decide that the price in time and work simply outweighs the satisfactions of the goal?

You have an alternative—an alternative both to giving up that dream and to enslaving yourself to it. *Find the touchstone and design another goal around it*—one you would be willing to work for. Get the same

---

*Nancy DuVergne Smith, "New Wrinkle Theater," *New Age* 4 (February 1979): 48.

satisfactions in quicker, simpler form. If the heart of doctoring for you is helping people, you might choose nursing, physical therapy, counseling, midwifery, massage, dance-exercise, or nutrition. If your touchstone is fascination with the scientific aspects of health and disease, you could go into medical pathology, scientific writing, or medical illustration. It's up to you. The real kicker is that you may come up with something better suited to you than the original goal!

When we think about what we want to do and be, our imaginations often get stuck with the standard roles available in society's costume closet: doctor, lawyer, merchant, chief. We choose one that sort of vaguely approximately fits us, and then we try to fit ourselves into *it* —instead of finding or making up something that's perfect for who *we* are. For example, when I was a little girl I wanted to grow up and star in Broadway musicals. My role model was Judy Garland. I couldn't have told you why, but I can tell you now: I craved attention and admiration and love. I wanted to get up on stage and sing my heart out for an audience and have them pour their love out for me.

As it happened, what I grabbed and got was being a therapist. And every time I walked into Group Laboratories, of which I was the president, I got looked at as if I were important. I was very famous on Ninety-first Street and Broadway. Nobody else had ever heard of me, but I felt like a star. I was giving everything I had, and I was getting all the love and respect I'd ever needed—not from a far-off audience, but from people I could love and touch. It gave me the strength to go on and invent the Women's Success Teams Seminars, where I can get up and perform in front of forty to three hundred people—and even go on TV.

The reason it all happened is that life tricked me into discovering my touchstone. If I *had* become a Broadway star, I might have loved it, but I doubt it. I think I would have hated it. I tried acting, when I was thirty and divorced and alone in New York with my kids. I scraped together a little money, enrolled in acting classes at HB Studio, and got a few parts in small showcases. And you know what? The only thing I liked about it was getting up onstage, turning people on, and basking in their love. I didn't like acting classes, I didn't like rehearsals, I didn't like theaters, I didn't like other actors—and I didn't much care for pretending to be someone other than myself. (That's how I'm different from a born actor.) If I hadn't had my kids, who kept me from traveling in summer stock productions, I might have gone on with it anyway, but I like to think that by now I'd have gotten tired of it and gone on to do exactly what I'm doing!

I designed the touchstone concept to encourage you to be just as inventive on purpose as I was by necessity and inspired accident. You can have the most fun of all designing a goal if you're in one of those "adolescences" I mentioned—the periods of change and self-discovery when you aren't at all sure what you want, and the world is wide open.

There are two "official" adolescences. One is the late teens and early twenties, when so many kids knock around trying out different jobs in different places in an unhurried search for something that feels right. The other is mid-life, when a man or woman has met the goals of the first half of life—raising kids, economic security, success in a profession —and may be free and ready for something totally new. But you really reenter adolescence whenever you go through a major life transition, like marriage, divorce, widowhood, your kids starting school—or meeting a long-held goal! Even losing a job, with its financial anxieties, can give you an opportunity to reexamine and redesign your life. Even early motherhood, with its heavy demands on time and restricted freedom of movement, changes your image of yourself and opens up new possibilities. Just reading this book may have pitched you headlong into an adolescence! (The root meaning of the word is "being nourished to grow.") If so, you may be having a lot of fascinating but confusing second thoughts about what you want in life. You may not even be able to define your touchstone—or to choose one out of all the possibilities that are calling to you.

You're in luck. The genius child in you is getting a fresh chance. You get to play around with *all* the talents and qualities you discovered in your Stylesearch, combining and recombining them like pieces of a puzzle until they click into a goal design that's uniquely yours.

Starting From Style: Alan and Victoria

The most important exercises to work with here are "The Private-Eye Game" and "Twenty Things You Like to Do." Your Detective's Report and Life Quality Profile give you a rich and compact portrait of your own genius. Is there a unifying theme running through that portrait that you could call your touchstone? Do different aspects of your style suggest some possible goal ideas? Can you invent ingenious combinations that get several of your qualities and interests into one package? Remember to use *basic brainstorming* to free your imagination. The wildest idea you come up with may be the one that gives you your goal.

Alan's Detective's Report revealed that he liked plenty of space, the textures of wood and stone, and natural foods. He lived in a small apartment in Chicago, but he'd taken the plaster off one wall to expose the brick, and painted the rest of his walls white to get as much light and spaciousness into the apartment as possible. He had lots of plants, and a big poster of a mountain view that was almost like a window into another world. The books on his shelves ran heavily to things like Thoreau and Rachel Carson and the Whole Earth Catalog.

Alan's Life Quality Profile told him first and foremost that, at 29, he wasn't living the kind of life he loved best. He lived in Chicago because he had gone to school there, and after school he'd gotten a job with an educational publisher, which he enjoyed. But he loved to be outdoors; he liked mountain climbing, though he hadn't done much of it (there isn't a decent-sized hill within 1000 miles of Chicago); he enjoyed doing things with his hands, but as a busy city person he hadn't had much time for that either. He liked to be alone. He loved to read. He didn't need a lot of money to be happy—and he'd *save* money on vacations if he lived out West. After looking over this portrait of himself, he summed up his touchstone as "Closeness to nature—in particular, the Rocky Mountains."

That didn't tell Alan anything he didn't already know—*but he'd never considered it a legitimate basis for designing his life!* Like so many of us, he'd assumed that the serious business of earning a living ruled out having what he loved most in the world for more than two or three weeks out of each year. He'd always figured he was lucky enough to have an interesting job. His Success Teams seminar convinced him of the importance of living a total life more in line with his genius. Challenged to design a goal, Alan said he thought he'd be happy as a national park ranger, fire lookout, forester, or tree planter. Even better, since it would work in his love for books, he could open a bookstore in a small mountain town—or start a small publishing firm specializing in field guides, backpacking manuals, and nature philosophy. Or, since he liked his job, he could explore the possibility of opening an office of his company in Denver, or transferring to the sales department and asking for the western territory.

Of course, no matter which of these potential goals Alan chose, there would be problems. He knew he'd have to face his father's disappointment if he chose a field like forest rangering that didn't make use of his education. Starting a bookstore or publishing firm required risk capital and entrepreneurial know-how he didn't have. And moving west for his own firm meant persuading his boss of the move's business value. But problems are not a reason to give up on having the life you want. *Choose the goal that sounds most exciting to you—even if it's the most "impossible."* Alan decided to start a small specialty publishing house. He made his target the incorporation of the venture with enough backing capital to survive for two years. (Always remember to state your goal in the form of a *target* that can be reached by a specific date.)

Victoria, the divorced, 42-year-old mother of four, loved to get her hands on fine antiques—which she couldn't afford. She'd inherited one beautiful old table from her aunt; otherwise, she'd decorated her house with the best things she could find in junk shops, a couple of which she had stripped and refinished herself. She loved to spend Sundays prowling around those shops among dusty old things that might turn out to be treasures. She was fascinated by the feel of living history old things gave her. Her favorite books were historical romances. She enjoyed giving parties with gourmet cooking, beautiful table settings, and good conversation—when she could get the younger kids into bed and find three matching plates that weren't chipped. She remembered her college years with nostalgia, because that was the only time in her life when she'd been surrounded by people active in the arts. She loved going to the theater.

Victoria had a lot of trouble and fun defining her touchstone. She finally expressed it as "Authentic historical atmosphere—the drama of the past in things, especially elegant things." But she didn't have any trouble coming up with goal ideas—she found about fifteen! Some of them were: become an antique dealer or interior decorator; open her own second-hand shop so the dust-covered treasures would come to *her;* become an auctioneer and run estate sales; do professional refinishing in her garage; design "period" sets for productions in a local theater; lead tours of the great castles of Europe—or of the historic homes in her own town; start a local historical society.

Victoria's problems were time and money, and they loomed large. She supported her kids by working as personnel manager for a large insurance company. Her job was fairly routine but secure, and she couldn't afford to give it up. But she realized that an occasional wistful ramble through the antique shops near Hartford was just not enough of what she loved. So I advised her to make her first target something she could start doing or learning *now,* in the time she had free— weekends and an occasional evening.

Victoria happily set herself not one but two targets: to start doing refinishing jobs for friends and neighbors on weekends (which would bring her both pleasure and extra income), and to enroll in an interior-decorating course in the city one evening a week, with an eye to a possible future change of career. On top of that, she's volunteering to design the set for her daughter's high-school Shakespeare play!

Victoria's situation brings up a problem you're likely to run into, too. What if, after doing the exercises in the first half of this book, you've got *too many* things you want to do? You can't possibly fit them into one lifetime; you'd need at least five.

Congratulations! You haven't got a problem, you've got an embarrassment of riches. I'm not going to tell you to make up your mind and leave the lost possibilities for your next incarnation, because nobody's ever succeeded in proving to me that there's going to be one. What I'm going to do is *give* you five lives—in imagination—as a guide to getting the most out of the one you've got.

FIVE LIVES—AND HOW TO LIVE THEM ALL

Think about it: if you had five lives, what would you do with each one?

I don't mean if you were five different people. I mean if you could be *you* five times over, and explore a different talent, interest, or lifestyle to the fullest each time.

This is an exercise, and like all the exercises in this book, it's flexible —you're supposed to tailor it to you. If you could manage nicely with three lives, take three. If you need ten, help yourself. I just picked five because it's a nice round number.

In one of my lives, I'd be exactly what I am. In one I'd be a nine-teenth-century botanist and spend all my time painting flowers. In another I'd be a theoretical physicist. In my fourth, I'd still be Judy Garland—no, something a little less intense and tragic: a musical-comedy star! In my fifth, I'd be a hermit and live alone on an island and write.

My writer friend Julia says that she would be:

1. A writer
2. A professional musician (this was "What She Might Have Been")
3. A linguist and world traveler
4. A naturalist or marine biologist
5. A wife/mother/farmer

Gene, a 47-year-old mortgage banker in a real estate firm, wanted four lives:

1. Head of the Department of Housing and Urban Development
2. A fishing guide
3. A novelist ("What He Might Have Been")
4. A radio announcer for major league baseball

Harriet dropped out of college twenty years ago to marry Gene and have five kids. She said if she had it to do all over again five times, she'd be:

1. The mother of five
2. A scholar of English literature
3. A painter
4. A dancer ("What She Might Have Been")
5. The boss of some large project or enterprise

Amanda, my editor, said she'd only need *two* lives. In one, she'd spend a lot of her time outdoors, riding, biking, gardening and "putting up," surrounded by animals of all kinds. (As a little girl she wanted to be a racehorse trainer.) In the other life she'd live in New York City, go to museums, concerts, and theater, give wonderful parties, study ballet—and be an editor. "The only trouble is," Amanda said, "which-ever life I was in, I'd miss the other one!"

That's just it. If you have to choose just one of your "lives," even if it's the one you love best, you're going to long for all the rest of them. Because *they are all vital parts of you.* The saddest phrase we ever got drummed into our heads was "Make up your mind!" There are people in this world who seem to be born for one single purpose, but they're the rare exceptions. Most genius is multifaceted. Even Einstein loved music as much as he loved physics. To ask him to choose between Bach and relativity would have been like asking, "Would you rather cut off your right hand or your left?" And it's the same with you. In each of your "lives" is something you love very, very dearly and need to get into your one life—*and you can.*

I have not decided yet what I'm going to be when I grow up, and I promise you that when I'm 80 I still won't have decided. What I plan to do is as many things as I can. What I plan to get is whatever I can get my hands on. As far as I'm concerned, there's only one answer to the question, "What do you want?" and that is, "Everything!"

In Mexico they have a wonderful saying: *"La vida es corta, pero ancha."* "Life is short, but it's wide." I'm not even so sure about the "short" part; have you really grasped the fact that you'll probably have twenty or thirty or forty more years to fill? In any case, there's a lot more room in your life than you think—room for everything in your "five lives" and then some. Finding that room is simply a matter of *making effective use of time,* and that means *planning*—the skills and techniques you'll learn in the second half of this book. Once you know how to use your days and weeks as the stepping stones to a goal, you will realize that time doesn't have to be a boat you're adrift in, or a treadmill you're running on. It's a raw material you can use the way a sculptor uses clay, and out of it you can shape not just one goal, but many.

So the first target you've chosen for yourself in this chapter is just that: the first. As your total life design unfolds, it will include *many* goals of different kinds, sizes, and shapes—from losing ten pounds by next month to traveling around the world ten years from now; from building your own dream house to block-printing this year's Christmas cards. *Anything you want can come true if you cast it in the form of a concrete goal.* And since the ultimate goal is a wonderful life, one that includes some of everything you love, I'd like you to try your hand at designing a *life plan*—a larger pattern of multiple goals that works in everything in your five (or three, or ten) "lives."

Before I show you some of the ways you can fit many goals into one life plan, I want to remind you again that you're not signing any contracts in blood. As you move through life, your perspective and priorities will change; new interests will appear on your horizon, and some of the old ones may fade. Your life plan five or ten years from now may not bear much resemblance to the one you draw up today. But it's always a good idea to have one. It's a way of reminding yourself that the time ahead of you is yours to create in your own image, however that image may change.

Sequential Goals: Switching Horses in Midstream

The most obvious way to fit more than one major interest into your life is to concentrate on one at a time and do them one after the other. People who change careers in mid-life—say, giving up an executive job to open a bookstore in Vermont—are following this kind of life plan. We are surprised and impressed when someone does that only because we've bought the fool notion that it is "normal" for people to make up their minds once and for a lifetime. There are many people for whom switching horses in midstream comes much more naturally. Like me: my lifestyle is to change goals every five or ten years. I can't think of a better way to live than to do something till I'm satisfied or bored with it and then do something else.

Sequential planning is a good way for a woman or man to combine intense involvements with family and career, or for a couple to alternate breadwinning and nurturing responsibilities and periods of study or creative work. A woman might decide to have her children early, and go back to work or school when they have reached school age—like Harriet, the mother of five, who finished college and entered a master's program in English when her youngest child was in junior high. Or, she might decide to achieve a certain level in her career before having her first child in her 30s. Travel is another goal it often makes sense to plan for after a professional or financial goal has been met. Julia's life plan for the next ten years includes all three: to write a book of her own, travel for a year or two and learn languages (one of her five lives was "linguist and world traveler"), then settle in the country and have a child ("wife/mother/farmer").

The advantage of sequential goals is that knowing the next juicy one is there and waiting spurs you on to meet the target date for your first goal. The pitfall of this kind of planning is that it can be used to postpone the goal you want—and fear—the most. And if you use it that way, it won't work, because you can put that goal off indefinitely. So it's a good rule of thumb to rank your Five Lives in order of importance to you—and then go for the most important one first, even if it's not the one you're living now.

Simultaneous Goals: Moonlighting

But what if two or more of your "lives" are equally important to you? Suppose you're a happily split personality like Amanda, who is half Kentucky bluegrass racehorse breeder and half cosmopolitan New York editor? Then you go for both at once! You become an editor moonlighting as a racehorse breeder, and vice versa.

Amanda has pictures of thoroughbreds all over her office bulletin board, including one of her "godchild"—a young filly owned by friends. She spends vacations and frequent weekends at the races in Saratoga or at Belmont. Like Clark Kent shucking his business suit for Superman leotards, she can switch from stockings and earrings to jeans and boots and back again with equal agility. The only way she feels she could improve on her double life is "more of both"—permanent dwellings in both city and country and an even deeper involvement in both her worlds.

My guess is that simultaneous goals work best when the two (or more) "lives" you're living are very different—because then each provides a refreshing change from the other. The "moonlighting" plan can also be a way of resolving the conflict between two touchstones that are notoriously hard to get together: financial security and creative satisfaction. In New York City there's a group of excellent jazz musicians who play club dates weekends and some evenings. On weekdays, they are . . . Wall Street stockbrokers!

Alternating Goals: The Patchwork Quilt

A variation on the "simultaneous" plan is to arrange your life so that you can devote alternating blocks of time to the pursuit of different goals. This comes very naturally to teachers, who have long summer vacations for traveling or mountain-climbing or creative projects or leading student tours; university types even get a whole sabbatical year off for research or writing. But you don't have to be an academic to plan your life in this pleasant patchwork fashion. Margaret, a nurse-midwife, works and saves money for two years at a stretch and then spends six months traveling through Europe or Asia. And Gene, the mortgage banker whose four lives included fishing, writing, and baseball, has invented what he calls a "businessman's sabbatical." Every few years he takes off from two to five months without pay and spends them tracking down fish in a quiet Florida backwater.

Multimedia Goals

Another way to have all your "lives" in one is to combine two or three interests into one goal. Amanda has published books on horseracing; Julia, who would have given one of her lives to marine biology, writes about whales; Gene plans to devote his next sabbatical to writing (life No. 3) about baseball (life No. 4); and Margaret could combine her profession with her love for travel by offering her much-needed nursing skills in different parts of the world. A multimedia goal can make you extra happy, because two or more of your talents are active at once, and no really important part of you has to wait on the sidelines.

I'll go further, and say that if you want to get the maximum joy and energy out of your life, *nothing you love should ever be left sitting on the shelf.* Everything you put down in your imaginary "lives" should be actively present in your life at all times, because you put it on that list for a reason. A talent or interest is a living part of you—like a hand or an ear or an eye. It needs to be used, it needs to be fed, or it will atrophy—and you'll be less than you're meant to be.

But how is it possible to keep five or six interests going at once? Many of us haven't even managed to develop one talent yet. We're fascinated and appalled by the spectacle of a "Renaissance person" like Buckminster Fuller or Margaret Mead—that's one of our definitions of "genius" as somebody different from the rest of us. What if you are the kind of person who needs to do one thing at a time? How on earth can you keep a love for horses alive while you're in law school, or learn to play the violin while you raise a child *and* write a novel? There just isn't that much time and energy to go around.

Main Meals and Side Dishes

The answer to the dilemma is: whichever interests are not included in your current main goal (or goals), make them "side dishes"—things you do every now and then just for pleasure. This is especially important when you're working toward a single goal that's a long haul. Don't say, "Oh, I'll own a horse someday when I'm a successful lawyer," or "I'll immerse myself in music *after* I finish writing this book." There will come moments when you just can't write or study or whatever any more—official or self-made vacations. Some of that time you are going to spend slumped in front of the TV set, or playing frisbee with the dog. All of us need time just to goof off. But some of it you can use to go horseback riding, or to sit and listen to music—whatever you've discovered you need in your life, even though it can't take first priority right now.

I'll give you an example: me. I'm operating at a very high energy level right now, going eighteen hours a day. I'm meeting my No. 1 goal with Success Teams; I have drive, designs, plans, and I love it. But I start crashing from dream deprivation if I don't also get some of the sweets in my other, secret "lives." So whenever I have some free time, I draw pictures of flowers! My walls are covered with them. I also like to read books about physics. I've found an island I can go to by myself when I really need to get away (my "hermit" life). And it is in my life plan within the next three years to be in an amateur musical comedy— something really silly, like *The Boy Friend.* I'm going to get up onstage and I'm going to tap dance and sing. There's no way to stop me, because I know it will make me happy.

An old childhood dream you've decided you don't want any more is almost always an indicator of something you still need in your life, because it goes very deep. Julia, for instance, said that under different circumstances she might have been a professional musician. As a small child she had a very exact musical ear, but nothing in her environment connected that talent with the fact that real, flesh-and-blood people make music. As a grown-up she would still like to learn to play the violin; she knows that with enough time and work she could get good enough to enjoy it. But full-time writing doesn't permit it.

What she can learn from this is that *she must have music in her life* —even if it's just to listen to. She'll feel happier and more alive if she listens to it a lot. She can always make it a future goal to study the violin when her current writing goals are met—but in the meantime, the musical part of her can be alive and singing even without an instrument.

"Side dishes" are delicious in their own right. They can also be the seeds of future goals, a way to keep something gently simmering on the back burner until you can move it up front. There's always room for them in your life, because they can be things you do once a week, once a month, once a year, or even just once. A "side dish" might be a weekly dance class, the history books you read in the evenings, a picture of a horse on your bulletin board, or even just the promise of a month on the beach compressed into one beautiful shell on your desk. It's a living reminder that life is not a miser, and you have the right to *everything* you love.

—5—

Hard Times, or The Power of Negative Thinking

All right—so you've found out what you want. To be perfectly honest, you want to own the world . . . or at least a nice big slice of it. Now let's be realistic. Can you get your house cleaned tomorrow?

Up to now we've been having nothing but fun. But now it's time to take a look at your Problems List. I invited you to postpone all the real-world difficulties so that you'd feel free to aim high; the only trouble with soaring in fantasy is that it's an awfully long way down to earth. Of course, you saw it coming. You're no dummy; you know there's a real world out there, and that high hopes and a great idea aren't enough. You need a track record, connections, know-how, money, guts—all kinds of things you may not have at all in the field you've chosen. To design your goal without taking this into account may have seemed to you a little like shoving everything under the bed to make your room look clean when you were a kid: the moment had to come when you (or your mother) lifted the bedspread, peered underneath, and groaned because the mess was still there.

OK. Let's take a good look at the mess. "I'll never get the money." "My husband won't like it." "I've got a wife and four kids to support." "I was always a lousy student." "I have absolutely no self-discipline." "I've never picked up a camera in my life." "Women don't advance in my company." "My children need me."

Whatever the problems on your list are, they're very real—and looking them in the eye can be overwhelming. This is the moment when you may crash. You may get depressed. And you may start to hate me for conning you into believing your most extravagent dreams could happen. That's OK. In fact, if you're down, I'm glad to hear about it. Not because I'm a sadist—but because if you aren't having some of those feelings *now,* I promise you they are going to hit you a day or a week after you close this book. And that would be worse, because then you'd have to cope with them alone. So this is the moment to confront "hard reality" and find out just what's making it so hard.

Glance through your Problems List once more. I can tell you without looking that some of them are real and perplexing problems that will take some energetic thinking to solve. And now I'm going to tell you something that will surprise you. *Those are the easy ones!* Those are the fun ones. They're purely a matter of strategy and game plans.

Suppose you want to get from point A to point B, and there's a river in between. What do you do? Well, you get a boat. You can't afford to buy one? You borrow one. You don't know how to row? You get a friend to row it for you. OK? OK. You've got a solution. It's as simple as that.

That is a *strategic problem*—the kind where you're asking, "How can I do it?" and you really want an answer. Strategic problems are hardly any trouble at all. They're discouraging right now only because you don't know how to find the answers. But there are answers. *There is no strategic problem that cannot be solved,* as you'll begin to find out in the next chapter. In fact, the whole second half of this book is designed to give you techniques and resources for solving strategic problems of every conceivable kind: time, money, know-how, contacts, credentials, space, equipment, and how to balance family responsibilities with your right to your own goals.

But there's another kind of problem hiding in your list that *can't* be solved by all the strategies and good ideas in the world. And unless we find out what that is right now, you won't even be able to tell what the real problems are, much less do any constructive thinking about them. Because this other kind of problem disguises itself as a strategic problem—and then that strategic problem mysteriously refuses to be solved.

Like this:

You want to get across a river, and you're brainstorming on it. You say, "Well, I could take a boat."

Then you say to yourself (or to anyone else who's trying to be helpful), "Yes, but I don't have a boat."

And then you say, "Mary has one. I'll borrow hers."

And then you say, "Yes, but I don't know how to row."

And then you say, "Well, I'll ask Mary to row it for me."

And then you say, "Yes, but Mary's very busy, and anyway I don't like to ask for favors."

And then you say, "I know Bill would do it. I drove him to the tree nursery last week, and anyway, he's in love with me. He'd help."

And then you say, "Yes, but I get seasick. I don't want Bill to see me that way."

I call this the "Yes-but" game. It is a sure-fire sign that what's really going on is *not* a simple attempt to solve a problem. You will reject every useful idea you or anyone else comes up with, "yes-butting" until you are purple with frustration and furious at whoever's trying to help you—and they'll be furious with you because you won't let them help!

The truth is, *you are not looking for an answer at all.*

And that's because the real problem isn't how to get across a river. You're no idiot; you can figure that one out as well as anybody. You just keep on saying, "Yes, but it's not that simple!" And you're right. It isn't. The real problem is very deep and painful and complex, and it has nothing to do with boats or rowing or seasickness. What it does have to do with is the *negative feelings* that come up every time you start thinking about going for your dreams.

That's where the hard part of "hard reality" really is. It's not in "reality." It's in your feelings. Half the time, when you say "I can't," or "It's impossible," or "I don't have this or that," all you're really trying to do is something very natural and healthy that has been forbidden by our culture.

You're trying to *complain.*

THE POWER OF NEGATIVE THINKING

Complaining—bitching, moaning, *kvetching,* griping, and carrying on—is a terrific and constructive thing to do. You've just got to learn how to do it *right.*

That sounds funny, doesn't it? You were brought up to believe that complaining is not nice and you should never do it. Of course, you do it anyway, but you don't like yourself when you do. Every one of us would like to be able to say, "I'm not a complainer." We're supposed to be able to pull in our belts, put off our pleasures, bear our disappointments, and face our fears without a squeak of pain or protest.

Hemingway called that kind of behavior "grace under pressure." I happen to consider it mildly psychotic.

The truth is that it just isn't human nature to feel good all the time. And when you're feeling bad or hurt or angry or frightened, you should be allowed to make a fuss and your body knows it!

I happen to believe in the efficacy of complaining the way some people believe in the efficacy of prayer. It's good for you. There are lots of times when you need it. And one of those times may be right now. Because the first half of this book has done something that's almost guaranteed to make you hurt and mad and scared—it's gotten your hopes up. Again. And now you're feeling pain for all the times you tried and it didn't work. For how hard it's been. For the lack of support. For all that lost time. You're feeling fear that you're going to get duped or disappointed again—that this book is just another hype and it won't work for you either. And pain and fear can make you fighting mad—at the forces that made you give up your dreams in the first place, and at me for reviving the hurt along with the hope. Who the hell do I think I am, to tell you you can have what you want?

Uncomfortable as they are, these are healthy feelings. I'd worry about you if you said meekly, "Thank you for turning me on to my fantasies." You'd have been turned on to them all along if you hadn't gotten slugged in the jaw a hundred times. The pain and anger you feel about that memory is a sign of life! After all, what you gave up was everything you loved best. And if *that* doesn't hurt, it's only because you're numb! The reawakening of hope is never painless. It's like running warm water over a frozen hand: your fingers hurt as feeling comes back to them. But do you say, "The hell with this. It felt better when they were numb. Let frostbite set in. Let them amputate."? Of course not! What you do is, you stomp around and cry and curse and swear. You start out in tears and end up laughing. And it *helps!*

Your dreams are just as important a part of you as your fingers. And you shouldn't have to put them back on ice just because it hurts to thaw them out. You ought to be allowed to stomp and holler and cry and swear—and have a good time doing it. That's what I call *Hard Times*.

But the hurt of old disappointments and the fear of new ones isn't necessarily the only kind of negative feeling lurking in your Problems List. There's another kind that comes up not because you're afraid to believe me, but because you're afraid you *do!* It's beginning to look like maybe this time you're really going to get your bluff called. And that means you're going to have to get out there and start doing some things that will make you very nervous. Like making phone calls to intimidating people. Like sticking a blank sheet of paper in the typewriter, or a blank canvas on the easel. Like walking in and asking politely but firmly for that raise. Like—maybe even—winning.

If you think you're nervous *now,* just wait till the next chapter, when you find out that you can—and should—start working toward your goal, not next week, not next month, not "someday," but *tomorrow.* Wait till all those too, too solid obstacles—the million bucks you'll never have, the family who will surely throw you out or die of malnutrition—start melting away, and you realize, too late, how safe you felt hiding behind them. A lot of times when you start reciting all the reasons why you can't get your goal, it's not because you really think you can't. It's because you'd really just as soon not. It's because you sort of hope you won't have to.

What you really are is *scared.* You're probably embarrassed to admit it, even to yourself, because you're a grown-up and you're not supposed to be afraid of anything. But there are a few thousand reasons to be scared when you start going for what you want. Some of them are part of the high cost of success in our society, especially for women. We got a look at those when we talked about the environment that creates winners—and the environment that doesn't: negative tapes . . . ignorance of ways and means . . . lack of support . . . guilt at leaving people in the lurch . . . fear of being left alone. It's murder trying to achieve your goals while you're carrying all those fears on your back, and with the help of this book, you won't have to. You're going to learn how to prepare for difficult situations like interviews. You'll find out that it's OK to fall on your behind and get back up again just as often as you need to. You'll learn to provide yourself with all the support you need: a team of real and imaginary winners who will help you out and cheer you on. And you know what?

You'll still be scared.

There is nothing in this world that's worth doing that isn't going to scare you. The moment you make the commitment to going for your dreams, you've begun to venture into the unknown. And the human organism's natural response to novelty and risk is adrenalin. Butterflies in the stomach. Wobbly knees. Pounding heart. It's commonly called stage fright, and it's just nerves, but it feels like a heart attack. Comfort is one of the things you can forget about right now. You're not going to have it any more. Excitement, company, help, and support, yes. Comfort, no.

So what do you do?

You do what every actress worth her salt does before she goes out on stage on opening night: you have a fit. You kick, stomp, and cry, "The lights are ghastly, the lines are awful, the playwright should be shot, the director's an idiot—I'm not ready, I *cannot* go on, I *will* not go on, I'm *leaving!*" And then you walk onstage under those lights . . . and you're fine.

That's Hard Times, too.

Hard Times is nothing but a good old-fashioned gripe session raised to the dignity and status of a ritual. Other cultures have made an art form of complaining. Look at the Flamenco gypsy's howl. Listen to the blues! The universal peasant poem is a string of curses directed at heaven . . . and what do you think the Bible means by "lamentation," anyway? A fancy word for bitching and moaning, in my book. All those people obviously knew something we don't. But we can learn to recognize and honor the need to complain—and then to be as openly, vividly, and *creatively* obnoxious as we can. It takes a little practice, because we've all been conditioned to be sweet and polite even when we're feeling like an alligator with a hangover. But you'll be surprised at how quickly your inhibitions vanish.

You can try it right now, in the privacy of your own mind. Take any item on your Problems List—it can be a perfectly serious obstacle to getting your goal, like a lack of money or schooling or too many family responsibilities. Sit down and really think about why that problem makes the whole idea totally impossible. You can take a sheet of paper and write down your thoughts if you like; title it "It Can't Be Done." It's a good idea to start out earnest, depressed, and a little whiny: "Even if I did get into school, I'd probably flunk out the first semester. I've always been a lousy student, I get headaches at the thought of sitting down to study."

Now, little by little, if you can—and you almost always can—start having fun with your negative feelings. Exaggeration, self-parody, melodrama, defiance, and obscenity are all useful weapons, and anything is a fair target: yourself, me, your goal, mother, flag, and country. "The truth is, I hate studying. It bores me and I can't concentrate and I hate *you* for suggesting it. I like things fine just the way they are. I'm too lazy to bother with all this. I think I'll eat a lot of chocolate and get fat." Say anything, as long as it's a mean, miserable complaint with some punch to it.

Did you notice that your energy level went up? Does your goal suddenly look a little less impossible? You haven't solved anything yet. The strategic problem is still there. Your doubts are still there. So why are you laughing?

Because you've dug down through all those heavy layers of "I can't," and struck a defiant gusher of "I don't want to and I *won't*." Depression is an energy crisis, and *negativity is energy*—pure, ornery, high-octane energy. It's just been so repressed and tabooed that we've forgotten something every 2-year-old knows: how good it is for us to throw a tantrum. We're all such good little girls, such brave, stalwart little boys, such polite little children—and inside every one of us is an obnoxious, exuberant little brat, just squirming to be let out. I've got one. So do you. That brat is your baby, and you'd better love her, because you ignore her at your peril.

If you had a child who was bursting with energy, and you dressed that child up in white and took her to church and tried to make her (or him) sit still and be quiet, that child would wreck the whole service. But if you put him (or her) in a pair of old Levis and let him run amok in the fields, roll in the mud, tease the dog, kick the cow, scream and holler, and take a nap, when he got up he might just go to church and behave himself.

Somewhere along the line our culture has sold us the absurd idea that we've got to have a positive attitude to succeed. We're afraid to be negative because we think it means we won't *do* anything. And yet the evidence to the contrary is overwhelming. A quick look at your own experience will show you how powerless positive thinking really is. Oh, it feels good—while it lasts. The first morning you get out of bed saying,

"I know I can do it, I know I can do it," it makes a whole new day for you. You walk around whistling to yourself, thinking, "God, I could run the world with this idea!" The second morning you know you're lying. You not only can't do it, you can't even get out of bed.

Trying to force a positive attitude is the surest way in the world not to get something done. A *negative* attitude, on the other hand, will get you to do it.

I call this The Power of Negative Thinking.

You can demonstrate it very easily if you have kids who hate to do their homework. (I've never met a normal, healthy child who loved it.) If you say "You've got to do it! Long division is good for you. Look, if you don't do your long division you're not going to get good grades, and then you won't get into college, and then what will happen to you?" I guarantee that your kids will lock themselves in the bedroom and read comic books. So next time, try saying this instead: "You're so right. Long division is repulsive. It's awful. So why don't you put your homework on the floor and jump on it? Hate it. Kick it around the room. Curse and swear at it. Use the dirtiest words you know. I'll go in the next room. And when you're all through, put it back on the table and do it." You'll find your kids will be laughing—and their long division will get done.

Of course they have to do it. They know they have to do it. *But they don't have to like it.* And neither do you.

The operative principle of Hard Times is, "Get it off . . . and then get on with it." *You've got to let negative attitudes and feelings happen.* Only then will you be ready for positive problem-solving, planning, and action.

Of course, there's only one little hitch I haven't mentioned yet. Throwing a tantrum isn't nice. Complaining isn't socially acceptable. Indulging in your grouches and fears may make *you* feel better, but what about the innocent bystanders around you? Their feelings may be hurt if they happen to get in the way of a stray expletive. "I hate this thesis, and I hate the goddam typewriter, and I hate you too!" They may worry that you really are going to have a nervous breakdown, or leave for Bermuda, or whatever threats you happen to fire off in the heat of the moment. They may think you're a little odd, if not certifiably crazy. What should you do about them?

Simple. Tell them exactly what you're doing—and invite them to be your audience and cheering section. Say, "This is Hard Times. I'm mad, nervous, fed up, and for the next five minutes I'm going to go totally bananas. Don't pay any attention to anything I say. You can stick your fingers in your ears if you like. It will all be over in five minutes." And then you run amok—and instead of ending in emotional wreckage, apologies, and tears, everybody ends up laughing. Once you learn this, you'll never forget it, and as soon as the people around you catch on, they'll start doing it too.

When you feel a Hard Times session coming on, you can tell your audience that there are three possible responses that will help you:

1. APPLAUSE. We should all develop artistic appreciation for each other's brats. Every really inventive complaint deserves cheers, laughter, and such comments as, "That's a beaut," or "That's a stinker." If several people get going together, a spirit of competition can develop. It's fun to see who can come up with the nastiest gripes, and such contests invariably end in laughter and really clear the air.

2. PARTICIPATION. The last thing anyone should do is argue with you or try to help you look at the sunny side. You don't need to be talked out of your negative feelings—if anything, you need urging on! Tell your audience if they want to say anything at all, for God's sake don't make it constructive. If they can pitch in and say something *de*structive, they're more than welcome. It's nice to hear yourself backed up by a friendly chorus of snarls and moans. Makes you feel less alone.

3. ADMIRATION. There's another reason why we sometimes complain that's a really subtle one. I used to do it, and it took me quite a while to understand why.

When my sons were small, it seemed like I spent half my life working my brains out and the other half griping about it. I'd march up to my kids and say, "Look at all the work I did. I got up at six, I made the beds, I did the dishes, I vacuumed and dusted the whole house . . . I'm exhausted!" And they'd feel terrible. They'd say, "Look, do you want us to do the dishes?" And I'd say, "No! I'm not mad! I just want . . . I don't know what I want!" I didn't mean to make them feel guilty and miserable. None of us knew what was going on.

And then one day it hit me. I didn't want them to do a thing. All I wanted was for them to say, "You know, you're really fabulous. How did you do all that?" And then I'd beam and say, "Oh, it was nothing."

The truth is, I was very proud of myself. But I didn't dare come right out and say so, because I was afraid I'd get shot down for being so conceited. None of us knows how to say, "Sit down. I want to tell you what I did all by myself against very tough odds. I want you to know I was Herculean." We're not allowed to brag, so we whine instead.

This kind of complaining is an appeal for admiring recognition. When you've had a hard row to hoe and you've hoed it, you deserve sympathy and praise. If this were the American frontier and you were Paul Bunyan or Wild Bill Hickok, you could boast about your heroic deeds and make a poem of it. But a Hard Times session will serve just as well. And if you tell your audience what you're after, they'll probably say, "Is that all? Why didn't you ask? I've been secretly admiring you all along—I just thought you were so strong you didn't need to hear it!"

So much of what we need just boils down to *permission*. Permission to feel what we feel—and say it. To let each other know. And to find out that what we feel isn't freakish, or destructive, or wrong. It's just human—and shared.

THE PRIVATE GRIPE

There will be times and places, however, when you won't be able to complain out loud. I don't recommend doing it with your boss, for instance—unless he or she is also a close personal friend. Many professional and business situations are what I call "on stage" situations, the kind where you have to keep up appearances even when you're quaking inside. You'll find some handy First Aid for those in Chapters 9 and 10. But meanwhile, you should know that the fact that you sometimes have to act like a Spartan doesn't mean you have to *feel* like one. If you can't bitch out loud, or there's nobody listening, or you've just got an incurable case of good manners, you can still let your brat out in private —and provide a sympathetic audience for yourself.

You can keep a Hard Times Notebook.

A small spiral notebook of the type secretaries use is ideal, because you can carry it in your pocket or purse. To set the tone, you might want to draw a nice negative face on the cover. Or find a picture of a lugubrious basset hound or somebody with a bad hangover, and paste that on. But this is optional. What really counts is the words you write inside.

As you proceed with the problem-solving and planning sections of this book, there will be many times when you feel like giving up the whole thing. Whenever that happens, get out your Hard Times Notebook and write down all the nastiest complaints you can think of. Let the brat, rebel, and cop-out in yourself have a field day. Record curses, confess fears, revel in all your own worst qualities, and plot fantasy escapes. The same rules apply as for complaining out loud—and for listening. Accept your own complaints with sympathy and relish. Have a good time, if you possibly can. Don't rationalize, apologize, explain, or argue with yourself. Above all, *never try to solve problems in your Hard Times Notebook.* This is the place for 100 percent unadulterated negativity. It will make entertaining reading when the fit is past and you're feeling good again—or the next time you're feeling rotten and need inspiration.

WHEN IT HURTS TOO MUCH TO LAUGH

But what about the times when you're hurting so bad you can't be funny? In some moods, past defeats and present problems seem overwhelming. It's no joke. And there are some life situations, like the loss of a job or a love, that are so hard that you can't be a brat about them. You'll laugh again later. Right now your only concern is to get through the rough time in one piece.

When you're in that state, suffering in silence is the worst thing you can do. You need the relief of complaining now most of all. And there's only one thing you need from whomever is listening to you: to be heard.

Real listening—quiet, sympathetic, and totally attentive—is one of the rarest commodities in our society. None of us knows how to ask for it, and very few of us know how to give it. You know there are plenty of times when all you need is to tell somebody how hard it's been, how you felt when s/he left you, when the kids were sick, when there was no heat. You don't want your problems solved. All you want is to see that click of recognition in another person's eyes that says your pain is valid and what you've lived through is real. Then you know you could go on. But for that to happen, someone has to listen with ears and feelings open—and mouth closed. How often have you really gotten that? More often, you either get well-meaning good advice—which you angrily and guiltily reject without knowing why ("If George is such a bastard, why don't you leave him?" "No, no, you don't understand!")

—or, if the other person can't think of any way to help you, her attention wanders out the window, up to the ceiling, anyplace but on you. I say "her attention" because most women are like this: if we can't cure another person's ills, we don't want to hear about them. And that's because we don't know that *listening is enough.*

Funny thing: men are better at it. They've always known about the healing power of that most ancient of psychotherapists, the bartender. He doesn't do anything but polish glasses and given an occasional grunt while his customer works his way deeper into his second double Scotch and his tale of woe. So when one man walks up to another and says, "Sam, I'm an alcoholic, my wife is leaving me, I've lost my job," Sam says sincerely, "Geez, Joe, that's rough"—which is precisely what Joe needs to hear. But I know perfectly well that if Joe walked up to me and began, "Barbara, I'm an alcoholic . . ." I'd go, "Oh my God. What do I do now? Let me talk to your wife. You can live in my house. I'll take you to the steam bath. I'll find you a job." Women are *fixers.* I've got to fix. Most of you have got to fix. We do it in the name of compassion—and it's heartless. What's more, it makes us feel, "Oh no, another person on my back!" And then we make the other person pay in subtle ways for help that she or he never asked for in the first place.

So when someone tells you a Hard Times story, it's much kinder not to say or do anything at all except show that person with your eyes that you are reliving the rough times with him or her, using all the resources of your imagination and feelings. If you have to say anything at all, you can say, "That sounds awful," or "Ouch." *That's all.* Otherwise, don't interrupt. She or he will be finished, really finished, in five or ten or at the most fifteen minutes. Real listening is the cure for chronic complaining. You know from your own experience that when you see in someone's face that your words have registered, you don't need to go on and on.

So make it a point to ask for this kind of healing attention when you need it. There are three little words that have been missing from our vocabulary: "Please just listen." (Note: tell your listener not to fake it, because then it won't work. If s/he is distracted, or just not in the mood, s/he should simply be honest about it: "Sorry, I just can't listen today." And the same goes for you when you're the listener.)

Can you use your Hard Times notebook for this kind of serious complaining if there's no one around to listen? Definitely—but you still need somebody to talk to. And sometimes the very best listeners are the ones you talk to just in your mind.

Some people still feel comfortable—and comforted—talking to God, Jesus, or a saint for whom they feel a special personal affection. But since religion has lost its central place in our lives, many of us don't have this source of comfort any more. It's too bad, because it was such a good one. I'm not suggesting that you do your complaining to a Supreme Being unless that really comes naturally to you. But I think those of us who aren't religious ought to have our "saints," too: kindly figures who loved and battled life, who lived through hard times of their own, who can give us their wisdom, humor, and understanding. Children often have imaginary friends they talk to, sharing their secrets and their sorrows. I know a painter who used to pray to Cézanne and Matisse when she was a girl! I think that's a skill we grown-ups ought to recover.

Is there one member of the "ideal family" you selected for yourself in Chapter 4 who is your favorite, or who lived through and triumphed over troubles not so different from yours? That person can be your personal "saint." You can probably guess who mine is, since I've already told you that Albert Einstein reminds me of my grandfather! If you don't already have pictures of your "family" members, at least get one of your "saint." Put it up on the wall above your desk, or wherever you'll be working on your goals. (If you don't already have a work space of your own, you should start thinking about finding one.) If your "saint" is an imaginary character from literature, find a photo or painting that looks the way you imagine he or she would look.

Now, when you're low and alone and need somebody to talk to, you can tell your troubles to Marlene Dietrich or Henry Thoreau. You'll be amazed at how much good it does. That's because your own private "saint" will never try to fix your problems, stare out the window in embarrassment, or tell you to cheer up. She or he will just listen, like God or a good bartender, looking back at you with that steady, warm, sad-merry gaze that says, "I know. I've been there. It's rough."

UP, DOWN—AND FORWARD

If your personal "saint" is a real or historical person, there's one more thing you can do that will help you over any rough spots on the journey to your goal. Read his or her biography—or even better, letters and journals, if they are available. You'll learn a fact that will surprise you—and encourage you. Famous people have suffered the same ups and downs as the rest of us. The only way they are at all different from you and me is that they didn't take the low moods as signals to give up. They sometimes felt like giving up, of course. And do you know what they did then? They complained. The private writings of accomplished people reveal that they did one hell of a lot of complaining. And I think it's one of the ways they got where they did. Because they kept going. And so they made the great discovery that you are also going to make: *success does not depend on how you feel.* Human moods have remarkably little to do with effective action—and it's a good thing, or we'd still be living in caves.

This is terribly important to realize, because deeply ingrained in our culture and our past experience is *the mistaken notion that you can only do well when you're feeling good.* You've had highs—those periods in your life when you just couldn't roll the dice wrong. You felt unafraid, self-confident, articulate, creative, and you knew you could do anything —for a day, a week, or even a month. Right? Well, that was just about the worst thing that has ever happened to you. Because then, as sure as night follows day, a low rolled in and wiped out your sense of progress, leaving you feeling like you were right back at zero. And ever since, you've been sitting around waiting for that high to come back so you could do it again. You probably assumed that famous people feel that way all the time—otherwise how could they have done what they did?—and that there's just something wrong with *you.* And publicly at least, famous people aren't telling, because they're afraid people will find out that there's something secretly wrong with them!

A peek into their private lives and feelings explodes the myth. If anything, the great souls and high achievers have had more emotional highs and lows than the rest of us. That's not because they were born with extra helpings of passion and drive (another myth)—it's because they're committed to realizing their life designs. That means they're out there in that high-risk area you're heading for. When you get there, you will not need antidepressant pills, bottled courage, or Norman Vincent Peale. You'll just need *structure* and *support.* That's what all true winners have had in one form or another, and it, not elation, is what keeps them moving forward. It's only because you haven't had that external support system that your low moods have been able to stop you before. And so we're going to spend the rest of this book constructing it for you.

But before we start, I'm going to equip you with one more useful tool for your success survival kit. It's a brief, simple notation you will put down at the end of each day, called an *Actions & Feelings Journal.* In it, you will trace the line of your own forward progress through all your ups and downs, and accumulate unshakable proof in your own handwriting that your progress does not depend on your moods.

You can keep this journal in another spiral notebook like the one you use for Hard Times, but a plain pad of paper will do. At the top of each page, write the following column headings:

DATE   WHAT I DID   HOW I FELT

Starting today, as you work with this book, make a brief note each evening of what you've done that day—no matter how small or unimportant it may seem to you. You might start with "Decided on my goal," or "Started Hard Times Notebook." As you draw up your game plan and start moving toward your goal, you'll be recording things like phone calls you made, letters you've written, visits to the library or employment agency, a helpful conversation with a friend, a page or a paragraph or even just a sentence toward the article or thesis you have to write. Just buying a pad of paper, some stamps, or a pair of new shoes for an interview is enough.

If you think you haven't done anything that led toward your goal, put down whatever you did do that day. Never write "Nothing." Write "Paid bills" or "Cleaned house" or "Went to the movies" or "Stayed in bed and ate a whole pizza all by myself." You need to begin to realize that *now that you have a goal, your whole life is heading toward it.* Even what look to you like backward steps are positive actions of another kind. They express some real and valid part of you, and they serve a purpose. Maybe you were pushing yourself too hard and needed a rest. Maybe you were feeling scared. Maybe your brat needed a whole day to him- or herself. Maybe you needed to give yourself a reward. That's OK. Just write down what you did. Don't judge it.

Under "How I felt," you might put "Great," or "Hopeless," or "I feel like I'm getting somewhere," or "Scared," or "Bored," or "Angry at all the time I wasted before," or even "Fed up with the whole thing."

Again, don't judge your feelings. Just record them as honestly as you can.

Even if you've never kept a journal before, this one is a cinch to keep —it just takes a few minutes and a few words each night. But try to make it a regular habit. The more faithfully you keep it, the more revealing it will be.

One purpose of your Actions & Feelings Journal is to keep a simple record of what you accomplish day by day. You can't imagine how important this is. Most of us have a very distorted notion of how things actually get done in this world. *We think that accomplishment only comes from great deeds.* We imagine our heroes striding toward their goals in seven-league boots—writing best-selling novels in three months, building business empires overnight, soaring to stardom out of nowhere—and this gives rise to painfully unrealistic expectations of ourselves. And yet nothing could be further from the truth. *Great deeds are made up of small, steady actions, and it is these that you must learn to value and sustain.*

Often you feel you've done nothing when you've actually done a lot. That's because what you did do seemed beneath notice—it was so small that it didn't "count." But it did—just as each stitch counts toward a finished dress, each brick or nail toward a house you can live in, each mistake toward knowing how to do things right. Directed action, no matter how small, moves toward its point. When you write down what you've done, you will have to realize you've done it—and you'll begin to see how small steps add up.

The second purpose of the Actions & Feelings Journal is to let you discover for yourself how your feelings and actions are related—or unrelated. You will find that they don't match up in any consistent, predictable, cause-and-effect way. You can often do as much when you're feeling negative as when you're sparkling. When I started keeping my Journal, I discovered that I often make the least substantial progress on my high days—I'm too busy celebrating, knocking on wood, wondering how long it will last, and so on. I also found that a really abysmal low often precedes a burst of growth or inspiration. When you *are* low, it's harder to appreciate what you've done. You may not have the jubilant sensation of progress even when you have the fact of it. That's why an objective record of your actions is so important. The daily entries in your Actions & Feelings Journal will represent *gained ground:* real progress you can see and savor, whatever your mood of the moment may be.

Being human, you can't always have a positive attitude—and you don't have to. You cannot be consistently self-disciplined—and you don't have to. You can get where you're going anyway, and have fun doing it. Are you feeling scared or mad? Get scared. Get mad. Is your self-esteem non-existent today? Don't worry about it. It's irrelevant. Look in the mirror and say, "I'm horrible, I'm a failure, I'm ugly. I'll never make anything out of myself." Applaud yourself. Enjoy your negative attitude. And then roll up your sleeves and get down to business.

Three

Crafting I: Plotting the Path to Your Goal

Hard Times clears the mind the way a thunderstorm clears the air. After a good gripe session the oppressive haze is gone, far things look near, and you're in the mood to come up with practical strategies for getting there. When you start plotting the actual steps to your goal, you'll understand why it was so important first to discover your emotional investment in "It can't be done." Because here's where you find out that it *can.*

I'm a down-to-earth woman, and this is a down-to-earth book. It's not about castles in the air—it's about the nuts and bolts and plans and principles of engineering that get castles built here on earth. But if there's one section of this book that comes close to being about miracles, this is it.

Down-to-earth miracles, that is.

Right now what you've got is a clearly-defined target and a list of the strategic problems that stand in your way. By the end of this section, you will have a step-by-step *plan* for getting to your goal—a bridge of actions connecting that distant dream to your doorstep. In other words, we're going to start turning obstacles into stepping stones.

What accomplishes this transformation? There are no magic wands, it's true. But you have two perfectly ordinary, absolutely priceless resources in your possession right now that can do as much as any magic wand in any fairy tale you care to name. One of them is in your head. The other is in your address book.

They are called *human ingenuity* and *human community*—or in plain English, a head full of brains and a room full of friends.

These two between them really have the power to move mountains. They can get you a million dollars, or they can get you what you want for $5,000 or $500—or for free. They can get you an introduction to Mikhail Baryshnikov. They can get you a working farm with six holstein dairy cows. They can get you a job in a new field without having to go back to school; they can get you into school and through it without a dime. They can get you the capital and know-how to start your own business. They can get you unstuck from a low rung on the corporate ladder. They can get you married. And I'll be showing you exactly how in the course of this section.

The technique for liberating ingenuity is called *brainstorming*. The technique for mobilizing community is called *barn-raising*. They are specific antidotes to the two mainstays of "hard reality": *conventional "wisdom"* and *pathological individualism*.

Conventional "wisdom" is the attitude that says, "It'll never fly." Then it goes on to say things like, "Only rich people can travel around the world first-class." Or, "You have to have an M.B.A. to get a good job in business these days." Or, "You can't make a living in the arts unless you're already famous." Or, "You can't make a successful business out of what you love." *All true winners are people who have taken conventional "wisdom" as a sporting challenge, instead of a pronouncement of defeat.* They assume that its rules were made to be broken, so they don't even stop to ask, "Can it be done?" They just ask, "How?"

Answers to that question start turning up as soon as you suspend all rules of conventional "wisdom" and look at each problem with pure, playful creativity, as if it had never been seen on earth before. That's brainstorming, and with its help you'll discover that some of the things you thought you needed to reach your goal—the really tough ones, like a lot of money, or a Ph.D.—may not even be necessary. You can invent alternative routes that are not only quicker and more direct, but closer to your path and a lot more fun.

Brainstorming will give you a wealth of ideas for the steps to your goal. But if a page full of good ideas were enough, everyone who's ever had a fit of inspiration—and that means everybody—would be rich and famous. So once you've pitted your native wit against conventional "wisdom," you will have to do the second thing enterprising people have always done: get help.

If this book has one single most important purpose, it is to mount a full-scale attack on the most destructive piece of conventional "wisdom" there is: "You've got to make it on your own." Nobody can. Nobody does. And yet we often hesitate to ask anyone for help, advice, or even instructions to the corner store for fear that it means we're "dependent." I know a grown woman, the mother of three children, who wanted to go back to college but couldn't sign up, because when she got to the campus she didn't know which building the registration office was in! She wouldn't ask anyone, because she thought she should know how by herself and was afraid she'd look like a fool.

That's what I call *pathological individualism*. I don't mean the marvelous *individuality* that makes each of us unique. I mean the cultural disease of extreme "self-reliance" that has cut us off from the most potent resource we have for achieving our goals: each other. The best ideas, the ones that really work magic, are the ones that draw on the knowledge, skills, and contacts of other people. I'm going to show you how you can mobilize your human resources to help you meet your goal. I call the technique "barn-raising," after the way people in pioneer communities pitched in to get each other's barns built in a day. A barn-raising is the closest thing I know to a magic wand. It turns the most "ordinary" group of people—friends, family members, co-workers, even strangers—into a gold mine of helping hands and minds.

Brainstorming and barn-raising together will give you the steps to your goal—steps you can start taking *tomorrow*. But you also need a way of organizing those steps into a map of your path you can actually follow. As you work through Chapters 6 and 7, you will learn to draw a special kind of visual plan called a *flow chart*—the heart of your Portable Success Support System. It is the tool that turns the dream in your head into *a structure outside yourself* that will guide your actions step by step and keep you on the track. Once that's been done, it takes only one more step to bring you to the threshold of action: setting *target dates* and putting your plan into a *time frame*. We'll be doing that in Chapter 8.

– 6 –
Brainstorming

You need three items before you're ready to start brainstorming: a pad of paper, a couple of pencils—and a problem.

Right now the problems on your list are probably stated in a form something like this: "I can't because I don't have X." For instance, Jill, 30, wants to move up to a management position in the accounting firm where she's worked as a secretary for four years. But she can't see any way to take that step without going back to school and getting an M.B.A.—which would take another two years she doesn't want to wait and $8,000 she hasn't got. Alan, a 28-year-old Chicago editor, wants to start his own small publishing firm, but he doesn't have the capital. Joyce, a 43-year-old mother, wants a paying job as a fund-raiser, but she has no previous job credits to put on her resumé—just one experience as a volunteer.

Credentials, experience, and money are among the most common obstacles conventional "wisdom" places in our paths—and often enough, when we look at the world around us, conventional "wisdom" just seems like common sense. But now that we've gotten the negativity out in Hard Times, you're ready to look at each of those obstacles in a more positive light: as a challenge to your ingenuity. And that change in attitude is as simple as a change in grammar.

"I can't because I don't have X" is a dead end. Your brain can't work with it. To turn it into a form your brain just loves to work with, take that one flat statement and turn it into a pair of leading questions:

1. How can I get it without X?
2. How can I get X?

Either of those questions can be the takeoff point for brainstorming. But it's almost always a good idea to start with question No. 1. Because the point isn't just to get to your goal by any means at all. It's to get you there by the quickest, most direct, most personalized route—one that will get some of the rewards of your goal into your life right away. When we talked about choosing a first target in terms of your touchstone, I told you that I want you to start doing what you love tomorrow —not five years from now, when you've made a pile of money or finished your Ph.D. This is the operative principle to keep in mind throughout your planning. Never take the long road if you can find a shorter one that will get you to the same place.

In the language of goals, this means that the only time to go straight into brainstorming with question No. 2—"How can I get X?"—is: one, if you're 150 percent sure that X is the only way to your goal (there's really no alternative to medical school if you want to become a doctor); or two, if X itself is something you love for its own sake, like wealth or scholarship or professional standing. Then it's not really an obstacle at all—it's one of your touchstones! With those two exceptions, never assume that conventional "wisdom" is correct until you've tried question No. 1.

For example, you may be depressingly certain that you have to have an M.B.A. to get a good job in business . . . or an M.S.W. or Ph.D. to do responsible therapy . . . or an M.A. in education to teach. In our ever more credential-happy society, there appear to be fewer and fewer doors you can walk through without a piece of paper, which will cost you thousands of dollars and thousands of hours. Well, I'll tell you something. At a conservative estimate, 75 percent of the conventional "wisdom" about credentials is pure gobbledygook.

In case you didn't know it, school is a big business. It's also a safe haven for those of us who just love to be in rehearsal. We can go to school until we're ready, and then go to school some more until we're *really* ready, instead of jumping in the water and starting to swim. Don't get me wrong. I'm not against higher education. I think everybody should go to college and study art and philosophy as an end in itself—like sending your mind to summer camp. But if you are heading for a specific goal and you're considering school as a means to that end, check your situation out carefully.

Is a degree an integral part of what you want to do—like becoming a research scientist or a history professor? Or is it an absolute necessity to get where you want to go? If you're in any doubt about this second question, do a little role-model research on the careers of the most interesting people in your field. Did the journalists you admire most go to journalism school? (Not likely.) Did all the male executives in your office or your business get hired with M.B.A.'s? (Ask around discreetly —and remember that nothing that's not required of a man can now be legally required of a woman.) Does your favorite poet or painter have a Master's in Fine Arts? If the answer is "no," the chances are excellent that you don't need a piece of paper to do what you want to do, either, and that you shouldn't waste your time and money getting one. Instead, grab yourself a plain old piece of blank paper and ask yourself, "How can I get it without X?"—X being more school.

Just this once, I'm going to give you some ideas to get the juices flowing. There are ways that I and people I know have achieved our goals outside the academy, and they all revolve around the idea that the best, directest, most exciting way to learn most things is *by doing them.*

CREATIVE HOOKY, OR: FIVE WAYS TO LEARN—AND EARN—BY STAYING OUT OF SCHOOL

1. Nerve. Otherwise known as talking your way through a door with nothing going for you but talent, cheek, and desperation. If you *know* what you'd be good at, there's nothing lost—and often much to gain —by just walking into wherever you want to be and presenting yourself. It's a little hard on the nerves, but you'll get plenty of help with that problem in the last section of this book.

This is the way my own career got started. When I came to New York, I had a B.A. in anthropology. Now there is nothing on earth more useless for getting a job than anthropology. You find me an ad that says "Wanted: B.A. in anthropology." I'd like to see it. I was what you might call highly unemployable. But I had to find a job that would feed my kids, and I was naive enough to hope for one that wouldn't starve my soul. I had the intuitive feeling that I would probably be good at working with people. So I screwed up my small supply of courage and answered one of those ads that said "Experience preferred." I noticed that it didn't say "Required," and anyway I figured that the experience of walking around on earth for thirty years ought to count for something. The job was as a counselor in a drug program, and I talked my way into it—probably because they needed manpower as badly as I needed the job.

I walked in there at nine the first morning with my knees shaking. By 5:00 P.M. I knew I hadn't been wrong. I might be green, but I was in my element. From there, one thing led to another. While I was still working at that job, I started group therapy. Within a year I had become an assistant-trainee of the head therapist. And then four of us split off from him and started Group Laboratories. Over the next eleven years I made a tidy living doing group and individual counseling; I was a consultant at three medical schools, teaching their psychiatrists and psychologists; and I got invited to speak and give creativity workshops all over the country. None of this happened because I had a piece of paper. It happened because I found the right swimming pool, squeezed my eyes shut, and jumped in. To this day, I have never gotten one unit of academic credit over the 108 units required for that B.A. in anthropology.

2. Volunteering. In a world of professionalism, where money is the measure of seriousness, volunteering has gotten something of a bad name. It's supposed to be amateurish, dilettantish, the sort of half-committed playing-at-work that society matrons do on alternate Tuesdays. I want to set the record straight right now. Volunteer work is one of the best ways there is to get your feet wet and gain experience in a new field—whether it's in a zoo, a hospital, a school, a museum, a neighborhood newspaper, a political campaign office, or a family farm. You don't need credentials or prior experience. You don't have to pay them a cent for your training. But what's best is that volunteering gets you started doing what you love right away, even if it's only once a week. Or—if you're trying out a tentative goal—it lets you get the living feel of a profession before you commit yourself to full-time work or training. And it equips you with experience, contacts, and references that will be useful if and when you do decide to make that commitment.

Volunteer work is the great cure for the classic vicious cycle, "Can't get experience without a job; can't get a job without experience." If you think unpaid experience doesn't count on a resumé, think again. If Joyce has done volunteer fund-raising while her kids were in school, then she's been a fund-raiser—and she should neither hide nor overemphasize the "volunteer" part when she applies for a paying job. *Experience is experience.* If you're like 22-year-old Jack, who spent a year of Saturdays and a summer vacation working with handicapped kids and had letters of reference to show for it, then you've got something at least as valuable to offer as an M.A. fresh from the books.

True, the M.A. may get paid a higher starting salary than you do—*if* she or he gets hired. On the other hand, you may get hired where an M.A. may not! Jack did. With a B.A. in English, he is now working as a resident counselor at a school for special children. Pieces of paper are a dime a dozen these days. People who've cared enough to get firsthand experience aren't. If the time comes when Jack decides he does want that piece of paper, his track record will make him a first-rank candidate for graduate school admission and financial aid.

Three years ago, Diane was a 24-year-old secretary with a B.A. in nothing special. Her secret dream was to be a city planner. She was totally unqualified; all she had going for her was a passionate love for New York City. She loved to walk around and savor the flavors of different neighborhoods, and she wished everyone could see and appreciate the city the way she did. But that special quality of vision wasn't going to get her into graduate school, and in any case, she couldn't afford to quit her job and study full-time. Even night-school classes were beyond her pocketbook. For the clincher, New York City happened to be going broke just then, and the city planning department was firing people, not hiring them.

That's a pretty staggering list of obstacles. Nonetheless, today Diane has an M.A. in city planning and a high-paying job with a major corporation. She works for the relocation office, introducing recently transferred executives and their families to the resources and delights of their new home. How did she do it?

In a brainstorming session, Diane came up with something she could do right away, and for free: take part in local planning-board meetings. She was so outspoken and enthusiastic in those meetings that within a few months everyone from block association leaders to city councilmen was calling her for ideas and advice. By the time she felt ready to apply for school, she knew most of the people who really make things happen in the city, and they all wrote her recommendations. She was awarded a full-tuition scholarship to Hunter College!

Diane's boyfriend was so thrilled for her that he offered to pay her rent so she could quit her job. But after one semester, she was hired into a teaching assistantship that paid her way. Diane was now not only studying *and* teaching city planning—she was already *doing* it every week on those local committees. And by the time she finished her Master's, her contacts and reputation were so widespread that she was offered a job in the first corporation she walked into.

That's how you take what you love most in the world and turn it into a career. Diane isn't "exceptional." She made a hit with local pols, professors, and potential employers simply because she was in her element. Her energy and imagination were irresistible, and yours will be too as soon as you're on your path. Volunteering is one of the best ways to get out there *now*.

3. *The Sorcerer's Apprentice.* The most ancient and natural way to acquire skills and knowledge is by hanging out with someone who's got them—watching, asking, helping. Before schools were invented, doctors, lawyers, and great painters all learned their trades this way. Psychoanalysts and carpenters still do. It's how I learned to be a therapist. There's an element of apprenticeship in any good education—but in many fields you can set up an apprenticeship for yourself.

My feeling is that there's hardly a person on this planet you couldn't walk up to and say, "I've followed your work for a long time, and I'd really like to learn from you. I won't cause you any trouble. I'll empty your wastebaskets, I'll clean up your workshop, I'll carry your gear. I just want to be near your mind." It's a rare curmudgeon who wouldn't be flattered and receptive. Most highly accomplished people want to share what they know with other eager minds. Seriousness of interest and a willingness to help out are the only real qualifications. A young potter named Juan Hamilton has become the assistant and close companion of the great painter Georgia O'Keeffe. Agnes Nixon, reigning queen of the soaps and creator of (among others) "All My Children" and "Another World," got her start sharpening pencils for Irna Phillips, who pioneered the soap opera form with classics like "Love of Life" and "Guiding Light." Young writers send their work for criticism to established writers they admire, and sometimes a close mentor-protégé relationship develops.

There are formal programs that have been set up to connect willing "masters" with would-be apprentices. The architect Paolo Soleri always has a staff of young paying guests who help him cast wind bells and build his "arcologies," or experimental desert cities. Writer May Sarton and others took part in a Union Graduate School program in which they acted as advisors for independent student projects. (For further information about apprenticeships see the "Resources" appendix at the end of this book.)

But you don't need a formal program to put you in touch with someone whose work you love. You don't even have to go in cold with a letter that may or may not be answered. In the next chapter you'll learn how you can get an introduction to just about anyone on earth you want to meet.

4. Starting from Scratch: The Independent Alternative. Another way to start out on your path without a degree is simply to sit down, draw up a plan for a mime class, political seminar, walking tour, art-therapy group, or editing service, and put ads in your local paper. That's the wonderful thing about doing what you love: you can do it wherever you are, because your resources are really inside yourself. All you need is talent, personal experience, love—and a carefully worked-out idea, or *program design.* How do you think *Weight Watchers* got started? Jean Nidetch wasn't a doctor or a nutritionist. She was a lady who wanted to be thin. She designed a package for other people like herself and turned it into a multimillion-dollar business.

Whether what you want is to be rich and nationally known or just to hold a weekly discussion group in your living room, remember that the key to survival and success for any independent program is *an angle.* What you've got to do is find and fill a specific need that nobody else has thought of filling. That's what Jean Nidetch did. That's what I've done with Success Teams. A therapist I know designed a series of seminars called "Who Takes Care of the Caretakers?" for therapists, counselors—and mothers! Two of the most successful small bookstores I know specialize in children's books and murder mysteries. Jake, a marine biology freak who didn't want to go to grad school, started a seaside nature museum for kids and got a grant from his city.

Just starting from scratch, you can develop involvement, competence, and authority in your field without one extra day of school. That's how it worked out for me. But once again, if you decide to go to school later on, you'll go in with two great advantages: a track record and hands-on experience.

5. *The Generalist/Popularizer.* I wish I could think of a better name for this one—maybe "the go-between." It's a strategy for anyone who's fascinated by the poetry of a technical field but hasn't got the knack or the patience for technical training.

Many professional people can use help communicating their ideas to the public. They're specialists in physics or nutrition or international law, not in the graceful use of the English language. And sometimes they're even too specialized to talk to each other. If you can write, or even just organize ideas, you can get up to your ears in any field without a degree. I know a man who spent ten years putting together the first textbook to coordinate psychology with brain physiology. Until he came along, the mind-and-behavior people had barely been speaking to the brain people, and vice versa. And I know a woman who got a large foundation grant to pull together all the far-flung branches of research on the learning disability called dyslexia. Her only qualification was that she was dyslexic herself, and cared desperately about finding a solution. A 20-year-old college English major who wanted to be a member of the first space colony decided to start by doing magazine interviews with scientists like Carl Sagan and Gerard O'Neill. A housewife interested in nutrition developed a newsletter for the food industry on federal labeling regulations. Writing, editing, interviewing, starting a specialized newsletter or a cable-TV talk show with a theme—any of these could be a wonderful way to gain admission to a world you love without the expensive ticket of a Ph.D.

Those are just a few examples of the kind of direct, ingenious route to your goal you can dream up if you take conventional "wisdom" as a challenge instead of a finality. We've been talking about credentials and schooling, but the same goes for any obstacle that looms large on your Problems List. I can't brainstorm every kind of goal and problem for you, or this book would go on for two thousand pages. But I don't have to. You have the prime source of all the ideas you'll ever need right between your ears. All you need is a tool for getting them out and putting them into organized form.

BRAINSTORMING TECHNIQUE

The brainstorming technique I'm about to teach you is a two-stage process. The first stage will be familiar to you from Chapter 5. You suspend reality and bat the problem around from here to the land of Oz, accepting every idea with uncritical delight, until you've come up with some really fresh thinking. I call Stage 1 "Woolgathering," and the wilder and woolier the better. This time you'll have the option of doing it either alone or with a little help from your friends—imaginary and real.

The second stage is something new. It brings the best of your windfall of wild ideas down to earth and puts them into practical, do-able form. You could call Stage 2 "Bridge-building," because that's exactly what it does: bridges the Grand Canyon between dream and reality, inspiration and action.

As a working example, I'm going to take what is probably the single most universal and exasperating obstacle conventional "wisdom" places in our paths. A woman in one of my seminars put it succinctly: "I just see a mountain in front of me, and its name is Money."

Now, money is a very peculiar substance. It doesn't behave according to the laws of physics. Any amount you *don't* have—whether it's $5,000 or $500,000—will appear to be a mountain. Almost any amount you do have will not appear to be enough to pay next month's bills! Money often seems to be an emotional substance—the very incarnation of "I can't." So, just to take a properly defiant attitude toward this obstacle of obstacles, let's start with a really big mountain—a million dollars. It will be a good warm-up exercise for your own brainstorming, because if you can stretch your mind around this one, your own money problem isn't going to give you too much trouble no matter how big it is.

Just suppose your goal happened to be to sail around the world on your own yacht. That would be a pretty far-fetched fantasy for most of us, and a natural item on your Problems List might be, "Only millionaires can afford yachts." ("I can't because I don't have X—I'm not rich.") So your question No. 1 would be, "How can I get a yacht (or access to one that would satisfy me) without a million dollars?" And question No. 2 would be: "How can I get a million dollars?"

Now, should you go into brainstorming with question No. 1 or question No. 2? That depends on only one thing: the *touchstone* hidden in your goal. I see three possible touchstones here:

1. Being rich for rich's sake
2. Owning your own yacht
3. Sailing around the world in style

Only if actually being rich is your touchstone should you start your brainstorming on Question No. 2!

I'm not saying you wouldn't like to be rich, mind you. Who wouldn't? But if what you're saying is, "If only I were rich, I could do this, and this, and that"—if, in other words, you want to be rich *as a means to the end* of doing what you really love—it's a much better idea just to go ahead and do it. Once you're in action, you'll have so much energy and imagination that you'll turn up one hundred ways to get rich by doing what you love—if you still care. (You may not, once you've found out that you don't need lots of money to live your good life.) But if you decide you've got to get rich first, it's a good bet you won't get rich—and you won't get what you want, either.

Obviously, a million dollars can be made. Plenty of "ordinary geniuses" like you and me have done it, and you can use brainstorming to figure out a way. But nontouchstone dreams, "means-to-an-end" dreams, have a funny way of never coming true. That's because they don't tap into the one real power source you've got: your heart's desire. People who really want to make money *make* it, because making money turns them on. The rest of us just let it turn us off to what we do care about.* But we don't have to. Human ingenuity invented money in the first place. Human ingenuity can find a way around it.

So let's assume in our hypothetical example that your touchstone is either "owning your own yacht" or "sailing around the world in style." We'll start with Question No. 1, and see how you could get that goal for very much less than a million dollars.

---

*Very often, we also let it shelter us when we're scared. Being poor is one of the best excuses not to go for your dreams. It gets you much more sympathy than being fat. Nobody knows how to argue with poverty. We're all much too bamboozled by money in this society.

STAGE 1: WOOLGATHERING

The different brainstorming techniques differ only at this stage in how you get your ideas, not in what you do with them once you've got them. There are three different ways to do "Woolgathering."

Brainstorming alone

Sit down with pencil and paper in a quiet place, where you can daydream undistracted. Across the top of the first sheet of paper, write the problem—for example, "How to get a yacht/sail around the world in style without $1,000,000?"

Now start writing down every idea that pops into your head, and I mean *every* idea. Don't rule out anything, no matter how far-fetched or frivolous it seems. If you wanted a yacht, "Go down to the boat basin at night and steal one" would be just fine. At this stage, don't edit or judge your ideas. It could inhibit your imagination, and you might miss a good one. Take as long as you like; keep going till you run dry.

If you have trouble shaking off the habitual limitations on your thought, first check and see whether a little Hard Times is called for. Discouragement or apprehension may be weighing you down. If not—and you just seem to need a spur to fresh thinking—there's a second technique for brainstorming alone that can really turn your mind loose.

Role-play brainstorming

In the "Seeing Yourself as Others See You" exercise in Chapter 4, you discovered that playing the part of another person can open up unsuspected stores of knowledge in your own brain. Besides being great fun, this is one of the best ways in the world to get fresh ideas.

Your everyday identity is itself a role you've been cast in by time and place and culture. It doesn't express your total human potential. You were born with the same basic equipment in your head as a Stone Age hunter, an eighteenth-century duchess, a Mississippi riverboat gambler, or a Japanese monk. You have the capacity to assume any of those points of view in imagination—and it's like looking at the world with new eyes.

You can use your imaginary "ideal family" as a cast of characters for role-play brainstorming, or you can try playing the roles of some diverse and far-out characters, like these:

1. an old mule driver
2. the queen of a foreign country
3. a mad genius
4. a Martian
5. a fool
6. the president of a giant corporation
7. a Samoan fisherman (Eskimo hunter, Watusi warrior, etc.)
8. an engineer who builds bridges in the Andes
9. a Texas oilman
10. a 5-year-old girl

To get into any role, just close your eyes and spend a few moments imagining yourself into the life and mind and environment of that character. Then look at your problem from his or her point of view and write down whatever solutions come to mind.

For example:

Albert Einstein: "Intelligent conversation is a very rare commodity. Perhaps there is someone who owns a yacht who would simply like to have you on board for stimulating company. Or perhaps there is something you can teach—about the stars, or the Greek Islands, or the Galápagos. What about a floating university or seminar? Surely someone would provide the boat and the funds for that."

Bette Davis: "Hell, I'd stow away and then charm them into letting me stay on board."

Samoan fisherman: "Whenever we need something, we make it ourselves. Of course, a dugout canoe is easier to build than one of your strange and foolish boats. I know, because they get wrecked on our coral reef from time to time. You could have one of those if you want. They're no use to us. You'd have to do some patching up, though."

You get the idea.

Role-play brainstorming will come to your rescue when you get stuck for ideas alone. But if you can get a bunch of *real* people to toss ideas around with you, all the better! Brainstorming is always done in groups in business, industry, and creativity workshops, and for a good reason:

each mind brings a different angle of vision to bear on the same problem. You've probably had the experience of effortlessly solving a dilemma for a friend who was totally blocked on it—or having a friend to do that for you. That effect will be multiplied if you can get four or five people to pitch in. Group brainstorming has the added advantage of being a natural takeoff point for a barn-raising, as you'll see a little later on.

Brainstorming with a group

The people you call in to brainstorm don't need to know the first thing about the area you've got the problem in. In fact, the less they know the better! On a brainstorming team, you want *inexperienced* people, because the experts in any field only know what *can't* be done. Naive people come up with the best ideas in the world. That means children too. Kids above the age of four are astonishingly creative, because they have no restrictions on their thinking at all. When 6-year-olds were asked to design a vehicle that could drive over rough terrain with big ditches in it, they reinvented the tank.

Older people are terrific too. They've known a world without television or jet planes or superplastics, and their minds are often slower, deeper, more resourceful. But anyone can play: your husband, your wife, your mother, your friends, the TV repairman. And they'll love it. Playing with ideas is the world's best party game. You can invite people over, serve wine and cheese, and make an evening of it.

The one rule you must be sure to establish is that at this stage of the game there are no rules. No holds barred—the weirdest idea is a welcome guest. Once you've put the problem on the table, your job is to sit there with your pencil and write every idea down. Don't let one of them escape. It might be the one you are looking for.

After a good brainstorming session of any of these three kinds, your list of ideas might look something like this:

OWN YACHT
1. steal a yacht
2. marry somebody who has a yacht
3. win a yacht in a contest
4. win a yacht in a poker game

5. buy shares in a yacht with a group of people
6. get an old hulk and fix it up

SAIL AROUND THE WORLD

7. stow away
8. make friends with somebody who has a yacht and get invited aboard as a guest
9. rent a yacht
10. trade the use of a yacht for something I have (living loft, country cabin, etc.)
11. get hired on a yacht as a:
    captain
    engineer
    crew member
    waiter/waitress
    bartender
    gourmet cook
    masseur/masseuse
    companion to elderly or handicapped person
    tutor to young children
    lifeguard/swimming teacher
    entertainer—musician, magician, singer, comedian, court jester, etc., depending on your talents and on what you're willing to do (Everyone —but everyone—has something to offer: a sense of humor, a great recipe for chocolate cake. . . .)
12. design a private educational tour for rich people
13. design a promotional voyage for a boat company
14. design an around-the-world goodwill mission for ecology or peace or an end to hunger
15. design a scientific expedition or "floating seminar": for instance, retrace the voyage of Darwin's *Beagle* for a travel agency or group

If it really was your heart's desire to sail around the world on a yacht, somewhere on this list you would find an idea that appealed to you— and one you could do without becoming a millionaire first. Of course, at this point you'd still have no idea how you were going to "get an old hulk and fix it up," or "retrace the voyage of Darwin's *Beagle*." Those ideas look almost as far-fetched as the original million dollars! But it's going to be the whole purpose of Stage 2 brainstorming to provide answers to the question: *"How?"* So don't worry if the most intriguing ideas on your Stage I list still look pretty far out. Just take it from me: if you really want it, it can be done. For instance, before you dismiss my yacht example as fairy-tale stuff, take a look at this:

"*Sofia,* an 89-foot, three-masted schooner and floating cooperative, is looking for crew members. Since being restored from very battered condition in 1969 . . . *Sofia* has hauled cargo in the Caribbean, fished in New Zealand, sunk in the Galápagos, and in nine years, sailed around the world. She's had 50 or 60 crew members, about ten at a time . . . Past members have usually put $1,500–$3,500 into the boat and become part owners."

CoEvolution Quarterly, Spring 1978

I found that clipping *after* I'd made up the example . . . and at about the same time, there was a news story on TV about a mysterious series of yacht hijackings! While I don't recommend piracy on the high seas, it does go to show that no idea is impossible.

The sample list of ideas above also shows you some of the general types of strategies you can devise for getting around the money obstacle —or drastically reducing its size:

1. There are plenty of ways to get things, even big things, without buying them:

  a. beg
  b. borrow
  c. steal
  d. trade
  e. win
  f. rent
  g. make

2. Sell yourself. Swap something you can do—gardening, magic, talking with old people or kids, telling jokes—for free admission to a world you want into. Two friends of mine longed to live in the country, but could see no way they'd ever have enough money to buy or rent the kind of place they dreamed of. So they advertised their services as caretakers—and are now living year round on a famous rock singer's farm!

3. Even if money is required for your project, it doesn't have to be

your money. Be the idea man or woman. Design a package and sell it to somebody who is a millionaire.

4. Share the cost of your dream with people you'd like to share your dream with. Basia, a textile designer in her 30s, confessed that she harbored a hopeless million-dollar fantasy of her own: to start an artists' community in her own villa in the south of France. Once I got her to drop her assumption that it was impossible, brainstorming quickly produced a solution: get together with several like-minded friends and share the rental of a villa. (Cost to each: about $2,000.)

See? Being poor is no excuse not to go for your dreams, no matter how big they are.

TRANSITION: EDITING YOUR LIST

OK. You've got a list of ideas for "How to get my goal without X" (or "How to get X"). You wrote down every idea that came along, so some of them are strictly whimsical. Some of them are workable ways of getting to your goal, but not things you think you'd particularly like to do. Then there will be a few ideas that look promising. I don't mean the most "possible" ones, I mean the ones that make your heart beat faster. They may still look pretty pie-in-the-sky. Your next job is to pick the one or two best ideas and then start bringing them down to earth.

Let's take a look at how a real-life person did it.

Mary, 27, the divorced mother of a 2-year-old daughter, had decided her first target was to go to medical school. Mary had been a premed major in college and had gotten good grades, but then she had fallen in love with a cellist who spent a good part of the year traveling with a professional string quartet. Since music was Mary's other great love, she had made the difficult decision to marry her musician and travel with him instead of going on in medicine. When the marriage didn't work (her husband fell in love with the new second violinist), she moved back home to her upstate New York town, where her married sister could take care of her daughter while she worked for an electronics company.

Mary felt that she'd chosen the wrong fork in the road and that, with no money and a small child to support, it was too late to go back. But she obviously still wanted very much to be a doctor! I urged her to make entering medical school her first target, and to put all the reasons for discouragement on a PROBLEMS list. They were formidable:

1. no money
2. my college science is very rusty
3. older women and mothers have trouble getting into med school
4. child care (if I have to leave this area)

I told Mary to take those problems through brainstorming one at a time. She picked "money" to work on first, because she was going to need money for everything: premed refresher courses, tuition, food, rent, child care. She did her brainstorming with her sister and a friend while their kids played under the dining room table. Her first list of ideas looked like this:

Problem: How to get through medical school without a dime of my own
1. get a scholarship
2. get a loan
3. win the New York State lottery
4. marry a rich man who will send me through school
5. join the Armed Forces and let them send me through school
6. get my story in the local papers and attract a wealthy patron
7. stand on the streets of New York City with a sign saying, SEND THIS MOTHER TO MEDICAL SCHOOL

That's how brainstorming often works. You think of all the staid, sensible, obvious ideas first, like scholarships and loans. Then come the "rescue fantasies": someone is going to come riding along in a white Cadillac and carry you away, or appear mysteriously on your doorstep with a check for a million dollars. Being free to give those fantasies a legitimate place on your list brings liberating laughter—and only then do the really audacious, original ideas begin to flow.

In fact, they'll look *too* original. When Mary first glanced over her list, she said, "Maybe I can get a loan, but I'm afraid it won't cover living expenses. Ideas No. 3 and No. 4 are just silly. As for No. 5—me, join the Army? No way. I'd go nuts in a week. I kind of like No. 6, but frankly it doesn't seem to have much chance of working, and besides, I've got too little nerve and too much pride to go begging. That really rules out No. 7."

Stop right there! When you reach this point with your list, *don't cross anything off.* Like Mary, you probably think you could throw out about nine-tenths of your ideas without further ado, but there are two very good reasons why you shouldn't do that yet. One is that even the craziest idea has something to give you before you abandon it. The other is that *pessimism about an idea's workability can masquerade as lack of interest in it.* And until you've probed a little deeper into each idea with the magic question "How?", you won't really know what the word "possible" means.

The first rule of transition brainstorming, either alone or in a group, is: *Never throw out any idea* until you have asked three questions about it:

1. What is the useful element (or elements) in this idea? (You must find something of value in each one.)
2. How can I (we) get around the impractical elements of this idea? (In other words, instead of being reasons to junk the idea, any snags would become a *miniproblems list* calling for a new round of Stage 1 "Wool-gathering.")
3. What further ideas does this idea suggest?

Let's see how Mary did it—and what surprises she turned up.

IDEA NO. 1: GET A SCHOLARSHIP

1. *Useful elements:*	No debts
2. *Problems:*	a. must have super-good grades and test scores
	b. I'm not sure there are scholarships to med school
How to solve:	a. go to night school and study like mad

	b. do some research on financial aid to med students
3. *Further ideas:*	Create a scholarship! Write to large corporations offering to let them do good for society and the cause of women and get great publicity by sending me through medical school!

Now that's an exciting idea, one that really set off fireworks in Mary's brain—and if she had just thrown out "Get a scholarship," she would never have thought of it! Mary didn't know whether anything like it had ever been done before, and she had no idea how corporations would respond to her approach. But the very fact that you're bold enough to try something brand new can impress the right people. And the time certainly looked ripe to offer big companies favorable publicity for their enlightened attitude toward women. So Mary set this idea aside as a promising one and continued with her original list.

IDEA NO. 2: GET A LOAN

1. *Useful elements:*	standard procedure, channels exist
2. *Problems:*	a. good grades, as above b. might not cover living expenses c. years of debt
How to solve:	a. & b. same as above c. unavoidable
3. *Further ideas:*	get a private loan, rather than an outright gift, from a wealthy individual (as in Idea No. 6 on list)

Ideas No. 3 and No. 4—winning the lottery and marrying a rich man —Mary recognized as outright "rescue fantasies," which had done their job of uncorking her imagination, and which she wouldn't really want if they *did* happen. She didn't want luck *or* love to solve her problem—she wanted it to come from her own ability and deserving.

IDEA NO. 5: JOIN THE ARMED FORCES

1. *Useful elements:*   training free
      living expenses provided

2. *Problems:*   I'd hate it!

    How to solve: no way

3. *Further ideas:*   Is there some other organization that would train me in exchange for service? Peace Corps? Government? Foreign government? Australia? Investigate

IDEA NO. 6: FIND WEALTHY PERSON VIA LOCAL PAPERS

1. *Useful elements:*   appeals to local pride

2. *Problems:*   a. unlikely to find a taker
      b. feels like asking for charity

    How to solve: a. try and see
      b. swallow pride—or decide I'm worth it

3. *Further ideas:*   Do "create a scholarship" idea and get a newspaper article written about that—send clippings to corporations—& even to national magazines!

IDEA NO. 7: STAND ON STREET WITH SIGN . . .

This idea may sound outlandish, but Mary's sister, who gave her the idea, told her the true story of a young man who staked out a corner of Fifth Avenue in a sandwich board that said, "Send This Nice Jewish Boy to College." He got enough money to go! (Of course, he had nerve —and an angle.) Mary had to admit it was enterprising and would have the advantage of not indebting her to one person, but it just wasn't her style. The further idea she got from it was, "Put an ad in MS. and other magazines asking for $1 contributions."

When you reach this point, you're ready to go into Stage 2 brainstorming with the idea or ideas you like best. Mary chose the "Create a scholarship" idea. (She decided that she'd also investigate the more conventional sources of financial aid.)

STAGE 2: BRIDGE BUILDING

Before you did any brainstorming at all, your situation looked like this:

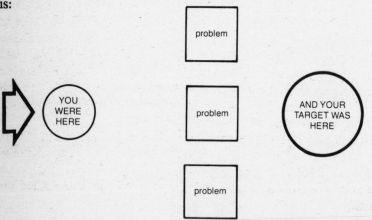

In Stage 1 brainstorming you transformed one of the problems into a *subgoal:* a specific way of getting one of the things you'll need for your goal. In Mary's example (her other problems, getting admitted to medical school and finding child care, can wait for now):

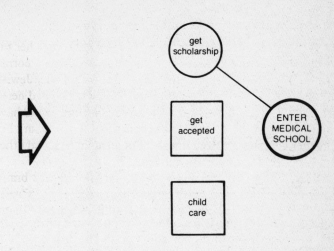

A subgoal is a first break in the wall of problems and the first link in your plan. *But it's almost as far away as your goal itself.* Mary wanted to win a kind of scholarship that didn't even exist yet except in her own imagination. You may have decided to get financial backing for your small business from an investor or "angel" you don't know how to find . . . or to sell a screenplay you haven't written yet . . . or to take an advanced painting class when you haven't made so much as a sketch in twenty years. There's still a big gap to get across before you reach that subgoal. What we've got to do now is build a solid bridge of actions over that gap, from the subgoal right to your doorstep. You'll be able to take your first step on that bridge *tomorrow,* confident that it will lead you step by step all the way to your goal.

There's only one way to build that kind of bridge, and that's the way you're going to do it in Stage 2 brainstorming: by *planning backwards* from your goal. If you've ever tried for your dreams before and been frustrated, the chances are good that you started out like this:

and then wondered why your best efforts petered out somewhere in the middle. You had energy and guts to spare, and even some excellent ideas. What went wrong?

There are three possibilities:

1. The steps you took were a waste of time because they were the wrong steps. They scattered your energy in fifteen directions instead of focusing it toward your goal.

2. Some of your steps may have been the right steps, but they seemed so small and insignificant compared to the size and distance of your goal that you couldn't see how they'd ever get you anywhere. So you gave up.

3. Your steps didn't come together right. You did the right things, but in the wrong order or at the wrong times. For instance, suppose you wanted to open a small bookstore. You went looking for a location, and found a perfect storefront at a reasonable rent. But you didn't have any money in the bank—and by the time you got the money together, the store had been rented. Or: you rented the store—and then it stood empty for two months, with money going down the drain, while you tried frantically to learn all you needed to know about the retail book business.

If that has happened to you, your basic mistake was thinking that just because *action* goes forward, from the present to the future, *planning* has to go forward too. It can't. Planning has got to go *backwards:* from the distant future to tomorrow . . . from the intimidatingly large to the reassuringly small . . . from the whole vision of your goal to its component parts, little things you can do one by one. "In reality, great deeds are made up of small, steady actions"—remember? But before you can put great deeds together in reality, you have to take them apart on paper to discover *what* small, steady actions, *in what order,* will really get you there. Here's how you do it.

Two questions are your tools for breaking down subgoals into the smaller and smaller steps that lead up to them. The first is, "Can I do this tomorrow?" If the answer is "No," the next question is, "OK, what would I have to get done first?" For instance, Mary's subgoal is to get a scholarship from a large corporation. Could she have that money in her hands tomorrow? Of course not. Well, what would she have to do first? She'd have to send letters to a whole bunch of corporations:

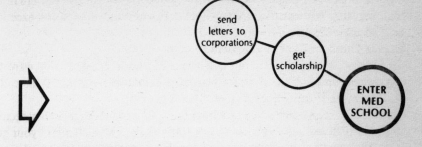

Can she mail those letters tomorrow? No. What would she have to do first? Draft a letter, and compile a list of promising corporations and their addresses. If she wants to use another idea she got out of her Stage I list—to have an article about her plan appear in the local paper and enclose clippings with her letter—she'll also have to arrange to get such an article published:

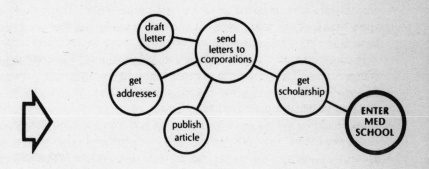

YOUR FLOW CHART

I'd like to stop for a moment and explain that this kind of visual framework for brainstorming—where you write the steps down in funny little circles, working from right to left—is called a *flow chart*. The one you will draw as you do your Stage II brainstorming is probably the single most important item in your Portable Success Support System, because it will not only help you think—it's also going to help you *act.* When it's finished, it will be a detailed map of the path to your goal, showing you exactly what you have to get done at each stage of the game before you can go on and do the next thing, and how the various "branches" of action have to come together.

I borrowed flow charts from business and industry, where they are used in coordinating the complex processes of manufacturing and marketing. In the Ford factory in Detroit, for example, body, engine, and transmission must each be assembled separately from subassemblies, which in turn are put together out of thousands of smaller parts; still other parts and finishings have to be imported from abroad. Flow charts are drawn up to insure that everything comes together properly, so that on the target date for the new season, a finished Ford rolls sparkling off the assembly line.

I've been using flow charts for my own personal "business" for several years, and I've found them every bit as indispensable to my success and my sanity as they are to Ford's profits. Once you know how to use them, I promise you you'll work one out for every project you ever have in mind, right down to planning a dinner party! You won't know how you ever got along without them. Of course, the flow chart you draw of the path to your goal will be much more flexible than its cousins in big business: a highly individual design, subject to revision and change. It will look and behave more like a living organism than an assembly line. But it will serve exactly the same purpose as Ford's: to guide you in getting your goal together.

A flow chart isn't finished and ready to roll until it completely bridges the gap between the present moment and your goal. That means that each of its main branches has to be worked down to *first steps: things so small and manageable you could do them tomorrow.* So let's go back and see how Mary completed her flow chart, following her through the process step by step.

Mary has three steps to ask questions about now. One: Could she draft a letter to corporations tomorrow? Theoretically, yes, she could. But in reality, she'll want to be further along in the process of brushing up her knowledge and applying to medical schools first. And that's another major branch of her flow chart, one she hasn't even started working on yet. What she can do tomorrow, though, is make preliminary notes for that letter, as a way of getting her thinking started and making the idea real to her.

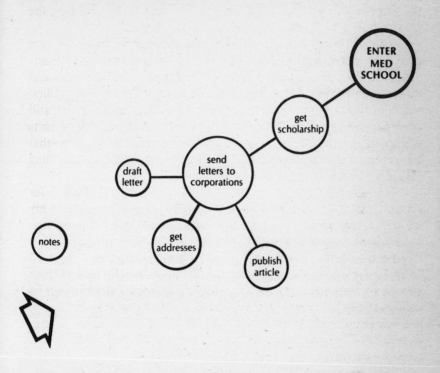

Two: Can she have a list of corporations' names and addresses tomorrow? No, she'll have to do some research first to figure out which corporations might be receptive and who would be the best person to contact in each one. Some of that research she can do in libraries, but some of it she'll have to do in another way, one we'll be talking about at length in the next chapter. (For now, I'll designate it in her flow chart by a question mark.) What Mary could do tomorrow is brainstorm on what kinds of corporations to approach: drug companies? Vitamin companies? Oil companies eager for a humanitarian image? (She felt there were ethical as well as practical questions to consider.)

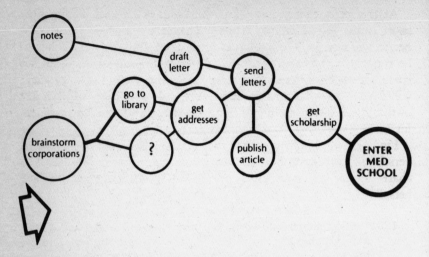

Three: Could Mary get an article about her plan into the local newspaper tomorrow? No, first she'd have to have a reporter come and interview her—and how on earth is she going to do that? Just calling up the paper and telling them about herself doesn't sound like such a hot idea. This is the place for another one of those question marks:

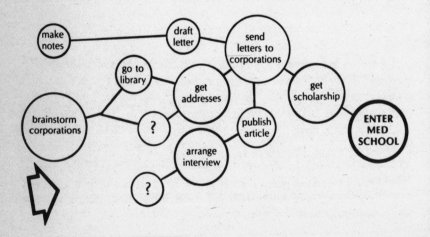

At this point, Mary has taken the "Money" branch of her flow chart as far as she can by herself. The next important branch for her to work on is "Get admitted to medical school"—and it has to be roughly coordinated with the "Money" branch so that the two come together in time. How Mary solves the child-care problem will depend on what medical school she goes to—if she stays in her own area her sister can help her out—so she can leave that problem for later.

I'm going to run quickly through the series of questions Mary asked herself, and show you how she incorporated the results into her flow chart—adding one more circle on the left for each answer she gave herself.

1. "Getting into medical school is a subgoal in its own right. Now, can I do it tomorrow?
   "Hardly.
   "What would I have to do first?
   "Well, I'd have to apply to medical schools."

2. "Can I apply tomorrow?
   "No. There are two things I'd have to do first: get high scores on the MedCATs (a general competence test for medical school admissions, like the college SAT's), and send for application forms."

3a. "Can I get high test scores tomorrow?
   Obviously not. First I have to take the tests."

3b. "Can I send for applications tomorrow?
   Not until I've decided which schools to apply to."

4a. "Can I take the MedCATs tomorrow?
   If I did, I'd flunk them! First I'd better take some kind of premed review course."

4b. "Can I decide which schools to apply to tomorrow?
   No, first I'll have to go to the library and read catalogs. (I can find out about regular loans and scholarships at the same time.) And *that* I *can* start doing tomorrow."

5. "Can I take a review course tomorrow?
   No—first I've got to find out where there is one. I can do that tomorrow, by making phone calls to all the local universities, colleges, and medical schools. Another thing I can do is dig up my old college class notes and start reviewing them on my own."

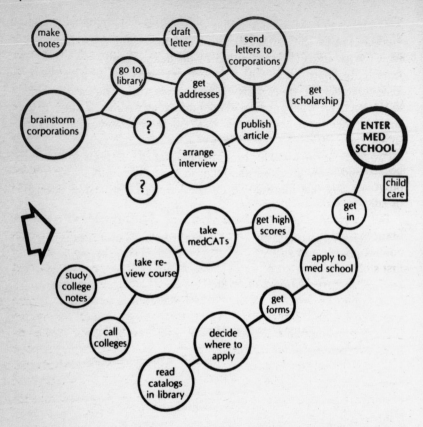

And that is an almost complete flow chart. It gave Mary five things she could start doing right away: make notes for a persuasive letter to corporations: brainstorm on what kinds of corporations to approach; make calls to ask about premed review courses; start reviewing her college science notes; and go to the library to check out med school catalogs. While she wasn't literally going to run out and do all those things the next day, they did give her plenty to do in the immediate future—small, manageable actions she could see were directly connected to her goal. If she ever had any doubts on that score, all she had to do was look at her flow chart!

Stage 2 brainstorming brings even the most unreachable goal within reach by breaking big achievements down into human-sized tasks.

There is *no* goal—I don't care if it's becoming President of the United States in twenty years—that doesn't break down to something as simple as going to the library or the newsstand or picking up the phone. Almost all goals begin with information-gathering, an act which requires no preparation and very little courage, yet sweeps you right up in the excitement and reality of your goal. Creative goals, like writing a novel or learning to paint, begin with a very modest qualitative and quantitative demand: "Write one *bad* page" or "Make 5 silly drawings of the cat." (More on this in Chapter 9, "First Aid for Fear.") Just because these first steps are so tiny, *you'll do them.* They'll get you up off your chair and out on your path where the prospect of a huge goal or subgoal would leave you sitting paralyzed.

But your flow chart isn't finished, as I said before, until all its major branches are broken down to first steps. Like Mary's chart, yours is bound to have a few holes in it—places where you get stuck short of first steps and have to write in a question mark. You may run into that kind of dead end in a much more drastic way than Mary did.

For example, Jeannette was a $150-a-week typist whose real passion was photography. Her dream was to travel through Appalachia taking pictures and to publish a book of those pictures. She knew that as an unknown photographer she didn't have a chance of getting a book advance, and that she'd have very little chance of selling a finished book even if she did find some way to finance her trip. So she went into brainstorming with a group of friends, and together they came up with a beautifully ingenious plan.

Suppose she got an old panel truck and turned it into a rolling darkroom? Jeannette could drive through Appalachia with Brownie cameras, teaching children to take pictures and develop them. As they explored and recorded their own world, she could photograph that luminous process of discovery—and put her pictures together with theirs. That would be a book with a fresh angle—and a good chance of finding a publisher. It was also the kind of project that was tailor-made to attract foundation funding.

However, this still left Jeannette stuck with a sizable money problem. Trucks, darkroom equipment, cameras, photographic paper, and just plain traveling all cost money—and getting foundation support takes time. It could be more than a year before Jeannette got her grant—or found out that she didn't get one. And she just didn't want to wait that long. She has a flow chart that isn't flowing. What can Jeannette do to break that bottleneck?

Then there's Alan, the Chicago educational-books editor whose goal was to open a small publishing house in Colorado, specializing in outdoors handbooks and literature. Alan had no capital of his own to invest in his business, and he decided to solve that problem by finding one or more investors or moneyed partners. After a great deal of thought, Alan's flow chart looked like this:

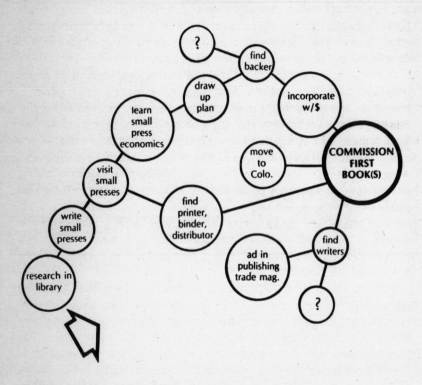

Alan was smart enough to realize that the best way to learn small-press economics was directly from the publishers who practiced them (that is, by apprenticeship), and he knew how to contact those publishers through directories that can be found in any library. But when it came to finding a backer, Alan was stumped. He didn't know anybody with that kind of money. When he brainstormed the problem, he got the wild and wonderful idea of getting an environmentally-aware celebrity like John Denver or Robert Redford to put his money and his clout behind Mountainbooks (as Alan was calling it). But that left him just as stuck as he was before, because he didn't know John Denver or Robert Redford, either, and he had no chance of meeting them.

When you come to this kind of impasse in your planning, you may get very discouraged. You may also feel embarrassed that you don't know how to pull the whole miracle off all by yourself. But I've got news for you. *You're not supposed to.*

Look at Christopher Columbus. A moment's thought will make it obvious that he did not discover America "on his own," and that there was no way he could have. There's no question that his vision, his drive, his desire was the galvanizing force of the expedition. But he was "dependent," first of all, on the brainstorming of Copernicus, who had come up with the ridiculous idea that the world was round. He was "dependent" on Ferdinand and Isabella for faith and financing, on shipbuilders for the *Niña,* the *Pinta* and the *Santa Maria,* on his crew, and on the inventors and makers of navigational instruments, the sextant and the astrolabe. If that's "dependency," then dependency is the foundation of human civilization. If you really think you should be an exception, good luck. You'll be the first.

What you have to do in this world you cannot do alone. Every successful human enterprise is a collaboration—a drawing-together of diverse resources and energies to achieve a single end. And you can and should do just that for your goal.

So when you've gone as far as you can on your own, it's time for a barn-raising.

−7−

Barn-raising

If you've done your brainstorming with a group, like Jeannette did, you're in luck. It's going to turn into a barn-raising spontaneously.

In all the years I've been working with creativity in groups, I have never once seen a brainstorming team come up with a bright strategic idea, like Jeannette's Appalachian plan, and then get up, put on their coats, and say, "OK, kid, good luck. You're on your own." That never happens. What does happen is what happened to Jeannette:

One of her friends said, "You know, a guy in my office has an old van he wants to get rid of. I'll bet he'd sell it to you for less than $200! It's in terrible shape, of course. But anyway, here's his phone number." And then somebody else said, "My best friend's brother is an auto mechanic! Maybe he'd fix the van for free if you did advertising photography for him, or portraits of his family. Let me call my friend and have her ask him." And then somebody else said, "Why don't you try to get a job in a photo store, so you can get stuff at discount? I think they even let you have the outdated film and photographic paper for free." Another friend knew a journalist who had gotten several grants, and offered to put Jeannette in touch with him for help writing up a grant proposal. The whole group agreed to ask everyone they knew to dig in their closets for old Brownies and Instamatics, and they decided to put together a list of addresses of people along Jeannette's proposed route who would be glad to let her stay overnight with them for free. Between them, Jeannette and five friends worked out a plan by which she could go ahead and set her dream in motion without waiting for a grant—

for less than a thousand dollars! And then they planned to throw a flea market to raise the money.

If you think this sounds incredible, try it. When your brainstorming team starts coming up with concrete suggestions, contacts, and offers of help, you'll find yourself scribbling as fast as you can to get down all the names and phone numbers—and within five minutes you'll have so many real and promising first steps that it takes your breath away.

When you've gotten your plan worked down to *specific needs,* that's the last moment when anyone wants to give up, go home, and forget all about it. On the contrary, that's when everybody leans forward and starts getting really involved. It suddenly looks like this fabulous thing might just happen. And it's not so much that people want a piece of the action. It's that they want to *give* you a piece of your action! Each member of your brainstorming team is realizing that she or he has something real to contribute: an idea, a contact, a skill. And each one loves the idea of being able to say, "See that house? See the third brick from the left in the third row from the bottom? I gave her that. I made it with my own hands."

In Chapter 6, we talked about the importance of identifying *emotional problems*—the hands-off kind that can only be helped by a sympathetic ear. But now we're dealing with *strategic problems,* the kind that call for helping hands. These are the problems that can be fixed—and we seem to take an uncanny delight in fixing them. You know what I'm talking about if you've ever given someone a lead that led to a job, or an apartment, or a part in a play, or a life-changing experience, or a love affair. Most of us remember and treasure every part we've ever played in someone else's survival, satisfaction, or success. And that's not because we're a bunch of altruistic saints. It's because helping each other is creative and it makes us feel good.

We're just beginning to realize that sharing skills and resources is a deep human pleasure and need, one that's wired into our survival just as much as hunger or sex. If our distant ancestors hadn't evolved an actual instinct for cooperation, they would have been eaten by saber-toothed tigers the first morning they crawled out of their caves. And the things that keep us alive always feel good. That's how nature makes sure we will do them.

Pioneer families and small farmers had to pool their labor to get their barns built, their crops plowed and harvested, their corn husked. In the process, they reaffirmed the bonds of community—and had a whale of a good time. Working together toward vital common goals strengthened their relationships as it lightened their labor. There was no split in their lives between love and work, self-interest and mutual aid. In our complex and technically advanced society, we no longer need each other's direct and personal help to survive. We're still dependent on other people, but the cooperation that keeps us alive has become abstract and impersonal. We can buy houses built by strangers. We can stand in line at the supermarket to buy our food. We can open the Yellow Pages and hire a doctor or a plumber. We exchange most goods and services for money instead of love. We've gained the freedom to pursue our individual goals—and that's a precious freedom—but we've paid a high price: the *community of purpose* that once fused work and relationship into a meaningful whole. Our most practical and satisfying way of getting things done is still *together*. And the proof is that so much of our potential stays stubbornly locked inside us as long as we try to tap it alone.

Our instinct for cooperation is still very much alive. It's looking for a job. Why not put it to work in the service of our individual goals? Sharing dreams and resources could be a wonderful way to surround ourselves with a "family" of winners—a community with a new common purpose: no longer the survival of all its members, but the fullest unfolding of each one's unique potential.

We don't have to go all the way back to pioneer days for a working model of that kind of "cooperative individualism." We have one right in front of our eyes. Our myths of "every man for himself" and "looking out for Number One" have just kept us from seeing it, because it's in the last place where we'd ever think of looking: *in the lives of successful men.* As a matter of fact, *it's the reason why they're successful!* Most of them take it so completely for granted that it doesn't occur to them to give credit where credit is due. Ask them and many will say, "Of *course* I made it on my own." But I can think of at least one high flyer from modest beginnings who's given the public lie to that Horatio Alger myth.

The popular notion is that this man single-handedly built up his family's little farm into a million-dollar business. The way he tells it, when he came home from the Armed Forces to take charge of the farm, a group of men got together with him, rolled up their sleeves, and said something like this:

"OK, son, the first thing you're going to need is a certain amount of money. Here's a loan. We figure it'll take about four years till you're in a position to pay it back. Harry here has a company that'll front you the starter seeds and fertilizer. I'm not growing anything on my lower forty, and I'll let you use it so you can get started. You can use my farm machinery too, here's the key to the shed. We've got marketing contacts in every town in the state, and old Sam has the trucks. Now if there's anything else you need, you just call on us, hear? We'll be droppin' by from time to time to see how you're doing."

And that's how Jimmy Carter, self-made man, got his start.

This system of cronies and contacts is called *the old-boy network.* It's an informal institution that many young men on the rise can call on to help themselves get established in their work. It operates both within professions—often in the form of the "mentor" relationship, where an older man takes a younger one under his wing—and between professions. It got its name from groups of men who had been classmates in school, and who kept in touch and helped each other out. The editor published the professor's book, the accountant finessed the executive's taxes, the lawyer saw the producer through his divorce, the banker got the entrepreneur a loan, the congressman threw the new Interstate to the contractor—and each man shared his ever-broadening contacts with the others.

That's how things really get done in our "individualistic" society— right at the top! Never mind the myths. *There's a network of helping hands behind every genuine success.* And do you know how Jimmy Carter ended his speech on the old-boy network?

He said, "I have never known a woman who had that."

He was only half right.

It's true that most women have been incredibly isolated in terms of our talents, dreams, and goals. Not *alone:* we'd go down to the river and beat sheets on the rocks together, or we'd meet at the laundromat, which amounts to the same thing. But until very recently, there were precious few women in a position to offer their sisters a handhold in the worlds of power, money, achievement, and adventure, and those few didn't initiate an "old-girl network"—a fact that was cited as proof of the old belief that women are competitive rivals, and that the good-buddy spirit of mutual aid is just one more piece of male equipment we were born without. Consciousness-raising groups gave the lie to the notion that women couldn't support each other, but that support rarely got beyond the emotional. We exchanged comfort and complaint, not contacts. And that gave ammunition to the belief that only the exceptional woman is built for action—and that she's not a nice person.

It's all myths. It's nonsense. Of course women will compete with each other—if two of them happen to be after the same job or in love with the same man! Men do that too, and it's as natural as when you've got two hungry people and only one cookie. Otherwise, women have always given each other, not only understanding and compassion, but enormous amounts of practical help. The fact is that *there has always been a women's network.* In the domestic and human sphere, where we felt competent and comfortable, women have shared recipes, remedies, outgrown baby clothes, tools, and techniques since time began. The traditional way to make friends in a new neighborhood was to go next door and borrow a cup of sugar!

Cooperation isn't our problem. It never has been. Women are able to share resources and skills quite efficiently, with a warmth and openness many men envy. Our only problem has been taking ourselves seriously—as full, fascinating people with dreams and gifts and goals. You've done that now. You've shaped a clearly defined goal out of the stuff your dreams are made of, and you've taken it seriously enough to work out a detailed plan for getting it. You're about to find out that that's all it takes to bring the "old-girl network" out of the kitchen and into the world—and to convince the old boys to go coed.

If you've been brainstorming by yourself, and your flow chart has some holes in it, you can call a group of people together to provide you with the missing pieces in your plan. You can throw a *resource party* —the modern equivalent of a pioneer barn-raising. And that will become the natural takeoff point for an ongoing *resource network:* an informal community of mutual aid, combining the clout and goal-orientation of the old-boy network with the versatility and comfort of the cup-of-sugar connection. In the last chapter, you learned how to build a bridge of actions from a distant goal to your doorstep. Now you're going to discover that you can build a bridge of helping hands to virtually any person, skill, or thing you need on Planet Earth.

HOW TO THROW A BARN-RAISING

To give a resource party, the first thing you need to do is sit down and ask yourself a simple question:

Who do you know?

That's another one of those tricky little questions like "Who do you think you are?" When we ask, "Who do you know?" most of the time what we're really saying is, "Are you well-connected? Do you have rich, powerful friends?" If you don't—and let's face it, most of us don't—you will probably answer, "I don't know anybody," meaning, "I don't know anybody who counts." And that's grounds for inaction.

I'd like you to forget that right now and take the question in its original, innocent sense. Who do you know? Who are your friends and relatives and acquaintances? Whose names and phone numbers are in your address book? *You've got the makings of a full-fledged, effective resource network right there.*

How many of those people should you invite to a barn-raising? In a pinch, you can just have lunch with your best friend, or even talk to her on the phone. Two heads, and two people's resources, are more than twice as good as one. But the more people you pull in, the more help and ideas you'll get, because everyone will be inspired by hearing what everyone else has to offer. Four or five is a good working number. Fifteen is about the most you can comfortably fit into your living room. (Anything over fifteen also calls for a slightly more formal procedure, so we'll talk about how to throw a large-scale barn-raising after I describe how the basic version works.) As with brainstorming, it's helpful, though not mandatory, to get people of a variety of ages, backgrounds, and occupations: someone from Montreal, someone in her sixties, someone in movies, a carpenter, a stockbroker, an encyclopedia salesman, a shrink. You can ask a few of your friends to bring along their most interesting friends—or their husbands or grandmothers. It's not necessary for everyone to know everyone else. Success Teams barn-raisings start with a roomful of total strangers.

A barn-raising not only gives fresh purpose to old friendships; it can be a great way of making new ones. I meet a lot of people who say, "I don't make friends easily. I just don't seem to attract people." I'll tell you the kind of people who do. *They're the ones who are on their own trip, who have a fabulous idea and are running with it.* They don't call people up and say, "Uh . . . whatcha doin' tonight, Marty?" They say, "I've got such and such to do, and I could use some help. Want to come over?" Everyone loves to be around them because they generate so much energy. We were taught that it was selfish to be on our own trips, much less to ask for help with them. That's nonsense. The truth is that *the most generous thing you can do for the people around you is generate energy.* So don't be shy about inviting people over to help you out. There will be plenty in it for them. You're not only going to give them the chance to share in your goal, you're going to give them inspiration and help with theirs. If there's anything *they* want or need in their lives right now—a piano teacher, a tenants-rights lawyer, a set of kitchen cabinets, a ride to Vancouver—a barn-raising is the place to ask for it.

Your get-together can begin and end with socializing, but in the middle it's got to be a business meeting, with everyone's attention focused on the problem at hand. You start things off by telling everyone, first, all about your goal, and second, everything you've figured out you need in order to get it. For instance: "My dream is to start a horse ranch and riding stable. I've already got my first horse, and she didn't cost me a fraction of what I expected. What costs is the tack! I need leads to second-hand saddles, bridles, and blankets that I can buy cheap or trade for riding lessons. I also need customers—people who would like to take private riding instruction for ten dollars an hour." Or: "I'm going to move out to Colorado and start a small publishing house called Mountainbooks. I've got to find a partner or investor with enough money to back the enterprise for two years. This is a shot in the dark, but does anybody know anybody who might have a personal contact to John Denver or Robert Redford? I also need personal contacts to small-press publishers and to writers who specialize in the outdoors and nature field." Be ready with pencil and paper, because the ideas will really start flowing.

There are two rules you've got to follow if you want your barn-raising to be effective. The first is: *Be as specific as possible about what you need.* (Unless you've gotten stuck for ideas and you want some group brainstorming, working with your flow chart should have helped you reach this point.) Asking for "help" doesn't work. It may get you sympathy, or some well-meaning suggestions that miss the mark, but eventually you'll just get a helpless shrug. But if you ask for a second-hand piano, a contact in the music business, or lessons in auto mechanics, it's like dropping a beckoning worm into a pond full of hungry bass: every mind in the room will rise to the bait.

I'll give you an example of how this works. Could you put me in personal contact with someone who speaks and writes fluent Chinese and could translate into English? It doesn't have to be someone you know personally; it could be a friend of a friend, or a waiter in your favorite Chinese restaurant, or a professor at a university where a friend of yours teaches. But I want a name, an address, a phone number, and the name of the go-between, so that I can go in and say, "So and so sent me."

I'll bet that the farthest thing from your mind just now was the people in your personal universe who know Chinese. But if you give it a few minutes' thought, I'll bet you'll realize that you can solve my problem. If, on the other hand, I had said, "I'd like to have a pen pal in Peking; can you help me?" the chances are that—unless I was making a clear request for brainstorming—you would have shrugged your shoulders and felt helpless.

Before you can get what you need, you've got to take responsibility for *knowing what you need.* Being clear and specific about your needs is one of the most important ways of treating yourself like a winner. It's also the signal to everyone else that you're serious about your goal. So if what you need is Hard Times—and an ill-defined problem often conceals fear or pain—ask for Hard Times. If you need ideas, ask for brainstorming. And if you need a tractor or violin, *ask* for a tractor or violin. The chances are excellent that you'll get it.

The second rule for getting the most out of a barn-raising is: *always ask for the most specific information you can get*—names, addresses, phone numbers, book titles, etc. Remember that what you are aiming for is to get your flow chart down to *first steps*—things you can do today or tomorrow. If you want to make the move from executive secretary to executive, and Anne says, "Hey, I know somebody who *did* it," don't say, "Wow, great!" Get that woman's phone number and write it down. If you need a write-up in the local paper and Bill's best friend's wife works there as a copy editor, get her number so you can call and ask if she knows a reporter. If Joe knows three magazines you should run classified ads in for your book-find service, write down their names and ask Joe if he has copies you can borrow tonight.

Do you feel like saying, "Hey, wait a minute! Not so fast!"? Right. That's because we're getting out of the nice, comfortable realm of fantasy and into the frightening realm of real action. You're going to *follow up* on the leads you get from barn-raising—tomorrow and the next day and the next. That's what makes your goal really happen. It can also make you very nervous. That's why the next section of this book is all about how to set up a support system that will keep you going when you feel like crawling into bed and pulling the covers over your head. But one of the best things about throwing a barn-raising is that you've already got some of the raw materials for your support system right there with you in the room.

I've mentioned the importance of accountability—of having someone else, like a teacher or a boss, who knows what you're planning to do and cares whether you do it or not. Just knowing that someone else's eyes have seen your plans helps to keep them from sliding back into the never-never land of dreams. Once you've told your friends that you're planning to write a novel or start a dairy farm, they'll be interested and excited—and hopeful, because if you can do what you love, maybe they can too. So they'll be rooting for you. And all of a sudden, if you don't do it, you'll not only be letting yourself down—you've done that before —but you'll be disappointing them, too.

Believe me, you will find this infinitely more effective than "self-discipline." And it works right down to the step-by-step level. Because if Anne should happen to call you next week and say, "Did you talk to that lady executive I told you about? What did she say?" you're going to feel pretty sheepish if you didn't call her. That may not be enough to get you to pick up the phone when the midweek willies strike (more first aid for them in the next section), but it helps. So whenever the person you get a lead from is a friend, it's a good idea to work on the "report back" principle. Say, "I'm going to call you next Sunday and tell you what happened." That's a firm date. Write it down.

When your barn-raising group has given you all the suggestions they can, it's the next person's turn to take the floor and tell what s/he wants to do and what s/he needs. As you go around the room, you'll be astonished at the variety of resources a small handful of people can offer each other for achieving goals of all kinds. Here are some of the kinds of things people I know have asked for—and gotten —in barn-raisings.

INFORMATION

I'm a great believer in libraries—and in librarians, bless them. You can go to the library in any moderate-sized town, college, or university and find out almost anything you need to know, from the regulations of the American Kennel Club to the Gross National Product of Paraguay. You can also accomplish wonders by browsing through a bookstore, if yours allows browsing. But before you spend precious hours searching for the facts and addresses you need, try a shortcut. Ask your friends.

Stacy had a bottom drawer full of poems she had always secretly thought were pretty good. She got up her courage and showed some of them to her friends, and they urged her to make it her first target to get at least one poem into print. Stacy was a school nutritionist in a small midwestern city, not a literary person at all. She had no idea who would publish the work of an unknown poet. One of her friends had taken a course in women's writing at a nearby community college and was able to give Stacy the names of the best women's literary magazines. She promised to check copies out of the college library so that Stacy could see the kind of work they printed and get their addresses.

Carol, a cartoonist, had signed up with a top agent and gotten some encouraging responses from TV people, but she needed a special kind of assistant: a gifted cartoonist who would be willing to work with someone else's concepts. She had no idea how to find such a person, or why that person would want to work with her. She brought up the problem at her barn-raising. One friend knew a professional illustrator who had done animated commercials. She called the illustrator and got the names of two trade magazines that deal exclusively with cartoonists. Another remembered seeing a recent magazine article by a freelance cartoonist that mentioned trade associations, and offered to track the article down. By following up on this information, Carol was able to place classified ads that led to interviews with three eager potential apprentices.

All of us have more odd bits of information floating around in our heads than we know we've got. We're constantly reading and overhearing things—TV features about women stockbrokers, newsletters on volunteerism, reports on new solar collectors or supersonic cockroach zappers—and filing them away, forgetting we even have them until someone else's need suddenly yanks them into the limelight. We can be eyes and ears and memory banks for each other. It's a lot less lonely than the library stacks, and it works just as well, if not better.

THINGS AND STUFF

"Pathological individualism" is the single factor that has done the most to give money its awesome power over our lives. Why be "self-reliant" and pay the going market price for all kinds of things we can help each other get for less—or for free?

Starting with that classic cup of sugar, *borrowing* is the world's most time-honored and legitimate way of getting something for nothing. Friends will very often be willing to make you the short-term or long-term loan of something they're not using. I know a penniless playwright whose first off-Broadway hit got written on an old mechanical Royal portable that had been gathering dust in a friend's closet. And a Siamese cattery that survived its first lean year because its owners could borrow a car to make trips to a wholesale pet-food warehouse.

My writer friend Julia is the most successful "borrower" I know. People just seem to walk up and offer to lend her things, and not just things, but whole houses. She needed a work studio for $100 a month or less; the third person she asked offered her the free use of an enormous gothic apartment with a view of the Statue of Liberty where she now writes her articles for a total cost of $25 a month in subway fares. (She stumbled on an exceptional situation—an empty apartment that its country-dwelling owners only used on occasional weekends. But that's just the kind of wonderful surprise that barn-raising can turn up! It's a more common solution to "borrow" temporary living or working space from vacationers in exchange for routine house, plant, or pet care.) Julia has also spent months writing in her parents' beach cottage, borrowing a neighbor's bicycle for trips to the grocery store. Most borrowers are equally enthusiastic lenders, and in return for all this bounty Julia arranged for me to use the same little beach house for free at a time when I was in desperate need of a cheap and solitary vacation. It gave her almost as much pleasure as it gave me.

When Shakespeare's Polonius told his son, "Neither a borrower nor a lender be," he was telling him to miss out on one of the small joys of life. Of course, he was talking about money. And money can be tricky. We'll be talking about that a little later. But there is rarely any problem about borrowing tools, books, tape recorders, tennis rackets, musical instruments, or a string of pearls to look classy for an interview —provided that they are not in active use and that you use them with care and respect.

Second-hand: Anything you can't borrow, or would rather have for your own, you can usually buy second-hand from someone you know or someone they know: a truck, a flute, a desk, a film projector. Ellen, who wanted to start a horse ranch, brought up her need for second-hand riding tack at her barn-raising. Within a week she had offers of two used saddles and three bridles, in good condition, cheap. Second-hand shops naturally mark things up. So do people who put ads in papers or throw garage sales for strangers. Friends give each other rock-bottom prices. The mark-up is in the pleasure of knowing that your old couch, camera, or Chevy van is filling a need in your friend's life.

Homemade: Do you need display shelving or a hand-lettered sign for your store, a handsome business card, a special costume for your stand-up comic act? Don't go out and buy them before you've checked out the talents in your network. If you can make a personal contact who knows carpentry or graphics or sewing, you'll get exactly what you want for less—and you'll be giving someone else the chance to do what s/he loves.

I know a free-lance sales rep in textbooks, the creator of her own business, who got a unique and beautiful business card designed by the friend of a friend, a graphics designer. Kate didn't charge Helen anything for the design (she was employed full-time), but she enjoyed it so much that she produced a whole sheaf of stationery designs for another friend who was starting a film production company. Both delighted noncustomers passed along so many inquiries—"Hey, who did your letterhead?"—that Kate wound up quitting her job and starting a free-lance custom design business.

Freebies: If you know someone who works in an office, s/he can sometimes bring you small quantities of pens, pencils, stationery, envelopes, rubber bands, and paper clips for free. Many a poet has broken into print on the strength of photocopied duplicates made on some more gainfully employed friend's office lunch break. My friends who breed Siamese cats got introduced to a restaurant manager who was happy to give them all the chicken gizzards that would ordinarily have wound up in the garbage. Free samples, out-of-date but still perfectly good merchandise (like dated film or photographic paper), and usable scrap (like mill ends from a lumberyard or empty fruit and egg cartons, the primary school teacher's and shoestring interior decorator's dream) can be carted away by people who work in many businesses. Get in touch with them and they'll give it to you.

Discount and wholesale: Here is another privilege that employees in anything from retail stores to giant corporations can often share with their friends. The old joke, "I can get it for you wholesale," is no joke if it saves you hundreds of dollars. One woman who was starting a small dance company on a shoestring got a personal contact to the friendly young manager of a hosiery store. He provides all the company's leotards and tights at wholesale prices in exchange for credit on their recital programs. A man I know who works for a large electronics corporation used his employee's discount privilege to buy videotape equipment for a friend who wanted to produce a series of health-information programs for community cable TV.

Shopping skills: Find that special person who knows where all the bargains are in your town. There's at least one in every network. I know a woman who has made it her business to find every thrift shop in a three-state area. Rae is a book designer with terrific taste, and she can make herself look like she just walked out of Saks Fifth Avenue for about $7. (I'll bet she loved to play dress-up when she was a kid.) She'll not only let you make the rounds with her—she'll design you from head to foot, just for the fun of it, if you've got a public appearance or an interview coming up.

Which brings me to another valuable kind of help you can get from your friends . . .

SKILLS AND SERVICES, OR MIXING BUSINESS WITH PLEASURE

Lorna, a weaver, ran a barely-surviving craft shop called Fabric Arts, selling weaving, knitting, crocheting, and macrame supplies. To meet her goal of getting the business into the black, she needed her shop remodeled, and she needed expert marketing advice. By announcing her needs at a barn-raising, she found a young interior designer and a marketing consultant who were friends of friends. The interior designer was willing to accept payment in kind—in hand-woven fabrics. The marketing consultant didn't charge her for his advice. In a couple of hours over coffee, he gave her some fantastic ideas—and invited her out to the movies the next week.

John, a psychiatrist who lives and sees his patients on a sailboat (believe it or not), had a further dream: to make his living by turning people on to nature. He got a bunch of people together for brainstorming, and they came up with a brilliant idea: he should promote himself as an expert on "success stress" (which, as an ex-workaholic himself, he was) and take small groups of executives on fishing and camping weekends as a form of play therapy. But how to do that and earn enough money to keep three children in school—and maintain a sailboat? His friends put him in touch with a professional PR person who was immediately delighted with the idea. Because John came to her through mutual friends, she didn't have to spend a lot of time interviewing or investigating him; there was an immediate feeling of warmth and "let's get to work!" She proceeded to prepare a campaign of press releases, media appearances, and newspaper interviews that would make him known and attract a clientele.

Whoever said that mixing business with pleasure was a bad idea? Since so many of us spend one-third of our lives doing business, it might as well be as pleasant and as personal as possible—and save us money besides. So if your goal calls for the know-how of an electrician, typist, editor, literary agent, publicist, lawyer, accountant, or auto mechanic, check out your network before you open the Yellow Pages. Services delivered on a basis of friendship, even a couple of times removed, are generally higher quality, lower cost, and a lot more fun than exchanges based strictly on money. If a friend or a friend's friend types your manuscript . . . or frames your drawings . . . or keeps the books for your store . . . or takes the pictures for your portfolio, you'll have the assurance of personal care and the added satisfaction of contributing to his or her survival. If you're setting up in business yourself, your friends will be your first and best source of customers and clients. Exchanging professional services with people you know does more than anything else to recreate the community of mutual aid that is such a natural form of human relating. And it often cuts costs even further by developing into a spontaneous system of barter—swapping services and skills instead of paying for them. (More on that a little later, when I talk about how to keep a considerate balance between giving and getting help.)

By supplementing your own skills, the skills in your network can save you time and energy as well as money. They'll set you free to concentrate on what you do best, instead of having to struggle with all the little side tasks that clutter up every goal. For instance, there are published books—good ones—that tell you how to write an effective resumé or grant proposal. I've listed the best ones I know in the Resources appendix at the back of this book. But if you know someone who's a whiz at resumés, you can get one written up in a pleasant evening over coffee, instead of wrestling with it for a week by yourself! If your network can put you in touch with someone who's applied for grants and gotten them, you'll get personal advice and feedback you can't get from any book. If you're applying to school and you draw a blank on one of those awful essay questions—"In 1,000 words or less, what are your reasons for wishing to enter the medical profession?"—you can get a friend with the gift of blarney to write it for you! In short, *you don't have to do everything by yourself.* Save your energy for what you love—and delegate as much of the rest as you can. You deserve help—and you don't have to worry about "using people" as long as you observe the "Safeguards for Barn-Raising" on p. 165.

If there are skills your goal requires that you really want to learn for yourself, like bookkeeping for your small business or auto maintenance for your delivery van, ask your barn-raising group to get you an introduction to someone who can teach them to you. For instance, if your goal is to open a bookstore because you love books, but you have no idea how to *keep books,* tap your network for an experienced small business owner who's willing to show you how to take inventory and use a ledger. (Again, I've provided a list of good books on starting your own business in the Resources appendix. But the best book is no substitute for the personal advice of a seasoned veteran.) If you're interested in photography but have never touched anything more complicated than a Brownie, get a photographer to give you a short lesson on f-stops and light meters so you can go out and start taking pictures tomorrow. A miniapprenticeship is the quickest and most direct way to get your hands on any skill, and barn-raising is the ideal way to set one up. Most people are as glad to share the secrets of their trade with a personal acquaintance as they are reluctant to teach them to a stranger or a customer.

Another valuable resource we can offer each other is something called *a day in the field.* This is especially important if you have one or more tentative goals that you think you might love, but don't really know much about. Suppose you're attracted to the life and work of a newspaper reporter, but you suspect that you got your idea of what it's like from the movies. It sure looks gritty and glamorous and exciting when Bette Davis or Robert Redford does it, but what's the reality?

The way you find out is, you ask your network to find you someone who works at a newspaper. And then you arrange to spend a day or two or a week hanging out with that person—soaking up the atmosphere of the newsroom, going along on assignments, carrying notebooks or cameras, toting coffee and copy. You won't be in the way. Most people love to talk about their work and enjoy the novelty of having an audience. It makes them feel like *they're* Robert Redford or Bette Davis! And that goes for doctors, stockbrokers, teachers, and craftsmen. Like volunteering, a day in the field is a great way to find out whether a particular goal is for you—and if so, to make contacts that will help you get your start toward it.

MONEY

Jeannette's Appalachian photography trip is a good example of how the exchange of ideas, goods, and services through barn-raising can reduce the cost of any plan to the absolute minimum. When you've reached that rock-bottom amount you've still got to have, your network will help you get it.

Friends can help you dream up and carry out fund-raising schemes, like Jeannette's did. They can find you a contact who's had personal experience with Small Business Administration loans. I know a couple who are close friends with the vice-president of a bank, an unpretentious sweetheart of a man; they have helped friends of theirs get bank loans by acting as references and go-betweens. If you have a promising scheme and a steady income, a friend will sometimes be willing to co-sign a loan with you or put up collateral—or even lend you the money directly. A woman I know put up her savings passbook for a doctor friend who had helped her through a difficult hospital stay and was now starting his own practice. And a young sculptor and his wife were able to buy a brownstone in Manhattan by arranging to borrow money at interest from a friend. If you know someone who has a few thousand dollars lying idle, there can be a special mutual advantage in this arrangement: you pay your friend less interest than you'd pay a bank, but more than he or she gets from a savings account. (Important note: a loan to or from a friend is a business arrangement. It should always be undertaken on the basis of financial reliability, not emotional trust, and the terms should always be drawn up on paper. That's not crass or cynical. It's the way to protect both your money and your friendship.)

If you're looking for a business partner, investor, or "angel," your network of personal contacts can find you one. There are an amazing number of mildly-to-massively wealthy people in this world who are looking for something interesting to do with $3,000 or $25,000—as a tax deductible contribution, a hedge against inflation, or just a sporting gamble. Where are they? They're hiding—for very good reasons. But even they have friends and cousins and grandchildren. And the odds are that someone you know knows one of them. It may take four or five or six links in the chain, but you can find that little old lady who loves murder mysteries and will back your little bookstore if you'll put up her name on a brass plaque.

I know people who've done it. Like the chess master—brilliant but broke—who opened his own chess shop with two partners: a former pupil and a fourth-generation multimillionaire who'd been in several business ventures with the pupil. And the theatrical director who financed a Shakespeare festival with a $14,000 gift from the grandfather of an actress in her company. Before you can look for a backer, of course, you've got to demonstrate your seriousness by getting your plan precisely defined on paper—and that means *figures.* And projections. It's the projections—where you expect to be in six months, one year, two years—that really turn on a creative entrepreneur. If you don't know how to do them, your friends will help you.* They'll dig up someone who's run a boutique, or managed a restaurant, or packaged a movie, and who can sit down and give you a short course on capital

*See the Resources appendix for books that give you sample business plans.

outlay, overhead, percentage points, projections, and whatever you need for a financially sound proposal.

CONTACTS, CONNECTIONS, CLOUT: "JOE SENT ME"

It should be getting very clear by now that the most important resource people can offer each other is *other people.* And it's never more important than when your goal is to get in through the door of a closed professional world. Not all goals require clout. But if yours does, your network will help you get it.

I'm sure you've heard those conversations about how hard it is to get a good job in business—or to get into medical school, or get a movie part, or get published, or get reviewed—that end with an angry sigh: "It isn't how good you are. It's *who you know."* Damn right it is! Some seeds have wings to travel on the wind; some have stickers for hitching a ride on animal fur or human clothing. The seeds of human genius happen to travel by a system of personal contacts. Why sit around bemoaning that fact when you can put it to work for you?

I'm not saying that how good you are isn't important. *It is.* It just isn't *enough.* Talent or merit alone will rarely get you past the smiling receptionist, the protective secretary, the wary agent, the routine hiring or admissions screening. A personal introduction to someone on the inside will. And that's not because magazine editors, movie producers, and personnel directors are "corrupt." It's because they're human. Like you, they tend to be a little suspicious of total strangers, but happy to meet anyone bearing the seal of approval of a respected colleague or a trusted friend. Personal introductions are the strength of the old-boy network. And by drawing on your own network, you should never have to walk into a job interview, publisher's office, or record company cold. At the very least, you'll go in with the name of a common acquaintance; at best, you can have an introductory phone call precede you.

Incidentally, this is one place where the generations can really be of help to each other. Your kid may be in school with the daughter of a film director; your friend's father may be a doctor who'd be willing to recommend you for medical school. You'll never know until you ask. And don't ever think this is "cheating." It's not a substitute for a strong sense of what you have to offer, or a willingness to be judged on your merits. It's simply the smart way to get your merits the recognition and opportunity they deserve.

If you're ambitious, there are two especially valuable kinds of inside contacts to ask for in any field. One is an equally ambitious young man or woman whose career needs complement your own. Ask your network to help you find and meet the brightest young agent or editor in town, on the lookout for new best-selling writers; a gifted young actress or director looking for scripts; a young record producer eager to turn an unknown talent into a smash hit; a young fashion designer looking for marketing help. And hitch your wagon to that rising star. When you're just starting out in your own career, this can be easier than getting the attention of someone already established, and the two of you together will have more than twice the chance of breaking into the big time.

Remember Andrea, the photographer who wanted to be famous for her portraits of celebrities? Since she was timid about marching straight up to big stars and major magazines, I suggested that she pick out a promising new rock star, follow his or her career, and offer her pictures to the editor of a young women's magazine that was just getting started. The singer would be grateful for the publicity, the magazine would be grateful for the scoop—and all three of them could get famous together.

The other kind of person you want to be put in touch with is the man or woman right at the top. If at all possible, get your novel manuscript to the editor-in-chief, your film script to the famous movie star, your marketing proposal to the vice-president in charge of sales. It may make you nervous (Chapters 9 and 10 will help you prepare), but it will save you time and uncertainty. Assistants and trainees may be friendly and sympathetic, but they hardly ever have the power to make decisions—especially positive ones.

This is where you will really need a personal introduction. People at the top, like people with money, are well protected against extra demands on their attention and time. They have to be. That's why letters of inquiry and phone calls to secretaries won't get you anywhere. But your network of friendships will.

Do you doubt that a modest gathering of friends in your livingroom could put you in touch with the likes of Robert Redford or an executive of IBM? Well, it can. It's already been mathematically proven that if you get any fifteen or twenty people together in a room and start asking them who they know, in five or six steps you can build a bridge of personal contacts to anyone—*anyone*—in the United States. Geography is no barrier. You can take a phone book from any town in the country—say, Bozeman, Montana—pick a name at random, and say, "All right, who knows somebody in Montana—or somebody who *knows* somebody in Montana?" And within five days you can have a message delivered personally to that sheep rancher or liquor-store owner in Bozeman. That's been done!*

I don't know if anyone has ever tried the same deliberate experiment across the tougher barriers of celebrity and power—getting together fifteen people in a room and asking for a personal contact with Marlon Brando or Jimmy Carter. But two friends of mine have done it in pursuit of their goals, and they're no more "well-connected" than most people. One, a man whose agent had failed to sell his exciting adventure novel to the movies, got copies of the book personally delivered into the hands of Telly Savalas and Robert DeNiro. The other, a woman journalist, arranged a rare telephone interview with the then ailing and reclusive Anaïs Nin through a network of trusted friends. If they could do it, so can you!

Given modern mobility and communications, every one of us has "connections." We just don't know they're there because they've never been plugged into the juice—the determination to reach a goal.

Let's just suppose I had written a screenplay, and I had a strong, irrational hunch that if Marlon Brando could see it, he'd do it. I wouldn't try to find out who Brando's agent was and mail it to him, because I'm no dummy. I know that that would be the surest way of getting my screenplay shipped back to me unopened and unread, with the unspoken message, "Who do you think *you* are—William Goldman?" What I'd do is, I'd take it to a barn-raising. And instead of asking my friends who they knew in Montana, I'd ask them who they knew in the movies. Once I'd gotten one or more contacts inside the movie biz, I'd say, "All right, now please find me someone who knows someone who knows someone . . . who's buddies with Marlon Brando." And just by following that chain of acquaintanceship, sooner or later I'd get my screenplay placed directly into Marlon Brando's hands. I wouldn't try to do it in five days, of course. I'd give myself, oh, maybe

*It's called the "small world experiment," and was done by psychologist Stanley Milgram.

six weeks, just in case Brando was on his island in the South Pacific.

I have a strong suspicion that there's no one in this world a chain of helping hands can't reach—however high, however far. If you still doubt that your own personal network will reach far enough fast enough, you can try expanding your barn-raising beyond the circle of your friends. But first, I want to deal with some of the problems you may anticipate arising when you start sharing resources with your friends.

SAFEGUARDS FOR BARN-RAISING

Most of the resources you can get from your friends in a barn-raising will make a minimal demand on their time and energy. But what if you're asking for a favor that will really cut into a friend's life space —like help writing a grant proposal or term paper, or painting a coffee-house, or getting a loan? Or what if *you're* blessed or cursed with skills many of your friends need, like editing or typing or carpentry or ther-apy? How do you keep from taking advantage—and being taken advan-tage of? Isn't there a danger that this barn-raising business could get out of hand and afflict our friendships with imposition, resentment, and guilt?

Getting and giving help is an art. It takes tact and sensitivity—and blunt honesty. Fortunately, there are two simple rules for restoring an optimum amount of community—enough to provide everyone with support and help without asking the impossible of anyone.

Rule 1: The Principle of Mutuality

"You scratch my back, I'll scratch yours" is the old, old secret of effective cooperation. And there's nothing crass or calculated about it. You don't help out a friend with the deliberate intention of putting him or her in your debt so you can demand something in return. You help because you care, and giving practical help is one of the most satisfying ways of saying so. But like all expressions of affection, this one has to be roughly equal and mutual, or a feeling of imbalance creeps into the relationship that makes both parties uncomfortable.

The economy of gratitude between friends is very deep and delicate and fascinating. When you help a friend, you establish a sort of fund of willingness to help you that you know you can count on if you need it. No one keeps books or writes up mental bills; each friend simply tries to keep the "account" more or less in balance. Most of us do this kind of balancing act instinctively. We know that simple favors are compensated by the pleasure of giving—and even so, we'll often take the giver out to dinner just to say thanks. But if we ask for a major investment of time or skill, we're aware that we're making a big draft on our "account," and we feel the need to make more substantial compensation. Here's where *barter* can really come to the rescue.

Informal barter is simply a matter of offering something you're able and willing to do in exchange for something you need. "If you'll help me with my resumé, I'll babysit for you when you have your interview." "If you'll build my bookshelves, I'll teach you to play the guitar." I know people who've traded professional typing for group therapy, scientific writing for free medical care, and clerical work for karate lessons. Most such "bargains" are spontaneous and approximate, made by feel rather than by a reckoning of hours spent or dollar value. After all, what someone else does for you gets its chief value from the fact that you can't or don't want to do it yourself, and that's a matter of quality, not quantity.

In case you're intrigued by barter as a cost-cutting strategy, I've listed some published accounts of both formal and informal swapping arrangements in the Resources appendix. But the principle of fair exchange isn't just a good way to save money. It's the best way of saving feelings—of getting help without guilt and giving it without resentment. In many close friendships, this kind of exchange takes place without a word being said. But if you're in any doubt, talk about it! Say, "I really appreciate your doing this for me, and I want to know what I can do for you in return." Your friend may not need to take advantage of your offer right now, but s/he will know s/he can, and that's what counts.

A word of warning, however. There are two kinds of people who seem to lack that instinctive sense of balance between giving and taking. I call them "mamas" and "babies." The terms have nothing to do with sex or age; there are male "mamas," and there are 55-year-old "babies." You will probably recognize someone you know in the portraits of them I'm about to draw. You may even recognize yourself.

Mamas are the compulsive fixers. They run through the streets hoisting people on their backs, and then they say, "See? Five hundred people on my back, and who ever carries me?" They are building up a case that they're all alone in the world with these tremendous burdens, but it never occurs to anyone to take care of them for the simple reason that *they never ask.* They don't know how. "Listen, I've got a problem, can you give me a hand?" is not a sentence that's ever in a mama's mouth. If you ask them, "Say, how's it going with such and so?" they get a stiff look on their faces and say, "Fine. Fine. I've got it all under control" —even if they're collapsing. And if you actually offer them help, they get terribly defensive, because what they hear is that you don't think they've been trying hard enough!

Mamas believe that they're supposed to do everything for themselves —after they finish doing everything for everybody else. If they can't accept help, by the same token they can't turn down a request for help. In fact, they will interpret a conversational complaint—like, "Gee, I'm having a rough time with my income-tax forms"—as the call of duty, and before you know it, they'll have taken over your life. That might be very convenient, if it didn't have a high price for mamas and their adopted charges alike.

Mamas need to help and help and help because they believe that's the only way to give and get love. (It's no accident that so many women are mamas—and that the majority of mamas are women.) But what happens is, first and worst, the mama's own dreams and talents get lost in the shuffle, because she or he is always giving them last place. And second of all, that kind of "love" really isn't very loving. Consciously or not, mamas regard their self-inflicted broods with resentment and sometimes contempt. That's not friendship. It is noticeably lacking in respect.

"Babies" are mamas' opposite number. They are the people who seem to lack all sense of moderation about asking for favors. The sentence that is always in a baby's mouth is, "I've got a problem. What are you going to do about it?" Babies have usually grown up as some-body's prize poodle. Lurking in the background is a parent who was going to prove what a good parent he or she was by taking such good care of that baby that it would never have to do a thing for itself. Babies believe that the way to love and get loved is to act cute and helpless. They know how to charm almost anyone into doing things for them that they would get much more satisfaction and self-respect from doing for themselves. Of course, it's the mamas who fall for it.

Mamas and babies are each other's natural prey. They're both con artists. They hustle each other. And they both miss out. Mamas are secret orphaned babies who can never relax and find out that life doesn't have to be so lonely and hard. Babies are private, angry adults who've been cheated out of feeling capable and needed. Neither mamas nor babies can marshal the resources to reach their goals, because mamas are always walking around on the cross, and sooner or later babies wind up wailing alone in the playpen.

You've got to be very careful of mamas and babies in barn-raising. If you run into one—or if you are one yourself—you've got to watch out that the mama doesn't take on everyone else's goals at his or her own expense, and that the baby doesn't turn the whole room into an army of private servants. There's a very useful little tool that serves both purposes.

If the magic word in brainstorming is "How?" the magic word in barn-raising is "No." Learning how to say it is the second safeguard for cooperation.

Rule 2: The Right to Say "No"

Every person in a barn-raising has the God-given right to say no both to offers of help that are unwanted or excessive, and to requests for help that he or she cannot reasonably fulfill.

Suppose, for instance, you're looking for a lawyer, and instead of just giving you a name and a phone number, your friend goes into a whole spiel about why her lawyer, Jane Jones, is the best, and it becomes more and more obvious that your friend is going to feel personally rejected if you detest Jane Jones on sight. You have the right to pick and choose what *you* want—not the obligation to make helpful people feel good. Real help is offered as neutrally as fruit on a tree, for you to take or leave as you wish. If you can use it, fine. If not, it doesn't mean you're rejecting the giver.

By the same token, if someone eagerly offers you a big chunk of help and refuses to accept any compensation at all, you're probably dealing with a mama, and if you accept the offer, you may pay in subtle ways. "No, I will *not* let you type my three-hundred-fifty page manuscript for free even if you've got nothing better to do" is one of the most important kinds of "No" you can say. You can insist on the principle of mutuality even—or especially—when the other person doesn't. It's better for you and better for the mama, who needs to learn to place a higher value on his or her own time and skills.

It's even more important, since so many of us have "mama" tendencies, to say no promptly, firmly, and without guilt when someone asks for a kind of help you don't want to give or don't have time for.

Sometimes, for instance, you will have to refuse professional services to friends, if giving them would jeopardize either your friendship or your profession. If you are in a position to make creative judgments—for instance, if you're the director of a local TV station, a talent agent, or a PR person—you've got to be very careful about acting as a resource for everyone you know. You must reserve the right to turn down material you can't work with, or even to refuse to consider something if you sense that more than an honest opinion is expected of you.

Similarly, if you have skills you'd rather not use—if, say, you can type really well, but you would rather die than type another word—don't ever feel obliged to volunteer them just because somebody needs them. You're not the only person on earth who can type, and you'll help just as much by recommending someone else who doesn't hate to type. Your friend will understand. After all, she doesn't want to type the damn thing either!

If a friend approaches you for a loan and you can't spare the money or can't be sure of getting it back, saying "No" is a kindness. In the long run it will only protect your friendship.

Finally, never, ever forget that *your time belongs to you and your goal first.* It's fun and exciting to be involved in other people's projects—but it must not be at the expense of your own. The time you can offer or trade to others should be spare time, after you've done your goal-work and anything else you need or want to do. True giving is from surplus, and the only way to keep your reservoirs full is to take good care of yourself.

The only people who will react to a "No" with real hurt and indignation are babies, and it should relieve your guilty conscience to know that a "No" is usually good for babies. It throws them back on their own resources—especially if you give them ideas and leads they can follow up themselves, instead of agreeing to do it all for them. Otherwise, an honest "No" between friends is an act of mutual respect, offered with regret and accepted with understanding, and often followed up by some joint brainstorming on alternatives.

On the other side of the ledger, you must respect your friends' right to say "No" to you—and don't let the possiblity make you afraid to ask. If it's so hard for you to ask that by the time you finally get up your nerve a "No" will kill you, you're doing something wrong—and you're putting an intolerable burden on the person you're asking. You should ask a *lot.* Just make your requests as *specific* and *direct* as possible, so your friends will know they have the option of saying "Yes" or "No" to the request, not to your whole existence. People love to be asked as long as they know they are free to say "Yes" or "No."

With these two safeguards in mind, you can now discover the magic of turning friendships into resources. It's like a connect-the-dots puzzle: the pattern of community is already there, but you don't see it until you draw in the lines of purpose. Most personal networks will reach as far as you need to fill in the gaps in your flow chart and get started toward your goal. But if you'd like to cast the net even wider on the first throw, you can invite your whole office, neighborhood, school, or town to a barn-raising in your conference room, church community hall, or school auditorium. Buy an ad in your neighborhood paper or on the local radio station announcing a resource-sharing gathering; put up invitations on every bulletin board you can find, and tell all your friends to bring *their* friends . . . the more people in a room the bigger the pool of possibilities, talents, and connections—and the higher the energy level. In Success Teams seminars, we start with a roomful of forty or fifty strangers and end up with a crackling resource network

When you've got a big group of people gathered together, you establish the rules:

1. Be as *specific* as you can about what you need.
2. *Do not* offer anything you are not truly willing and able to give.
3. If you can provide what someone else needs, or use what someone has to offer, raise your hand and give your name. Write down each other's names and get together after the formal part of the meeting is over.

Then each person gets up in front of the group, introduces him- or herself, and says, "I'm Ellen Johnson. I'm a Gestalt therapist trained at Esalen, and I'm starting my own workshops. I need clients and loft space. Does anyone have any ideas?" "I'm Joe Jones. I'm a sculptor, but I make my living by carpentry. I'll build anything out of wood for a reasonable price. I could use contacts to art galleries that might show my work. Does anyone have any ideas?" "I'm Mary Smith. I want to go to dental school, and I'd like to talk to a woman who's actually done it." "My name is Joy Greenberg. I've written a screenplay, and I'd like to get a production together and act in it myself! I need lots of advice, any contacts in the movie business, and maybe financial backing." And so on around the room.

When everyone has had a turn, the formal meeting breaks up and everyone goes looking for the people whose names they've written down. Ideas, leads, advice, and phone numbers are exchanged over refreshments. It happens to be a great way to meet people, as well as goals. Many of the participants will stay in touch and develop fruitful professional and/or personal relationships. If you ask everyone who comes to write his or her name on a master list by the door, you can call a "reunion" in three or six months to see what's actually happened as a result of one evening's barn-raising.

Once you've got a master list of interested people, it's a very short step to starting a *resource bank*. This is a bit of a project— one that could even become a fascinating goal in its own right for anyone interested in the interconnections that bring community alive. The simplest way to start a resource bank is to ask everyone on the list to fill out a large file card with: name and address; goals; specific needs; and resources to offer. This last category should include not only professional skills and services, but hobbies, interests, abilities, experience, anything the person knows and loves: fluency in Spanish, time spent living in Greece or Alaska, knowledge of cooking or ballet or backpacking. It should *not* include any skills he or she does not want to share. Whoever takes responsibility for the resource bank then has a brain-teaser of a job: devising a filing or cross-referencing system.

In Success Teams, we started out by giving each name on the master list a number. Then we could file the cards in numerical order and make a separate, alphabetical classification of skills and resources. After each resource we'd list the numbers of the cards on which that resource was offered—like this:

Animals: 5
Carpentry: 17, 29
Cars: 10, 27
Greece: 19
Public Relations: 15
Spanish: 10, 12, 23, 36
Typing: 8, 43, 61

That way, when a request came in by mail or phone ("I need to meet someone at the Ford Foundation," "I need to know people who raise Labrador retrievers"), we could just look up the appropriate numbered cards and give the caller names or phone numbers. Whenever someone new called in, we'd say, "Would you like to be part of our resource bank?" and, if the answer was yes, we'd fill out a card for that person.

We've got over 2,000 participants now, and we're working on computerizing the network. Our goal is to make it nationwide, with a geographical cross-referencing system, so that you can call a toll-free 800 number at any time of the day or night and get the name of someone in Chicago with a kennel full of Labradors; or a recording engineer in Seattle; or someone in Houston who has pink canaries and will ship you one by Christmas; or the only woman plumber in Sacramento; or someone who's taken that new career-counseling course and can tell you "It's great," or "Don't waste your money." We're going to have our own network all over the country.

I've put our address under Resources, in case you'd like to send in a card and plug into *our* network. I've also given the names of books that list some other experiments in community-wide and nationwide resource-sharing: education, information, and employment networks, barter organizations, apprenticeship clearinghouses, etc. You might want to investigate and see whether one of them meets your needs— or you could use any or all of them as models for setting up your own local resource-sharing system.

There are infinite variations on the theme, but the theme itself— lending each other helping hands—is an ancient good idea whose time has come again.

–8–
Working with Time

After a successful barn-raising, you should be able to finish your flow chart, with every major branch of action developed right down to first steps. You don't actually have to write all your first steps into the chart —you'll probably have too many to squeeze them all in. Just complete the basic structure of your chart.

Then make a separate list of your first steps, checking them off as you get them done and adding new ones.

Like Jeannette:

FIRST STEPS	GOAL
call mechanic	publisher accepts
call A	book
call friends	
look	
network	
get maps	

or Mary:

FIRST STEPS	GOAL
notes	enter medical
research corporations	school
call B	
study for exams	
call about review course	

The purpose of a flow chart isn't to map out every tiny detail of your plan. We're going to be using other tools for that, like a pocket calendar. The flow chart is to guide you so that you'll always know what *phase* of your plan you're in, and exactly what you have to get accomplished at that phase before you can move on to the next.

Flow charts are as individual as fingerprints: no two are alike. Try drawing your own on a sheet of blank paper. Once you've done that, you've turned your dream into a *structure*: a logical sequence of actions designed to lead you step by step to your goal. But that structure hasn't begun to exist in reality yet. A flow chart is like an architect's blueprint: it's a lot more specific than a mental image of your dream house, but it still isn't the house—it's only a guide for building a house. To turn it into a reality you can live in, you've got to start building. And the only way to build a dream is brick by brick, action by action, day by day, *in real time.* So our next task is *to map your flow chart onto time.*

That will mean, first of all, setting a target date: an actual day, like January 1, 1981, by which you'd like to have your goal and think you might be able to get it. Then you will mark a wall calendar with target dates for each major phase or step in your plan, corresponding to each circle on your flow chart, so you have a rough schedule to measure your progress against. And finally, you'll start assigning the small specific actions that really make it all happen to specific days in your pocket calendar, so that they actually get done, one by one.

Before you can start working with time, however, you've got to have the time to work with. If you think you don't, there is a very simple way to solve that problem. Just get into action. Start fitting little bits of your goal-work into your life however you can. And it's like being in love: the time will find itself.

Whenever people complain to me that they can't afford to do what they love full time, I tell them, "Start doing it in your spare time and watch what happens." Ellen, an elementary-school teacher on a small salary, dreamed—and despaired—of having her own horse ranch. I told her that as a first target she ought to have a horse to come home to evenings and weekends. She thought horses were terribly expensive because every birthday of her childhood she had asked her mother for one and her mother had said, "We can't afford it, dear." So I suggested she schedule some first steps of the "go-out-and-find-out" variety. To her astonishment, she found a wonderful, gentle 11-year-old bay gelding for all of $150! She stabled him in her tiny backyard and paid for his feed by giving riding lessons on weekends.

Having that horse changed Ellen's life and her whole personality. She was such a joyous teacher that word spread all around her New Jersey area, and the demand for riding lessons grew to the point where she needed—and could afford—a second horse. Next year she's going to be teaching riding full time.

The same thing happened to Diane, the city planner, who started her career by going to block-association meetings in the evenings after work. And the same thing will happen to you. If your goal is to make your living by doing what you love, start doing it just for love.

Whenever someone still protests that I don't understand, she or he really has no time, I say, "Try a Hard Times session." Because "I don't have time" can be an emotional problem. It means you're scared, and keeping very busy is your way of staying safe. You'll be learning techniques for defusing that kind of fear in the next two chapters. But in the meantime, you can go ahead and start freeing blocks of time for your goal-work. The way to do that is by analyzing the way you spend your time now—and then pinpointing those time-filling, time-killing activities where the fear and pain are hiding. I call them *avoidance patterns*, and it's from them that most of your new time will come.

PRESENT PATTERNS OF SPENDING TIME

Most of us have very little idea of how we actually spend our time —and it can be pretty hair-raising to find out. But if you think you have a time problem, I really recommend doing this next exercise if you can stand it, because *the way you spend your days is the way you spend your life.* It's right here, in the little details of your days, that you will have to make the changes if you want your life to change. And before you can change those details, you've got to take a good frank look at what they are.

Try to record, without flinching or falsifying, *what you actually do with your time* every day for a week. This is even harder than keeping track of every penny you spend to figure out where the money is going, but it can be done. Fill in this chart:

PRESENT PATTERN OF TIME SPENT			
	Morning	Afternoon	Evening
Sunday			
Monday			
Tuesday			
Wednesday			
Thursday			
Friday			
Saturday			

Most people have one of two reactions to what they find out: 1) "I had no idea I was wasting so much time!" Or, 2) "What's going to be on my gravestone is, "Good Person. S/he kept a lot of people clean, well-fed, and happy." We will call 1) The Procrastinator, and 2) The Good Woman/Good Provider.

The Procrastinator

If you have discovered that a lot of your time is going down the drain of avoidance patterns, don't be too hard on yourself for it. Above all, *don't make any drastic resolutions to reform.* You know perfectly well that "I'll never watch another late movie or read *Cosmopolitan* again!" leads straight to a guilty orgy of whatever it is you're not supposed to be doing. It's an invitation your inner brat cannot resist. The strictest Puritans are the worst and sneakiest time-wasters, because they demand so inhumanly much of themselves that their brats are in a constant state of rebellion.

The fact is, you cannot get rid of your avoidance patterns—and you shouldn't. You need them. You have to have some self-indulgent goodies—a few late-night movies, some time to read paperback best-sellers, drink beer, talk on the phone, or do nothing at all. The whole trick is to schedule them. That's right, absurd as it may sound, *schedule your avoidance patterns,* so that you can look forward to them, instead of allowing yourself to fall into them whenever the impulse strikes.

Unless you are a mother with two children under the age of 3—in which case you'd better find another mother to swap afternoons with —your "Present Patterns" has probably turned up at least an hour or two a day that you habitually fill by napping . . . or watching football games or soap operas . . . or rereading the morning papers . . . or cleaning a closet or desk you already cleaned last week. It's probably a time when you're alone, a lull between storms of activity and demand: lunch hour at work, afternoon before the kids come home, evening after they're in bed. That's the ideal kind of time for working on your goal —but you need the idleness and relaxation, too.

So here's what you do. First, pick one of those time periods and mark it off simply as *time that belongs to you.* (Note that you're not stealing time from anything or anybody else—not yet. Right now, all you're doing is making official and positive something that's already true in fact.) Try to define its borders—say, from 1:30 to 3:00 P.M. in the afternoon. If you use the kind of pocket calender that shows the hours of each day, draw a red line around those hours and label them, *"My time."*

You don't have to set a formal block of time aside every day, unless you want to. It can be once or twice or three times a week—but try to make it the same time every day or every week, like "One-thirty to three P.M., Tuesdays and Thursdays." That's because ritual is a terrific antidote for procrastination. Setting a definite and regular time for getting certain things done makes it much likelier that you will do them, as you well know if you pay your bills on the first of every month. I happen to think you owe yourself at least as much promptness and reliability as you owe the phone company. If you forget to pay them, they just shut your phone off. Forget yourself for long enough, and you'll shut your soul off. So you establish a regular time period that's just for you. I don't care how short it is at first.

Now, *divide that time period in half.* The first half is your time slot for doing whatever goal-work you'll schedule into each week: writing a paragraph, sketching the cat, running over to the library, making phone calls. The second half is strictly for goofing off. *Promise* yourself that when half your time is up, you'll drop whatever you are doing for your goal and start reading *True Romances* or watching "Columbo" with a vengeance. I promise you that you'll eventually break that promise, but never mind. It's there for as long as you need it.

That's how you start getting goal time out of "wasted" time, like gold out of dirt. And a start is all you need. Once you really get going on your goal, a lot of other things you thought you absolutely had to do are suddenly going to start taking second, third, and eighth place. Like housework, for instance.

The Good Woman/The Good Provider

I've got a couple of radical statements to make about housework and other role-related "shoulds." The first is: If you love keeping a house shining clean, cooking, and taking care of people (or mowing the lawn, washing the car, and weeding the garden), do it. Have a good time, and don't let anybody tell you that you should be doing something more Important and Creative. But if you find you're bored and overwhelmed by the *sameness* of it all, stop. I did. And I found out that a lot of things I thought were important—like a clean floor and a full refrigerator— weren't. My friend Joe made the same discovery—just in reverse. Joe had grown up with the male myth of the Good Provider. That meant that it was a real man's responsibility to get a secure high-paying job and work long hours, so he could supply his wife and children not only with food, shelter, and clothing, but with ten-speed bikes, Florida vacations, and Airstream trailers. A man who would really rather spend long evenings at home, make jewelry in his garage, and take the kids camping in a 6-year-old Volkswagen bus was considered shiftless, self-indulgent, and an evader of responsibilities. It cost Joe a bleeding ulcer to quit driving himself in an accountant's job he hated and start keeping books at home part-time while he worked on his cabinetmaking and woodcarving. He discovered to his surprise that his kids felt proud when they earned the money for something they wanted, and that his wife infinitely preferred the pleasure of having him at home to the convenience of having two cars.

So my second outrageous pronouncement about housework . . . or any other paying or nonpaying job—is:

If you don't love doing it, *stop.*

You're only going to live once. *You must have what you want.* So draw up a list of all the things you think you have to do. Then cross out everything you would cross out if you were going to die in six months! And then stop doing them. Your house may not run right. Your lifestyle may go through some interesting mutations. But no one is going to die, no one will get scurvy, no one's teeth will fall out—and no one is going to throw you out on the street for not being a Good Woman or a Good Provider.

Of course you need to take care of other people. It makes you feel connected, and it's rewarding to protect and nurture living things and watch them grow. But *you have no right to give away everything.* If you have two children and a husband or a wife, that's three people you need to love, but there's a very important fourth one—you. There shouldn't be *any* second-rate children in your house. If you treated yourself like a favorite child you would know how to help your husband learn to be nurturing and attached . . . your wife to be a person in her own right.

You would help your children see you as someone who loved life, loved them, and encouraged them to love themselves.

"Selfish" people love with all their hearts. They may not take care of their loved ones from the cradle to the grave, but they do something better: they give them the gift of self-respect and strength and freedom. Self-sacrificers create bonds of guilt. If your children look into your eyes and see delight, they've got a good world. If you're so tired and angry you can't enjoy them, what they're going to feel is, "I don't care about my Christmas present or my lunch. Why don't you ever smile?"

Just try this exercise and ask yourself how you felt about your own parents:

OBLIGATIONS

Did you ever feel guilty about either of your parents? How do you think you would have felt if your mother or father had done a little less for you and a lot more for her/himself?

Here's how some other people answered:

John, 32 years old: "If my mother, instead of making all the beds and making sure I had my lunch, had kept coming in to me—when my bed was unmade and nothing was picked up—and telling me how excited she was about some poem she was writing, I think I'd have had the best life in the world! I think that I'd have felt so enthusiastic about her, so free to go out and do what I wanted, so happy to have some real company instead of a devoted maid who made me feel sad and guilty, that I'd have adapted to the rest."

Harriet, 45 years old: "I can think of no greater single pain in my life than knowing that my mother, 'because of us,' was less than she could have become. And I can think of no greater gift she could have given us than to have been a full, complete, and happy person—because if she had, then I would have had a much easier time finding the full and happy person within myself."

Grace, 27 years old: "My father was the martyr in my family. There were four of us kids, and he worked for years at a routine job to keep us in braces and vacations. I didn't really know what he believed or felt, except that he thought it was good to be the way he was—self-denying for other people's sake. I could never enjoy the "selfishness" he made possible for me, because he made me so ashamed of it. There's a happy ending to this story, though. After we all got out of school my father went through an incredible transformation. He quit his job, pooled his savings with another man, and started a restaurant and jazz club! It's almost as if he was inspired by the changes in his kids' lives and values. I love him so much. I swear, I would have worked my way through college if he could only have been himself when I was growing up."

How would *you* like to have had no guilt about your mother or father?

How would you like your kids to have no guilt about you?

OK. Now let's get back to planning.

YOUR PLANNING WALL

We've talked about finding time for yourself. Now you're also going to need a space that's all your own: one wall of one room in your apartment, house, or garage, preferably with a desk or a table in front of it. If you've got a real space problem—you share a bedroom with your mate, and you've got a small living room and kitchen and that's it—buy a cheap folding screen with which you can temporarily block off one corner of either room. Use the screen, or a moveable bulletin board, for your wall space.

That's your *planning wall,* and on it you're going to put up a series of charts that will map your plan of action out *across time*—month by month, week by week, day by day—like a general mapping out both the broad strategies and the details of his campaign.

The reason for blazoning your plans across a whole wall, instead of hiding them away in a drawer or a notebook, is that you can glance up at any time and see exactly where you are in your flow chart, whether you're ahead of or behind the schedule you've set yourself, what you have to get done *this week,* what you have to do *tomorrow.* (And when you get to knock off work for a while.) When it's all right in front of your eyes, constantly updated, you won't ever get lost—and you won't be able to run away from it! This wall is going to be your conscience and your guide, your security blanket and your boss. And your planned vacation. You might as well have fun designing it.

You can cover your wall with corkboard, and put up your charts with bright-colored push pins. You can stick them on the wall with masking tape, and tear them down and tape up new ones every time your plans change. Or paper a whole wall with glossy shelf paper, and scribble all over it with water-color markers that can be wiped off. Or use the side of a metal filing cabinet—or your refrigerator!—and tack up your plans with magnets. No matter how you design your wall, though, put up a picture of your personal "saint"—the person you chose in Chapter 5 to inspire you and cheer you on. (You can put up pictures of your whole imaginary "family" of winners from Chapter 3, if you want a really substantial cheering section.) You can "report back" to that imaginary friend as a way of acknowledging your own progress whenever you don't have a real friend waiting in the wings to hear how things went.

The real meat of your planning wall begins with:

Your Flow Chart

This belongs right in the center, because it's the master plan that coordinates everything else. If you're one of those wonderful maniacs who plans to pursue more than one goal at a time, like running for City Council and learning to play the piano, you can put up two (or more!) flow charts in different colors.

On the left-hand side of your flow chart it should say "Tomorrow." Now you're going to pick a *target date* and write it under your goal, over on the far right. (You might also like to draw or cut out a picture that symbolizes your goal—a published book, a well-dressed executive at her desk, a house in the country, a horse in a field—and put it up at the end of your flow chart. Some people find that it helps them keep their goal in their mind's eye.) That date is the other end of your "bridge" of actions, and it is what makes it a solid bridge, of a measurable length, with a real destination, not a rainbow with its other end in the clouds.

Of course your target date can only be a rough estimate. After all, we're planning without facts. Once you get out there, a hundred things can roll in that there's no way of predicting—from an unforeseen problem that sets you back two months to a fabulous job offer that advances you six. Life is full of chutes and ladders. Even without major surprises, you'll almost certainly have to adjust your target date simply because you can't know in advance how long things are going to take. For instance, you may have thought you could write a book at the rate of ten pages a day, and then discover that you can only write ten pages a week—or vice versa. In other words, you can and probably will change this date—*but it is very important to set it anyway.* Here's why.

Anybody who's ever gotten married knows that setting the date is a declaration of serious intention—the promise that makes the goal real. Because a date is also a deadline, and you know from experience that that makes the difference between acting like you have all the time in the world and getting yourself in gear.

A 17-year-old boy was standing in line to apply for college. He turned around and discovered that standing right behind him in line was a white-haired old man.

The boy said, "Excuse me, are you . . . I mean, I don't mean to be rude, but what are you doing here?"

"Why, I'm applying for college," said the old man, smiling.

"Would you mind if I ask you how old you are?" said the boy.

"I'm seventy-four."

"But . . . don't you realize that you'll be seventy-eight by the time you graduate?"

"Son," said the old man, "I'll be seventy-eight anyway."

That's the whole point. You'll be 78 anyway. You can do a thousand fabulous things between now and then. If you get with it. And a deadline will make you do that.

If setting deadlines for yourself has never worked before, it's because you kept those dates in your head (or your pocket calendar, where you never look six months ahead). *In your head there is no time!* In your head it is always now. That's why you need a planning wall. On it, you're going to be able to see time blocked out ahead of you as clearly as a hopscotch game, with instructions for each square, each "now."

Only two words of caution about setting your target date. Don't set it so close that it's totally impossible. That's a dirty trick to play on yourself—it will only make you feel inadequate. You are not a machine. You've got to allow some time for Christmas and summer vacation, for laziness, love, and fun. But on the other hand, don't set the date so far away that it gives you lots of slack "just to be safe." You want some pressure and urgency. This piece of work isn't less important than a term paper for your professor or a report for your boss. It is more important, because it's for you. If, after your best efforts, your target date turns out to be "unrealistic," you'll change it with no sense of failure. But if you give yourself three years to write your book, you'll never know what you could have done in one.

Your Goal Calendar

A GOAL CALENDAR is a large sheet of paper divided into boxes, one box for each month between you and your target date.

It can be a six-month goal calendar:

	Jan.	Feb.	Mar.	Apr.	May	June
1980						

or a two-year calendar:

1980												

	Jan.	Feb.	Mar.	Apr.	May	June	July	Aug.	Sept.	Oct.	Nov.	Dec.
1981												

or whatever you need.

Now look at the major steps of your plan—the circles on your flow chart. Important: If your goal is something like writing a novel that doesn't have clearly defined steps—just demands a steady pace of work —invent some big steps: "Finish first draft," "Finish 100 pages," "5 chapters." You will need these landmarks, both to regulate the pace of your work so you don't hit a panic two weeks before target, and to reward you with a frequent, reachable sense of accomplishment. Assign each of these steps a target date of its own, and write *those* deadlines into your goal calendar.

Again, you're going to be doing some fairly wild guessing. It doesn't matter. You can change every one of these dates, if necessary, as you find out what the realities are, but they are guesses you must make in order to get yourself in motion.

Your goal calendar is really what maps your flow chart onto time, giving you a tentative schedule against which you can check your pace and progress.

Jeannette—the would-be traveling photographer—really had a first target: the day of departure for her trip to Appalachia, with a fully-equipped rolling photo lab, a list of places to stay for free, and enough money for traveling expenses. When she got back from her trip, she could draw a new flow chart for the process of putting together and selling her book. So she set a target date for her departure: June 15, 1979. She chose that target date not only to allow enough time to get everything together, but so that she would be driving through Appalachia in summer, when children were out of school.

To leave on June 15 there were three things Jeannette would have to have—goals she would have to meet: equipped truck, addresses, and money. Jeannette decided to allow a good four months before departure for fixing up the old van she planned to buy—two-and-a-half months for the mechanical repair work, and six weeks for converting it into a darkroom. So the van would have to go into repairs no later than February 1. While it was being repaired, she would have time to send out a call through her network of friends for second-hand cameras, as well as for places to stay along her route—which meant, of course, that she'd also need to get her route planned out in February. She then had January to take advertising pictures for the mechanic in trade for repairs. She decided to aim for a pre-Christmas flea market on November 25 to raise the money to buy the truck. She also realized that her best chance of getting a job in a photo store would be during the pre-Christmas rush—and that a lot of film and photographic paper would probably go out of date on January 1. Jeannette marked all of these deadlines on her calendar. She had now organized the tangle of tasks on her flow chart into neat blocks of time that didn't overlap too heavily in any one month, and her calendar for the nine months between her starting point and her target date now looked like this:

call mechanic call re truck call friends start looking	organize flea mkt. by 25th look for photo store job	buy truck	advert. pix for mechanic try to get old. film, paper, etc. after 1st	start fixing truck by 1st	network call for cameras	outfit truck network call for cameras	outfit truck Lab	
call re grants				grant applica-tions			$	
			get maps	plan route	network call	network call	addr.	
Oct.	Nov.	Dec.	Jan.	Feb.	Mar.	Apr.	May	June 15

For Mary, whose goal was to get into medical school, drawing a goal calendar required meeting an outside-world timetable. So Mary had to do a little research. What was the deadline for medical school applications each year? When were applicants informed about their admission? When were the MedCATs given? When did review courses start?

Mary had begun working toward her goal in March, 1978. A few phone calls to nearby universities quickly informed her that this semester's review courses were already under way, that the MedCATS were given in June and December, and that the deadline for medical school applications was in September. Mary realized that she would have to take the review course starting in the coming fall, and that since she had to work and couldn't possibly study full time, she would probably have to take it over a time span of two semesters. She couldn't apply to medical schools until the fall of 1979, and that would make her target date for entering school the fall of 1980. Mary had a two-and-a-half-year goal calendar!

Now you can begin to see how different a flow chart is from a goal calendar—and how necessary both of them are. Your flow chart gives you the *logic* of your plan. Your goal calendar gives you the actual *timing*, accounting for reality factors like Christmas rush and summer vacation, test dates and application deadlines—and just how long things are likely to take. Your flow chart works each branch of action down to first steps, things you could do tomorrow. Your goal calendar lets you know which of those first steps you *should* start doing tomorrow.

When you've completed your calendar, you've got your plan planted firmly in real time. You've defined your *first steps*—clear-cut, short-term tasks with fairly pressing deadlines. Now you can focus in on those and forget about everything further down the line for the time being. You've entrusted it all to paper; it's there, it's real, it's not going to go away. You don't have to try to carry the whole structure around in your head. Any time you need to know if you're on schedule, you can look ahead at the next deadline on your calendar. And any time you need to be reminded why you're doing what you're doing, you can just glance up at your flow chart and see exactly where today's small action fits into the context of your plan.

Scheduling Your First Steps

Right now you've got your list of first steps to launch you on all the branches of your plan: places to go, people to see, numbers to call, information to look up. Your goal calendar makes it clear to you which of these first steps must take immediate priority and which can wait. What you're going to do now is tack up a list of those immediate-priority steps on your planning wall—and then start scheduling them, one by one, into the days of this week, next week, and the week after that.

We're going to schedule one week at a time. Some of the steps you take may turn out to be blind alleys, and you'll have to come up with new ones to replace them. (For instance, Jeannette might call and find out the man with the broken-down van has already sold it. Then she'd have to start looking for another one: asking her friends, checking classified ads in the paper, putting notices on bulletin boards, etc.) On the other hand, one step may hit the jackpot and catapult you into the next phase of your plan, making five other steps unnecessary. (Jeannette might walk into a photo store and strike up a conversation with a store manager who couldn't give her a job, but liked her plan and was willing to donate old film and paper.) Once you get into action, each week is really going to be a whole new ball game.

Weekly Calendar

You're going to put up a fresh weekly calendar each week, at your own personal Sunday night planning meeting (see p. 239). Use a week-at-a-glance calendar, or hang a whole pad of paper on your planning wall and just tear off each week as it's finished.

How many of the steps on your master list you can schedule into any week depends, of course, on how much time you've been able to set aside for goal work. Jeannette had a full-time job, but she'd cleared most lunch hours, one hour two evenings a week, and Sunday afternoons. Her list of first steps read:

1. Call Ned in Susan's office about van
2. Call Abby's brother about van repairs
3. Call friends to arrange flea-market planning meeting
4. Call Tony A. for advice on grants
5. Check Yellow Pages for photo stores near my office
6. Start looking for photo-store job
7. Call Abby: report back

Obviously, after talking to Tony about grants, checking out the Yellow Pages, and having her flea-market meeting, she'll have a number of *follow-up* steps to add to her master list on Sunday night and to start scheduling on her next week's calendar.

Mary, by contrast, had an even fuller schedule of responsibilities—and only one immediate first step to schedule over the next four months: reviewing her old college science notes. Your weekly calendars may look like Mary's if your job is to make slow, steady progress toward a subgoal like researching a particular business or topic—or a goal like writing a book. (If your life is as crowded as Mary's, you may also want to schedule your relaxation time to remind yourself that you need and deserve it.)

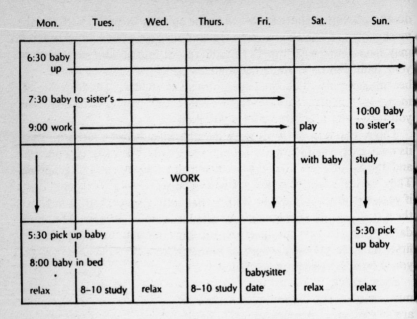

	Mon.	Tues.	Wed.	Thurs.	Fri.	Sat.	Sun.

The next step is very easy—and very important. You transfer the information from the weekly calendar on your planning wall into your purse or pocket calendar. *This is the step that really gets things done.*

Purse or Pocket Appointments Book

This little calendar is the piece of your planning machinery that travels around with you and reminds you what you're supposed to do at lunchtime today and at 3:00 P.M. tomorrow. Most of us already use pocket calendars to remind us of business lunches, dentist appointments, birthdays, and social engagements. If you don't, I recommend starting now—you'll discover that a pocket calendar is at least as indispensable as a wristwatch. If you do use one, you know that writing something in that calendar virtually assures that you will do it. And that's because you've got an *appointment.* Not an option; not something you may or may not do depending on whether you remember, whether you feel like it, and the weather; but something you've contracted to do at a particular time. In this case, the contract is with yourself—the most important person in your life, and the one person to whom you may never have accorded the simple respect you give your doctor or your date. But once you write a goal step in your pocket calendar, it becomes as real as a doctor's appointment. And like a doctor's appointment, unless there's a blizzard, it doesn't make much difference how you feel—when the time comes you'll do it.

This is that wonderful thing called *structure*. It has a momentum of its own, and it will keep you rolling along with it through all your ups and downs. You don't have to be solemn and military about these plans. They are an aid to help you get what you want—and they will. Even if you sometimes skip a scheduled step, you'll get many, many more of them done than if they weren't assigned to specific days in your calendar. (When you have no structure, you can just bury the whole idea the first time you get discouraged or scared.) And as you do those steps, you'll be making real progress toward your goal.

Each phone call you make, each article you read, every office or museum you visit, forges another link in the chain. Many of these steps are so small that you don't need "self-confidence" or "self-esteem" to do them. And yet they're going to give you the self-esteem of cumulative accomplishment—the only kind there really is. At the end of each day, you can note down what you did in the Actions & Feelings Journal you started keeping in Chapter 5. At the end of each week, you can look back at your weekly calendar and see how many things you've actually done. (Whether they've all worked out or not, they will have given you what you need most: the experience of goal-directed action.) And then you can check your progress against your goal calendar and see how far you've already come. If you're making more rapid progress than you anticipated, shift your deadlines forward. If you're slipping behind schedule, step up your pace—scheduling two steps a day instead of one or using Saturday afternoons as well as Sundays—or decide that your deadlines are unrealistic, and push them back.

You'll make many other changes in your planning wall. You may get a totally unexpected job offer; you may fall in love and go off on a two-month cruise to the Bahamas; you may decide to change your goal. So you'll pull down all your charts and start over. You may want to draw a new flow chart halfway through your plan, when the details of the later stages are much clearer. What I'm giving you here isn't an absolute, it's a flexible set of skills for building large plans out of small, steady actions *without losing sight of either the detail or the whole.* Gloria, 36, who had conceived a complex and ambitious plan to found a textile-design and learning center, had this to say about it:

"My plan seems big and I'm nervous about it, but I know there's one thing that's going to make me feel secure, and that's my planning wall. Even if there are unknowns ahead that frighten me, I'll feel fine now that I understand how to work with these different kinds of charts. I'm a visual person in my work, and it really helps me to be able to see it all in black and white."

Speaking of the detail and the whole, there are two more items that are very handy to have on your planning wall. They frame the whole vista of time, from your very next step to the far horizon, and remind you that to make the best of your one stay on Earth, you've got to think both large and small.

The Next Five Years

At the end of your Goalsearch, when we did "Five Lives," I encouraged you to think about a larger life plan that includes all your dreams and goals. Here's where you put that life plan into a real time frame. Of course, you have no way of knowing what you'll really be doing—or wanting—in five years. But of all the forces that will be operating on your life over those years—chance and love and loss and luck, health and economics and history—your wish and will, your own unfolding, should be one of the strongest. And it can be. That's what this book is all about.

Here, for instance, is what my writer friend Julia put down:

1980	1981	1982	1983	1984
write	write	live in Mexico learn Spanish	house in country have baby	study violin

Having this sketch of the next five years on your planning wall serves two purposes. It gives you an extra nudge to meet your deadlines, because it reminds you of all the adventures that are still waiting for you. And as you log in solid progress toward your current goal, those future dreams are also going to start looking much more real and possible. Your reach will grow with your grasp as you realize from experience that you really can shape your destiny with your own hands.

The Next Step

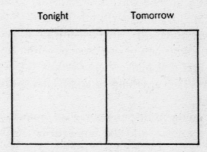

Tonight | Tomorrow

Like your weekly calendar, this is most conveniently drawn on a pad of paper you hang on your planning wall. You can tear the top sheet off every day and fill out a new one, entering the information from your weekly calendar.

It may seem redundant to write down again what you're going to do tonight or tomorrow when you've already got your actions laid out day by day on your wall and in your pocket calendar. But it can be tremendously helpful, and I'll tell you why. First of all, it lets you clear your mind of everything but what you have to do the next day. You can focus on that one action and make sure you're prepared for it. If you have a phone call to make at lunch hour from the office, you'll want to make sure you've got the number written in your pocket calendar. You may want to run through what you're going to say, or even make cue notes for yourself. If you have an interview coming up, it might be a good idea to rehearse it, and to pick out what you're going to wear so you won't be frantic in the morning. I'll have a lot more to say about preparation in the next chapter. It's one of the world's greatest antidotes for the shakes.

Second, a tonight/tomorrow sheet is a forceful reminder that action is always *now*. The present is where it's got to be happening, or it isn't going to happen at all. The most important action in your whole plan isn't that big meeting next week, or even your goal—it's what you're going to do *tomorrow*. Your goal is only as real as that step! Handle it as best you can, and your goal will take care of itself. Don't handle it—and the biggest talent or the best imagination in the world won't budge you one inch off dead center.

That's reassuring, in one way. You can forget all about the exaggerated fantasies of glory and fears of defeat that gather around a large ambition like angels and devils, and concentrate all your creative energy on the text of one phone call or one page of prose. But in another way, that first call, or that first blank sheet stuck in the typewriter, is going to scare you more than anything in your wildest dreams.

Because it's real.

What are you going to do for your goal tomorrow?

This is where the fear—and the fun—really starts.

Four

Crafting II: Moving and Shaking

−9−

Winning Through Timidation, or First Aid for Fear

Up to this point, everything you've done—with the possible exception of throwing a barn-raising party—has been on paper. If you haven't been too nervous, it's because you haven't had to do anything dangerous yet.

The structure you've built on your planning wall has led you right up to the threshold of action, and it has taken away a lot of your old excuses for not acting—like not knowing where to start, or despairing of ever getting there (your flow chart shows you exactly how you are going to get there), or thinking you'll get around to it someday. So having a structure makes it a lot likelier that you will act. But it can't *make* you act at the moment when you encounter what Carlos Castaneda's Don Juan called "the first enemy"—*fear*.

Fear strikes when you feel as if you'd been so busy building and climbing a ladder that you forgot there was a thirty-foot diving board at the top. All of a sudden you're teetering out at the end of that board, with your toes curling over the edge, and the loudspeaker is booming, "Hello! Are you ready?" And as the spotlight hits you and the drums begin to roll, you feel like yelling, "Wait a minute! I thought we were just having fun! I didn't know I was actually going to have to *jump!*"

That may not happen to you the first day you start work on your goal, because many first steps are as small and simple as just walking down the steps into the shallow end of the pool. There's nothing particularly intimidating about a trip to the library or the newsstand. But you keep taking those little steps, and one day very soon you're going to find yourself out on the end of your first thirty-foot board. It may be a job interview, or a dramatic audition, or the first day of a class, or the day you finish your nice safe research and have to start writing. But whatever it is, it will have an element of *the unknown* (you've never done this before); a strong *investment* (both your dreams and your self-image are at stake); and a corresponding *risk* (you may get hurt, mess up, make a fool of yourself, find out you're not good enough).

The funny thing is, you may or may not know it when you encounter the first enemy. The physical symptoms of fear are unmistakable: icy hands, wobbly knees, blushing, stammering, a runaway heart, and a seasick stomach. The body has a candor that's refreshing, if sometimes embarrassing. But the mind is much sneakier. It thinks fear is beneath its dignity, so it will try to save face by persuading you that you're not scared at all—you just suddenly remembered you had pressing business elsewhere. Since it's important to know when you are dealing with fear, I'm going to show you some of its most common disguises, so that you'll be able to unmask it in a flash.

KNOW YOUR ENEMY

If you've ever had any of the following thoughts, feelings, or experiences in the course of trying to do or get what you want, you have met fear. Put a check mark beside the ones that are familiar to you, because you're going to be meeting them again very soon.

☐ An overwhelming desire to sleep: you're suddenly so tired

☐ An overwhelming desire to eat: you're suddenly famished

☐ An overwhelming attraction to the paperback rack: you must read *Love's Tender Fury* or the latest Travis McGee mystery *now*

☐ The soothing thought, "I've got plenty of time. It can wait till tomorrow."

☐ A suddenly blank mind: you were fermenting with plans and ideas, now you're the Village Idiot

☐ A sudden ferment of plans and ideas about eighteen other dreams you'd rather have first, before this one ("Gee, I've never been to Europe . . . I can always start my business when I get back.")

☐ A sudden loss of interest in your goal: it fascinated you in theory, but in reality it's boring, not for you at all (NOTE: Hidden fear will try to trick you into changing your goal whenever it starts getting challenging. That's why so many of us have picked up and dropped so many activities—not because we're "dilettantes" who can't make up our minds.)

☐ A sudden conviction that you don't have what it takes for this goal ("Whatever made me think I was aggressive enough for a job in sales? I'm really a very shy, retiring person.")

When fear strikes—whether it's bare-faced or in one of these disguises—what's to stop you from saying, "I've changed my mind. I'm not ready yet"? What's to stop you from tearing up all your charts, stuffing them in the wastebasket, kicking this book into a corner, and deciding that goals are just a bad ego trip and you'd rather join a Zen monastery or get pregnant instead?

I'll tell you what's to stop you from letting fear stop you. *Everything in this section.* Because I happen to believe that missing out on your dreams and never finding out what you're capable of is a hell of a high price to pay for peace. You have the right to get what you want and become all you can be—and sometimes that means you have a right to *act* even when every nerve in your body is screaming "Stop!!" The secret is to turn the "first enemy" into a stimulating companion, advisor, and friend.

Fear is the natural companion of creative action. There is only one way to live free of fear—and that is to live without hope, change, or growth. Do you want to know what "self-confidence" really is? Just think about how you feel when you're doing something you've done so may times you could do it in your sleep—like tying your shoes. That is self-confidence, and that's all it is: know-how verging on boredom. Do you remember the first time you tied your own shoes? You weren't self-confident then. You were nervous, excited, and unsure. But you mastered shoe-tying, and you soon moved on to bigger things in which, once again, you had no self-confidence—like arithmetic . . . and jitterbugging . . . and driving a car. That's the game we're playing. That's the law of human growth. Would you like to do nothing but tie your shoes again for the rest of your life so you'd never have to feel nervous again?

There's no way around it. When you start moving, you start shaking. Every time you try anything new, anything that really summons and stretches your capacities—in short, anything worth doing—you're going to feel uncertainty and self-doubt as well as challenge and exhilaration. That is the healthy fear called *stage fright,* and I'm going to let you in on what all accomplished people know: how to live with it and love it. It's a good friend that lets you know you're on the right track, that what you're doing is big enough for you. There are easy ways to make yourself move right through it, and as soon as you do, it turns into pure excitement.

For many of us, however, stage fright is complicated by another kind of fear, much deeper and more disabling. I call it *survival fear.*

Survival fear is most common in "first-generation winners"—people whose families didn't know how to prepare them for action. The people it doesn't afflict are the rare ones who've had lots of loving support and who've been shown *how* to do things, so they could start getting experience early. To those lucky people, the unknown is just ... the unknown. There could be a lady or a tiger behind that door, but they're prepared for either one. They've handled both before. They know they can call on reinforcements in an emergency. They aren't going to open that door without nervous palpitations, but you can bet they're going to open it. They have had the security human beings need for risk and adventure.

For those of us who haven't had emotional and practical backing, however, the unknown is the part of the map with the dragons in it. When we don't know what's coming, we expect the worst. If you feel a mistake or a failure would be so devastating that you don't even dare try, that's survival fear. So is the paralysis that strikes when you demand a performance of yourself that's far beyond your skill and experience—like trying to write the Great American Novel the first time you sit down to write. If you think someone you love will be hurt or hate you or divorce you if you start getting what you want, that's survival fear, too.

All survival fear is exaggerated. It gets its intensity from a child's-eye view of the world that many of us were never helped to outgrow. Of course one mistake isn't going to be the end of you. Every great novelist, salesman, doctor, or anything else began as an inexperienced beginner.

And it's an extremely rare husband who's really going to divorce his wife for painting instead of ironing his shirts. Your *mind* knows that. Your *feelings* don't. The best antidote for those feelings is the adult experience of going ahead and doing the thing and finding out that nothing so terrible happens after all—*but it's precisely that experience that the fear prevents us from getting.* So we're caught in a vicious cycle, a lot like the old circular saw about a job: "Can't get self-confidence without experience; can't get experience without self-confidence."

How can you tell stage fright from survival fear? With just a little encouragement and Hard Times, you can push right through stage fright. Survival fear is too strong. You can't bluff and brave your way through it—and for a very good reason. As exaggerated as it is, that fear has a real message for you. It's trying to tell you that there's something you need and have got to get before you can afford to take risks and have adventures. It may be practical preparation or emotional support; it may be permission to lower perfectionist standards or to make mistakes. The message will be different for different people. But whatever it is you need, if you don't get it and you try to go ahead without it, you really will get hurt. And your body knows it.

So the only way to break the vicious cycle of survival fear is to *respect the fear and pay attention to it.* If you decode the *survival message* and take care of your need, all that's going to be left of your fear is stage fright—and that's the easy part.

SURVIVAL MESSAGE NO. 1: PREPARE

Suppose you have something to do that you've never done before —say something that involves presenting or selling yourself, like going for a job interview, asking for a raise, or taking samples of your handmade greeting cards around to gift shops. You're scared. Being scared just makes you feel more inadequate, more sure that you're going to lose the power of speech and trip over your own feet. So what you usually do is try to fight the fear, either steeling yourself with will power or relaxing yourself by deep breathing. That doesn't work very well, and the reason it doesn't is because it misses the most important point: you have never done this thing before, and *you don't know how.*

In this situation, self-doubt is not a weakness—it's a valuable warning signal. It's telling you you're about to go off the thirty-foot board without ever having had a diving lesson in your life, and that's dumb! The worst thing about Positive Thinking is that it tries to override this natural signal and push you into the arena full of blind, unfounded confidence. That can get you so badly hurt that you'll never try again. *A positive attitude is a rotten substitute for knowing what you're doing.* If I told you, "You're wonderful, you can do it!" and sent you into the ring against Muhammad Ali, I'd be guilty of murder. The least I could do for your self-doubt in that case would be boxing lessons.

The survival message here is an urgent request for *preparation: information, instruction,* and *rehearsal.* You aren't supposed to be born knowing everything—although some men and most women think they are. If you don't know something, say, "I'd better find out." Don't say, "There's something wrong with me, and if I ask, everybody will know."

Information and Instruction

This is where you can really *use your network.* If you have a difficult phone call, interview, or sales pitch coming up, find someone who's done that kind of thing and ask: "What should I say? How do I act? What should I wear?" Get a close approximation of the actual words you're going to say. *Write them down.* If you like, you can use them as a little script for rehearsal, or as cue cards for a phone call.

Another thing you need to know is the questions that are likely to be asked of you, so you can be ready with the answers. If the owner of a gift shop likes your greeting cards and then asks you, "Advance or consignment? And what's the retail discount?" you don't want to stand there opening and closing your mouth; it doesn't look professional, and it feels awful. Again, someone who's had experience is the source to go to. If you're scheduled for a job interview in a particular company, it will help you to know as much as you can about that company in advance: what its priorities and objectives are, what kind of ability and personality they're looking for, even what kinds of questions they ask in their job interviews! Read about the company. Talk with somebody who works there. You'll get a better sense of what you have to offer in the context of that company, and you'll impress the interviewer with your initiative and interest.

Rehearsal

It may seem silly to you to actually practice a phone call or interview, but it's one of the most reassuring things you can do if you're nervous. Knowledge hastily filed in your head is more likely to desert you under the pressure of stage fright than knowledge you've programmed into your behavior so it's at least semiautomatic. Actors know that. They don't just memorize their lines and then walk on stage opening night. They rehearse.

It helps a lot to have someone to rehearse to, who plays the other part, throws you your cues, and helps you shape up your performance. It's good practice to stand up in front of someone and talk, whether it's your mate, your child, or a friend. (The next chapter will tell you how to enlist that kind of help.) But there are also two very useful kinds of rehearsing you can do by yourself, in fantasy.

SuperMe/SuperFool

Know how you sometimes lie awake in the safety of your bed imagining the perfect conversation or argument, in which you are devastatingly witty, utterly poised, and say all the right things? And how, on the other hand, when you're in the throes of stage fright, you imagine utter catastrophe? Both kinds of fantasy have a purpose. They are instinctive efforts to *prepare.* Here's how you can help them help you.

Whatever it is you've got coming up, sit back in a comfortable chair, close your eyes, relax, and imagine how you'd do it if you were perfect. A flawless performance by the person you wish you were, the person you've only seen in movies and daydreams . . . who doesn't exist.

Now change the scene. Shut your eyes, tense up, and imagine the worst disaster that could possibly befall you. You walk into the office smiling with your hand stuck out, trip over the rug, and fall on your face. You stutter. The magazine editor, leafing through your short story about the death of your dog, starts to laugh. You forget your own name. Whatever. Just make it a real pratfall—the worst.

Now open your eyes.

This exercise will bring you the great relief of realizing that *you're not either one.* SuperMe doesn't exist, it's true—but SuperFool doesn't either. Since you can't possibly be perfect (and no one else is either), why torture yourself trying to be, or punish yourself for failing to be? On the other hand, no matter how badly you mess up, you'll never live down to your SuperFool fantasies. So you can stop worrying on that score. You've now explored the most extreme possibilities, and you can be sure that the reality is going to fall somewhere in between. But you can get a few helpful hints from your SuperMe fantasy. That paragon may have come up with some genuinely elegant ideas, gestures, or lines. It was your imagination that scripted them—it won't be plagiarism if you use them!

Role-Play the Opposition

It will help you to be prepared for an interview or encounter if you sit in a chair and imagine that you are the person you're going to meet, watching *you* come into the room. You've had practice at this way back in Chapter 3—"Seeing Yourself as Others See You." That time, you wrote down everything nice that the person you were role-playing could see in you. This time, however, you are role-playing a prospective employer, backer, retailer, or customer—someone who has wants, needs, and expectations you will have to meet if the encounter is to be a success. Useful questions to ask yourself are: "What is this person looking for in the way of an employee/investment opportunity/retail item? Would s/he be more impressed by a conservative, casual, or strikingly original appearance? What kinds of questions is s/he likely to ask? How do I look to this person? Is there a mismatch between his or her expectations and the way I present myself? If so, what is it and how can I fix it?"

I disagree with people who think it's possible to be "overprepared." I really don't think there is such a thing. Just as long as you don't forget that the real situation will be different from your practice sessions, that it remains fundamentally unpredictable, preparation can do you nothing but good. There are going to be enough unknowns in the actual encounter without adding unnecessary ones! Preparation doesn't cure stage fright, but it does make you feel a lot more secure than if you were walking into a strange situation cold. And once you've had some experience, you won't need as much preparation, because your experience will be your preparation.

SURVIVAL MESSAGE NO. 2: LOWER YOUR STANDARDS— AT FIRST

This is the merciful message fear is trying to get across to you whenever you freeze with your paintbrush in midair . . . or your fingers an inch above the typewriter keys . . . or your mouth open to make your first insurance sales pitch. No matter how prepared you are for your first day on a new job, or the first real page of a novel you've been making notes on for months, this is different. This is *real*. You've never done it before, and if you expect yourself to do it the first time with the finesse of someone doing it for the thousandth time, you'll be in trouble. You won't be able to do it at all.

There are many reasons for becoming this kind of premature perfectionist. You may have had overly high standards imposed on you as a kid. Or, like me, you may have been told that you were a wonderful genius who could do anything in the world, but never told *how*. Or maybe you grew up in what I call an "audience family": people who regard great achievements as the effortless products of a superior species, and can't see the long, slow, human process of development that leads up to them. Any of these early experiences can create a humiliating gap between your fantasy of what you *could* do and the reality of what you *can* do.

Your vision of what you could do isn't necessarily wrong. The problem is that your vision and ambition have outgrown your experience and skill. To give them a chance to catch up, you have to allow yourself to do what you never got a chance to do as a child: *start at the beginning*. I know it feels funny to be an adult beginner in our precocious society, but there are wonderful rewards. The world is kind to beginners the way it's kind to preschool children. They get lots of help and praise, and they're allowed to play.

Professional First Steps: 'Fess Up, Don't Mess Up

Bernadette, 46, had passed her real-estate certification course with flying colors, but it was her first day as an agent and she was facing her first customer. The man had asked a routine question about mortgage rates, and Bernadette knew she was supposed to have the answer at her fingertips. But her mind had gone blank. The seconds ticked past as she waited for the man to realize that she wasn't a competent professional at all, just an impostor pretending to be one. Then she'd lose the sale. But finally she had to say something, so she admitted, "This is my first day on the job. I'm sorry, I'll have to look that up."

The customer said, "Oh, are you just starting out in this business? Great! I'll have to bring my wife over to meet you. Now that our kids are growing up, she's wondering whether it's too late to get some kind of professional training."

You know from your own experience that if a tour guide, taxi driver, or librarian fumbles around, takes too long, and makes mistakes, you get annoyed—unless he or she tells you, "It's my first day. I'm new at this." Then you immediately become sympathetic and curious! If it's the other way around and you're the one in the hot seat, the worst thing you can do is try to act experienced and suave. The strain of keeping up the act will make you twice as clumsy and prone to mistakes. Admitting you're a beginner, on the other hand, instantly creates a warm, relaxed, low-risk atmosphere in which—paradoxically—your performance improves. Even medical students new on the wards, who are terrified of hurting someone with a misplaced needle, are often soothed and reassured by the patients themselves! You won't be a beginner for long. More will be expected of you even a week or a month from now. But by that time you'll be ready for it.

Creative First Steps: Start Badly

When you're starting a first creative project or beginning the study of an art or craft, what I want you to do is lower your standards until they disappear. That's right. You're not supposed to be any good at the beginning. So you might as well give yourself the liberating gift of joyously expecting yourself to be *bad*.

Forty-three-year-old Matthew wanted to take up drawing and painting again after a twenty-year lapse, but he found all kinds of excuses not to start. The biggest thing stopping his hand was the fear that he wouldn't be any good. So I told him that his first step was to go home and do a bad drawing of the cat, the coffeepot—anything, just as long as it was *bad*. He had to do at least one terrible drawing every night for a week. The point was simply to get his hand moving—by getting rid of the paralyzing expectation that he demonstrate a skill he couldn't possibly have. And it worked. He looked through his first sheaf of "bad" drawings with surprised pleasure. Of course they weren't that bad at all.

Elaine, a 30-year-old English teacher, did not want to be an English teacher all her life. She had a secret fantasy of becoming a best-selling mystery writer, which she was embarrassed to confess because she had never been able to get past page 1 of a thriller. The solution for Elaine was to set herself the unthreatening task of writing just ten *bad* pages a week, working early in the mornings before school. She is now 150 pages into her first book, and she's having so much fun working out the intricacies of the plot that she's forgotten to worry about whether it's good or not. When it's finished, maybe she'll revise it and get it published to hosannas and dollars, or maybe she'll decide to put it away in a drawer and write another one, using everything she's learned from the first. But she's a working writer now, instead of a wishful thinker, and her talent is getting the exercise it needs to grow.

First steps are supposed to be small and manageable, remember? That's what makes it possible to do them. And "Become a good painter" or "Write a best-seller" is not a small, manageable step. It's a major goal. If you ever want to get there, take my advice and make your first steps something like, "one *bad* page a day" or "one roll of *bad* photographs a week." You will tighten up your standards later— when you have the experience to match them. In the meantime, remember the lesson of SuperFool: the worst you produce can't possibly be as bad as the worst you can imagine. And you might also like to remember this cheerful piece of advice from Robert Townsend: "Anything worth doing is worth doing badly."

The Graduated-Risk Principle

Raising a talent or ability is like raising a child. When you start out, you need to be allowed to make any kind of mess you want. No one should criticize you—least of all yourself. As your competence grows, it can be given simple tasks to master, then gradually harder ones; it can be introduced little by little to wider and more discriminating audiences. You've got to pace new challenges and demands so that your skill gets stretched a little more each time, but never snapped or hopelessly outdistanced. A good basic principle is: "Your reach should always be one step ahead of your grasp." You can build this kind of graduated risk right into your planning.

The safest arena is solitude. You don't want to get stuck there, but it's the place to start if other people's eyes make you feel judged and self-conscious. Robert, a New Journalist, developed his own distinctive style by keeping journals that no one ever saw. Matthew didn't have to show his first "bad" drawings to anyone. When no one is watching, you can play freely, and that freedom of movement is crucial for discovering and developing the natural direction of your talent. Training and discipline can come later.

Unless your creative goal is just for your own private pleasure, the next step should be to set a *target date* for venturing out and showing your work to someone else. Make it your family or a close friend—someone who is not an expert in your chosen field. At this stage of the game you don't want professional critical judgment, you want loving appreciation. You need to experience the world as a welcoming place. Your family and friends will think you're fabulous, and their praises and suggestions will help you discover that it's safe to be your growing self in front of others' eyes. Only then can you move into a more impersonal and demanding arena.

After Matthew had been showing his drawings to his friends for a few weeks, he wanted to start getting some training, but he still got the shakes at the thought of being up against other students in the competitive atmosphere of a classroom. He realized that he knew a woman painter who taught in her home, so he arranged to take private lessons for a while. After just a month he had gotten enough guidance and encouragement from that teacher to sign up for drawing classes at a small art school. From there he "graduated" a few months later to painting classes at a major art school.

Matthew had to cope with the fear of not being good enough, and he was only studying painting for his own pleasure! That's how tyrannical our inner critics are. But what if your goal requires that you meet a combination of inner and outer standards—like Andrea, who wanted to become a famous photographer? Her first goal was "To publish one or more photographs of celebrities in a quality national magazine." And one of her problems was, "I'm afraid I'm not good enough." Since creative "self-confidence" breaks down to nothing more mysterious than practice and graduated outward confirmation, you can brainstorm it just like any other strategic problem. That's what Andrea did.

"Problem: I can't because I don't have X—X, in this case, being 'Knowing I'm good enough.' Then Question No. 1, 'How can I get it without X?' becomes, 'How can I get my goal without knowing I'm good enough?' I can't. If I don't have at least some confidence in my ability, I know I'll never even approach a magazine editor. I don't want to make a total fool of myself. So I'd better try Question No. 2: 'All right—how can I get X? How will I know when I'm good enough to show my work to magazine editors?' "

Notice that that's a question like "How will I know when I'm a movie star?" It cries out for a *target*—a clearly-defined action or event. If Andrea waited till she felt good enough, she'd never march up to an editor's door, because that kind of subjective self-confidence vanishes like a mirage in the throes of stage fright. So what Andrea did was to set up an *external confirmation* of her ability that she'd have to accept even if she was terrified: "I'll know I'm good enough when a professional photographer whose work I respect tells me so."

Now Andrea could ask herself, "How will I know when I'm good enough to show my work to a professional photographer?" She set an adequate but firm limit to the amount of "safe" practice she allowed herself: her answer was, "After three months of taking pictures and showing them to my friends." At that point, she could ask her network of friends to give her a personal introduction to a photographer, which would put the "test" in an informal context and make it less intimidating.

The fact is, however, that no matter how prepared you are, *each time you move to a higher level of performance or a more exacting audience, you're going to get scared all over again*—like a diver who's gotten very comfortable on the three-foot board, but feels sick the first time he has to go off the ten-footer. If it's true that you cannot be overprepared, it's equally true that you will never be ready. That's why you had to set definite dates for each step in your plan. The moment comes when you've got to act, ready or not.

I sometimes think the biggest single difference between men and women is that if a boy is scared of something, he has to do it anyway or face ridicule, while a girl is allowed to chicken out without too much disgrace—and sometimes even with approval. Timidity is supposed to be "feminine." Of course, that ethic is changing now. But it's one of the reasons why so many of us grown women missed out on the experience that would have freed us from the witch's tower of inaction, fantasy, and fear.

I want you to have the experience of moving right through fear. Because there's only one way to get really burned—and that's to stop because you're scared. *That's what* real *failure is.* Look back over your life, and I think you'll find that your cop-outs have cost you much more than your worst mistakes. When you fell on your behind, at least you learned that the ground is hard and you're not made of glass. But when you quit, you didn't learn anything.

Let's suppose that you've taken care of Survival Message No. 1 or No. 2. (There's a third powerful survival fear—the fear of being alone —that we're going to deal with separately, because you can't deal with it by yourself.) All that's left now is the last barrier: stage fright. You bust through that once, and you're home free. The next four steps are to help you do it.

HARD TIMES REPRISE: BE SCARED

If you feel scared before you make a difficult move, don't fight it. Let yourself be scared. It's your body's natural response to novelty and uncertainty, and it's designed to tune you up to peak readiness—not to paralyze you. It's only the fear of fear that can do that, not fear itself.

The hard time is the day or the hour *before* you go into action. This is when all the frank physical symptoms of fear show up. You may feel like you're going to have a heart attack, or not make it to the bathroom. But all that's really happening is that you're anticipating, the energy of readiness is revving up, and it doesn't have an outlet yet. So give it an outlet. Move. Pace the floor, punch the wall, shred paper, shiver, dance. Make noise. Moan, complain, growl, swear, scream, and cry. I will never understand why we were taught that we had to behave like Mature Adults under these circumstances. Let's dispense with maturity. If you're doing difficult, scary, grown-up things that are right for you, that's enough. You shouldn't have to act like a grown-up too. You have the right to act like an absolute infant—right up to the moment when you walk through that door or the voice on the other end of the phone says "Hello?"

Obviously you can't allow yourself to fall apart in an "onstage" situation. A bad mood under fire is the luxury of losers. So just do your falling apart beforehand—and afterwards! Throw a tantrum in the wings before you make your entrance—it will get the energy flowing. Then, when the heat is on, be a pro. When you come "offstage" and it's all over, you can go to pieces—you have that relief to look forward to. Minimize the heroics. It will help you concentrate them where they really count—in the action itself.

TASK THERAPY

When the moment comes, and your hand is on the doorknob or your toes are wiggling out over thirty feet of space, follow one simple rule:

DO IT RIGHT, DO IT WRONG, BUT DO IT.

Squeeze your eyes shut and jump. Because a wonderful thing happens then. Your focus shifts from yourself, your nervousness, and your imagined inadequacies to the task at hand.

The trouble with the debate about "self-doubt" versus "self-confidence" is that it has you thinking about yourself at all. You may have noticed that at the times when you're feeling best, you do very little thinking about yourself. You are a background of awareness, not an object in the foreground. You only focus attention on yourself when you feel bad. And then, of course, you can't see anything else. It's hard to tear your eyes away from the worry: "What's *wrong* with me? Why am I depressed/scared?"

Insight therapy takes those questions seriously and seeks the causes in your past. It's fascinating and helps you feel better, but it doesn't necessarily lead to action. "Task therapy" says, "All that's wrong with you is that you're human. You're full of mixed feelings and unresolved conflicts. So what? You've got a job to do. Do it." The funny thing is that the minute you switch your attention from the unsolvable problem inside you to the solvable problem in front of you, you feel a surge of energy and relief. And afterwards, looking at what you accomplished in one hour will do more to heal your self-doubt than ten hours of self-analysis.

DON'T BE AFRAID OF MISTAKES

"Yes, but what if I make a terrible mistake? What if I fail?"

Well, what if you do? What's so terrible about that?

Many grown-up people feel that one failure, setback, or mistake will be a sign of ultimate defeat and worthlessness. But look at any child learning to walk! That child will have to fall down at least a hundred times before it masters the art, and instinctively it knows it. Watch what any 1-year-old does when she falls down. She has a fit—not so much in pain as in impatience and fury. Then she crawls over to the nearest chair leg, pulls herself up, and tries again. If that child fell down once and gave up, she would never learn to walk. And that's a beautiful model for every kind of learning.

You will never learn or accomplish or create anything of value if you cannot let yourself make mistakes. All successful people know this. You tell a top achiever in any field, "I failed. I feel like giving up," and she or he will say, "You're crazy." Herman Melville, of *Moby Dick,* went so far as to say, "He who has never failed somewhere . . . cannot be great. Failure is the true test of greatness." And this is from a *Quest* magazine profile of rock climber Royal Robbins:

It's disturbing, perhaps, to think of Robbins, one of the greatest climbers alive, as losing his hold and falling—after all, if *he* falls, what about us? —but the reason has nothing to do with lack of ability. Robbins falls when he attempts something that is at the very limit of his powers, and it is his nature always to extend these limits. He expects a fall and is prepared for it.*

There is a strange and comforting relationship between failure and preparation. It's a common assumption that if you really try your hardest to get something and don't get it, you'll be shattered—so it's safer not to risk going all out. That is totally false. The exact opposite is true. If you've prepared for every contingency you can imagine, and then it doesn't work out, you won't feel so bad. You'll just say, "Damn! Well, three cheers for me, I really tried," and go on to the next thing. *You never feel really bad when you've given something your best shot.* You may be disappointed, but you don't blame yourself. But if you haven't given it your best shot, you feel terrible. Because you never really know whether you could have done better . . . but you do know you could have done more. Win or lose, all-out efforts leave you feeling clean and good about yourself.

REWARD YOURSELF

I do not happen to be a believer in the cliché that "Virtue is its own reward." As far as I'm concerned, the reward for virtue should be at least a chocolate sundae, and preferably a cruise to the Bahamas. Virtue is damned hard work and frequently uncomfortable. Yes, the results are satisfying in themselves—immensely so. But the satisfaction of accomplishment is much too complex, adult, and uncertain a reward to promise the frightened child in you. S/he needed something simple, sure, and sweet to look forward to, like a lollipop after getting a shot. And I bet you never said "No, thanks," to the lollipop afterwards because your relief and pride were enough! You took all the goodies you could get. And you still should. The more you give yourself, the less vitamin deficiencies you'll have.

There are not one but two kinds of rewards you should plan to make a regular feature of your success program.

The first is the kind of reward you earn. You get to look forward to it before you do a hard thing, and then to savor it afterwards. It could

*James Salter, "Man Is His Own Star: Royal Robbins and the Art of Pure Ascent," *Quest,* vol. II, no.2, March–April 1978, p. 28.

be a big helping of your favorite food—or your favorite avoidance pattern: an old John Wayne movie, a fat paperback family saga, a long-distance phone call. It could be a daydream of lying on the beach on the most beautiful island in the Caribbean, or of the life you'll lead when you've reached your goal. It could be a day in the country, a hot oil massage, a new pair of earrings, or that fishing rod or Picasso poster you've been wanting for so long. Give yourself little extravagances for little steps, big ones for big steps, and a real whopper when you reach your goal: a whole new wardrobe or a set of matched golf clubs or a fabulous vacation. This kind of reward keeps things sweet instead of Spartan and prevents you from developing a permanently stiff jaw on your way to success.

The second kind of reward is the kind you should give yourself often just because you're you, and worth it—whether it's cooking a gourmet meal for yourself, taking a long, hot bath, or buying yourself a new sport jacket, a jazz record, or a theater ticket. This kind of reward is as important for the health of your self-image as physical exercise is for the health of your body. You must treat yourself like a first-class person, no matter what you've done or not done.

Don't ever punish yourself for skipping a step—or ten steps—in your plan by cutting out these little ways of being good to yourself. You need them more than ever when you're feeling down. They remind you that you have every right to be on earth and enjoy it just because you're alive. You need and deserve some pleasure at all times. When you've accomplished something, you get an extra helping on top of that for having been willing to undergo the discomfort of risk and change.

So, to sum up my six-point program for coping with the shakes:

1. *Survival Message No. 1:* PREPARE. Get information, advice, instruction, and practice.
2. *Survival Message No. 2:* LOWER YOUR STANDARDS—AT FIRST. Begin in a risk-free arena and gradually work your way up.
3. BE SCARED. Use Hard Times to release fear and tension before and after a difficult step.
4. TASK THERAPY: Focus your attention on the task, away from yourself.
5. DON'T BE AFRAID OF MISTAKES. They hurt you much less than stopping for fear of them.

6. GIVE YOURSELF REWARDS. Be nice to yourself at all times and extra nice to yourself when you've done something hard.

SURVIVAL MESSAGE NO. 3

Now, however, we have to talk about the third survival fear and its message. I'm talking about the fear that success will be cold and lonely —that gut feeling that you'll leave your friends and loved ones behind, or that they'll be mad at you for being "selfish" enough to put your dreams and plans first. "It's lonely at the top" is a common cliché, one powerful enough to scare many women and men away from the highest peaks of achievement. But it's even truer to say that it feels like it's going to be lonely *outside*—outside the comfortable, if constricting, nest of other people's expectations. When you start moving, changing the status quo, you shake up everyone around you, too. And yet, that is the moment when you need their support the most.

You need much more emotional security for risk-taking than you do if you stay within the safe, predictable bounds of habit. Going for your goals involves not only uncertainty, change, and the unknown, but a new and scary feeling of being visible. You are no longer hidden behind a low profile that attracts little attention, expectation, or envy. You're laying your real self on the line, making promises you'll be expected to keep, and making waves people are bound to notice. And that feels dangerous. But if you have even one positive partner around saying, "Your idea is wonderful. You're wonderful. Stick with it. I'm with you," you've got the warm weight of another body right beside you on that line.

I don't know if anyone's ever done a statistical survey, but I have the impression that the overwhelming majority of successful men get this kind of support from their wives (with booster doses from their secretaries and sometimes their mistresses). I can't remember reading a book by a man the acknowledgments of which didn't end something like, "And last, but not least, my wife, without whose unfailing support and help . . ." A well-turned-out woman smiles beside every senator, and it's a truism in the business world that an unmarried young executive is handicapped for the climb. There is also the fact that the majority of widowers remarry within a year or two of their loss. They can't make it alone and they've got sense enough not to try. Less well known is the fact that successful women have had exactly the same kind of support in their lives, sometimes from a woman friend, but very often from a man. Look at Virginia Woolf and George Eliot. Look at Bella Abzug and Jacqueline Susann!

Where does that leave those of us who aren't getting that kind of support? In trouble. In double trouble, because at the moment when we need *more* love and encouragement—when we start moving out for our goals—we're likely to get *less*. If you're a woman, your husband, lover, and/or kids may react angrily to the rerouting of so much of your attention away from them. After all, they've been used to getting the whole pie! That not only leaves you all alone out there, it puts you under fire at a time when you're shaky enough already. It can make you feel like giving up your goals or your family, neither of which is a very happy solution. There are men who have this problem too—men whose wives are willing to support some kinds of success but not others, the secure or managerial but not the creative or domestic, the executive but not the carpenter or restaurateur.

If you are one of those women—or men—your survival fear is real. The fear of being alone becomes a self-fulfilling prophecy if you think you have to walk out or sue for divorce in order to be free to pursue your goals! That fear isn't a weakness, to be overcome by toughening up and caring less. It's a survival message: "You can't go for your goals without emotional support. So *get* it." That's going to take some strategy. The next chapter tells you how.

– 10 –
Don't-Do-It-Yourself

A lot of women these days are talking about getting all the support for their professional goals from other women. I think that's fine, up to a point. There's no question in my mind that women can and should be a primary source of support for each other, especially when they're just beginning to exchange old roles for new goals. Later on in this chapter, I'm going to give you a format for sharing goal-support with a friend—a format men can use equally well to make going for their goals less of a solitary struggle.

FAMILIES: TURNING RESISTANCE INTO SUPPORT

For women who live with men and/or kids, however, those people are very important and dear. No matter how much new emotional nourishment we're getting from women, we still need our families or lovers, too. It's sad to leave them, and it's sad to live with them in a state of armed truce, defensive about our goals and resentful of their demands. We really want them on our side. What we don't realize is that they want to be on our side, too, if we would only give them the chance. But we're so guilty and frightened about *putting ourselves first* that we've got our dukes up from the word go, expecting nothing but trouble. And people who expect trouble usually get it.

And what about the men who love and puzzle over women who are trying to change their lives? And the men (*and* women) who would like to liberate their talents and loves, but feel responsible for economic dependents? What about the male poet and teacher in the middle of a divorce who told me, "I felt as if I had to do all the living, as well as all the earning, for two"? We know now that the rigid breadwinner/ nurturer split along sex lines has been as oppressive for many men as it has for women. But it's difficult to change any behavior that since childhood has spelled "love," whether it's clean socks or a regular paycheck. Here are some of the strategies—developed by my usual scientific technique, trial and error—for making it through the rough transition in roles with your sanity and your relationships intact.

Let Them Be Mad

When I decided to start Women's Success Teams, I told my husband about it, with some trepidation. He scowled and said, "I don't like that. I don't like women working with women. It worries me."

I panicked.

"What do you mean, you don't like it? How can I go ahead if you don't like it? What am I supposed to do now?"

He looked at me like I was slightly bananas and said, "Whatever you want!"

I said, "What do you mean, do whatever I want? You'll be angry!"

He said, "So what? You get mad at me frequently, and I do what *I* want! Where did I get all this power to stop you from doing things? So I'll be mad! The fact is, women working together make me nervous. I'll get over it. Why do I have to love it right away?"

And I thought, Well. He's right. How did I get to be such a sissy?

Just about every grown-up person still has a scared little kid hiding inside. That's why we so often react to our mates as if they were our fathers or mothers. We give them much more power over us than any adult really has over any other adult. We don't go home and say, "Hi, I've decided I'm going to be a veterinarian." We're afraid they'll be mad at us. So instead, we say, "Can I be a veterinarian? Please? Is that OK with you? Will you still love me?" And then when we don't get total, instant, 100 percent approval, we feel like we've been stopped. We say, "He won't let me do what I want," or "They're forcing me to choose."

I call that the "S/he won't let me" syndrome.

If you think someone won't let you do what you want, take another look at yourself. Because *he or she can't stop you.* You are not 4 years old, and that person is not your parent. S/he's just a person and s/he's scared. The people who love you are bound to be at best ambivalent about the changes you're making in their lives. They liked having everything nice and safe the way it was, and change makes them nervous!

Of course, what's really killing you isn't so much that you have to start doing things for you. It's that you're going to have to *stop* doing certain things for them. In the time-planning chapter, we've already dealt a blow to the guilt many women feel when they stop taking total care of everybody from the cradle to the grave—and some men feel when they stop being the Iron-jawed Provider. But of course there's survival fear there too, very deep. We're afraid that if we stop delivering the way we've always delivered, they'll never love us again. That's why, if they get mad or grouchy, we overreact—with terror or rage.

What they really deserve is compassion. These are people you love, don't forget it, and they're in trouble. All of a sudden, this man and these kids have got to become aware of a few facts of life which, thanks to you, they never had to think about before—like, when you wear something or eat off it, it gets dirty, and then what? To make matters worse, they have been trained to associate *care* with *love*—at the price of feeling eternally guilty toward their mothers. And you've fallen right into the trap. You've been giving them lots of attention and service. Now all of a sudden a lot of your energy is going someplace else. That feels to them like you're going away. And when they express their apprehension in the form of resentment, all of a sudden you feel oppressed!

Or: all of a sudden this woman and/or these children have got to become aware of a few facts of life which, thanks to you, they never had to think about before—like, when you want something it costs money, and money takes work. And work is sometimes scary, hard, or dull, and then what? To make matters worse, they may have grown up associating *financial support* with *love*—at the price of feeling eternally guilty toward their fathers (and sometimes their mothers too). And you've fallen right into the trap, carrying the whole household on your shoulders. Unfortunately, most men endure this trap in silence till they crack, and then they run off with another woman who represents the free and romantic side of them.

Do you see what a crazy thing we're doing to people we love? We're adding insult to injury out of our own insecurity and guilt. We've got a new love in our lives, which is a threat to them for starters; we've stopped taking the old compulsive kind of care of them; we've thrown their lifestyle into total disorder—and on top of it, we're ready to kill them or leave them! Of course they're going to blame and resent our new goals, because it looks to them like that's where all the trouble started.

Don't give up your goals. Go ahead and make the changes. Come home and announce that you're going to be writing a novel or running for City Council, not making beds or folding the laundry any more; or that there will have to be some changes around here because Dad wants to get out of the wholesale sporting-goods business and become a college philosophy teacher. *And give them the right not to like it.* Let them be scared and mad. Let them sulk and throw tantrums. Instead of getting all up in arms, say "I know, it's rough." Give them some time to get used to it. And one day somebody's going to look at you sheepishly and say, "You know, this is kind of fun. I like it a lot better than I thought I would."

We all need to learn a new language for love—a language that speaks not in socks, pancakes, and paychecks, but in shared fascination with physics or poetry, delight in each other's uniqueness, and *mutual* practical and emotional support. If you think your family loves you for the role you play, there's only one way to find out. Throw the role to the winds and go right through the fear of losing love. You aren't going to lose it. All you're going to lose is some peace. And only sissies think they're the same thing.

Working It Out

I've been talking about the *emotional* turbulence of changing roles, and how you can anticipate and weather it. But what about the *practical* rearrangements? In any shared household, certain things have to get done. The bills have to be paid, food, clothing, and other necessities have to be shopped for, and somebody has to bring in enough money to pay for them. And while people can survive on a bare minimum of cooking, housecleaning, and laundering, life is a lot more pleasant if those things get done at least some of the time. If you can't afford a maid, who's going to do them?

There's been a lot of talk about drawing up marriage or living-together contracts in which each person's responsibilities are spelled out very explicitly. You can do that if you want, but in my experience, imposing rules doesn't work as well as *defining common dreams, needs, and priorities*—in other words, finding a shared touchstone.

Economics: The Family Goal Conference

What if you are the primary breadwinner in your family—man or woman, partner or single parent—and your goal involves a temporary or permanent drop in either the amount or the regularity of your income? Carl, a married cartoonist, wanted to give up his newspaper job and try to make it as a free-lancer. Laura, a divorced teacher with two grammar-school children, wanted to make a living by marketing her own coloring books. Herm, the father of six, wanted to leave the real-estate firm where he was a vice president and take a lower-paying job with a nonprofit housing organization that got its funding renewed from year to year.

If that's you, the people you live with are simply going to have to make some changes. Either they will have to make their own economic contributions to the household, if they're old enough—like the teenager who takes a paper route to pay for her bicycle, or babysits to supplement his allowance—or they'll have to decide on what aspects of their lifestyle they are willing to economize. That sounds harsh. In practice, it's fun. If you sit down with your partner and/or kids and give them a full voice in the decision making, they're not going to feel deprived, threatened, or abandoned. They're going to feel like partners in an adventure.

Carl and his wife Sherry sat down and agreed that they would both actually enjoy the challenge of living more simply and self-sufficiently. They planned a move from their big-city apartment to a small lakeside town where rents were low and they would be able to catch fish and grow a vegetable garden. Sherry decided to contribute a little extra income by finding an outlet for her knitting and crocheting.

That's a fairly extreme example of two people who were willing to make a major overhaul of their lifestyle. What if you're not? Laura stayed where she was, in a Minneapolis apartment; she and her daughter and son decided to bake bread and cook "from scratch" and exchange homemade Christmas presents—things Laura would have more time for when she worked at home. Herm's wife got her first paying job —something she had been wanting to do for a long time—and his three youngest kids, who were in college and high school, gladly agreed to work summers for money instead of just for fun, so that their father could do what *he* loved.

The questions to ask when you sit down for a couple or family goal conference are very much like the questions you asked to arrive at your pared-down ideal day:

1. Which elements of our current lifestyle do we *need?* (Living space, health insurance, and—in some cities—private school might be examples.)
2. Which elements do we *want?* (An annual trip to the ocean, pets, a color TV? These items may be adjustable, or ingenious substitutions can be found by brainstorming.)
3. Which elements could we do without or economize on? (Our own washing machine, lots of eating out, second car, summer camp, private health-club membership instead of YMCA?)

Like your adjusted ideal day, this strategy isn't meant to be a permanent compromise, or to prune life down to the bare essentials. It's meant to get your priorities straight—in this case, your *shared* priorities. If you love each other, one of the things that's important to you is to have each other be happy. So each of you should define those areas where you're willing to compromise and the ones where you can't and won't. ("I don't mind eating out less, but I *refuse* to give up going to the movies." "Mama, I'd rather babysit every weekend than stop my ballet lessons.") Now ask yourselves two more questions:

—What long-term goals do we have in common? (Each other's happiness, more money, a house in the country, a trip to Europe, etc.)

—What is each of us willing to do *now* to help reach those goals? (A small sacrifice, a part-time job, help with the housework, etc.)

Housework: How Not to Nag

Note that I said, "Help with the housework." One of the things men and kids are going to have to pitch in and do if they want a happy lady and/or a second income is a share of the shopping, mopping, dishwashing, and bed- and dinner-making. And I promise you that they're going to make all sorts of noble resolutions at your family goal conference, none of which are going to get kept. What do you do then?

I think it's safe to say that the great majority of working women have tried to keep the peace by continuing to take the lioness's share of responsibility for the household. We usually justify this by saying, "If I don't do it nobody will," or "It takes more energy to keep nagging and reminding them than to do it myself." But often what we're really doing is striking a bargain: "If you let me have my job (school, boutique, literary magazine, painting class), I promise I'll still be just as good a wife/mother as I was before." In other words, we're keeping one foot in the old role just to be safe.

I think that's a mistake, because anyone who earns love doesn't believe in it when she gets it anyway. You've got to find out that you are loved just for being you. (Then you can cook an occasional meal or wash the dishes because it's fun and relaxing for a change, or because it's your turn.) I personally believe in making the change abrupt. If that makes you feel guilty and scared, *be* guilty and scared—you have the right to feel what you feel. But don't give in. Brave it out.

Your family wants a clean house? There are four strategies for dealing with that one.

Democratic Chaos: If you're cheerful and willful and can play blind like me, and step over debris, you can simply say, "You're absolutely right. Everybody should have a personal maid, including me. However, since none of us has got one, I guess we're just going to have to do the best we can."

Just think of yourself as one in a household of roommates who are muddling through. No one person is the foreman. When you wake up one morning and say, "Oh, my God, nobody's got any clothes," the laundry has to be done, and somebody has to do it. You can fight over who's going to do it. Nothing makes a kid feel better than being able to say, "Hey ma, it's your turn to do the dishes, and you better do them!" It really brings it home to them that you're not that slave they used to feel so guilty about. Nobody's the "mother" in my house any more. We were just three kids in a mess until I got married again; now we're four kids in a mess. We hassle over whose turn it is to walk the dog. It's a warm, noisy household.

The Compassionate Autocrat: What if you have a lower clutter tolerance than I do, and you need cleanliness and order around you to hear yourself think? Don't fall into the trap of doing all the housework yourself because it's easier and takes less time than getting them to do it. There is a way of getting them to do it that takes no time at all. Like this:

The dishes need washing. Instead of saying, "You never help me!" or "You must help. That's the rule. This is discipline," walk up to the man or child who is reading or watching TV and say, "Please do the dishes. *Now.*"

He or she will stand up with a loud sigh, slam the book shut, kick the television, throw you an evil glance, and start moving toward the kitchen with about as much enthusiasm as if it were the guillotine.

At this point we usually say, "Oh, forget it!"

We have so much trouble asking for help that when we finally do ask, we're hurt if we don't get enthusiasm! Well, you don't need enthusiasm. You just need the dishes washed. So use the key sentence from Hard Times. Say, "I don't blame you. I don't like to wash the dishes either. *You don't have to like it, you just have to do it.*" And if they grumble and swear all the way through the dishes, when they finally slam the towel down on the counter, you say just two words:

"Thank you."

I Need You to Take Care of Me: Here's what my days were like when I first got to New York: I got up at 7:00, made breakfast, made my kids' lunch, took them to separate schools, went to work, came home, shopped, made supper, and screamed at them all evening because I was so exhausted. That obviously wasn't working very well, but it went on for a few years, both because my kids were still quite small and because I needed to be this frontier mother to hold myself together.

Then one evening I looked at my 8-year-old and 5-year-old, who were watching TV, and I thought, Hey! I'm working two full-time jobs, staying up half the night, and here are these two strong healthy kids who aren't doing anything. I opened my mouth to lecture them, like I usually did, but then I shut it again. I thought, You know . . . I'm complaining, but it really gives me a wonderful feeling to make their lunches because I know it makes them feel loved and not lonely. But what makes *them* feel that good? My God. They're being cheated. *They need to make my supper!*

So I ventured, "I'm so tired when I come home from work at night. It would really make me feel good if you made my supper."

And they lit up! They went to the supermarket the next day and shopped, did all the cooking, set the table, and when I got home from work and they saw my face, they felt like a million dollars.

During the years we were alone together, those kids were what kept me going, and they know it. They cooked my dinner, they made my lunch, they even occasionally cleaned house. And they felt valuable and loved—and proud and protective, because I was just one little lady, and I needed them to look out for me. They say, "You'd never have made it without us."

I am convinced that that's one of the major reasons why those kids grew up OK: somebody needed them. We don't give that to our children. We give them everything else, and then we wonder why they're not satisfied. I think it's because they need to feel needed. They need to know that they are truly important to someone they love—helpful, capable, and necessary.

Love Your Life: The most important strategy isn't a strategy at all. *Be really happy at what you're doing.* That's when you're irresistible to your family, because you're off their backs, and you're cheerful, enthusiastic, and loving. That's when they start willingly cleaning the kitchen, doing the laundry, cooking dinner. They don't cook, clean, and wash *first* and then say, "OK, now you go to school and work, and we'll take care of everything." It's the other way around!

All they really want is your loving attention—in any form. They want to feel needed, involved, and included. Therefore, the best and simplest way to have both love and success is to let your people help you with your goal. Let them pitch in with practical help and emotional support. Instead of a rival that divides you, make your goal a shared project that brings you closer together.

Sharing Ownership of Your Plans

Sharing your goal may require a little bit of psychological judo, especially at first. It took me a while to figure this out. I used to walk into the house with my jaw stiff and my boxing gloves on, and announce, "I've got a fabulous idea. I'm going to start a worm farm and make lots of money!" Then if anyone just said, "But do you really think that will work?" I'd burst into tears and say, "See? See? I never get any support," and stomp out and give the idea up. That was very unfair of me. I was shutting them out completely, and then expecting them to smile and applaud like a paid packed house.

When you walk in with a flawless plan, *everybody feels left out.* I know I do. When somebody says, "I have the most fabulous idea," no matter how helpful I'd like to be, I start thinking, "What has that got to do with me?" But if somebody says, "I have this idea, but I don't know if it's going to work—so-and-so hated it," I roll up my sleeves and say, "OK, what is it?" Then I've got a place.

That's very important to do with your family—and your friends and co-workers, too. *Share your hopes, fears, and failures, not just your triumphs.* Triumphs always shut people out, no matter how much they'd like to join. So don't try to sell them the positive aspects of your idea. Say, "I have an idea, but it's only half-baked. I think anybody can shoot it down, and I don't know what to do about it." And let them talk you into it!

This is where you can really put negativity to work for you. It isn't a trick, because those doubts are there. Don't try to hide them, use them! It works like a charm. Judy, 29, told me, "This had never dawned on me before; I always thought I had to present a confident front. Instead, this time I went home and told my husband I'd been thinking about starting my own craft gallery, but I was afraid I wouldn't be able to pull it off. I expected him to criticize me. And what do you know, just like I'd pushed a button he said, 'You can do it. Here's an idea. Why don't you try . . .'"

As you saw in Chapter 7, other people have so much to offer once you invite them to get involved. Men—husbands, lovers, colleagues—love giving suggestions and help. They often have skills, experience, and connections women don't, and being asked to share those things with us makes them feel big and kind and wise, like older brothers. They'll write your resumé for you, photocopy it in the office, teach you corporate strategy, get their friends to write you references on impressive stationery. Kids are especially fabulous at ideas and legwork. Their heads and feet are quick. They'll come up with brilliant solutions to problems that had you stumped, and they'll run around on their bikes sticking notices up on bulletin boards. Trust them to help you with actual procedures, and to figure out their own ways of doing the jobs you assign them. This is very important. The more problems you give people to solve on their own—unsupervised—the more commitment and enthusiasm you get.

It doesn't have to be done the hard way. People will give you all the help and support you need if you just give them a place in your garden.

As far as I'm concerned, the goal of goals is a system in which you and the people you love act as each other's mutual support team. There are only two problems with it. One is that it takes time—and turmoil —to get there, and in the meantime you need something to keep you moving toward your goal. The other problem is that it doesn't work for people who live alone. If your family or partner is still in the throes of adjustment to the new order, or if you happen to be single, what do you do?

You call your friendships to the rescue.

In particular, you find someone who's in more or less the same bind as you (and believe me, we're all in some version of the same bind), and you make a compact to help each other out—a conspiracy to succeed together. I call it the Buddy System.

THE BUDDY SYSTEM: TEAMING UP FOR SUCCESS

The Buddy System is a way of creating your "ideal family" in miniature. It's the most compact and efficient way I know to give yourself the kind of support system I've been describing throughout this book. Its principle is simple: you and a friend make it your shared goal to meet both your individual goals. It works because it's about a thousand times easier to have faith, courage, and good ideas for someone else than it is for yourself—and easier for someone else to have them for you. So you team up and trade those positive resources: your buddy provides them for you and you provide them for her or him.

How do you pick a buddy? She or he can be a close friend or roommate, but doesn't have to be. A new acquaintance or a neighbor can be just as good. This is an action-oriented arrangement first and foremost, and an intimate friendship only if you want it to be. Your buddy will be giving you emotional and moral support, yes, but for a purpose: to keep you in motion. In fact, if you are close friends, you're going to have to keep the long, rambling, heart-to-heart talks out of the business part of your relationship and save them for after hours.

Almost the only requirement for a buddy is that she or he be someone whose mind and values you respect and whose ideas and goals intrigue you. His or her goals don't have to be in the same field as yours, or even in a field you know anything about. I know a concert pianist and a department-store buyer who helped each other reach their goals! On the other hand, I also know a husband and wife, both book editors, who are each other's informal "buddies." (You can make a family member your buddy; I'm just putting the system in terms of friendships because they are often a firmer and steadier source of support, outside the emotional fireworks of intimate love.) So there are no rules. Just beware of picking someone who intimidates you, who is considerably more advanced in his or her career than you are, or who never admits to being doubtful or down. The buddy system, unlike the mentor system, is a relationship of equals.

You and your buddy will be able to give each other three overlapping kinds of help:

1. First and most important is *expectation*—the knowledge that someone is waiting to hear whether you did what you said you'd do and how it went. A buddy fills the need for that vital someone outside you who steadfastly believes in the importance of your goal and expects you to stick with it, as if you were doing it for him or her and not just for yourself. It's like my Ideal Environment fantasy of a boss who would make me do what I really want to do even when I don't feel like doing it!

Each week, you will tell your buddy exactly what steps you've scheduled for the following week, day by day. And s/he will tell you what's on his or her schedule. (See *Weekly Business Meeting,* below.) The next week, you'll report in and tell each other what you did or didn't do. It's as simple as that—and it makes all the difference in the world.

Elaine, the English teacher who wanted to be a mystery novelist, decided to start writing her first book at the rate of ten pages a week. She knew she was going to be meeting with her buddy every Thursday night, and she couldn't walk in there empty-handed. So as often as not, those ten pages got written on Thursday morning. But they got written. And at the end of eight months, this woman who had dreamed of writing for years but never done it had produced a 350-page manuscript.

The buddy system *works,* where attempts at "self-discipline" usually end in self-loathing. Alone, you can always find good excuses for falling off your schedule, but the minute you've got somebody else to answer to, it becomes a lot harder to fool yourself. Your buddy isn't your externalized "conscience" so much as the appointed representative of your best self. Once you've empowered her or him to keep you on the track, you don't have to try to sustain constant enthusiasm. You are free to be human—sometimes lazy, sometimes ornery, sometimes depressed—and still get things done.

2. You and your buddy will give each other the emotional support so necessary for staying with any plan: a sympathetic audience for HARD TIMES when you're down, someone to hold your icy hand when you're in the throes of stage fright, and above all, companionship in the enterprise of goal pursuit. Help over the rough spots is a necessity, but sharing the positive excitement of goals is a delight, as women and noncutthroat men are just beginning to discover. You can't always get that from your mate or kids, at least not at first when they may still perceive your new goal as a rival. With a buddy, you can share not only the weight of your problems, but the crackle of ideas, the camaraderie of work, and the festivity of success.

3. Finally, you and your buddy can provide each other with lots of *practical help.* You'll be each other's core brainstorming and barn-raising team. When either of you has a tough strategic problem to solve, you can put your two very different heads together and they'll be twice as good as one. Your buddy will lend you the unused paints and brushes in her closet, or her fur coat when you need to look rich. You can

role-play her for her upcoming interview—and even make phone calls and pretend you're her if she hates the telephone more than anything on earth. He'll get his sister the journalist to write an article about your dance studio; you'll get your lawyer uncle to give him a reference for law school. You can share whatever ideas, contacts, materials, and skills will help you both meet your goal of mutual success.

The best format for all this give-and-take is a regular one: the *weekly business meeting*—supplemented whenever necessary by the *three-minute booster phone call.* First, though, you'll need to have an initial get-together to share your plans and set a joint target date.

Bring your flow chart, goal calendar, and the coming week's calendar to this first meeting—unless you prefer to do some of the detailed planning in this book together with your buddy. In either case, get a broad overview of each other's plans and a sense of the major time blocks for each of you. The later of your two target dates will become your *joint target date*—the day when both of you will have achieved your goals. Make a verbal contract to stay together until that date. Like all target dates, it is tentative and can be readjusted any time the circumstances warrant, but you've still got to set it. When that day arrives you can have a party—and then renegotiate whether you want to stop or to stay together because you've got six new goals to work on!

Now pick an afternoon or evening when you'll both be able to meet at the same time every week. It's important to be in frequent, regular touch—a contact you can count on and look forward to. And it is very important to make these business meetings an open, official, high-priority part of your life—not something you just sneak in when you have time. *The commitment to your buddy is a commitment to yourself and your goals.* It doesn't have to take up more than an hour a week, but family demands and social activities should be planned around it, not vice versa. If you're out of town or you have a sick child or some other good reason why you can't make it, you will report in to your buddy by phone at the regular time.

Before you end your setting-up meeting, go over your next week's calendars with each other. You write down what your buddy is planning to do each day. She writes down what you are planning to do each day. If either of you thinks you could use a "booster" phone call on a particular day, write that into your schedules too: "You call me Wednesday evening to find out whether I called the director of the museum. I'm going to call you Friday noon to see if you wrote your poem." (Note: don't always wait for your buddy to ask for a "booster" call. You ask him when he thinks he might need one. A little loving push every now and then is very much a part of the buddy system. So is the snarled reply, "For Chrissake get off my back!" Because you'll be urging each other to do things that are uncomfortable, an occasional flare-up of resentment is inevitable. It's just Hard Times. Handle it with awareness and humor.)

Now for your weekly procedure.

Weekly Business Meeting

I call this a business meeting because it is exactly that. It is not a kaffee klatsch; it is not a beer-and-football party; it is not a consciousness-raising group. It is a goal-oriented strategy session, and the minute it turns into anything else, it's not going to work.

The problem is, you're friends. You like each other. And it's very hard for people who like each other to get down to business, because they have such a good time together. On top of that, you may not be used to practical talk about goals, achievements, plans and problems, all of it taking place "between friends." Sometimes we have a lot of trouble taking ourselves and each other seriously in that dimension. Women especially tend to slide over into the realm of feelings, personalities, and relationships, where we feel at home and can go on for hours. To prevent this from happening, you've got to make your business meetings stick to a couple of rules.

1. Be on time. This sounds like a small thing, but it's the essence of self-respect. You try not to be late for an appointment with your doctor or your boss, because you respect them and you want the feeling to be mutual. Well, your weekly business meeting is an appointment with your future—with the person you can become. So no matter how you feel on the meeting day, try hard to be on time. And expect the same from your buddy.

2. Use a clock or a kitchen timer. This will structure the meeting and help you keep to the point. Each of you gets a maximum of half an hour, divided up roughly as follows:

5 minutes: Report in. Tell what you did—or didn't do—in the past week, and if you did it, what were the results. Your buddy will have it all written down from the previous week and will expect a report on each item. If you haven't done any of the things you said you were going to do, that isn't the worst thing in the world. You just come in and say, "I didn't do anything." But usually you did do something, and you just don't realize it. You start out, "I didn't do anything. Oh, well, I did call so-and-so, but he wasn't in." And so you get the confirmation you can't always give yourself that you've really done a great deal. (Here your buddy is fulfilling the same report-in and feedback function that an Actions & Feelings Journal fulfills when you're working alone.)

20 minutes: Problems and solutions. Now tell about any problems you ran into, and invite your buddy's suggestions. But watch out: if the problems you bring up have an *emotional ingredient*, air it out in a Hard Times session first, or your attempts at problem-solving will be a spectacular failure. Here's where you'll have to be alert and attentive to each other. You can't always pick up on the need to complain in yourself, but there's no mistaking the "yes-but" game or that heavy, dragging tone in someone else's voice. Try to have fun with Hard Times. Complain until you feel lightened and ready go on, but *set yourself a limit of 10 minutes.* Even bitching and moaning can be done efficiently in the service of your goal! Then get down to brainstorming and barn-raising.

Five minutes: Scheduling. Update your master list of unscheduled actions, adding any suggestions from your buddy that you want to act on, and then lay out your next week's plan of action: what you're going to do on what day. Be sure to write in any booster calls you're expecting from your buddy, because knowing those calls are coming in will keep you on the ball. Your buddy should write down a copy of your schedule, including the times s/he's promised to call you. And then it's his or her turn.

After this basic one-hour business meeting is over, you can do things like rehearse an interview or draft a resumé (you'll be very up for it); you can sit around and fantasize about how great it'll be when you both have your goals; you can open a bottle of wine and gossip all night; or you can go home. I really want you to experience what it's like to walk out and say, "I'll see you next week and tell you what happened—and I'll talk to you Wednesday on the phone."

The Three-Minute Booster Phone Call

A phone call from your buddy in the middle of the week can give you a shot of courage and motivation when you need it most: just before you've got to do something difficult, or just after you've done something difficult, or both ("Are you ready to leave for your interview? OK, I'll expect you to call me the minute you get out of there and tell me how it went"). I don't mean only those calls you've promised to make at your weekly business meeting, but also an occasional impulsive holler for help, advice, congratulations, or just to touch base. If you and your buddy make it part of your verbal contract to be available to each other over the telephone, it will help both of you not to feel alone. But like any other mutual-aid arrangement, it can get out of hand. If the person you team up with has any "baby" tendencies at all (see Chapter 7), after a while you're going to cringe every time the phone rings. Again, the best preventive is a rule.

No call should be more than three minutes. Besides being cheaper, this three-minute limit will remind you to value both your own time and your buddy's. Now that you have a goal, you are living in a *time frame,* and for women and other former nonwinners that's a whole new ball game, one that's going to take some practice. People who don't live in a time frame have nothing to do but pour out their concern for each other and take care of each other for years, but people in a goal-directed work situation have to distinguish between linear time, which is for getting things done, and free or "global" time, which is wide open for play and feeling. Linear time has to be used efficiently; global time can be squandered, like "mad money." You can call up your buddy, say "This is the business call I said I'd make," talk for three minutes, and then call back and talk all night if you like. Just so you get it into your head that business is business.

One more suggestion. If your buddy ever calls up and starts going on and on in a negative way, remember, whatever you do, *don't try to fix the problem,* or you'll never get off the phone. If s/he says, "My husband/wife doesn't love me, I'm too fat, " don't offer help. Saying,

"Oh, no, you're not too fat, maybe you can get another wife/husband" will only trigger the "Yes-but" game. Just listen a little more and then say, "What can I do to help? You tell me." That little sentence is magic. If more people knew about it, Ma Bell might go broke.

Intensive Care

I don't know where you first heard the term "the buddy system." I picked it up in grade-school swimming class, where you had to keep an eye on another girl and she had to keep an eye on you to make sure neither of you drowned. There are times when your success buddy can be a bona fide lifesaver, too.

I mean those bad moments when there's something you've got to do and you know you can't do it. The very prospect of calling a Montessori school and asking if they need a teacher's aide gives you appendicitis. Or you've got a thesis deadline coming up and you've got that sinking sensation that you're not going to make it; your mind goes blank when you so much as look at the blank sheet of paper in the typewriter. Or you're supposed to go in for an interview and you have a strong feeling that when you reach the door you're going to turn around and go home and eat a whole bag of Fritos. What you have to do is just too hard, or you're mysteriously and horribly blocked.

This is known as a *crisis.* Sooner or later it happens to everyone, and there are three danger points in the pursuit of your goal when it's particularly likely to happen:

Crisis Point 1: *At the beginning,* when the field you're venturing out in—or maybe directed action itself—is new to you, and you have no solid experience of success to counteract your fantasies of disaster.

Crisis Point 2: *Whenever you have to do something you don't want to do in order to get to something you do.* No matter how ingeniously you've done your brainstorming, almost any goal you head for is going to require a few steps you don't much care for. Like practicing scales when you want to play jazz improvisations. Like taking a calculus course when you want to be a marine biologist. Like finishing your thesis. (Nobody wants to finish a thesis.) These can cause major crises of inaction, because in the short run it feels nicer to sit behind the roadblock and daydream about your goal than to grapple with the roadblock so you can go get your goal. A roadblock is also handy to hide behind if the idea of actually getting your goal is still a little scary. I'd wager that most chronically unfinished theses owe their long lives to a combination of these factors.

Crisis Point 3: *When you face the jump to a new level of risk or visibility.* I know a burgeoning writer who had a field day with her first steps, but froze up on the day she reread what she'd written and realized that not only was she serious about her work, she was actually good. And Andrea felt very comfortable with her camera after three months of taking pictures on her own, but the day she made an appointment to show her prints to a professional photographer, she freaked out. That's only natural.

I've told you the story of Matthew, the man who hadn't painted for twenty years and whose goal was to get back into it for his own pleasure. He progressed without a hitch from making sketches on his own to taking private drawing lessons in his home, and finally to life-drawing classes at a small art school. Heartened by that triumph over timidity, he enrolled in a painting class at a prestigious art school —and he crashed. He walked in and walked out again and said, "I can't do it. Everyone in there can paint but me."

The first thing I said to him was, "You can't stop now. When you're through being scared, that's different. Right now you get to panic, you get to feel lousy, you get to hate yourself, but you don't get to stop painting!" And that's the first rule for you, too, any time you hit a crisis. Never, *never give up or change your goal when you're feeling scared, discouraged, or depressed.* Once you get past the rough spot and you're feeling good again, you are free to change your goal if it really isn't doing much for you. But *not while you're down!* When you're down what you need more than anything else is to keep going, but it's awfully hard to do that alone. You'll make it if you have someone to hold your hand every step of the way. That's *Intensive Care.*

What Matthew did was to get a buddy to go with him to that painting class every night for a week. To be more precise, his friend Sharon dragged him to class and to make sure he went in the door. Sharon would be waiting for him two hours later when the class was over, and they'd go out and have a stiff drink together. The second week Matthew went to class on his own—a little unsteadily, but he went. He met Sharon after class a couple of times, but mostly he just checked in with her on the phone right before class to say, "Here goes." At the end of those two weeks Matthew called Sharon up and said, "Thank you for making me do it. You couldn't drag me away from that class now."

You don't have to be working in the buddy system to set up Intensive Care for yourself, though it helps. But in a pinch you can ask a good friend or family member to see you through a crisis. It's important for them—and you—to realize that this isn't a full-fledged nervous breakdown. It's just a temporary case of stage fright, and you need somebody to shove you lovingly out under the lights. With that understanding, if you're facing a difficult interview or performance, you can have someone come with you right to the door and be waiting to give you a big hug and a hot bowl of soup when you come out. You can also ask for *crisis calls.*

Crisis calls are indicated when you can just feel that you've got a bad week coming up. You might say to your buddy (or appropriate substitute), "Help. I've got a thirty-page proposal to write this week and I can't." Or your buddy might spot the signs of an impending crisis. So she or he says, "All right, I want you to call me at nine every morning before you sit down at the typewriter. I need to hear from you at eleven with at least one paragraph written. And then I want to hear from you at four." In a crisis, your buddy gets to give you orders just like a schoolteacher. (Remember s/he is "the appointed representative of your best self.") That way, when you're blocked, you're not alone with it. You have someone to get you started in the morning and someone to report to at the end of the work day. Frequent crisis calls also help to break up an imposing task into manageable units: one paragraph, one page, one phone call at a time.

You won't need Intensive Care very often. In fact, once may be enough. Once you've had the experience of keeping going through a crisis, the world will be a different place for you. You'll have a solid, tangible achievement to be proud of, and you'll be less afraid of your fears—if they couldn't stop you this time, why should they ever stop you again? But to crash through that barrier the first time, you need help. Matthew needed it. I needed it. And I still want a loyal team on my side whenever I've got something grueling or scary to do—or something wonderful to celebrate.

Let the lone cowboy walk off into the sunset. He's a movie myth and the director is yelling, "Cut!!" Real cowboys rode the range in twos and threes, so they'd have somebody to help them out when a cow got stuck in the mud . . . and someone to drink coffee and play guitar with at night. Sharing goals works. It's based on the way we are.

I ran into Matthew about a year after he successfully weathered his crisis, and I asked him, "How's your painting going?"

He said, "You know, thanks to Sharon, I really did what I wanted to do. I carried a sketch pad around with me all the time, and I filled our apartment with canvases. I've got to put some of them in storage now to make room for the piano. That's right, I'm buying a piano! I've found someone to give me lessons. Of course, I'm scared to death.

"But I know now that I can do anything."

–11–
Proceeding

You've got all your planning machinery in working order, and you've got a set of helpful hints for starting up again any time you're stalled. Only one thing remains, and that is to show you how to turn the key and get it all rolling. What I'm going to give you now is the *weekly and daily procedure* that really puts your plans into action.

Here's what you have to work with:

ON YOUR PLANNING WALL:
1. your personal "saint"
2. Flow Chart
3. Goal Calendar
4. First Steps
5. Weekly Calendar
6. the next five years
7. the next step: tonight/tomorrow

PORTABLE:
1. Purse or Pocket Calendar
2. Actions & Feelings Journal
3. Hard Times Notebook

Here's what you do every week:

SUNDAY NIGHT PLANNING MEETING

This is the night on which you meet with yourself and prepare for the entire week ahead. It may take as much as an hour, or even more, but it's vitally important. No sensible business would proceed without planning meetings, and you've got to learn to treat getting what you want as top priority business.

I've picked Sunday night because it fits in with most people's work week, but if your schedule is different, it could be Monday night or Thursday night just as well. If you are working in the buddy system, your weekly business meeting with your buddy will take care of some of the steps below. I've indicated which those are, so that you'll know which ones you will still have to come home and do for yourself to keep your plans up to date.

Step One: Looking Back. Review what you got done the past week, referring to your Weekly Calendar and Actions & Feelings Journal to refresh your memory. (This step is taken care of by the report-in to your buddy if you've got one.) Now tear off the past week's page to reveal a clean new one.

Step Two: Flow Chart and Goal Calendar Update. Check to see where you are now on your flow chart and goal calendar. If you're using colored push pins, move them ahead to your present position. Pay special attention to the *closest approaching target date* on your goal calendar. Does it look like you're going to make it? Many unforeseen problems and/or opportunities may have come up in the past week. If you're falling behind schedule, what can you do about it? Can you step up the pace of your actions, or will you have to push back your target date? Or can you actually move it forward? This is the time to make any changes in your flow chart and goal calendar—either of target dates or of actual plans—based on what's happened out there in the world.

Step Three: List of First Steps. Look at your list. You will have updated it in your *Daily Procedure* (see below) as new ideas and leads came in, but now make any further additions you can think of and cross out any steps that have become unnecessary.

Step Four: Problems. Did you run into any snags last week? Are there any upcoming steps on your list that you feel puzzled or pessimistic about? This is the time for the Problems List, and as always, dealing with it is a two-stage process. (Both stages will be taken care of by your meeting with your buddy if you've got one.)

a. Hard Times. If you're feeling discouraged, tired, or anxious, open your Hard Times Notebook—your private, negative, ornery, un-American "I Hate Success" book—and start writing down all the reasons why it can't be done. Look at the picture of your personal "saint" and say, "I hate you. Go jump in the lake with your bloody encouragement." Say, "I'm a woman and I shouldn't have to do anything," or "Nobody else ever works this hard to get rich. Tomorrow I'm going to sell out to the highest bidder." Sooner or later, if you keep it bright and are very bad, you'll start to laugh. At that point, say, "Oh, what the hell," and turn your attention to the strategic problems.

b. Brainstorming—and Barn-Raising. Now, turn your ingenuity loose and play around with possible solutions to the problems. If you need input—fresh ideas, practical help—reach for the telephone and call someone in your resource network. Enter the results on your list of First Steps.

Step Five: Next Week's Plan. Two parts here, too (you'll do them with your buddy if you have one):

a. Weekly Calendar. Assign the actions you've decided you can get done this coming week to *specific days and times* on your fresh new Weekly Calendar page. Don't forget also to schedule any crisis, booster, or report-back calls to your buddy or to a friend who's given you a lead.

b. Purse or Pocket Calendar. Transfer the coming week's "appointments" into your portable calendar.

Steps Six, Seven, Eight and Nine will be the same as Steps 1, 3, 4, 5 in the *Evening Procedure* below *(Journal, The Next Step, Rewards, Dreaming).*

DAILY PROCEDURE

Evening:

1. Journal. Enter in your Actions & Feelings Journal what you got done today and how you felt.

2. List of First Steps. Add any new steps you've come up with as a result of today's actions to your List of First Steps.

3. The Next Step. Tear off yesterday's tonight/tomorrow sheet and fill out a new one. What do you have scheduled for *tomorrow?* What do you have to do *tonight* to prepare for it—lay out your clothes, lay out your paintbrushes and paints, make sure a phone number is in your pocket calendar, rehearse an interview in your mind? *Now do it.*

4. Rewards. Give yourself something nice: a hot bath, an hour of reading, a late movie, a glass of brandy, your favorite record, your favorite fantasy.

5. Dreaming. The last thing before you go to sleep, lie awake in the dark and imagine yourself in your Ideal Environment—the one from Chapter 3 in which you would be your best self. Go to sleep enjoying that thought.

Morning:

1. Set your alarm for ten minutes early, so you don't have to leap out of bed in a panic.

2. After breakfast, go to your planning wall and look at the next step. That's all you have to do today, and you are prepared for it. Remember that it may turn up nothing, or it may turn up a hundred new possibilities. There's no way of knowing until you do it.

3. Look at your flow chart and see where this one small step fits into the whole plan that's leading you to your goal.

4. If your goal or job takes you out into the world, pack up your pocket calendar and Hard Times Notebook, take a look at your kindly personal "saint," and you're on your way. If you're doing your goal work at home, sit down, take a deep breath . . . and begin.

— EPILOGUE —

Learning to Live with Success

Congratulations. You're there.

Where? Maybe this is the day when you've actually reached your first target. Maybe you've arrived at the first major milestone on your way to it—you've written a whole chapter, gotten through a job interview and felt good about it, lost ten pounds, drawn up a business plan, or learned to use a camera. Or maybe you're just at the end of your first week—or day—of directed action. *Each small step you accomplish is going to feel like success*—not just the big ones.

Winning is a process, not a product. And as soon as you get out on your path, you're doing it. Now you've got to learn to live with it. That isn't quite as breezy as it sounds. You may not be used to being out there making things happen, and it can sometimes give you a headache. But it's worth it. It feels so much better than the depression and boredom you suffered just sitting around. And there's an art to making it easier for yourself.

1. Hurray for Me! Don't ever let anyone tell you that there's anything wrong with self-congratulation. When you've done something hard, you deserve cheers, from yourself and everyone around you. When you've done something hard and it's worked, you deserve a banquet! You may remember that when you were setting your target and your target date, I told you that you would need to be able to know beyond a doubt when you had arrived—at your goal and at each big step on

242

the way. I can tell you now that part of the reason was so you would know when to celebrate!

Pausing to savor your own accomplishments and feel proud of yourself isn't "conceited" or "self-indulgent," the way our Puritan culture taught us it was. It's food for your unfolding self. And you don't need to worry about "resting on your laurels." You've got to rest on them a little bit, if only to catch your breath! Then you'll want to move on. So enjoy this moment of triumph, in private and with the people you love. Give yourself one of those big rewards we talked about in Chapter 9. Take a vacation. Throw a party.

2. *Fake It* . . . The party's over. It's the morning after. You got the job of your dreams—and now you have to walk in there at 9:00 A.M. and *do* it, and not just tomorrow, but every day after that! You got the contract; now you have to write the book. You came through the audition with flying colors, and they gave you the part; now you're going to have to get up in front of a real live audience and act.

Each new level of success (and this is true of even the smallest steps) brings new tasks, new challenges, new stresses, as well as new opportunities. The operative word is *new.* You're navigating in unknown waters now. But don't think that means all your old, familiar fears and uncertainties are going to vanish as if by magic. No way! You bring them right along with you, and they will be doing plenty of kicking and screaming long after the rest of the world considers you a dazzling, invulnerable success. If your history is anything like mine, for a long, long time you're not going to believe you can do something even when you've just done it and the evidence is right in front of your eyes.

So I would like to share with you my simple, one-sentence formula for how to live with success:

FAKE IT TILL YOU GET USED TO IT

The first time I was invited to be on national television, I said, "Yes!" —not because I was ready, but because it was too good a chance to pass up. (Success, no matter how long you've waited for it, always comes before you're ready for it.) Then I freaked out. "I can't do it. I'll open my mouth and nothing will come out. I'm too fat." And so on. But by this time I knew a thing or two. So I made a resolution—the very rare kind that really *is* written in blood: "I will not, repeat, will not sabotage myself, no matter how much I may want to."

I got everything ready—the clothes I would wear, my plans for what I was going to say. Then I was hysterical for two days before the show. On the big day, I pulled myself together, walked in, carried it off almost as smoothly as an old pro, thanked everyone (they were very impressed), went home and got hysterical again. Nobody who watched the show ever knew that they had been watching a total fake. Only my family, who had to live with me backstage, knew that there were *two* Barbara Shers.

There are two tricks to faking it. One is the Hard Times before-and-after technique you learned in Chapter 9. You need to express your hysteria without ruining your performance. So just do it in the wings! Be your nervous self until they call your name, and then go out there and be a pro.

The second trick is *costumes*. Every actor and actress knows that getting into costume is a tremendous aid to getting into a role, and that there's a huge difference between the last rehearsal in jeans and leotards and the first one in full dress. You can do the same thing. If you are now, by definition, a doctor, lawyer, wilderness guide, salesman, businesswoman, executive, or college teacher—that is, if you're doing the thing—*dress the part even if you don't feel like it.*

I know two former college roommates, now both successful—one a lawyer, the other an executive—who made the mistake of waiting until they felt self-confident in their professional roles to start dressing for them. They may actually have slowed down their careers, because dressing like a college kid or a stay-at-home mother creates a vicious cycle: it provokes the people you work with to treat you as someone not quite grown up or serious, and you'll respond in kind. On the other hand, something magical happens when you look in the mirror and see someone you don't recognize as ordinary you. (By the way, there's an "ordinary me" hiding behind the confident face of every celebrity, bar none.) Even if you still feel ordinary inside, believe me, the ham in you will rise to the occasion.

Note: The days when you least feel like dressing for the part are the days when you absolutely must do it. For two reasons. One: When you're feeling great, you can look rotten and nobody will notice because you'll be so radiant. When you're feeling down, you need outside help. Two: If you drag yourself groaning to the mirror and get your makeup on or your tie straight, you'll start feeling better.

Sooner or later, the day will come for you that came for me: I'd bought a dress to fool everybody . . . and I put it on . . . and suddenly I realized that the only person I'd been fooling was myself. *I belonged in that dress.*

3. Until You Get Used to It. The scenario of my first TV appearance repeated itself, with decreasing intensity, for about a year. It got a little easier each time. And now? Now I'm absolutely greedy about it! I love to show off and can't wait for my next chance. I speak in front of large groups, go on TV and radio, and have a wonderful time. My stage fright has diminished to a pleasant champagne-like tingle. Nobody knows I've changed but my very patient family, who no longer have to put me together like Humpty Dumpty beforehand and pick up the pieces afterwards.

When you reach this point, you've really arrived. You'll wake up one day and realize that you are living a version of the Ideal Day you dreamed about all those months or years ago, when you first started moving. It may or may not be just the way you imagined it, but in one crucial respect it's different—and better: this is real. There's something else that's better about it, too. You're not alone, the way you once feared you would be. On the contrary, you have to take the phone off the hook every once in a while to get some peace. Success is sexy. It puts roses in your cheeks, a swing in your stride, and a warmth and enthusiasm in your presence that people can't resist. If you ever notice that someone you care about is feeling left behind, don't feel guilty. Grab that person, say, "Stop crying in your beer, get up out of that chair and come with me! I want your company. If I did it, believe me, you can. I'll help."

At this point, it is also in the nature of the human animal to say, "What next?" Remember, I told you that when you had attained self-confidence in one thing, you would start looking around for something new to do in which you would have *no* self-confidence. But you've got something much more important than self-confidence now. You've got experience and skills. When my friend Matthew said, "I know now that I can do anything," that wasn't a delusion of grandeur. It was a statement of fact. He could go on from painting to playing the piano because he had acquired a *metaskill:* he had learned how to learn, he had gained mastery of the process by which things get done. When you reach your first goal, you've done this too. Now you've really got the luxury of choice.

Look at the next five years on your planning wall. Are you ready for the next goal? Do you still want to run a printing press, or would you rather study the Spanish Civil War? Do you want to go on running a business or would you like to be a beachcomber for a while? The shape of things has changed. Your efforts have changed it. So what about the shape of things to come? What would you like to do now?

What I always do is imagine a new Ideal Day, in detail and in full color. It is always completely different from the last one, and often quite the opposite of the life I'm living. That helps me set my course for the *next* two years.

You've discovered the ultimate secret all winners know: that "the journey, not the arrival, matters." Being on your path is what it's all about. Each destination you reach only opens out into wider horizons, new and undiscovered countries for you to explore.

Resources

This resource section has one ambition: to have something in it for everyone who reads this book. The books, pamphlets, magazines, organizations, and people listed here will tell you more about brainstorming, forming resource networks, volunteering, apprenticeships, surviving role transitions, and so on. I've also tried to connect you with the best existing associations, networks, newsletters, clearing houses, and counseling services that I know of to help you reach your goal. This section will be a brainstorming aid, directing you to many sources of fresh and ingenious goal ideas. And it will give you the sources you need to pursue a specific goal, whether it's a career in engineering or puppetry, your own florist shop or a grant to support you while you paint.

Obviously, this kind of listing can never be complete. You may know of something I should have listed and didn't. If you do, write and tell me about it and we'll put it in the next edition. But many of the resources I've listed are wonderful precisely because they lead to a thousand *other* resources. An asterisk appears next to books that have unusually good reference sections and periodicals and organizations that act as information clearing houses. Books I've found particularly helpful (mostly down-to-earth, step-by-step "how-to" books) also have an asterisk.

Resources are listed in alphabetical categories. Some are cross-referenced and appear in more than one category.

APPRENTICESHIPS AND INTERNSHIPS

Career Internship Program, Carol Feit Lane, 115 East 87 St., New York, N.Y. 10028. (212) 831-7930.

Carol Feit Lane's 12-week workshops are offered in the adult education divisions of New York University and the New School; she also runs private groups and works with individuals. Her program: (1) self-assessment—skills, interests, and fields you can use them in; (2) placement in an unpaid internship, lasting from a few months to a year, in which you can develop a new skill or get acquainted with a new environment (e.g., a law firm); (3) follow-up: making the transition to paid work—how to market yourself, write a resumé, get interviews, etc. Carol negotiates actual internships for people in the New York area and advises people in other parts of the country on how to set up their own. For further information see Carol's article in *Working Woman* magazine, Jan. 1979.

Goddard College, Plainfield, Vt.

Students of all ages in Goddard's nonresidential B.A. and (new) M.A. programs draw up a "learning contract" with advisors. An apprenticeship with an eminent thinker, writer, or professional can be written into the contract. (See also EDUCATION, DESIGNING YOUR OWN.)

The Learning Connection, Uniondale, Long Island, N.Y. 11553.

Federally sponsored. Makes connections between "teachers," "learners," and "sharers." Working on a full-fledged directory. (516) 538-9100.

National Apprenticeship Program, U.S. Department of Labor, Manpower Administration, Washington, D.C. 20210.

Primarily for the unionized trades. (See NEW, p. 249.)

Shared Experience

A program for college students only, sponsored on many campuses by the Western Electric Company. Students are carefully interviewed and matched with experienced mentors in their field of interest.

The Newspaper Fund, P.O. Box 300, Princeton, N.J. 08540.

For information on internships in journalism.

Paolo Soleri, Arcosanti, Scottsdale, Ariz. 85253.

A wonderful avant-garde architect who will advise people on apprenticeships.

NEW: Nontraditional Employment for Women, 105 East 22nd St., New York, N.Y. 10010. (212) 420-0060.

Publishes a newsletter and acts as a network for women interested in blue-collar trades. Helps women get apprenticeships in such unionized trades as carpentry, machinists, etc.

FURTHER INFORMATION OR HELP IN ARRANGING APPRENTICESHIPS

Catalyst, 14 E. 60 St., New York, N.Y. 10022. (212) 759-9700.

A research organization and information network funded to support the concept of women and work. Offices in many cities.

The Guide to Career Education: If Not College, What? by Muriel Lederer. The New York Times Book Company. Rev. ed. 1976.

For sources of training other than college. Each chapter has an excellent reference section.

ARTS, MAKING A LIVING IN THE

Artist's Market, edited by Kirk Polking and Liz Prince. Writers Digest, 9933 Alliance Rd., Cincinnati, Ohio 45242.

Careers in Art. National Art Education Association, 1916 Association Dr., Reston, Va. 22091.

Careers in Music Therapy. National Association for Music Therapy, Inc., P.O. Box 610, Lawrence, Kan. 66044.

Careers in Education. National Commission on Teacher Education and Professional Standards, National Education Association, 1201 Sixteenth St. NW, Washington, D.C. 20036.

Includes music and art education.

How to Make Money with Your Camera by Ted Schwartz. HP Books, P.O. Box 5367, Tucson, Ariz. 85703.

How to Produce a Successful Theater Festival. Creative Book Co., P.O. Box 214998, Sacramento, Cal. 95821.

How to Sell Your Artwork by Milton K. Berlye. Prentice-Hall.

National Federation of Music Clubs, Suite 1215, 600 S. Michigan Ave., Chicago, Ill. 60605.

Opportunities in Acting. Vocational Guidance Manuals, 620 Fifth St., Louisville, Ky. 40202.

The Performing Arts in America, edited by Diana Reische. H.W. Wilson Co.

Photographer (no. 51). Department of Human Resources Development, Mail Control Unit, 800 Capitol Mall, Sacramento, Cal. 95814. Free.

Starting and Staging a Successful Community Arts Festival. Creative Book Co., P.O. Box 214998, Sacramento, Cal. 95821.

Sunshine Artists, Sun County Enterprises, Inc., Drawer 836, Fern Park, Fla. 32730.
   Lists and rates outdoor and community art fairs.

Van Nostrand Reinhold Manual of Film-Making by Barry Callaghan. Van Nostrand Reinhold Co.

Your Future in Music by Robert E. Curtis. Richard Rosen Press, Inc., 29 E. 21 St., New York, N.Y. 10010.

BARTER

Barter: How to Get Almost Anything without Money by Constance Stapleton and Phyllis C. Richman. Charles Scribner's Sons.

"The Barter Revival" by Robin Snow. *New Age* magazine, Jan. 1979, back issue no. 44. $2.50 from New Age Circulation Dept., P.O. Box 1200, Allston, Mass. 02134.

The Boston Trade Exchange, 10 Post Office Square, Boston, Mass. 02114.
   A formal barter network.

The International Trade Exchange, 7656 Burford Dr., MacLean, Va. 22101.

Will help you find or establish a formal barter network in your own locality.

The Mother Earth News. P.O. Box 70, Hendersonville, N.C. 28791.
This fabulous bimonthly runs a regular "$uccessful $waps" column in which readers send in reports of their own ingenious barter ideas and experiences.

BRAINSTORMING AND CREATIVITY

Applied Imagination by Alex Osborn. Charles Scribner's Sons.

Best of Both Worlds by Fran Goldman and Renee Taft. Distaffers, Inc., Suite 1130, Western Savings Fund Building, Philadelphia, Pa. 19107.

The Five Day Course in Thinking by E. DeBono. Basic Books.

Intuition by R. B. Fuller. Doubleday.

New Think: The Use of Lateral Thinking by E. DeBono. Basic Books.

On Knowing by Jerome Bruner. Atheneum.

The Opportunity Explosion by Robert Snelling. Macmillan.

The Universal Traveler: A Soft-Systems Guide to Creativity, Problem-Solving and the Process of Reaching Goals by Don Koberg and Jim Bagnall. William Kaufmann, Inc., 1 First St., Los Altos, Cal. 94022.

CAREER INFORMATION

GENERAL INFORMATION AND GUIDANCE

Careers Tomorrow newsletter. The World Future Society, 4916 St. Elmo Ave., Bethesda, Md. 20014.

Catalyst, 14 E. 60 St., New York, N.Y. (212) 759-9700.
Ask for list of publications on careers and list of career counseling centers. Catalyst has a large central career library.

Chronicle Guidance Publications, Inc., Aurora St., Moravia, N.Y.

Creative Careers for Women by Joan Scobey and Lee Parr McGrath. Simon & Schuster.

*I Can Be Anything: Careers and Colleges for Young Women by Joyce Slayton Mitchell. Bantam.

Office of Education, Bureau of Adult Education, Vocational and Library Programs, Washington, D.C. 20202.

Vocational Guidance Manuals, 620 S. Fifth St., Louisville, Ky. 40202.

Vocational Guidance Manuals, c/o National Textbook Co., 8259 Niles Rd., Skokie, Ill. 60076.

Washington Opportunities for Women, 111 20 St. NW, Washington, D.C. 20006. Drop-in-counseling services in seven cities.

SPECIFIC CAREERS (A PARTIAL AND ARBITRARY LIST)

Advertising

Advertising: A Guide to Careers in Advertising 1975. American Association of Advertising Agencies, 200 Park Ave., New York, N.Y. 10012.

111 Jobs for Women in Advertising. The Women's Advertising Club of Chicago, Chicago, Ill. 60606. $1.

Airline/Pilot

Airline Pilot (no. 374). Department of Human Resources Development, Mail Control Unit, 800 Capitol Mall, Sacramento, Cal. 95814.

Banking

National Association of Bank-Women, Inc., 60 E. 42 St., New York, N.Y. 10017.

Broadcasting and Journalism

American Women in Radio and Television, 75 E. 55 St., New York, N.Y. 10022.

Broadcasting the News. National Association of Broadcasters, 1771 N. Street NW, Washington, D.C. 20036. Other radio and TV career pamphlets also available.

Women's National Press Club, National Press Bldg., 529 14 St. NW, Washington, D.C. 20004.

Cartooning and Comics

Career Package. The Newspaper Comics Council, Inc., 260 Madison Ave., New York, N.Y. 10016.

National Cartoonists Society, 130 W. 44 St., New York, N.Y. 10036.

Construction

National Association of Women in Construction, 346 N. Beachwood Dr., Los Angeles, Cal. 90004.
   Engineers, architects, steelworkers, etc.

Ecology, Conservation, Parks and Wildlife Management

Ecology and Your Career. U.S. Department of Labor, Bureau of Labor Statistics, Washington, D.C. 20212.

How to Start a Neighborhood Recycling Center. Ecology Center, 2179 Allstone Way, Berkeley, Cal. 94704.

Making a Living in Conservation: A Guide to Outdoor Care by Albert M. Day. Stackpole Books, Cameron & Kelker Sts., Harrisburg, Pa. 17105.

National Recreation and Parks Association, 1404 New York Ave. NW, Washington, D.C. 20005.

National Wildlife Federation, 1412 16 St. NW, Washington, D.C. 20036.

Working towards a Better Environment—Some Career Choices. Environmental Protection Agency, 1626 K St. NW, Washington, D.C. 20460.

Education

Doing Your Own School. The Great Atlantic & Pacific School Conspiracy. Beacon Press. 1973

Careers in Education. National Commission on Teacher Education and Professional Standards, National Education Association, 1201 Sixteenth Street NW, Washington, D.C. 20036.

Opportunities Abroad for Teachers. Department of Health, Education and Welfare, Washington, D.C.

Engineering

Aids in Choosing Engineering as a Career. Engineers Council for Professional Development, 345 East 47 St., New York, N.Y. 10017.

National Association of Women in Construction, 346 N. Beachwood Dr., Los Angeles, Cal. 90004.

Society of Women Engineers, United Engineering Center, 345 E. 47 St., New York, N.Y. 10017.

Florist, Grower, Horticulturist

The Society of American Florists, 901 N. Washington St., Alexandria, Va. 22314.
  Has newsletter with how-to details.

Horticulture—A Satisfying Profession. American Society for Horticultural Science, 914 Main St., St. Joseph, Mich. 49085.

U.S. Department of Agriculture, Washington, D.C. 20251.
  Catalog of pamphlets on how to start a greenhouse or nursery.

Geography

Society of Women Geographers, 1619 New Hampshire Ave. NW, Washington, D.C. 20009.

Interior Design and Decoration

American Institute of Interior Designers, 730 Fifth Ave., New York, N.Y. 10019.

The Painting and Decorating Contractors of America, 7223 Lee Hwy., Falls Church, Va. 22046.

Law

National Association of Legal Secretaries, 146 N. San Fernando Blvd., Burbank, Cal. 91502.

Part-Time, Day-Time Law School. The Women's Committee, New England School of Law, 126 Newbury St., Boston, Mass. 02138.

Life Insurance

National Association of Life Underwriters, c/o Union Central Life Insurance Co., 225 Broadway, New York, N.Y. 10007.

Modeling

Everything You Wanted to Know about Modeling and How to Become a Successful Model. Models Mart Ltd., 17 E. 48 St., New York, N.Y. 10017.

Model (no. 144). Department of Human Resources Development, Mail Control Unit, 800 Capitol Mall, Sacramento, Cal. 95814.

Nutrition and Dietetics

American Dietetic Association, 620 N. Michigan Ave., Chicago, Ill. 60611.

Photography

How to Make Money with Your Camera by Ted Schwartz. HP Books, P.O. Box 5367, Tucson, Ariz. 85703.

Photographer (no. 51). Department of Human Resources Development, Mail Control Unit, 800 Capitol Mall, Sacramento, Cal. 95814. Free.

Public Relations

Careers in Public Relations. Career Information Service, Public Relations Society of America, 845 3rd Ave., New York, N.Y. 10022.

Puppetry

Puppetry Journal. Puppeteers of America, Inc., Box 1061, Ojai, Cal. 93023.

Real Estate

National Association of Real Estate Boards, 155 E. Superior St., Chicago, Ill. 60605.

Sciences

American Institute of Biological Sciences, 3900 Wisconsin Ave. NW, Washington, D.C. 20016.

American Institute of Physics, Education Division, Graduate Physics Bldg., State University of New York, Stony Brook, N.Y. 11794.

Free pamphlets: *Wise Use of Science* and *Should You Be a Physicist?*

Test Yourself for Science. U.S. Department of Health, Education and Welfare, Office of Education, Division of Higher Education, Washington, D.C. 20202.

Secretarial

National Association of Legal Secretaries, 146 N. San Fernando Blvd., Burbank, Cal. 91502.

National Secretaries Association International, 1103 Grand Ave., Kansas City, Mo. 64106.

CORPORATIONS, SURVIVAL AND SUCCESS IN

The Career Game: A Step-by-Step Guide up the Ladder of Success by Charles Guy Moore. Ballantine Books.

Effective Business and Technical Presentations by George L. Morrisey. Addison-Wesley, Reading, Mass. 01876.

How to prepare and present your ideas clearly and forcefully: flow charts, flip charts, graphs, statistics, etc.

*The Effective Woman Manager: Seven Vital Skills for Upward Mobility by Nathaniel Stewart. John Wiley & Sons.

Executive Jobs Unlimited by Carl Boll. Macmillan.

Fitting Management Development to Company Needs. American Management Associations General Management Series No. 174, 135 W. 50 St., New York, N.Y. 10020.

The Gamesman: Winning and Losing the Career Game by Michael Maccoby. Bantam.

*Games Mother Never Taught You: Corporate Gamesmanship for Women by Betty Lehan Harragan. Warner Books.

Handbook of Management Tactics: Aggressive Strategies for Getting Things Done Your Way by Richard Buskirk. Hawthorn Books.

How to Manage by Objectives by John W. Humble. Amacom Executive Books, 135 W. 50 St., New York, N.Y. 10020.

Management by Objectives and Results for Business and Industry by George L. Morrisey. Addison-Wesley, Reading, Mass. 01867.

Men and Women of the Corporation by Rosabeth Moss Kanter. Basic Books.

Moving Mountains, or The Art of Letting Others See Things Your Way by Henry M. Boettinger. Macmillan.

Negotiation: The Art of Getting What You Want by Michael Schatzki. A Signet Book, New American Library, New York, N.Y. 1981.

Organizing Your Job in Management by Carl Heyel. American Management Association, 135 W. 50 St., New York, N.Y. 10020.

The Practice of Management by Peter Drucker. Harper & Row.

The Professional Woman, edited by Athena Theodore. Schenkman Publishing Co.

Strategy in Poker, Business and War by John McDonald. Norton.

The Woman's Guide to Management: How to Get to the Top and Stay There by Edith M. Lynch. Cornerstone Library, 1230 Sixth Ave., New York, N.Y. 10020.

Woman's Guide to Management Positions by Wilma C. Rogalin and Arthur R. Pell. Monarch Press, 1 W. 39 St., New York, N.Y. 10018.

COUNTRY LIVING

Country Journal. 205 Main St., Brattleboro, Vt. 05301. $15.00 Monthly, 12 issues. (802) 257-1321.
    Articles, recipes, practical hints.

Cash from Your Garden: Roadside Farm Stands by David W. Lynch, Garden Way, Charlotte, Vt. 05445.

Farmstead Magazine. Home Gardening & Small Farming. P.O. Box 111, Freedom, Maine 04901. $15/Year (8 issues).

First-Time Farmer's Guide by Bill Kaysine. Straight Arrow Books.

Five Acres and Independence by M. G. Kanes, Dover.

How to Make a Living in the Country (Without Farming) by William E. Osgood. Garden Way Publishing, Charlotte, Vt. 05445.

How to Shoe a Horse by Marion C. Manwill. Arco Publishers.

The Manual of Practical Homesteading by John Vivian. Rodale Press, Emmaus, Pa.

*Mother's Bookshelf. P.O. Box 70, Hendersonville, N.C. 28791.
A free periodical catalog of self-sufficiency books—beekeeping, goat farming, homesteading, log cabins, you name it.

*The Mother Earth News. P.O. Box 70, Hendersonville, N.C. 28791. Bimonthly, $18/6 issues.
Ongoing how-to information and encouragement for back-to-the-landers.

Profitable Earthworm Farming by Charlie Morgan. Shields Publications, Box 472, Elgin, Ill., 60120.

Wildcrafting: Harvesting the Wilds for a Living by Jack McQuarrie. Capra Press, 631 State St., Santa Barbara, Cal. 93101.

See also HOME BUSINESS, SMALL BUSINESS, SELF-EMPLOYMENT.

CRAFTS, MAKING A LIVING IN

Ceramics Monthly. 1609 Northwest Blvd., P.O. Box 12448, Columbus, Ohio 43212.

Crafts for Fun and Profit by Eleanor Van Zandt. Doubleday.

The Crafts Report: The Newsmonthly of Marketing, Management, and Money for Crafts Professionals. 801 Wilmington Trust Bldg., Wilmington, Del. 19801.

Craftsman Survival Manual: Making a Part-Time Living from Your Crafts. Spectrum Books, Prentice-Hall, Inc., Englewood Cliffs, N.J. 07632.

How to Make Money with Your Crafts by Leta Clark. William Morrow.

Jewelry Art by Henry Wilson. Hub Material Co., 387 Washington St., Boston, Mass. 02124.

Selling What You Make by Jane Wood. Penguin.

EDUCATION, DESIGNING YOUR OWN

INFORMATION SOURCES

Adult Education Association of the USA, 1225 19 St. NW, Washington, D.C. 20036.

College On Your Own by Gail Parker and Jean Hawes. Bantam.

The Guide to Career Education: If Not College, What? by Muriel Lederer. The New York Times Book Company. Rev. ed. 1976.

Guide to Independent Study through Correspondence Institutions. National University Extension Association, 1 Dupont Circle, Suite 36D, Washington, D.C. 20036.

The Learning Connection, Uniondale, L.I., N.Y.
A federally sponsored clearing house connecting individual "teachers," "learners," and "sharers." (516) 538-9100.

The Lifelong Learner by Ronald Gross. Simon & Schuster, 1974.

"Lifelong Learning," *New Age* magazine, back issue no. 33. $2.50 from New Age Circulation Dept., P.O. Box 1200, Allston, Mass. 02134.

National Home Study Council, 1601 18 St. NW, Washington, D.C. 20009.

Study Skills: A Student's Guide for Survival by Robert A. Carman and W. Royce Adams. John Wiley & Sons.
A self-teaching guide.

The Weekend Education Source Book by Wilbur Cross. Harper's Magazine Press.

The Weekenders by Max Gunther. Lippincott.

SPECIFIC NONRESIDENTIAL DEGREE PROGRAMS

Note on accreditation: Some of these programs offer accredited degrees; others are working toward accreditation. Accredited programs have attained membership in their regional association of colleges and universities, but some states recognize and honor degrees the associations don't. To find out whether a particular program is accredited, and whether you need an accredited degree for professional standing in your field, write to the program, or write or call The Mentor Academy (above).

Ben Franklin Academy (definitely accredited), P.O. Box 1776, Dept. PT 2, Washington, D.C. 20013.

Board for State Academic Awards, 340 Capitol Ave., Hartford, Conn. 06115.
Administers exams, gives college credit for self-study, certified.

Thomas A. Edison College, Forrestal Road, Princeton, N.J. 08540.

Has a Life Experience Credit Course. You can get up to two years of academic credit by taking specially designed exams.

Empire State College, SUNY, Saratoga Springs, N.Y. 12866 (Mentor program).

External Degree Program, California State University, 5670 Wilshire Blvd., Los Angeles, Cal. 90036.

Friends World College, North American Campus, Plover Lane, Huntington, L.I., N.Y.

Goddard College, Plainfield, Vt.
Nonresidential B.A. and M.A. programs. You negotiate your own "learning contract."

Heed University, 1720 P. Harrison St., Hollywood, Fl. 33020.
Has a Ph.D. program.

Nova University, Ft. Lauderdale, Fla. 33314.

Regents External Degree Program, State University of New York, 99 Washington Ave., Albany, N.Y. 12230.

University Without Walls, Antioch College, Yellow Springs, Ohio.
The granddaddy of them all, with satellite programs all over the country.

The Walden University, Naples, Fl. 33940.
Has a Ph.D. program.

FLOW CHARTS

Effective Business and Technical Presentations by George L. Morrisey. Addison-Wesley, Reading, Mass. 01876. (If you want to see how the pros use 'em.)

GOALSETTING

If You Don't Know Where You're Going, You'll Probably End up Somewhere Else by David Campbell. Argus Communications, 7440 Natchez Ave., Niles, Ill. 60648.

What Color Is Your Parachute? by Richard N. Bolles. Ten Speed Press, P.O. Box 7123, Berkeley, Calif. 94707.

Where Do I Go from Here with My Life? by John Crystal and Richard N. Bolles. Seabury Press, New York.

HOME BUSINESS, SMALL BUSINESS, SELF-EMPLOYMENT

COMPREHENSIVE GUIDES: HOW TO

Complete Guide to Making Money with Your Ideas and Inventions by Richard Paige. Prentice-Hall.

Cutting Loose: A Civilized Guide for Getting Out of the System. Saturday Review Press.

Fortune in Your Head by N. Russell Dock and William R. Sanderson. Boardman, New York.

How I Made a Million Dollars with Ideas by George J. Abrams. Playboy Press, Chicago, 1975.

The Home Office Guide by Leon Henry, Jr. Arco Publishing Co.

How to Run a Small Business by J. K. Lasser. McGraw-Hill.

How to Start a Money-Making Business at Home by Laura Robertson. Frederick Fell, Inc., 386 Park Avenue South, N.Y. 10016.

How to Start, Finance, and Manage Your Own Small Business by Joseph R. Mancuso. Prentice-Hall.

Includes sample business plans of the kind you'll need to guide you—and to interest investors.

How to Start Your Own Business by William Putt. M.I.T. Press.

How to Succeed in Business before Graduating by Peter Sandman and Daniel Gordenson. Collier Books.

Jobs: How People Create Their Own by William Ronco. Beacon Press.

Profits at Your Doorstep: A Complete Guide to Setting up a Successful Business in Your Own Home by Judith Weber and Karol White. Barnes & Noble.

The Pure Joy of Making More Money by Donald M. Dible. The Entrepreneur Press, Mission Stations, Drawer 2759V, Santa Clara, Cal. 95051.

Small Business Management Fundamentals by Dan Steinhoff. McGraw-Hill.

Small-Time Operator: How to Start Your Own Small Business, Keep Your Books, Pay Your Taxes, and Stay Out of Trouble! by Bernard Kamaroff. Bell Springs Publishing, P.O. Box 322, Laytonville, Cal. 95454.

Spare-Time Fortune Guide by D. Newcomb. Prentice-Hall.

Starting and Managing a Small Business. Small Business Administration, 1441 L St. NW, Washington, D.C. 20416.

A Woman's Guide to Her Own Franchised Business by Anne and Levy Small. Pilot Books, N.Y., 1967.

The Woman's Guide to Starting a Business by Claudia Jessup and Genie Chipps. Holt, Rinehart & Winston.

Working for Yourself: How to be Successfully Self-Employed by Geof Hewitt. Rodale Press, 33 East Minor St., Emmaus, Pa. 18049.

You, Inc.: A Detailed Escape Route to Being Your Own Boss by Peter Weaver. Doubleday.

TAXES AND TECHNICALITIES: HOW TO

Accounting, Tax, Retirement, & Estate Aspects of the Psychotherapist's Practice by George Greenspan. Charles C. Thomas.

Fear of Filing. Volunteer Lawyers for the Arts, 36 W. 44 St., New York, N.Y. 10036.
　A guide to taxpaying for the self-employed.

How to Advertise and Promote Your Small Business by Connie McClung Siegel. John Wiley & Sons.

IRS Pamphlets: Tax Guide for Small Businesses (no. 334); *Information on Self-Employment Tax* (no. 533); *Record Keeping for a Small Business* (no. 583).

Call your local IRS office for the address of the center nearest you that has these materials.

Small Business Administration

Not famous for actually giving you money, but does come up with many other useful items—like free courses. Write for Pamphlet SBA-115 to: The Small Business Administration, P.O. Box 15434, Fort Worth, Tex. 76119. When you receive the pamphlet, call your local office for their schedule of courses.

IDEA BOOKS: WHAT TO

Big-Time Opportunities & Strategies That Turn Pennies into Millions by F. Franz, Sr. Prentice-Hall.

Buffet Catering by Charles Finance. Hayden Publishing Co., Rochelle Park, N.J.

Catering Handbook by Edith & Hall Weiss. Hayden Publishing Co.

Dozens of Ways to Make Money by Yvonne Mickie Horn. Harcourt Brace Jovanovich.

The Data Search Guide to Low Capital Startup Computer Businesses. Datasearch, Inc., 730 Waukegan Rd., Suite 108, Deerfield, Ill. 60015.

The Family Circle Book of Careers at Home by Mary Bass Gibson. Henry Regnery Co.

Free Enterprise magazine. 800 Second Ave., New York, N.Y. 10017.

How I Turn Junk into Fun and Profit: As Told to Uncle Milton by Sari. Wilshire Book Co., 12015 Sherman Rd., N. Hollywood, Cal. 91605.

How to Earn $25,000 a Year or More Typing at Home. Frederick Fell, Inc., 386 Park Ave. South, New York, N.Y. 10016.

How to Make Money in the Flea Market: A Practical Guide for Dealers and Customers by Joan Burstein and Lorianne Norris. Dutton.

How to Make Your Own Greeting Cards by John Carlis. Watson-Guptill Publications, 1515 Broadway, N.Y. 10036.

How to Run a Paperback Bookshop by S. Gross and P. Steckler. Bowker.

Jobs for Weekends: How to Make It the Best Experience of Your Life! by Roberta Boesch. Berkley Publishing Co., N.Y., 1978.

Job Ideas for Profit, for Pleasure, for Personal Growth, for Self-Esteem by Ruth Lembeck. Prentice-Hall.

Landlording: A Handy Manual for Scrupulous Landlords Who Do It Themselves by Leigh Robinson. Express, Box 1373, Richmond, Cal. 94802.

Making Money in Your Kitchen: Over 1600 Products That Women Can Make by Helen Stone Hovey. Wilfred Funk Publishers.

The Mother Earth News. P.O. Box 70, Hendersonville, N.C. 28791.

The Mother Earth News Handbook of Home Business Ideas & Plans. Bantam.

Mother's Bookshelf. P.O. Box 70, Hendersonville, N.C. 28791.

  Free catalog of self-sufficiency books.

No Experience Necessary by Sande Friedman and Lois Schwarts. Dell.

101 Businesses You Can Start and Run with Less Than $1000 by H. S. Kahm. Doubleday.

101 Practical Ways to Make Money at Home by the editors of *Good Housekeeping.*

100 Surefire Businesses You Can Start with Little or No Investment by Jeffrey Feinman. Playboy Press.

132 Ways to Earn a Living without Working for Someone Else by Ed Rosenthal and Ron Lichty. St. Martin's Press.

  A fabulous resources section.

On Your Own: 99 Alternatives to a 9–5 Job by Kathy Matthews. Random House.

Retailing Principles and Practices, edited by G. Rickert. McGraw-Hill.

A Typing Service in Your Own Home by Patricia M. Willbank. Arco Publishing Co.

MAIL ORDER

How Mail Order Fortunes Are Made by Alfred Stern. Selective Books, Inc., 712 S. Missouri Ave., Clearwater, Fla. 33516.

How to Start and Operate a Mail Order Business by Julian L. Simon. McGraw-Hill.

Mail Order Moonlighting by Cecil C. Hoge, Sr. Ten Speed Press, Box 7123, Berkeley, Cal. 94704.

Mail Order Retailing by Small Enterprises. Superintendent of Documents, U.S. Government Printing Office, Washington, D.C. 20402.
Small Business Administration Pamphlet.

Planning and Creating Better Direct Mail by John D. Yeck and John T. Maguire. McGraw-Hill.

Selling by Mail Order. Superintendent of Documents, U.S. Government Printing Office, Washington, D.C. 20402.
Small Business Administration pamphlet.

See also COUNTRY LIVING.

INFORMATION

The Basic Guide to Research Sources by Robert O'Brien and Joanne Soderman. New American Library.

Bowker Catalog. Bowker.

Encyclopedia of Associations. Gale Research Co., Book Tower, Detroit, Mich. 48226.

*Finding Facts Fast: How to Find Out What You Want to Know Immediately by Alden Todd. William Morrow.

Finding Facts: Interviewing, Observing, Using Reference Sources by William L. Rivers. Prentice-Hall.

Guide to American Directories by Bernard Klein. B. Klein Publications, Inc., P.O. Box 8503, Coral Springs, Fla 33065.

The Modern Researcher by Jacques Barzun and Henry F. Graff. Harcourt Brace Jovanovich.

Readers' Guide to Periodical Literature.
In all libraries.

Reference Books: A Brief Guide by Mary N. Baron and Marion V. Bell. Enoch Pratt Free Library, Publications Office, 400 Cathedral St., Baltimore, Md. 21201.

Research Centers Directory, edited by Archie M. Palmer. Gale Research Co., Book Tower, Detroit, Mich. 48226.

Statistics Sources, edited by Paul Wasserman and Joanne Paskar. Gale Research Co., Book Tower, Detroit, Mich. 48226.

Subject Guide to Books in Print. Bowker.

Available at library and in bookstores.

U.S. Government Publications, Superintendant of Documents, U.S. Government Printing Office, Washington, D.C. 20402.

Last but not least, have a talk with your librarian. She or he is a very special person to have on your brainstorming team, because s/he knows where to find information and probably studied library science because s/he was interested in too many things to settle on just one!

INTERPERSONAL SKILLS AND STRATEGIES FOR ROLE CHANGE

Games Mother Never Taught You: Corporate Gamesmanship for Women by Betty Lehan Harragan. Warner Books.

The Two-Career Family by Linda Lytle Holmstrom. Schenkman, 3 Mount Auburn St., Cambridge, Mass. 02138.

When I Say No I Feel Guilty by Manuel J. Smith. Bantam Books.

INVENTIONS AND PATENTS

Fortune in Your Head by N. Russell Dock and William R. Sanderson. Boardman, New York.

An Information Aid for Inventors. Department of Commerce, 14 St., Washington, D.C. 20235.

Inventions, Patents & Their Management by Alf K. Berle. Van Nostrand Reinhold.

The Inventor's Patent Handbook by Stacy V. Jones. Dial Press.

The Inventor's Source Book: How to Turn Ideas into Inventions by Susan N. Hartman and Norman C. Parrish. Inventors Resource Center, P.O. Box 5105, 2901 College Ave., Berkeley, Cal. 94705.

JOB, GETTING THE RIGHT

HOW-TO

The 8-Day Week by John Ward Pearson. Harper & Row.
Four days on, four days off.

Getting Yours by Letty Cottin Pogrebin. Avon Books.

Go Hire Yourself an Employer by Richard K. Irish. Doubleday/Anchor.

How to Find a Job by Donald E. Larson. Ace Books.

Job Finding Techniques for Mature Women. U.S. Department of Labor, Manpower Administration, Training and Employment Service, Washington, D.C. 20210.

The Job Handbook for Post College Cop-Outs by L. Handel. Pocket Books.

*28 Days to a Better Job by Tom Jackson. Hawthorn Books.

WHAT-TO: IDEA BOOKS AND LISTINGS

The Independent Teenager: 350 Jobs for High School Students by David M. Rubin. Collier Books.

Teen-Age Job by Ruth Lembeck. David McKay Co.

1,001 Job Ideas for Today's Woman by Ruth Lembeck. Dolphin Books.

Job Information Service, Office of Technical Support, U.S. Employment Service, U.S. Department of Labor, Washington, D.C. 21210.
Up-to-date, computerized listings of job openings.

Employment Abroad. Council on International Education Exchange, 777 U.N. Plaza, New York, N.Y. 10017.

Federal Jobs Overseas (Pamphlet 29). Superintendent of Documents, Washington, D.C. 20402.

How to Get a Job Overseas. Research Associates, Box 889-MA, Belmont, Cal. 94002.

Opportunities Abroad for Teachers. Department of Health, Education and Welfare, Washington, D.C. 20203.

Summer Employment Directory of the U.S. National Directory Service, Inc., 252 Ludlow Ave., Cincinnati, Ohio 45220.

KIDS, MOTHERS, AND WORK

Day Care: How to Plan, Develop and Operate a Day Care Center by E. Belle Evans, Beth Shub, and Marlene Weinstein. Beacon Press.

Doing Your Own School. The Great Atlantic and Pacific School Conspiracy. Beacon Press.

"Great Ideas for Women Who Work," *Family Circle* magazine, Sept. 1978.

How to Go to Work When Your Husband Is Against It, Your Children Aren't Old Enough, and There's Nothing You Can Do Anyhow by Felice N. Schwartz, Margaret Schiften, and Susan Gilotti. Simon & Schuster.

The National Association for the Education of Young Children, 1834 Connecticut Ave. NW, Washington, D.C. 20009.
   Pamphlet—*The Essentials for Developing a Good Early Childhood Program* —for those interested in opening day-care centers.

The Two-Career Family by Lynda Lytle Holmstrom. Schenkman, 3 Mt. Auburn St., Cambridge, Mass. 02138.

Working Mothers Bibliography. BPW, 2012 Massachusetts Ave. NW, Washington, D.C. 20036.

Working Woman magazine.

"LATE" STARTS

FOR INSPIRATION

Never Too Late: My Musical Life Story by John Holt. Delacorte Press, N.Y., 1978.

Late Bloom: New Lives for Women by Luree Miller. Paddington Press (Grosset & Dunlop).
   Tales of "housewives who became doctors, lawyers, scholars, antique dealers, as well as a photojournalist turned Buddhist nun."

"Second Acts" by Herbert B. Livesey, *Quest/77* magazine, July–Aug. 1977.

Starting: Early, Anew, Over and Late by Helen Yglesias. Rawson Associates, 1976.

Starting in the Middle by Judith Wax. Holt, Rinehart & Winston.

The author published her first success—a Watergate parody—at age forty-two.

FOR TRAINING, IDEAS, CONTACTS, HELP see also APPRENTICESHIPS AND INTERNSHIPS and CAREER INFORMATION.

Back-to-Work Seminars, National YWCA, Dr. Aurelia Toyer, 600 Lexington Ave., New York, N.Y. 10022.

Career Internship Program, Carol Feit Lane, 115 E. 87 St., New York, N.Y. 10028. (212) 931-7930.

Catalyst, 14 E. 60 St., New York, N.Y. 10022. (212) 759-9700.

Continuing Education Programs and Services for Women, Pamphlet 10, Women's Bureau, Department of Labor, Washington, D.C. 20210.

Job Finding Techniques for Mature Women. U.S. Department of Labor, Manpower Administration, Training and Employment Service, Washington, D.C. 20210.

Displaced Homemakers, Network, Inc., 755 Eighth St. NW, Washington, D.C. 20001. (202) 347-0522.

Newsletter reports nationwide.

Office of Education, Bureau of Adult Education, Vocational and Library Programs, Washington, D.C. 20202.

Part-Time, Day-Time Law School. The Women's Committee, New England School of Law, 126 Newbury St., Boston, Mass. 02138.

The Career and Volunteer Advisory Service. Project Reentry, 14 Beacon St., Boston, Mass. 02108 (617) 227-1762.

Help Yourself to a Job: A Guide for Retirees by Dorothy Winter. Beacon Press.

The Retirement Daybook by Hyman G. Weitzen. Chilton Book Co., Chilton Way, Radnor, Pa. 19889.

"New Images of Aging," *New Age* magazine, back issue no. 45. $2.50 from New Age Circulation Dept., P.O. Box 1200, Allston, Mass. 02134.

The Gray Panthers, 3635 Chestnut St., Philadelphia, Pa. 19104. (215) 382-3300.

Branches in almost every state. People of all ages working to defeat "ageism" in all sectors of society.

SAGE (Senior Actualization and Growth Explorations), 1713A Grove St., Berkeley, Cal. 94709. (415) 454-7042.

MISCELLANEOUS SKILLS

Establish Yourself as an Authority by Sol H. Marshall. Creative Book Co., P.O. Box 214998, Sacramento, Cal. 95821.

Hobby Collections A–Z by Roslyn W. Salny. Crowell.

How To by Peter Passell. Farrar, Straus & Giroux.

How to Analyze Handwriting. Falcon, Cornerstone Library, 1230 Ave. of the Americas, New York, N.Y. 10020.

How to Design and Decorate an Eye-Catching Booth by Ben Berkey. Creative Book Co., P.O. Box 214998, Sacramento, Cal. 95821.

How to Do Your Own Painting and Wallpapering by Jackson Hand. Popular Science, Harper & Row.

How to Repair Small Gasoline Engines by Paul Dempsey. Tab Books, Blue Ridge Summit, Pa. 02139.

How to Write and Deliver a Speech by John Ott. Cornerstone Library, 1230 Ave. of the Americas, New York, N.Y. 10020.

Let's Go Prospecting! by Edward Arthur. P.O. Box 395, Joshua Tree, Cal. 92252.

The Weekend Camper by Dan and Inez Morris. Bobbs-Merrill.

Wines, Cordials and Brandies: How to Make Them. Vanguard Press.

MONEY, GETTING (GRANTS, ETC.)
AND MANAGING

American Woman's Economic Development Corp., 1270 Ave. of the Americas, New York, N.Y. 10019.

Annual Register of Grant Support, edited by Deanna Sclar. Marquis Academic Media, 200 E. Ohio St., Chicago, Ill. 60611.

The Bread Game. Glide Publications, 330 Ellis St., San Francisco, Cal. 94102.
A specific how-to guide for getting grants.

Business and Professional Women's Foundation, 2012 Massachusetts Ave. NW, Washington, D.C. 20036.
$70,000 annual loan fund for graduate business education.

How to Save Money Through Group Buying by Albert Lee. Stein & Day.

Industrial Cooperative Association, 249 Elm St., Somerville, Mass. 02144. (617) 628-7330.
Establishing a revolving loan fund to assist small businesses which are operated as worker cooperatives. For further information contact Steven Dawson.

The Joy of Money by Paula Nelson. Bantam.

National Association of Investment Clubs, P.O. Box 220, Royal Oak, Mich. 48068.

The Seven Laws of Money by Michael Phillips. Random House.

Sylvia Porter's Money Book. Avon Books.

Up Your Own Organization: A Handbook on How to Start and Finance a New Business by Donald M. Dible. The Entrepreneur Press, Mission Station, Drawer 2759T, Santa Clara, Cal. 95051.
Includes a thorough guide on investment and venture capital groups.

Grantsearch, Leigh F. Wright, 2674 Johnson Pl., Baldwin, N.Y. 11510. (516) 223-4117.
An extraordinary new service.

NETWORKS

ORGANIZATIONS

The Briarpatch Network, c/o Glide, 330 Ellis St., San Francisco, Cal. 94102. (415) 431-8395. Contact: Shali.

A coalition of businesses, nonprofit organizations, artists, and individuals interested in "right livelihood," humane economics, and a blend of diversity and community. Acts as a support system for people running nontraditional businesses; can refer you to someone who can advise you on starting such a business. Send $8 (plus $1.50 postage) for *The Briarpatch Book*, a compilation of philosophy, advice, and modest success stories. Make checks out to Glide.

World Future Society, 4916 St. Elmo Ave., Bethseda, Md. 20014. (301) 656-8274.

A worldwide network of people interested in various aspects of the future. Publishes a newsletter, *Education Tomorrow*, and three magazines: *The Futurist*, *The World Future Society Bulletin*, and *Future Survey*.

PERIODICALS

The magazines listed here *act* as networks, offering resources and inviting reader participation.

CoEvolution Quarterly, Box 428, Sausalito, Cal. 94965. Quarterly, $14/yr. (4 issues).

A surprise box of ideas, tools, skills, minds, learning, funding sources, etc., from the folks who brought you the *The Whole Earth Catalog*. You may now order either C.Q. "Bold" (which includes occasional sexually explicit material) or "Lite" (which omits it for those offended thereby).

The Mother Earth News, P.O. Box 70, Hendersonville, N.C. 28739. Bimonthly, $18/year (6 issues).

A gold mine of information on land, self-sufficiency, building, crafts, solar energy, gardening, food preservation, etc. Readers participate heavily, sending in recipes, designs, anecdotes, and questions, and making contacts.

New Age. Monthly, $18/year, back issues $2.50 each from *New Age* Circulation Dept., P.O. Box 1200, Allston, Mass. 02134.

Of special interest are issues no. 33, "Lifelong Learning"; no. 40, "Right Livelihood"; no. 44 on money and New Age economics; no. 45, "New Images of Aging." Editorial address: New Age Communications, Inc., 244 Brighton Ave., Allston, Mass. 02134. This magazine sensibly and critically documents new ideas and values embodied in gentle, human-scale institutions. Each issue is a practical resource bank for a different theme and includes a listing of current conferences, workshops, seminars, fairs, retreats, etc., on a wide and practical range of topics.

Savvy (The Magazine for Executive Women).

Will send you a complete nationwide listing of networks of interest to women (examples: Women in Sales Association, Women Entrepreneurs in San Francisco, National Association of Bank Women, New England Women Business Owners). Send a $2 check or money order and a stamped self-addressed envelope to: Professional Connections, Savvy Magazine, 111 Eighth Ave, New York, N.Y. 10011.

NEWSLETTERS, GETTING THEM AND MAKING THEM

Fundamentals of Layout by F. H. Willis. Dover Publications.

The Newsletter Clearinghouse, 44 W. Market St., Rhinebeck, N.Y. 12572.
Publishes *The Newsletter Yearbook/Directory,* edited by Howard Penn Hudson.

*Practical Guide to Newsletter Editing and Design by LaRae H. Wales. Iowa State University Press.

PUBLICITY

How to Advertise and Promote Your Small Business by Connie McClung Siegel. John Wiley & Sons.

How to Get Big Results from a Small Advertising Budget by Cynthia S. Smith. Hawthorn Books.

Profitable Newspaper Advertising by Edmund C. Arnold. Harper & Row.

Promoting Your Cause by Howard Bloomenthal. Funk & Wagnalls.

Publicity: How to Get It by Richard O'Brien. Harper & Row.

Syndicated Columnists by Richard Weiner. 888 7th Ave., New York, N.Y. 10019.

PUBLISHING YOURSELF, MAGAZINES AND BOOKS

American Book Trade Directory. Bowker.

A list of booksellers, publishers, and wholesalers.

The Art and Science of Book Publishing by Herbert Bailey, Jr. Harper & Row.

Bookbinding: Its Background and Techniques by Edith Diehl. Kennikat, 1965.

Bookmaking: The Illustrated Guide to Design and Production by Marshall Lee. Bowker.

Community Journalism: A Way of Life by Bruce M. Kennedy. Iowa State University Press.

*COSMEP (Committee of Small Magazine Editors and Publishers), P.O. Box 703, San Francisco, Cal. 94101.

COSMEP Bookstore Survey, COSMEP, P.O. Box 703, San Francisco, Cal. 94101.

Country Editor by Henry Beetle Hough. Chatham Press, Old Greenwich, Conn. 06870.

Creative Bookbinding by Pauline Johnson. The University of Washington Press.

Directory of Little Magazines, Small Presses and Underground Newspapers, edited by Len Fulton and James Boyer May. Dustbooks, 5218 Scottwood Rd., Paradise, Cal. 95969.

Editor and Publisher, 850 3rd Ave., New York, N.Y. 10022.

Periodical with ads for used equipment and newspapers for sale all over the country.

Folio: The Magazine for Magazine Management, 125 Elm St., New Canaan, Conn. 06840.

Fundamentals of Layout by F. H. Willis. Dover Publications.

The Home for Unpublished Books, R.D. 2, West Winfield, N.Y. 13491.
   Write to Everett Adelman for information.

How to Produce a Small Newspaper: A Guide for Independent Journalists by the editors of the *Harvard Post.* Harvard Common Press, The Common, Harvard, Mass. 01451.

How to Publish, Promote and Sell Your Books by Joseph V. Goodman. Adams Press, 30 W. Washington St., Chicago, Ill. 60602.

How to Publish Your Own Book by L. W. Mueller. Harlo Press, 16721 Hamilton Ave., Detroit, Mich. 48203.

How to Write and Publish Your Own Book, Course, Song, Slide Chart, or Other Printed Product and Make It Go! by Duane Shinn. Shinn Music Aids, 5090 Dobrot Way, Central Point, Ore. 97501.

How to Write Non-Fiction That Sells by F. A. Rockwell. Henry Regnery Co.

The Newspaper Fund, P.O. Box 300, Princeton, N.J. 08540.
   Internships and information.

Practice of Printing by Ralph and Edwin Polk. Bennett.

Preparing the Manuscript. Ulda Olsen. The Writer, 8 Arlington St., Boston, Mass. 02116.

The Print Center, Inc., Box 1050, Brooklyn, N.Y. 11202.
   Books and other printed materials at half price.

Printing and Promotion Handbook by D. Melcher and N. Larrick. McGraw-Hill.

Printing with the Handpress by Lewis and Dorothy Allen. Van Nostrand-Reinhold.

The Publish-It-Yourself Handbook: Literary Tradition & How-To, edited by Bill Henderson. Pushcart Book Press, Box 845, Yonkers, N.Y. 10701.

Reporting Today: The Newswriter's Handbook. Stein Cornerstone Library, 1230 Ave. of the Americas, New York, N.Y. 10020.

"Self Publishing: The Do-It-Yourself Way to Success," *Writer's Digest,* Aug. 1978.

The Self-Publishing Writer: A Quarterly Journal for Writers by Joanna Gregg, P.O. Box 24, San Francisco, Cal. 94101.

Small Press Record of Books. Dustbooks, 5218 Scottwood Rd., Paradise, Cal. 95969.

The Small Publisher's Book. COSMEP, Box 703, San Francisco, Cal. 94101. Free to members of COSMEP.

Words into Type by Marjorie Skllin and Robert Gay. Appleton Century-Crofts.

TEEN-AGERS

The Independent Teen-ager: 350 Jobs for High School Students by David M. Rubin. Collier Books.

Teen-Age Job by Ruth Lembeck. David McKay Co.

TIME MANAGEMENT

Getting Things Done by Edwin C. Bliss. Bantam.

VOLUNTEERING

Women and Volunteering by Herta Loeser, The Career and Volunteer Advisory Service, 14 Beacon St., Boston, Mass. 02108.

See also Carol Feit Lane's Career Internship Program under APPRENTICE-SHIPS AND INTERNSHIPS and Project Re-entry under "LATE" STARTS.

WRITING, EDITING, COPYRIGHTING, AND GETTING PUBLISHED

American Newspaper Women's Club, Inc., 1607 22 St. NW, Washington, D.C. 20008.

Dial-A-Writer, American Society of Journalists and Authors, 123 W. 43 St., New York, N.Y. 10026. (212) 586–7136.

Getting Started . . . in Journalism: A Mini-Course by Herscel O. Engebretson and Jack Gillespie. Educational Impact, P.O. Box 355, Blackwood, N.J. 08012.

The Complete Guide to Editorial Freelancing by Carol L. O'Neill and Avima Ruder. Dodd, Mead, & Co.

*A Complete Guide to Writing and Selling Non-Fiction by Hayes B. Jacobs. Writer's Digest, 9933 Alliance Rd., Cincinnati, Ohio 45242.

A Copyright Guide by Harriet F. Pilpel and Morton Goldberg. Bowker. 4th ed.

The Craft of Interviewing by John Brady. Writer's Digest, 9933 Alliance Rd., Cincinnati, Ohio 45242.

The Elements of Style by William Strunk, Jr., with E. B. White. Macmillan.

Employee Publications by William C. Halley. Chilton Book Co.

*How to Get Happily Published: A Complete and Candid Guide by Judith Appelbaum and Nancy Evans. Harper & Row.

How to Write a Book about Your Specialty by Thomas F. Doyle, Jr. Creative Book Co., P.O. Box 214998, Sacramento, Cal. 95821.

How to Write Non-Fiction That Sells by F. A. Rockwell. Henry Regnery Co.

Jacques Barzun on Writing, Editing and Publishing by Jacques Barzun. The University of Chicago Press.

Literary Market Place. Bowker.

A Manual of Copyright Practice by Margaret Nicholson. Oxford University Press, 2nd ed.

Available at your library.

1000 Tested Money-Making Markets for Writers by Walter G. Oleksy. Barnes & Noble.

Opportunities in Publishing Careers by John Tebbel. Vocational Guidance Manuals, Inc., 620 S. Fifth St., Louisville, Ky. 40202.

Reporting for the Print Media: A Workbook by Fred Fedler. Harcourt Brace Jovanovich.

Reporting Today: The Newswriter's Handbook by M. L. Stein. Cornerstone Library, Inc., 630 Fifth Ave., N.Y. 10020.

The Word Guild, 119 Mt. Auburn St., Cambridge, Mass. 02138.
Will help you find a collaborator.

Words into Type by Marjorie Skillin and Robert Gay. Prentice-Hall.

Writing and Selling a Nonfiction Book. The Writer, 8 Arlington St., Boston, Mass. 02116.

Writing Book Reviews by John E. Dewry. The Writer, 8 Arlington St., Boston, Mass. 02116.

Writing, Illustrating and Editing Children's Books by Jean Colby. Hastings House, 1967.

Writing the Modern Magazine Article by Max Gunther. The Writer, 8 Arlington St., Boston, Mass. 02116.

Writing without Teachers by Peter Elbow. Oxford University Press.

ABOUT THE AUTHORS

Barbara Sher, a therapist and career-counselor with a private practice in New York City, is the founder of Women's Success Teams. She has been a lecturer at New York University and the New School for Social Research, a time-management consultant and problem-solving consultant to Mt. Sinai Medical School, the New York City Board of Education, and major corporations, and is President of Group Laboratories.

Annie Gottlieb's journalism has appeared in *The New York Times Book Review, Village Voice, Quest, Viva, Mademoiselle, Ms.*, and elsewhere. She is co-author of a novel, *The Carpathian Caper* (with Jacques Sandulescu), and lives in New York City.

Photography Is...

Photography Is...

Wyatt Brummitt

AMPHOTO
American Photographic Book Publishing Co., Inc.
Garden City, New York

The author and the publishers wish to express their thanks to Thomas H. Miller, John Fish, and Charles Evans, all of Kodak, for their expert and unstinted cooperation.

Library of Congress Catalog Card No. 73-82106
ISBN 0-8174-0559-3

Manufactured in the United States of America

Contents

...The General Idea

Back in the 1870's George Eastman made some photographs. He used a big, clumsy camera perched on a cranky, unreliable tripod. His fragile glass plates had to be emulsion-coated by hand (in the dark, of course) and rushed, still wet, into the waiting camera. Then, with the exposure made, the plates had to be rushed back into the dark for immediate processing. It was a messy, tedious, frustrating, uncertain, temper-rousing, clothes-ruining process. And George hated it.

But he liked photographs. And he had a hunch that if the whole process could somehow be simplified, at least for the user, photography might just possibly become very important, not only to those who used it but to those who provided photographic goods and services.

He played his hunch. And by 1890, after an incredible expenditure of hard work, he evolved what he called his system of photography, for which he created the deathless slogan *You press the button—we do the rest*. The phrase captivated the whole world, partly because it was catchy but mostly because it was true. And modern photography was born.

Since then, photography has grown and evolved beyond anything George Eastman dared to dream. It has also become frightfully scientific, complex, standardized, specialized, and infinitely adaptable. Yet to many millions of snapshooters photography still appears to be ridiculously simple. And the photographic industry cheerfully (and logically) perpetuates the illusion.

Yet, behind all of today's superb, smoothly functioning equipment, the fine, fast films, magnificent color media, and swift, sure processing, there is a great and fascinating world of complexities, technicalities, and ingenuities. Some of them we should know about.

Photography Is... seeks to illumine a little of the background and to render its readers a little less innocent, photographically speaking. It holds to the notion that there is somewhat more to picture making than an agile trigger

7

finger, and that most of us would like to produce better photographs than the merely adequate, and usually dull, results of utterly innocent snapshooting.

Photography Is . . . emphasizes photographic *ends* over photographic *means*. Its objective is to help the reader attain better pictures, more eloquent pictures, more individual and more useful pictures.

Photography in color is, of course, immensely popular; it's bound to be. So, more or less as might be expected, there's a bit of back-lashing going on. Some photo-sophisticates are re-discovering black-and-white photography, and in the process they are also discovering that monochrome has unique satisfactions, both in its results (or *ends)* and in the degree of personal control it affords. So, despite the popularity of color, *Photography Is* . . . doesn't try to pretend that black-and-white photography is either passé or played out.

Some of the technical material, with the supporting graphics, is reproduced here with the kind consent of the Eastman Kodak Company, which has been and continues to be the fountainhead of so much photo-technical data. To Kodak and its cooperative people, my thanks.

Herb Archer, photographer, produced scores of the black-and-white photographs used herein, under pressure of both time and Rochester's notorious weather. He rates, and gets, my sincere thanks. And thanks be for and to Pauline Hansen, my former assistant at Kodak, who has continued to assist, cheerfully, loyally, and delightfully.

WYATT BRUMMITT

1
You Have
A Camera

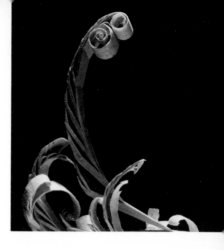

You have a camera, of course. But, why? For picture making, obviously. Okay, then, what *is* a picture?

Well, four thousand years ago cavemen scratched pictures on the walls of their caves. Somewhat later, Michelangelo painted magnificently on the ceiling of the Sistine Chapel. In our own era, D. W. Griffith lined up a million or two snapshots to make a movie drama called *Intolerance*. And last Saturday Johnny Whoozis made a picture of his dog, Spot.

Fig. 1-1.... why Spot is so special.

In each case, the pictures told something. The cavemen told of the animals they had seen or hunted; Michelangelo told us something of his religion; Griffith tried to tell us of humanity's strange and ancient inhumanity; and Johnny wanted to tell us why Spot was so special.

The word for all this is *communication.* An artist or a photographer, if he is successful, communicates. He sends an idea and, depending on his skill, that idea reaches the viewer. So the camera is, therefore, a means of communication.

But it does more than that. It conveys *two* messages—the primary, obvious one and, whether he likes it or not, an impression of the sender or communicator. From the picture he made, we get a pretty good idea of the kind of person he is; whether he enjoys what he sees or finds everything dull; whether he cares about what he depicts or merely feels that he should prove he *was* somewhere or saw something. And, finally, it tells us whether or not the photographer has sense enough to picture his subject so that it makes sense, so that we understand it.

It follows, then, that the user of a camera is much more important than the camera itself. This means you. You are the most important part of any camera you may ever own. Your eyes, your imagination, your sensitivity, and your skill are the essentials. Back up those fundamentals with some understanding of the physics, the optics, the chemistry, and the techniques of photography, and your ability to communicate is increased, your effectiveness sharpened.

So, photography is (1) a means of communication and (2) a reflection of your own personality. It is a means of expression. Your photographs express you, characterize you, as surely as does your handwriting, the way you talk, or the kind of friends you choose.

As a matter of fact, when we make photographs we are being creative. That's a much abused word, but it is still an important one. For creativity is one of mankind's greatest gifts, one of our greatest satisfactions. We are at our best, we are enjoying life most, when we are making, building, creating something—a piece of cabinet work, some weaving, a cake, music, a nicely adjusted carburetor, or a picture.

And the better the cabinetry or the cake or the music or the picture, the more certainly you will have made use of the disciplines of the art, whatever it may be. It is only when the disciplines become second nature to you that you can ad-lib effectively; before then, far-outness will probably look silly.

One thing more. Every beginner in photography, as in any other kind of creativity, feels that he would achieve masterpieces if only he had fancier equipment—a better camera, another set of filters, specialized and faster film, a deluxe darkroom, and so on. All of this is good. Equip yourself as well as you can, within reason. But gadgets do not make pictures. You do.

Keep your eye on ends, not means. I have known many photographers, the best of whom bothered least about collecting carloads of expensive, complicated, and sophisticated equipment. And the better they were, the surer they were that their best reliance was themselves.

SOMEWHAT LIKE AN EYE...

In some ways a camera is a remarkably good imitation of a human eye.

In an adjacent diagram are drawings of a camera and an eye, both greatly simplified. Both the camera and the eye are enclosed chambers, with a lens in the front and a light-sensitive area on the back wall. In both, the function of the lens is identical; it gathers rays of light from the viewed scene and transmits them, in an expanding cone, back to the light-sensitive area. In the eye, the image formed by the rays of light is televised by a very complex system of nerve reactions to the brain, which, being tuned in, says, "Oh yes, I see."

In a camera the rays of light transmitted by the lens fall on the surface of the light-sensitive film, which reacts chemically so that the image can subsequently be made permanent and usable.

Both the camera and the eye have a device, in or at the lens, that controls the volume of light transmitted. In an eye it is called the iris; in a camera it is a mechanism called the iris diaphragm. Both the eye and the camera are happiest with a moderate volume of light; too much is blinding and too little provides inadequate information.

There are other parallels and similarities between eyes and cameras—matters of focus and adaptation to varying intensities of light—but there is a *difference* between them that is much more important than all the resemblances. And that difference is the fact that a camera, no matter how shiny and complicated and expensive, is dumb, dumb as a chunk of mud.

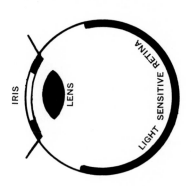

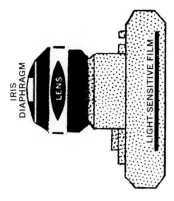

Fig. 1-2a, b. Your eye and a camera are much alike, physically or mechanically. But in use they are different. The camera takes in whatever scene it is pointed at, and unless forcibly restrained, carefully records everything in sight. Your eye, however, disregards most of a scene as it searches for some meaningful detail—a face, a sign, a flower, or whatever. In short, the camera records—the eye scans.

Fig. 1-3. The Wave. One minute they were just rough shavings, sliced with a spoke-shave, on the workshop floor. Minutes later, piled up and dramatically lighted, they became the makings of a picture. Moral: There are picture potentials in almost anything, if you look for them.

A camera cannot refuse to have anything to do with a scene that is inane or pointless. It cannot insist on another vantage point that might make a scene more meaningful. It cannot even suggest the simplest considerations of composition. It can do only what you ask it to do; the responsibility for what the poor old camera "sees" is strictly up to you.

Being dumb, the camera has no imagination. It cannot use the visual shorthand that we all use, all the time. For example, someone approaches us on the walk. In a single glance we recognize something about him that we identify—his grin, his voice, the way he walks, that beat-up old jacket, or whatever—and we say "Hi, Joe."

Your camera cannot do that. To it, Joe is a complete stranger. So the camera gives Joe the full treatment, laboriously recording every visible detail from head to toe. And it will go through exactly this same detailed operation the next time it "sees" him.

When, overnight, you have landed in a strange town, you can sense a little of what cameras have to face, all the time. You see details of buildings, cars, busses, people, churches, schools, and so on—details you seldom or never note in your own home town. At home, you take everything for granted. You look at specific details only when there is some immediate reason for doing so.

It follows, then, that one of the best approaches to photography is to learn to see. Exercise your sense of sight. *Look* at things. Acquire the habit of scanning a scene, appraising and appreciating its qualities. For, unless you savor what you see, unless you get a bounce out of the unadvertised beauties, the ironies, the design of the visible world, you cannot expect your camera to give you any but commonplace, ordinary pictures. If you enjoy *seeing,* you may reasonably expect to make pictures others will enjoy, too.

2
A Confusion of Cameras

The selection of a camera was once a simple matter. If you had a few dollars and were interested primarily in sunny Sunday-afternoon snapshots, and not much more, you bought a box camera, probably one of the classic Brownie cameras. The Brownies operated on the principle of the happy medium. They had an average shutter speed of about 1/40 sec., an average lens speed rated at about $f/11$, and were fixed-focus to give you reasonably sharp pictures of everything beyond six feet. Thus, you were all set for average shots of average subjects in average light.

If you had a few more dollars, you acquired a folding roll-film camera. Many of these cameras had multi-speed shutters, faster lenses with variable settings, and provision for selective focus. They came in assorted sizes and colors, and used conventional paper-backed roll film. Many of them were capable of excellent results.

There is probably an old camera of some sort somewhere around your place. Get it out, and play with it. If it is of a size for which black-and-white film is still available, make some pictures with it. The very shortcomings and limitations you encounter will help you decide on the kind of camera you want or need now.

The modern explosion in cameras and camera technology was detonated by the development of modern film. In other words, if film had not been greatly improved and if color had not come along, we might very well still be using cameras much like those of 1935 and before. But film *has* improved, and color is no longer a novelty. So, today, we need cameras capable of more accurate exposure control, greater lens speed, and higher mechanical precision.

If you have recently visited a large photo supply shop or leafed through one of the big photographic magazines, you will have been amazed and bewildered by the variety of cameras offered, by the complexity and ingenuity of their engineering, by the many devices designed to give you precise control of all the factors governing exposure and picture making, and by prices that range all the way from moderate to hair-raising.

15

Fig. 2-1. Kodak's famous Brownie box camera of 1900. It was extremely simple (embossed lines on the top of the camera indicated the view embraced, thereby eliminating a viewfinder) and sold for $1. Subsequent versions of the Brownie showed a few refinements, cost very little more, and served to introduce millions to the joys of snapshot photography.

Fig. 2-2. The first camera George Eastman produced was this "Detective Camera." For 1886 it was compact, almost miniature; by today's standards it was big and clumsy. Incidentally, it did not succeed (photo, courtesy Smithsonian Institution, History of Photography Collection).

Fig. 2-3. Along about 1914 this Autographic Kodak Special Camera was a real aristocrat among folding cameras. The Autographic feature permitted the user to inscribe pertinent data on the back of the film at the time of exposure.

Because of the proliferation of cameras and the constant and rapid changes in camera technology, it is futile to describe here any but basic classes of cameras, and to do it in terms of the size of film they use. Let's begin at the large end of the scale.

SHEET-FILM AND FILM-PACK CAMERAS

Sheet film is generally available in a few standard sizes—from $2\frac{1}{4}'' \times 3\frac{1}{4}''$ up to $5'' \times 7''$ and $8'' \times 10''$—but in a broad variety of types or emulsions, both monochrome and color. Conventional film packs are made in only two or three sizes, black-and-white only.

Traditionally, sheet-film cameras are called *view cameras,* because they are close kin to the bulky old boxes once used by earnest photographers who wrestled any weight and endured any hardship to capture the views, the scenics, and the landscapes that were once photographic staples. Today, such cameras are much less bulky. They are sold without lens or shutter, on the assumption that you will provide that which is best for the kind of work you want to do. (See p. 47, A Lens for Your Camera.)

Fig. 2-4. While modern view cameras are very precise chrome-and-black-leather creations, I still enjoy my old, beat-up Korona View Camera. With an $f/7.7$ lens and a more-or-less exact shutter, it is still capable of many of the odd jobs that come along, an ever-present help in time of trouble.

View cameras generally provide direct focus and view finding on a groundglass screen in the camera's film plane. Many of them offer the luxuries of rising-falling lens mounts and swing backs so that you can correct or distort perspective as you please. Some of them have an extra-long bellows extension so that you can work at very close range for frame-filling shots of small objects.

Your lens may have its own integrated mechanical shutter, or you may find yourself resorting to the ancient squeeze-bulb system or even the primitive method of controlling exposure with the lens cap.

View cameras are not hand cameras; they assume the use of a tripod or some such steady support. You'll find a view camera almost indispensable for studio work, a means of doing many a job that otherwise would require endless contriving and making-do. Because the film is in sheets, which you load in individual or twin film holders (septums), you can make one or two trial shots and develop them at once. With a big image on a generous piece of film, your contact prints are large enough for many uses and your enlargements come up easily, with minimum grain and strain. If you need to retouch or otherwise doctor a film, it is relatively easy on a larger negative.

Sheet film is heavier and thicker than roll film, hence easier to handle. Manufacturers usually cut notches on the upper right edge of sheet film so that, in the dark, you know when the film is emulsion side up and, according to the code, what kind of film it is.

ROLL-FILM CAMERAS

Roll film is an arbitrary term for film that is supplied in spooled rolls and used directly in a camera, without benefit of magazines, cassettes, or cartridges. Generally, it has an opaque paper backing. It is to be had in a variety of sizes—upward from 1½ inches or thereabouts—and long enough for a dozen or sixteen exposures. It is produced in a full variety of monochrome and full-color emulsions.

A few of today's roll-film cameras are so simple that they resemble the cameras of a generation or two ago. But most of them are very modern and sophisticated, sleek, shiny, and precise. They incorporate all manner of optical and electronic devices to measure and control exposure, plus superb lenses, accurate (sometimes electronic) shutters, and very impressive price tags.

Within the general category of roll-film cameras there are two major divisions: *conventional viewfinders* and *reflex finders*. By conventional I mean merely that the finder is a little optical system, quite apart from the camera's own optics, which gives you a small but reasonably accurate version of what the camera lens can be expected to "see." It may or may not be provided with a range- or focusfinder, plus a provision for the correction of parallax. (See p. 31, Parallax.)

Reflex finders, on the other hand, give you a full-size (*i.e.,* the size of the film format) image of the to-be-pictured scene via either the camera's own lens (this is a single-lens reflex or SLR) or a coupled twin lens (obviously, a twin-lens reflex). When you focus on your subject through a reflex finder you thereby focus the taking lens, or the camera itself. Both types of reflex cameras can be fitted with special wide-angle and long-focus lenses; both have, year after year, been improved and refined; and both can be had at a variety of prices, from un-cheap to very costly.

Fig. 2-5. One of the classic roll-film cameras, the Kodak Medalist. It combined the precision, the fast lens, and the wide range of shutter speeds of a good miniature camera with the larger format of 120 ($2\frac{1}{4}$-inch) film. It incorporated a rangefinder but no light-metering device.

Fig. 2-6. A good modern twin-lens reflex camera, the Mamiya C220. Its lenses are rated at $f/2.8$, its shutter speeds range from "bulb" to 1/500, and it has sufficient bellows extension to permit close-ups at $1\frac{1}{2}$ feet. It accommodates either 120 or 220 film for negatives $2\frac{1}{4}$ inches square. The standard 80mm lens-pair can be replaced by any of eight other short- and long-focal length lens-pairs, from 55mm to 250mm.

35MM CAMERAS

The classic miniature camera, the 35mm, is a direct descendant of the professional motion-picture camera. Right from the start professional movies have been made on raw (unbacked) 35mm film (about 1⅜ inches wide). The first 35mm still camera, in fact, was practically extemporized as a means of testing new batches of 35mm film. Later, it became the tool and the symbol of so-called "candid photography." With the coming of better, finer grain film and, especially, color film, the 35mm camera came into its own as a popular amateur camera. A whole new industry developed to supply cameras, accessory lenses, projectors, screens, and the automated processing that color film, particularly, required. The 35mm film, edge-perforated and without paper backing, is usually supplied in metal cassettes or magazines that are, themselves, loaded into the cameras. After exposure, the whole length of the film, normally 20 or 36 exposures, is rewound into the cassette for subsequent processing.

The old, original Leica camera was the honored ancestor of all 35mm's. It was simply a small, well-made camera equipped with a relatively fast lens and an accurate shutter. Viewing was accomplished by means of a secondary, miniature optical system.

Today, such simplicity is rare. Instead, you will find complex little mechanisms incorporating all sorts of light-measuring devices and interlocked controls for lens aperture and shutter speeds. Even the time-honored spring-loaded shutter systems are being challenged by electric (electronic, actually) shutters. In fact, you need almost daily bulletins to keep abreast of progress in 35mm technology.

The standard image size of the 35mm camera is 24×36mm (about $1'' \times 1⅜''$). Obviously, prints of that size are of little use, save for test prints of one sort or another. Enlargement is normal procedure. But 35mm positives, especially color, are naturals for projection, as slides, onto a screen for group viewing.

Among 35mm cameras we have, again, conventional and reflex viewing systems. Conventional viewing, to repeat, refers to a separate but integrated optical system that gives you a reduced image of what's out in front, plus coupled range finding in many cases. The single-lens reflex (SLR) camera utilizes the camera's own lens, bouncing the image received up to a viewing screen. There are various schemes by which this contortion is performed but, by today's technical standards, they are all perfectly practical.

Almost all of the better 35mm cameras now incorporate some sort of light-sensing or measuring system. In some, the sensing element is behind the lens; in others it is back at or near the focal plane; and in a few others it is out front on the face of the camera.

Fig. 2-7. A Single-Lens Reflex 35mm camera (Kodak Retina Reflex III) with light-metering unit on the face of the camera.

Because enlargement—either in printing or in projection on a screen—is a basic assumption in 35mm photography, precision in the manufacture and use of a 35mm camera is necessary. Errors of any kind get enlarged, right along with the image—and that's too bad. In selecting a 35mm camera be guided by the reputation of its maker, by the integrity of the dealer, and, if at all possible, by a first-hand test.

One of the pleasures of 35mm photography is the very wide variety of top quality accessories offered you. Within recent years many magnificent special-purpose lenses have been created. Hence, be sure that the camera you choose is one to which special lenses can be fitted without difficulty.

Fig. 2-8. Special-purpose lenses are available to extend the usefulness of most 35mm SLR cameras. Here's a modest quartet of long- and short-focus lenses available for the Kodak Retina Reflex III Camera.

There are sundry variations on the standard 24×36mm format of the 35mm cameras. Some give you half frame, 24×18mm, and others a square image, 24×24mm. Another variation is the 28×28mm format of Kodak's Instamatic cameras.

A NEW CONCEPT

The Instamatic Camera was created and evolved by Eastman Kodak as a full and final escape from the old and sometimes fumbly business of loading a film into a camera. The goal was a camera that could be loaded simply by inserting a film magazine—without subsequent threading of the film onto a take-up spool or, later, cranking the film back into its little round case.

The trick was solved by enclosing both the film supply and the take-up spool inside the same magazine. One merely dropped a film magazine into the opened camera (couldn't miss because it fitted in one perfectly obvious way), closed the cover, and started making pictures. And then, when the exposures were all made, it was just as simple to open the camera, lift out the magazine, and hurry it off to the processing lab. You never once saw the film.

But this ingenuity was only part of the system. For the Instamatic cameras, Kodak created a bevy of films—monochrome and both color print and color transparency films. Furthermore, subtle mechanical "codes" were built into the cassettes for each type of film so that the camera would be kept informed, so to speak, as to the nature of the loaded film. Thus, exposures were automatically modified to meet the existing needs.

Since the inception of the Kodak Instamatic cameras in 1963, the system has been refined and expanded. But the objective has never varied—sure and simple picture-making by everyone, always.

Fig. 2-9. A standard Kodak Instamatic Camera, with Magicube flash.

Color slides produced with Instamatic cameras are the standard $2'' \times 2''$ size. And there are several sizes of color enlargements any Kodak dealer is prepared to order for you.

Incidentally, the Instamatic program and others that followed meant drastic changes in the various Kodak and other processing stations, all over the world. Somehow, they survived.

The simplest and least expensive of the Instamatic cameras closely approximates the basic philosophy of the old Kodak Brownie cameras, in addition to capabilities of which the Brownies never dreamed. And the more complex and expensive models are first-rate miniature cameras.

The Instamatic concept has been licensed to other manufacturers, so that there are non-Kodak as well as Kodak cameras embodying the essential idea. All of them, of course, use the same little plastic, pre-threaded film cartridges.

Instamatic cameras use especially perforated 35mm-wide film and afford an image area 28mm square. This squareness can be a small problem, because there is no question that a succession of square pictures, as in a projected travelog, tends to become monotonous. Expert Instamatic users, therefore, make a conscious effort to seek and to use strong compositional factors—forceful lines or implied movement—to minimize the monotony of the format. Or, they resort to variously proportioned masks which, when fitted over the image area of the film, achieve an arbitrary, ex post facto kind of composition.

INSTANT, AUTOMATIC COMPETITION

Inevitably, other simplified, more-or-less automatic film-using systems appeared. Several concerns, especially in Europe, concentrated on the *Rapide* system, which utilized the familiar 35mm film cassettes but eliminated much of the old film handling. Other ingenious systems are bound to come along. So far, however, none of these remarkably clever devices has managed to come up with anything half as exciting as basic photography, in which you match your eye, your imagination, and your skill against the ambient light and the limitations of a chunk of machinery.

SUB-MINIATURE CAMERAS

These are the tiny cameras that, theoretically, are the special joys of international spies and other snoopy types. But that theory is full of holes....

Very small, very inconspicuous cameras have always had a special fascination for manufacturers and for some photographers. Even before he produced the first Kodak camera, George Eastman came up with something he called the Detective Camera (it was, by the way, a magnificent flop), and other of his contemporaries produced cameras so small that they could be hidden in the head of a cane, in a pocket watch, or even in the crown of a Derby hat.

But that kind of juvenility has almost disappeared. For truly serious and practical photography can be—and is being—done on tiny areas of today's vastly better, finer-grained, high-acutance films. The entire, and flourishing, home-movie industry is predicated on the fact that 16mm or 8mm film is big enough for excellent work. In the still-camera field, some Minolta and Rollei camera models permit serious picture-making with film images 14×20mm in area; the little Minox has done very well on the basis of an 8×14mm image area.

Kodak's Pocket Instamatic cameras gave a tremendous boost to sub-miniature photography. The general idea, of course, was an extension of the Instamatic camera idea, with all the ease of operation and certainty of the original Instamatics. There had been so-called "pocket" cameras for many, many years, but this one really lived up to its name and its billing. Moreover, the Pocket Instamatic camera does very well indeed, for the lenses are good, the controls quite specific, and the built-in features remarkably trouble-free.

The Pocket Instamatic camera, like its larger brother, uses monochrome or color film in very small, pre-threaded cassettes. The image area on the film is 13×17mm, which, obviously, gets away from the squareness of the larger Instamatics. The simplest, lowest priced of the Pocket Instamatic cameras operates at a fixed aperture and its mechanical shutter has two speeds, 1/100 sec. for daylight and 1/40 sec. for flash. The other members of the PIC line have electronic shutters and, as the prices go up, increasing sophistication in lenses and exposure control. All of the Pocket Instamatic cameras offer picture making on an improved version of Kodak's famous Verichrome Pan film plus three kinds of color: Kodacolor II for color prints and Kodak Ektachrome-X and Kodachrome-X for color transparencies.

Transparencies produced with these little cameras are returned from processing in 30×30mm slide mounts ready for use in the handsome Kodak Pocket Carousel Projector, which has slide trays that hold 120 slides. So projected, the images are bright, clear, and large enough for family enjoyment; but when the little slides are projected in a standard Carousel Projector (they have to be fitted into snap-in $2'' \times 2''$ adapters), the image is conspicuously small.

It is entirely possible that the miniaturization process will continue. But it poses a problem for the serious amateur. For, the smaller the film and the image, the greater becomes our dependence upon automatic processing and on a raft of devices and automations that de-personalize the whole business.

PICTURES-IN-A-MINUTE CAMERAS

The integral processing cameras produced under the Polaroid name are extremely ingenious; for some purposes they are also very useful. Studios use them to check lighting set-ups or models or sets; advertising art directors use them to prove or disprove the feasibility of a visual brainstorm; travelers find them excellent means of note-making or, sometimes, of winning the good will and interest of otherwise standoffish subjects; party hosts find that instant pictures make memorable souvenirs, and so on.

But for the student of photography, the instant-picture camera presents a problem or two. For one thing, it involves no usable negative. So, extra prints or enlargements have to be made by round-about means. For another, the sheer magic of the process conceals the techniques that any *bona fide* photographer must know and understand, whether his ultimate work is in the field, studio, or lab.

Polaroid film is made in both color and monochrome types. The cameras vary widely in cost, according to the refinement of their optical equipment and exposure controls.

Dr. Edwin H. Land, presiding genius of the Polaroid-Land operation, is a daring innovator. As this is written he has unveiled the prototype of a whole new line of even faster picture producers which, we are assured, approach the ultimate in personal photography. And Land is not alone; Kodak and others are expected to bring out still more remarkable, more sensational picture-in-a-minute cameras.

This is all very fine...for button pushers.

OKAY, WHICH CAMERA?

There is no one, single, "best" camera. But there are cameras that better meet your particular needs and interests than others. So, the selection depends upon what you expect and demand—and can pay for.

If you want to have a hand in every aspect of the picture-making process, you'll pass up the highly automated miniatures.

If you travel a lot, you'll prefer a compact, sturdily engineered outfit. Some travelers we know carry two identical cameras, just in case one breaks.

If you need to picture distant or inaccessible objects, your camera must be capable of swift and easy acceptance of special long-focus lenses.

If you're a sports fan, your camera should be capable of high shutter speeds.

And so on.

You probably have a camera of some sort right now. How far can you make it go in encompassing the work you need or want to do? Chances are, it will go pretty far. Okay, keep ahead of it.

3
Good and Bad Camera Habits

Good habits, photographically speaking, are based on ordinary common sense backed by a few scientific considerations. For the most part, photographs begin as intensely personal things—as ideas, as something you want to share or show or shout about. But to achieve your purpose, you must apply procedures established by experience and science.

This is another way of saying that photography *as an art* offers endless scope for inspiration, daring, and originality. It is when the *science* of photography is called on to realize personal, volatile aspirations that it becomes necessary to behave, to observe the lesson that all the scientists, the artists, the technicians, and the innovators of the last century and a half have learned, sometimes the hard way.

We can be thankful to all those people; what they learned can save us a lot of frustrations and headaches. This chapter deals with some of the simpler, more obvious rules of the road; others may emerge as we go along.

Just as a good driver knows his car, knows the feel of it, knows what it can and cannot be expected to do, the mature photographer knows his camera. He knows its limitations, and exults in his success within those limits. He operates from the strength of knowledge, not from the weakness of wishful thinking.

One of the best ways to begin this knowledge, this understanding, is with some quiet study of your unloaded camera. Put it through its paces, get the feel of its various controls. If your camera is so made that the back can be removed, flatten a piece of good tracing paper in the film plane and in a darkened room, with a candle or a bare electric light as your subject, watch what happens as you run the gamut of exposures. Then with the shutter wide open, as for a time exposure, watch the image on the paper as you rack the lens back and forth. I don't like to suggest anything drastic but, if you haven't misplaced the manual that came with the camera, read it. Can't do any harm.

27

CAMERA HOUSEKEEPING

The better you know your camera, the better care you will give it.

The first rule is: *don't tinker* with the mechanism. Any good camera is a precision instrument, a combination of applied optics and miniaturized engineering. If something goes wrong, it is unlikely to respond nicely to the application of rule one for unskilled technicians, *i.e.,* bang it. In normal use, a camera should go for a year or so between inspections and servicings, but don't expect it to go on forever. If or when something happens, get it to a competent service center right away. Have it cleaned, checked, and adjusted. *Never* attempt to lubricate any camera action, the shutter especially. That's inviting real trouble.

On the other hand, there are some aspects of camera care that are definitely your responsibility. Care of the lens is one of them.

Your camera's lens is valuable and vulnerable. It is precisely ground to an exact formula; in most cases it is a combination of several optical elements, some of which are cemented together with a resin. And you know what happens when heat and resin meet. The resin gets soft, loses strength, and because of its softness attracts dust. So, protect that lens of yours from heat and dirt.

One does not clean a good lens by breathing humidity thereon as a prelude to a brisk wiping with the nearest handkerchief or shirt tail. A small, soft, and very clean brush is your first reliance. If there remains any stubborn grime, some sort of solvent cleaner is needed. Do not use ordinary window-cleaning fluids; they leave a residual film of their own. Get a small bottle of lens cleaner from a reputable source and use lens tissue or a bit of perfectly clean, soft linen to carefully clean the exposed glass. Don't scrub. And *do not* use ordinary eyeglass-cleaning papers: they can erode the special coating so carefully applied to modern lenses.

Most of the grease found on dirty lenses comes from fingers, so establish a firm habit of never touching the lens surface, and don't let the kids play with it. Dirt and grit get into a camera all too easily anyway, especially when it is "safely" stowed away on a shelf or in a drawer. So, provide for the protection of your camera when it is not in use. If you have a lens cap, use it. And if you have a camera case, keep the inactive camera tightly encased in it. Go ahead, be finicky—it pays.

A camera case is almost a necessity. It's the best possible physical protection your camera can have, idle or at work. It absorbs casual bumps and shocks as nothing else can.

Dust can seep into the interior of a camera, where it is attracted inevitably to the smooth, faintly gelatinous surface of any film that may be in place. And dust on film means tiny, unerasable specks and spots. So give your camera an interior cleaning once in a while, using a soft camel's hair brush or a gentle air brush. While the camera's open, check the inside surface of the lens; it can get dusty, too.

One of the worst camera habits is to keep your camera in the glove compartment of a car, whether while at home or on the road. It's so convenient, so easy, and so dangerous. It gets really hot in there from sun heat and from motor heat—and heat, remember, is your camera's natural enemy. The ledge between the back of the rear seat and the rear window is just as bad. In a parked car on a sunny day, that ledge is a broiler.

Assuming the camera is in a stout, tight case, it should be safe underneath one of the front seats of your car or in a pouch strapped to the back of a seat. Determine where in your car the camera is coolest and safest, and form the habit of keeping it there.

Fig. 3-1 (left). Don't! It's so easy and convenient to stow a camera in your car's glove compartment.But—don't do it, because it gets much too hot in there. Fig. 3-2 (right). Do! Properly encased and slung over the back of a front seat, your camera is safe from excessive heat. It would be even safer, from prying eyes, under the seat.

Here are a few other good habits, mostly matters of common sense plus the advice of the camera's manufacturer. (To repeat, you might even break down and *read* that manual he so carefully prepared.)

1. Load film only in subdued light, never in full sunshine. Sheet film, of course, requires full darkness.

2. Have a definite place for the storage of your camera. Be sure that it is well away from heat or hot water pipes, and kept dry and not violently dirty.

3. When the camera is not in use, relax its mechanical tensions, if any. A spring-loaded shutter, for example, should be left uncocked.

4. If the kids in your place are hopelessly fascinated by your camera, fight them off. I gave my boy a simple camera for his very own, and the strategy worked.

5. A good camera deserves about the same kind of attention as a good watch. Most of us have our watches cleaned and checked once a year or so. A camera rates the same kind of care. The dealer who sold it to you can undoubtedly arrange for good, fast service by qualified experts. Consider the cost of that service as a kind of insurance; it pays dividends.

HABITS OF CAMERA USE

Most of the foregoing is defensive or preventive. Now let's consider some habits of camera use.

Maybe you haven't had your camera out for a week or so, but now you need to use it. Okay, do you know what kind of film it is loaded with? Um, you *think* so. But you can be sure if you have made a habit of sticking an identifying tab somewhere on the outside of the camera as you load it. Some people use the end of a film carton, stuck on with a bit of transparent tape; others use little pressure-sensitive labels with the film's name and ASA rating written thereon. The exact method you use doesn't matter, but you do need something of the sort. Otherwise, how can you calculate exposures?

Double exposure prevention is built into most modern cameras (often with an override control that permits double exposures if you want them), but if your camera is not so equipped, form the habit of winding the film on to the next exposure position after making a shot. When the habit becomes automatic, your worries are over.

Always carry enough film with you for a few more pictures than you expect to make. Opportunities sometimes develop that cannot be counted on to recur.

As you probably know, most professionals make a lot of exposures for every one that results in a profitable picture. By amateur standards, all those shots may be good, but one may be—for its intended use—much better than the others. It's the better shots that pay the rent.

Your camera kit should contain a filter or two, tailored to the kind of film you use and the nature of the picture-making project. (See Chapter 5.) Filters, by the way, should be as well cared for as lenses.

IT'S WHAT'S OUT FRONT THAT COUNTS

Sometimes, when you riffle through a batch of a stranger's prints, you get the impression that the camera user either had no viewfinder on his camera or, if there was one, he paid no attention to it. Horizon lines are at all sorts of crazy angles; trees, telephone poles, and street lamps combine to confuse or even to hide the real subjects; lighting is so ignored that obviously important subjects are relegated to deep, unrevealing shade, and so on.

Use that viewfinder. You may have to *learn* to use it, especially if it is an optical finder and you wear glasses. Experiment to make quite sure that the camera "sees" what you see—or think you see. An extra few seconds study of what your viewfinder shows you will pay off, and handsomely.

full second's exposure. There are cameras, by the way, so poorly designed that the shutter-tripping action is at right angles to the axis of the lens; thus camera shake, save at high shutter speeds, is almost built-in. The best exposure control is one which moves in the direction of, or against the firmest natural support for the whole camera.

A tripod is the final answer to camera shake. A flexible cable release is next best. In dire emergencies, good photographers have been known to hold their cameras tightly hugged to a lamppost or anything else reasonably firm.

It may be useful to determine for yourself whether or not you have any tendency to camera shake. Make a series of hand-held shots of some sharply defined object, something that has good clean lines in several directions. Vary the shutter speeds through 1/15, 1/30, 1/60, and 1/125 sec. Then, when you have the finished negatives, either examine them with a good magnifying glass or make a set of uniform enlargements and study them. It's a good bet that the higher the shutter speed the higher the acuity or sense of precise detail.

CONSIDER THE WEATHER

With decent regard for camera and film, there is no "season" for picture-making. The hazards of heat have already been mentioned, but cold can present difficulties, too. Shutter actions have been known to slow down over long periods of intense cold. But more insidious is what happens when you bring an ice-cold camera indoors; inevitably you have condensation, inside and out. So, allow time for the condensation to disappear, especially on the lens, before you resume picture-making. Common sense will guide you through most such matters—if you follow it.

ABOUT ACCESSORIES

Your camera's lens is undoubtedly more capable, more versatile than you suspected when you first began to use it. But it does have its limitations. There will come times, for example, when you want to picture something at very close range, a distance shorter than your camera is designed to handle. Fortunately, a variety of suppementary lenses is available; these supplementaries, fitted right over the camera lens, give you really sharp images at very close range. Each such lens supplement has a definite limit of usefulness; none can be used haphazardly.

Similarly, the capability of your camera to capture distant objects can be extended by lens attachments. These can extend the versatility of your camera considerably; but better results in both close-ups and distant shots can generally be attained by replacing the regular lens with specific short- or long-focal-length lenses. Today a good photo shop will offer you a great variety of these special-purpose lenses, at prices that are very reasonable—relatively speaking. For normal photography, there is little excuse for getting a whole battery of these beautiful big and little lenses. For a while, work within the limits of your camera as it stands, and then add other lenses or lens attachments as your needs become more and more specific.

Incidentally, astute enlargement of a negative made with the regular lens can often eliminate the need for a fine, fancy, and costly long-focus lens. The finished picture will look just exactly as good.

There are, as you may have discovered, far more fascinating accessories, attachments, gadgets, and whatnots than most of us can justify buying, much less paying for. So resist the temptation to get another accessory as the guarantee of that perfect picture you—and all of us—want to make. Dealers will love you if you weaken. But I have news for you; you simply can't catch up with all the shiny new gadgets from all the manufacturers, all over the world.

Finally, don't count on luck. The only sure thing about luck is that it will leave you in the lurch, just when you need it most.

4
Light and Lenses

Sometimes it almost seems that *light* doesn't matter any more. Lenses are so fast, so big, and so good. And films have become so sensitive that they get along with a very meager diet of light.

But the fact remains, however, that without light of some sort there can be no photography. No light, no picture.

Okay, we have to have light. But what *is* light?

Light is one of many types of energy, all of which travel radially, in waves, from their points of origin. For a very simple demonstration of wave action, drop a marble into any convenient pool of water and watch the resulting waves spread out in expanding, concentric circles. Sound is another form of wave energy, much faster than waves in water but sensationally slower than the wave action of radio impulses.

As it happens, radio waves travel at very high speed—the speed of light, which is 186,000 miles/sec. That's fast. It is also one of the great scientific constants. Astronomers measure distances in space in "light years"—the distance traveled by a ray of light in one year.

But the fact that light waves and radio waves travel at the same speed doesn't mean that they are alike. They differ, most importantly, in their wave length. Radio waves vary in length from several hundred yards down to a few inches. And visible light has relatively short wave length—from .00008 to .00004 cm.

SHORT WAVELENGTHS					1 CM. LONG WAVELENGTHS		
COSMIC RAYS	GAMMA RAYS	X-RAYS	ULTRA-VIOLET RAYS	INFRA RED OR HEAT RAYS	HERTZIAN WAVES		WAVES USED IN RADIO BROADCASTING
				VISIBLE LIGHT			

37

Here's a greatly simplified representation of the spectrum of radiant energy. Visible light occupies a very thin section or band in the spectrum but, thin as it is, it is all-important to photography. Within that band there are differences of wave length that signify differences in the kind or color of the light. And photography recognizes and uses those differences.

The fact that, to the left in the diagram, there are various and very much shorter forms of radiant energy is of no immediate concern to us—except that we should note that, in many forms of specialized photography, photographic film is the basic tool by which they are made evident, for study and analysis.

LIGHT IS...

There are five basic, and generally useful, facts about light.

1. Light travels in straight lines—an infinite number of straight lines radiating out from the point of origin.

2. Light can be deflected or reflected, as by a mirror. And the good old rule of Physics I that "the angle of reflection equals the angle of incidence" holds comfortingly true.

Fig. 4-1. High noon light, and lots of it, illuminates the wall of this old mission from almost directly overhead, creating an interplay of bright and shadowy areas. Handling light is the essence of photography.

3. Light can be bent (refracted) by a prism and sent off on a new path, a fact that is essential to the concept and design of lenses, rangefinders, binoculars, and so on.

4. Light can be absorbed. A piece of black felt absorbs most of the light falling on it, reflecting only a little; whereas a shiny white surface reflects most of the incident light, absorbing very little.

5. Light can be systematically filtered so that some of its component qualities are absorbed or blocked, without effect on the rest.

Photography makes constant use of these characteristics. It is concerned, just as our eyes are concerned, with light that has been partly absorbed and partly reflected from objects. The reflected light flies, straight and true, to the lens that refracts it. And, if you seek some special effect, you use a filter on the lens.

This is all, obviously, oversimplified. So, beginning with lenses, let's get down to some specifics.

We think, generally, of a lens as a complex bundle of glass shapes, encased in a metal barrel. We know a good lens is expensive but we also know that it is worth what it costs, because really fine photographs depend upon fine lenses. Photography, as we know it, simply couldn't exist without lenses.

That's all demonstrable, valid, and true. But it is not quite the whole truth.

PICTURES THROUGH A PINHOLE

You can make and use a camera that has no lens at all. Of course, you have to relax a bit in your demand for sharpness and fast shutter speed, but you *can* get pictures. You use, instead of a complex bundle of optical glass elements, nothing but a fine pinhole in a sheet of cardboard or very light metal.

The pinhole camera is the direct descendant of the old *camera obscura,* known to many early physicists and experimenters (including the fabulous Leonardo da Vinci). It was represented in various forms, the simplest of which was an enclosed chamber with a small hole in one wall. Light streaming through that hole formed an image (inverted) on the inside of the opposite wall, an image of goings on outside that amazed, fascinated, and sometimes scandalized the beholders.

Here's how the pinhole camera works. Waves of light broadcast, for instance, from a lighted candle enter the pinhole and, continuing on back in straight (unrefracted) lines, reach the light-sensitive film. An infinite number of rays from that candle strike the front of the camera, but only those landing squarely on the pinhole get through and reach the film. At the end of a longish exposure, a flap is dropped over the pinhole and the film removed and developed. You will not only have an image, but a pretty good one—maybe not critically sharp but otherwise clean and undistorted.

KODAK POCKET INSTAMATIC CAMERA LENSES

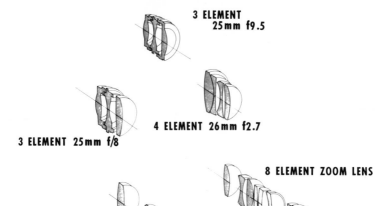

3 ELEMENT 25mm f9.5

4 ELEMENT 26mm f2.7

3 ELEMENT 25mm f/8

8 ELEMENT ZOOM LENS

POCKET CAROUSEL PROJECTION EKTAR LENSES

Figs. 4-2 and 4-3. There is absolutely nothing casual about a good lens. Each of its elements is carefully ground to conform with the painstakingly developed formula for that specific lens. The lenses diagrammed above were designed for the Kodak Pocket Instamatic Cameras and Projectors. Several popular 35mm cameras can be fitted with an even wider variety of special-purpose lenses, as below.

In order to shorten the exposure time, we enlarge the hole. Seems reasonable. But now we get an image that is much fuzzier than the first. Why? Because many, many more rays of light have zipped through the enlarged hole and, with no lens to guide them, have splashed themselves over a much larger, much less well-defined area of the film.

The pinhole camera is a charming photographic plaything. It even has its uses. Because the pinhole has no fixed focal length, you can make long- or short-focus shots ad lib, a fact that has been utilized to obtain soft, pictorial shots of otherwise difficult subjects—a tall building or a monument, for instance. Pinhole images have tremendous depth of field but lack sharpness. For real photography, in short, we need a lens.

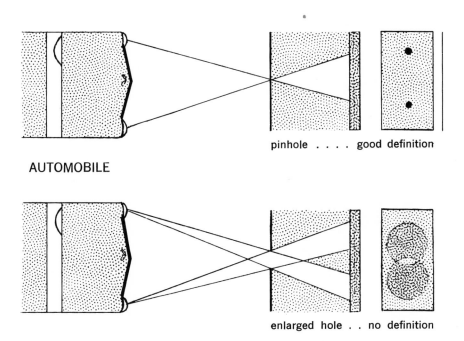

pinhole . . . . good definition

AUTOMOBILE

enlarged hole . . no definition

Figs. 4-4a & b (next page). Pin-hole picture 1 (top). The hole, made with the point of a fine needle through a thin aluminum sheet, was about 1/75 inch. The exposure was six seconds on Kodak Plus-X film in a 4″ x 5″ sheet-film view camera. Pin-hole picture 2 (bottom). For this, the pin-hole was enlarged to about 1/10 inch, with corresponding decrease in exposure time. Same film, same camera, and simultaneous development. Any larger hole would have produced unrecognizable blurs.

Fig. 4-4a (above). Fig. 4-4b (below).

The fact that light is bent or refracted as it passes from air to glass or glass to air is basic in lens design. An extreme, and simplified, closeup of refraction may help to clarify what happens. Here an enlarged light ray travels in air

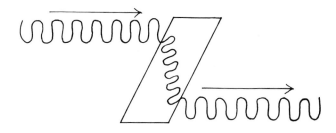

and encounters a slab of glass, set at an angle. Because glass is more dense than air, the light is slowed down or bent a little; it is bent, moreover, toward the side of the wave that first meets the glass. Similarly, on emerging from the glass the light tends to resume its original direction, being almost literally pulled that way by the braking action of the part of the wave that is still in the glass. This uneven pull is somewhat like what happens in a car with faulty brakes; when the brakes grab hold on one side before the other, the car swerves to the side first slowed down.

By changing the angles or slants of the glass surfaces, front and back, very specific changes in the course of the light can be achieved. Assuming that the glass is a prism (see diagram), the light takes two changes in direction, always toward the thicker part of the prism.

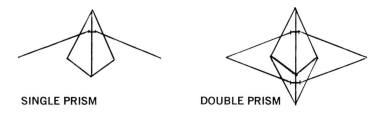

SINGLE PRISM   DOUBLE PRISM

Now, put another prism in place, base to base with the first. And look what happens. Along comes a second ray of light from the same point, entering the lower prism; obeying precisely the same physical rules, it is bent back upward so that it meets the one that came through the upper prism. They meet, as the song says, not really by chance. It is scientifically foretold.

Having gone this far, take the next step. Get a lens maker to produce for you, in a single piece of glass, a complete circle of prisms, all base to base. This combination of a practically infinite number of prisms, all ground to a scientific nicety, gives a vastly greater convergence of light rays from any one point. If there is film at the place where the rays all meet, we gain by the impact of far more light than was possible with the pinhole camera's tiny openings, which, theoretically, could accommodate only one ray from any one point. Obviously, therefore, much shorter exposures can be used. That's a big step ahead.

But the very fact that an accurately made lens bends light in a very definite, predetermined way introduces another problem—the problem of focus. As long as the subject being photographed is at a certain specific distance, and as long as the lens-to-film distance coincides exactly with the plane in which the lens reunites all those light rays, all is well. But when either of those distances is changed, there's trouble.

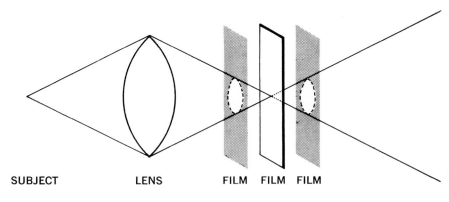

SUBJECT   LENS   FILM   FILM   FILM

Here's what happens when the lens-to-film distance is changed. All those light rays, remember, are converging in a cone-shaped bundle, the apex of which is at a precise distance from the center of the lens. And when the distance between lens and film is changed, the apex of the cone is either in front of or in back of the film plane. As a result, the light cone's impact on the film becomes a cross section of a cone—a circle. The name for this, in photography, is *circle of confusion,* and a better, more realistic description would be hard to find. For when rays from millions of points in a pictured scene are imaged on the film not as points but as little, overlapping circles, confusion is what you get.

Much the same situation arises when the lens-to-*subject* distance is changed while the lens-to-film distance remains unaltered. For the angle between the paths of a ray of light as it enters and exits from a lens is practically the same, no matter what the distance may be between the source of that ray and the lens. It may help to think of a lens as a sort of pivot or fulcrum on which the bent ray of light teeters. The closer the subject, the farther back is the point of convergence; and the farther the object, the nearer the converging point.

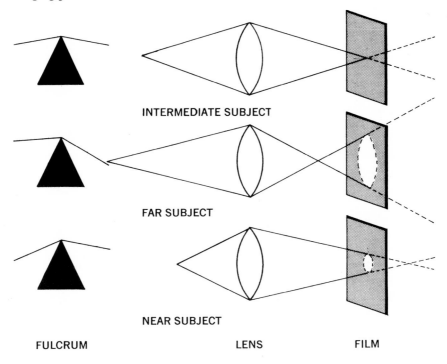

INTERMEDIATE SUBJECT

FAR SUBJECT

NEAR SUBJECT

FULCRUM   LENS   FILM

Obviously, then, if the film is placed at the converging point for rays from one subject distance, objects at greater or shorter distances will be imaged as circles of confusion rather than as points.

Fixed-focus cameras have small lenses and produce their best, or sharpest, results when used to picture objects about 15 feet away. In manufacture, the camera's lens-to-film distance is adjusted for picture-making at that distance. And points imaged on the film from other distances appear, as you rightfully suspect, as circles of confusion. But, because of the small lens, those circles are so tiny that the resulting unsharpness isn't enough to bother an uncritical snapshooter. There is, under these conditions, very little difference in the angles of light coming to the lens from points a dozen or a hundred feet from the camera.

With larger lenses, this fixed-focus setup is impossible. If a camera with a relatively large lens is focused for work at a 10-foot range, objects 50 feet away are way out of focus.

Therefore, a means has been devised to make the lens-to-film distance variable, so that light rays from any specific distance can be converged on the film as points rather than as circles of confusion. This is what you do when you focus a camera. You simply change the lens-to-film distance as your subject distance requires. For closeups you need maximum lens-to-film distance; for long shots, beyond a hundred or so feet, the critical distance from lens to film is much less. Your camera is fitted with some sort of mechanism to give you easy and accurate control of that critical distance.

A GOOD MODERN LENS IS A GEM

Lens design is a problem in physics and mathematics. It used to take teams of specialists months or even years to make all the laborious computations involved in the creation of a new lens. But today the work can be programmed for computers to produce the necessary answers in a matter of hours or days.

Lens *making* is more of an art. Traditionally, fine lenses were produced from silica (sand) glass by craftsmen who jealously guarded their formulas and procedures. The secrets of production were not revealed in patents but were passed on, within families or small groups from generation to generation. German lenses, up to about 1940, enjoyed a great reputation, which was built on secret—almost occult—family procedures. But, along in the late 1930's and early 1940's, Kodak and a few other research organizations came up with new kinds of glass made from various "rare earths"—compounds of tantalum, tungsten, and lanthanum, with little or no silica. These new lenses had very high refractive (light-bending) indices plus low dispersion (spreading of the individual colors of light). The art of lens making became a science.

Fig. 4-5. On the left, a simple, inexpensive lens; on the right, a costly, complex one.

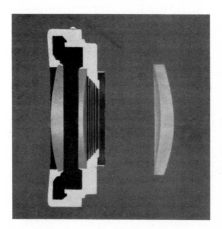

Today, the whole lens-making industry has been opened up. Fine lenses are being made not only in the United States, but in Japan, Germany, France, England, and even behind that Curtain.

Another factor in the production of today's good lenses emerged at about the same time as "rare earth" glasses. This was the discovery that a specific kind of chemical coating of air-glass surfaces of a lens tended to minimize flare and actually increase light-transmitting properties. Today coated lenses are general, but remember that coating does not miraculously transform a poor lens into a fine one; the lens itself must be good.

A good modern lens is a remarkable achievement to be cherished and used with full appreciation of its many qualities.

A LENS FOR YOUR CAMERA

The business of fitting a lens to a camera is not at all haphazard. It must be done with care; otherwise the result can be grotesque—as grotesque as a submarine diesel engine "fitted" to a Volkswagen.

Any lens has two major optical characteristics that the photographer must know before he buys or starts to use it: *focal length* and *f/number*.

Focal Length (F) is almost a self-defining phrase. It means, simply, the distance from the optical center of the lens to the plane (called the focal plane) where approaching parallel rays of light are brought to a point by the lens, so that a sharp image is formed.

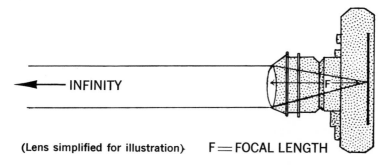

INFINITY

(Lens simplified for illustration) F = FOCAL LENGTH

Since all rays of light approaching a lens from a point at infinity are parallel, *focal length* is the distance of the image from the lens when the subject is at infinity. Even though focused on a closeup subject or even removed from the camera, the focal length of the lens never changes, for it is a result of the fundamental design to which the lens was ground. (So-called "zoom" lenses complicate the picture a bit, but a predetermined focal length is quite as important for them as for any other lens.)

The optical rule-of-thumb for fitting a lens to a camera is this: the focal length of the lens should be roughly equal to the diagonal of the camera's image area or frame. For example, the diagonal of a $2\frac{1}{4}'' \times 3\frac{1}{4}''$ (6×9cm) image area is about 4 inches. Hence you will find most $2\frac{1}{4}'' \times 3\frac{1}{4}''$ cameras fitted with lenses that approximate 4 inches. Some cameras, especially view cameras, are sold without lenses; you provide the lens yourself. The rule of the diagonal will help simplify your lens selection.

PERSPECTIVE

Perspective is the apparent relation between objects, as to position and distance, as seen from any given viewpoint. Lenses of differing focal lengths give you the same perspective but, because they vary in the area they cover, they create different effects. The longer the focal length of a lens, the narrower is its field of view. Yet if you enlarge a negative made with a short-focus lens, cropping it to include only the area covered by the longer-focus lens, you come up with pictures having essentially the same perspective. The difference in the apparent perspectives of long- and short-focus lenses is really one of relativity. A long-focus lens appears to shorten the distances between objects and dimensions along the axis of the lens; a short-focus lens appears to exaggerate those distances, making nearby objects seem disproportionately large.

Both long and short focal-length lenses have their very specific and important uses; a bird, a hundred feet away, is best photographed with a long-focus lens, whereas an interesting but cramped room demands, for its proper presentation, a wide-angle, short-focus lens. For general work, however, stick to the lens best suited to your camera, a lens with a focal length about as long as the diagonal of the frame.

You can, of course, "play" with lenses to produce weirdly exaggerated effects. Try using a short-focus lens too close to the subject; foreground objects now become relatively gigantic. Such tricks are, of course, part of the seasoned photographer's repertoire, but even for him, and certainly for most of us, they are at best only sometime things.

NOW, ABOUT $f/$NUMBERS

The second major basis on which a lens is described or rated is that of its $f/number$, $f/8$, for example. It is a simple, mathematical way of stating the relationship that exists between the maximum effective opening or the iris of a lens and its focal length. On this relationship a good deal depends; primarily it provides a guide for measuring the intensity of the light passed by the lens onto the film. The f/number system provides a common standard for exposure calculations with all cameras and under all conditions.

The f/number is simply the statement of a fraction, with f representing the focal length of the lens and the *number* indicating how many times the full effective diameter of the lens goes into the focal length. A moment ago we mentioned $f/8$. That means, then, that the widest useful diameter of the lens is one-eighth of the focal length. Obviously, then, an $f/4$ lens of the same focal length has twice as large useful iris diameter, and an $f/16$, one only half as large. But because we are dealing with light falling on the whole area of a lens, it is area we must think of, not diameters. And, as you'll remember from Geometry I, when you double the diameter of a circle, you increase its area by four.

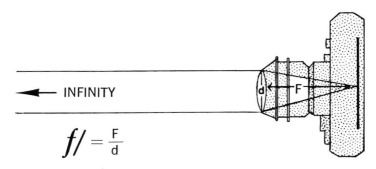

INFINITY

$$f/ = \frac{F}{d}$$

Thus the $f/4$ lens mentioned above admits four times as much light (in any given time) as the $f/8$, and the $f/16$ lens only one-quarter as much. Accordingly you tailor your exposure times; one-quarter as much time for the $f/4$ and four times as much for the $f/16$. Thereby you get the same amount of light to the film under three different lens conditions.

One of the things about f/numbers that tends to confuse some people is the fact that the smaller the number, the "faster" the lens. If you keep in mind the idea that an f/number is merely a fraction, the alleged mystery subsides: one-quarter of an apple is smaller than half that apple.

Practically every good camera lens has an iris diaphragm built into it— an ingenious little mechanism of overlapping metal leaves by means of which the effective aperture of the lens can be varied. Because the various stages in the opening or closing down of the diaphragm are marked around the rim of the lens barrel, you have immediate information as to the f/number setting.

For example, a lens that is wide open at $f/4$ (an $f/4$ lens, obviously) is marked so that progressive stopping down can be fixed exactly at points where the f/ratio is $f/5.6$, $f/8$, $f/11$, $f/16$, $f/22$, or $f/32$. Those particular ratios are used because they give you a fairly precise and important mutual relationship. Closing down the diaphragm from one f/number to the next in this series—$f/1$, $f/1.4$, $f/2.0$, $f/2.8$, $f/4.0$, $f/5.6$, $f/8$, $f/11$, $f/16$, $f/22$, $f/32$, $f/45$, and $f/64$— reduces the intensity of the light falling on the film by *one half*. If you are mathematically curious, you will have noted that from $f/1.4$ on each of the numbers in that series is so chosen that its mathematical square is almost exactly twice the square of the preceding number. It is on this convenient basis that exposure systems have been worked out in conjunction with exposure meters of one sort or another. More about this later on.

BUT, WHY STOP DOWN A LENS?

If you have a fine $f/4$ or faster lens, why bother to stop it down? Shouldn't you be happy about it, and use it wide open all the time? Well, you have about 200 horsepower in the family car's engine. How often do you call on all those horses to give, for all they're worth? With a lens you use your full power even less often, because most of the time you will find yourself working with openings somewhere along in the middle of the scale—$f/8$, $f/11$, $f/16$, and such. But why? Why this deliberate disdaining the full power or speed of your lens?

For several very good reasons, that's why. The first is a matter of *depth of field:* an optical phenomenon that can be defined as the distance, at any given lens setting, between the points nearest to and farthest from the camera that appear to be sharply in focus. Under some circumstances the depth of field can be very great; in others, practically nil.

The sketch below indicates what depth of field means; with the focus sharp on the fourth tree you get acceptable sharpness a little nearer to and farther from the camera, assuming a medium lens aperture.

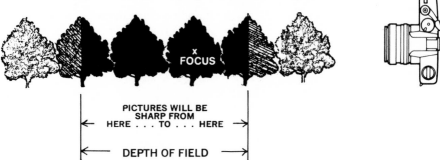

But sometimes we want to use a very small aperture or even the largest of which our lens is capable. Then what? Consult the next two diagrams.

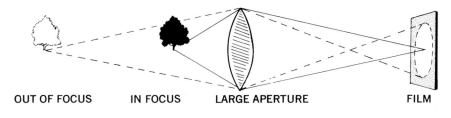

OUT OF FOCUS IN FOCUS LARGE APERTURE FILM

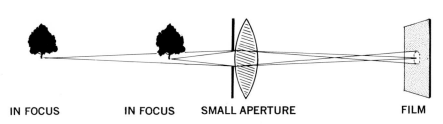

IN FOCUS IN FOCUS SMALL APERTURE FILM

Think back to those cones of converging light mentioned in the paragraphs on focus. When the lens aperture is relatively large, the angle between the rays converging from any point is correspondingly wide. With such a fat cone, the circles of confusion fore and aft of the focal plane become quickly apparent, and objects in front of or beyond the focused object are imaged in terms of circles of confusion, or blurs. By using a very small aperture, $f/22$ for example, those fat cones are so slenderized that far more points in the pictured scene come through as slim pencils of light that appear almost as points-in-focus. This is precisely what photographers mean when they say that they *stopped down* to get maximum depth of field. They increased the range of objects that were acceptably in focus.

"Acceptably in focus" is, of course, a relative term; what is acceptable under some circumstances is intolerable under others. An image destined to be greatly enlarged, either in printing or by projection onto a screen, needs to be sharper than an album snapshot. Within limits, however, the human eye tends to accept a degree of unsharpness. It is within these limits of negligible circles of confusion that depth of field is calculated. Into such calculations go, as you might suspect, such other factors as the focal length of the lens and the f/number or relative aperture employed. Published data are usually in terms of average conditions for each particular lens. From experience with all the conditions involved, it has been determined that an allowable maximum circle of confusion has a diameter of $1/1000$ of the focal length of the lens. Thus, for a 2-inch (50mm) lens, the circle of confusion should not exceed $1/500$ inch; for a 5-inch (250mm) lens, $1/200$ inch is considered tolerable.

DETERMINING DEPTH

Some cameras have depth-of-field indicators, little dials or scales by means of which you can determine the extent of fore and aft sharpness in any picture-making setup. As you study such a scale, you will discover a phenomenon; depth of field tends to *decrease* very rapidly as you get closer and closer to your subject. For example, when using a good modern lens in an average-size camera, you'll note that when you focus on an object 25 feet away, your depth of field at, say, $f/4.5$ extends from about 21 to 37 feet, and at $f/16$ from about 13 feet to infinity. But when you focus on a subject only 6 feet away, the depth of field at $f/4.5$ is only from 5¾ feet to less than 7 feet, and even at $f/16$ it is still a small range, from 5 to about 7¾ feet.

The reason for this interesting state of affairs will be found in another consideration of circles of confusion and in careful viewing of the sketches below.

Two objects at a distance of 30 and 32 feet register on the film at very nearly the same point; but similar objects within 3 and 5 feet of the lens are imaged in quite separate planes and therefore defeat simultaneous focusing. So we have a rule: the closer the subjects are to the lens, the greater the separation of their images, and the less, or the shallower, the resulting depth of field.

Depth of field can be calculated using four factors. They are listed here, together with their effects when the other three are held constant.

1. *Focal length.* The shorter the focal length of the lens, the greater the depth of field. Miniature (35mm and smaller) cameras have short focal-length lenses and, therefore, afford images with greater depth of field.

2. *f/number.* The larger the f/number (i.e., the smaller the opening) the greater the depth of field.

3. *Distance focused on.* The farther the subject is from the lens, the more will be in focus in front of and beyond that subject.

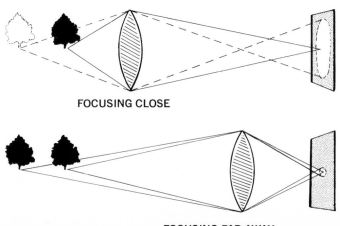

FOCUSING CLOSE

FOCUSING FAR AWAY

4. *Circle of confusion.* The larger the circle of confusion to be tolerated before the image is pronounced unsharp, the greater the depth of field.

Putting three of the depth-of-field factors into mathematical combination, the *hyperfocal distance* (the shortest distance at which the far limit of the depth of field extends to infinity) can be calculated; then, using this value as a mathematical stepping stone, the *depth of field* can be determined.

$$\text{Hyperfocal distance (in feet)} = \frac{\text{The focal length (in inches) multiplied by itself}}{f\text{-number x circle of confusion (in inches) x 12}}$$

(The 12 converts the answer from inches to feet)

$$\text{or in formula} \quad HF = \frac{F^2}{f \text{ x c.c. x } 12}$$

Having determined the hyperfocal distance you can calculate the near and far points of sharp focus for any focus-distance setting, the fourth "depth" factor.

$$\text{Near Point (in feet)} = \frac{\text{Hyperfocal distance x distance (d) focused on (in feet)}}{HF + (d - \text{Focal length in feet})^*}$$

$$\text{Far Point (in feet)} = \frac{HF \text{ x } d}{HF - (d - \text{Focal length in feet})^*}$$

Note the necessity for expressing the focal length in feet to keep all units alike.

Depth of Field (in feet) = Far point − Near point

Example

What is the depth of field when using a camera with a 6-inch lens at $f/8$ focused at 10 feet and assuming a tolerable circle of confusion (c.c.) of 1/200 inch?

$$HF = \frac{F^2}{f \text{ x c.c. x } 12}$$

$$HF = \frac{36}{\dfrac{8 \text{ x } 1 \text{ x } 12}{200}} = \frac{36}{\dfrac{96}{200}} = 36 \text{ x } \frac{200}{96} = 75 \text{ feet}$$

$$N.P. = \frac{75 \text{ x } 10}{75 + (10 - .5)} = \frac{750}{75 + 9.5} = 9 \text{ feet}$$

$$F.P. = \frac{75 \text{ x } 10}{75 - (10 - .5)} = \frac{750}{65.5} = 11.5 \text{ feet}$$

Depth of Field = Far Point − Near Point
Depth of Field = 11.5 − 9 = 2.5 feet

There is a perfectly to-be-expected misconception about depth of field and the importance of stopping down. Many an earnest amateur cherishes the notion that a small lens aperture produces finer detail not merely over a deep field but even on the subject focused on. He religiously closes down to the smallest possible opening even if he's shooting a billboard head-on. As far as the rendering of detail within the billboard, he might just as well use his lens wide open, for the rendering of detail within a flat plane is done quite as easily by a good lens at $f/4.5$ as at $f/32$—provided it is accurately focused.

As was said at the beginning of this section, you may seldom need the top speed of your lens. But as you use it, you may discover that your lens seems to give you most satisfying and consistent results at some aperture well below the greatest. Theoretically, such behavior in a good lens cannot be justified; actually, it does happen—and only experience, plus study of the results, can determine for you what your optimum aperture is.

Figs. 4-6 to 4-8. On the next three pages, a depth-of-field experiment, using an 80mm lens on a $2\frac{1}{4}$-inch-film-format camera. Numbered discs were placed three feet apart, beginning about four feet from the camera. The crossed disc represents the point of focus.

Figs. 4-6a, b, & c. Focus on extreme foreground.
a. (upper left). At $f/4.5$ only foreground is sharp.
b. (upper right). At $f/8$ sharpness drops off beyond disc II.
c. (below). At $f/16$ sharpness extends almost halfway back.

Figs. 4-7a, b, & c. Focus on disc IV.
a. (upper left). At $f/4.5$ sharpness runs from about disc III to VIII.
b. (upper right). At $f/8$ sharpness is fair from disc II to IX.
c. (below). At $f/16$ the whole range is acceptably sharp.

Figs. 4-8a, b, & C. Focus on disc X.
a. (upper left). At $f/4.5$ sharpness begins near disc IV.
b. (upper right). At $f/8$ sharpness begins near disc II.
c. (below). At $f/16$ everything is reasonably sharp.

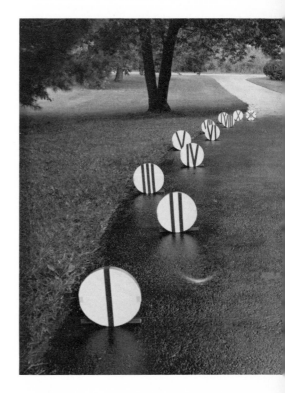

Summary. It would appear, therefore, that a conventional exposure of about $1/125$ sec. at $f/8$, optimum depth of field in a scene 35 feet deep is obtained by focusing on a point about a third of the way back. To achieve maximum depth, the lens needed to be closed down to $f/16$ or $f/22$, apertures which required shutter speeds on the dangerously slow side for a hand-held camera.

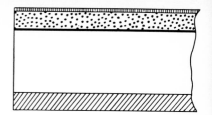

5
Film

We take modern photographic film for granted, as naturally as we do electric light. There is no reason in the world why we shouldn't. But, once in a while, we might spare a small grateful nod in the direction of our predecessors who, only a few generations back, revolted against the heavy, cumbersome, fragile, messy, and miserable means to photography that were all they had and all they knew.

In those days there was no such thing as a casual photographer. Either you were so dedicated to photography that you put up with its complicated, awkward, cumbersome processes—or you didn't have anything to do with it.

Moreover, because you had to sweat and endure the tears of frustration that were implicit in the old wet-plate process, you took the time and the trouble to make sure that every exposure was as nearly right as possible. There was no such thing as a casual bracketing of exposures, no easy confidence that you could compensate in the darkroom for your shooting boners. Because they had to be so careful, many of the old wet-plate photographers turned out exquisite photographs. They simply could not afford—in terms of hard, frustrating work—to be snaphappy. So, next time you rip off a long sequence of exposures in a few minutes, you might have the simple decency to be grateful that, thanks to a few tough and persistent people, progress has progressed.

Irrespective of its historical or technical background, modern film is remarkable. It is light, convenient, stable, relatively inexpensive, and so loaded with potential that it gives you command of practically any picture-making situation.

Ever look at a piece of undeveloped film in full light? It's usually a disappointment, for that supple bit of plastic with its dull, creamy coating gives away few secrets of its inherent magic. Ordinary film consists of a support of flexible plastic on which that coating resides. You can easily scratch the coating, or wash it off with warm water. On the back of the film there is a dye coating, blue, red, or green. It's not very impressive. All of film's almost miraculous virtues remain hidden.

THE EMULSION

To keep things uncomplicated, let's concentrate for the present on the emulsion of an ordinary, everyday black-and-white film. It achieves its usefulness because it carries, suspended in that creamy, gelatinous coating, millions of microscopically small crystals of silver bromide. Silver bromide itself is light-sensitive, and made more so by the addition of certain sensitizing agents. It registers its encounter with light by turning black—but not until it is helped to do so by the chemistry of development.

This sensitivity, this response to light, is the foundation of the whole structure of photography—the science, the art, and the down-to-earth practical citizen that is photography.

Film manufacture is one of the most scrupulously controlled processes in industry. Maximum cleanliness is vital in every step, many of which have to be taken in complete or nearly complete darkness. Light, dust, and chemicals have to be under rigid control. Temperatures have to be maintained at precise levels, relative humidity must be constant, the thickness of the coatings must be uniform, and so on throughout the whole manufacturing process.

For some highly specialized work, glass plates are still used; the requirements of their users are such that high precision is a basic necessity. Modern glass plates are a far cry from the plates used in pioneer photography.

THE SUPPORT

Modern film support or base is generally a plastic, most commonly cellulose acetate. Its sole function is to provide a firm, transparent, adequately flexible, and chemically stable foundation for the light-sensitive emulsion. It is non-flammable, tough, resistant to distortion or shrinkage, and capable of withstanding the repeated dunkings of processing without a whimper.

In the early days of film, the base was nitrocellulose—practically gun cotton. It was explosively flammable and dangerous in manufacture, in use, and in storage. That's why movie theatres were required to have fireproof projection rooms, for the juxtaposition of the flaming arc light and the nitrate film was open invitation to trouble.

In the manufacture of film base, cotton is first treated with acetic anhydride and subsequently dissolved in chemicals of which ether and wood alcohol are the major constituents. The result, after repeated purification processes, is a thick, clear syrup. To the people who make and use it, it is "dope." It is, of course, highly volatile.

For dope to be useful as film base, it must be spread evenly on a clean, perfectly smooth surface and allowed to dry while its volatile ingredients are evaporated. In modern production, the necessary smooth surface is the highly polished 4-foot-wide rim of an enormous (20-foot) wheel. As the wheel turns slowly, dope is fed onto the mirror-smooth surface of the rim by a mechanism that assures uniform spread and thickness. Because the big wheel is totally enclosed, temperature and ventilation can be controlled all the way around. Before the wheel has made a full revolution, the freshly deposited dope has dried and strengthened enough so that it can be gently peeled from the shiny surface and led off, in great loops, through seemingly endless alleys in which it is subjected to further sequences of temperature, humidity, and airflow. It winds up, literally, on great shining, tremendously heavy spools, ready for storage or for use.

Film manufacturers have batteries of these gigantic machines, each attended by its own team of expert technicians; their skill is in their use of the controls rather than in manipulation.

There are various thicknesses of film base. Sheet film needs relatively thick and firm support, miniature and standard motion-picture films need a medium base, and roll film or film-pack films require a thinner fundament.

FILM MANUFACTURE

The preparation of light-sensitive photographic emulsions and the mating thereof with their appropriate supports is another story. It begins with silver, the finest silver obtainable. At Kodak Park, where the Eastman Kodak Company makes its film, about ten tons of silver are used every week. Add the tonnage of silver used by other manufacturers, and you begin to understand why the production of silver and the photographic industry are so closely related.

The first step in emulsion making is enough to break a miner's heart; for the shining, pure bars of silver are dissolved in nitric acid. Silver nitrate is the chemical result. Then, as the water in the solution evaporates, crystals of silver nitrate are formed; these crystals are subsequently washed and purified.

Meanwhile, gelatin (chemically superior to the kind used for desserts and salads) has been prepared to function as the vehicle for the light-sensitive emulsion. It is warmed to a syrupy consistency, and the silver nitrate and potassium bromide added to it. At this stage operations must be carried on in almost complete darkness, for the silver and the bromide combine to form light-sensitive silver-bromide crystals. The potassium and nitrate unite as potassium nitrate, which is removed from the gelatin by washing. Thus, the crystals of silver bromide are left alone in the embrace of the gelatin. Photographically speaking, this is the emulsion.

The "wedding" of the emulsion to the film support is a complex operation; it is only sketched here. Because the emulsion is light-sensitive, darkness is necessary in preparation. First, the emulsion is warmed to a liquid state and kept at a precise temperature and level in big troughs wide enough to take the full width of the spooled base. The base is led down, into the trough, and then up and out; in the course of this maneuver it picks up a skin of emulsion. It is difficult, with the process so simply stated, to understand how coatings of uniform thickness (1/1000 inch when wet; much less when dry) can be maintained; but because they *have* to be, they are. The film and its new coating are then chilled to effect controlled cooling and uniform setting. From long, dark drying tunnels, the coated film finally winds up in big, covered rolls.

Before it can be cut and packaged, the coated film must receive at least two more coatings. One, the *anti-halation* backing, has the job of absorbing strong rays of light as they jab down through the emulsion; without this backing, those rays would tend to reflect back up from the back of the film base and create fuzzy halo effects around the strong highlights. The other coating is simply an outer protective coating, the utility of which is obvious. Both the anti-halation coating and the top coat are dissolved away during processing.

Another coating goes on the base ahead of the emulsion simply as adhesion assurance. It is indicated in this greatly enlarged schematic of a cross section of simple film.

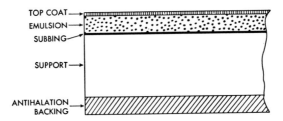

In the making of color and special-purpose films, this basic scheme is complicated unbelievably.

FILMS AND FILMS

Photographers shop talk endlessly about film. Everyone seems to have his own favorite; obscure trade names are tossed around with studied casualness.

6
Developing Film

So you have "taken" a picture, or a whole roll of pictures. Wrapped in mysterious invisibility, the latent images of all those pictures lie in the emulsion of the film. To make them useful (and to satisfy your suddenly overpowering curiosity as to how they "came out"), you take the next step; you develop the film. This involves placing the film in a chemical solution—the developer—for a specific time, after which it is rinsed in water or a stop bath and transferred to a third bath, the fixer. After another few minutes, you switch on the light and peer anxiously at the wet, shiny film.

And there, sure enough, are your images. Or...*are* they? For they're an odd-looking lot. Then you remember that a developed film is a *negative;* an image in which all the brightnesses of the pictured scene are reversed. That which you know was white or highlighted now appears black, while the deepest shadows and blackest blacks are almost perfectly clear in the negative. All very interesting, of course, but hardly a picture, in the normal sense. So?

So you repeat the cycle. This time you expose another piece of sensitive material to light that has passed through a negative. You make a negative of a negative; and two negatives produce a positive. If the new positive is on paper, it is called a print; if it is on another piece of film, it becomes a positive transparency. In either case, you have a recognizable image, a picture.

All this has a pleasant sense of magic about it, heightened by the darkness of the darkroom and the moments of suspended animation while you wait for processes to be completed. But, like most magic, it turns out to be quite simple.

The sole purpose of development is to make real, visible, and permanent the shy, retiring, and invisible latent image. Chemically, the development process is specific. The active ingredients of the developer attack the exposed grains of silver bromide and reduce them to metallic silver and a form of bromine. The silver is deposited, in place, on the film support and the unwanted bromine is liberated, to be washed down the sink.

Now, to be specific....

67

Figs. 6-1a & b. A good negative and a print from it. In the negative, the brightnesses of the original scene are reversed; in the positive, normal relationships are restored.

DARKROOM AND EQUIPMENT

Neither your darkroom nor your equipment need be elaborate. Any room from which *all* outside light can be excluded will serve as a good darkroom. It must be really black dark. To test your room, get in it and close all the doors and openings. After several minutes, as your eyes adapt to the darkness, look around you for tiny cracks or light leaks. If you see any, cover them with bits of opaque tape. Then, pick up a sheet of white paper from the table or bench. If you can see it at all, your room isn't really dark.

Ideally, everyone should have a permanent darkroom—a little room with a sink and running water, a couple of benches, and storage shelves for paper, chemicals, and for the equipment you have, or hope to have. There should be electrical outlets for safelights and white lights, enlarger, and so on, plus some form of ventilation.

Short of that ideal, however, you can initiate yourself into the mystique of photographic-processing very easily—if you're willing to improvise. Many a good photographic career has been launched in a bathroom, a fruit cellar, or a stuffy, under-the-back-stairs closet.

Darkness, to repeat, is the first essential. Your equipment will depend on the kind of film you're using; if it's, say, 35mm film, you'll need one of those little, round tanks; ditto for roll film; for sheet film, you can get along very well with three shallow trays. Because sheet film is so simple and basic, let's assume that you have a sheet of exposed panchromatic film in a film holder or septum. To develop it you need:

1. Developing and fixing solutions, in well-stoppered bottles.
2. A graduate or liquid measure, 16-ounce capacity.
3. An accurate solution thermometer.
4. A safelight, with a dark green filter (Wratten Series 3).
5. Four clean glass or enamel trays, an inch or so larger in both dimensions than your film.
6. A timing device of some sort, audible or luminous, but not illuminated. (Personally, I have trouble seeing anything useful on the dial of my luminous-handed watch, so I rely on the audible timer.)

You will find that most photo shops have small kits that provide most of your starting equipment; some even include the chemicals. Be sure your safelight is really safe, and can be adapted, by changing filters, for both film and paper processing.

The Developer

As a modern photographer, you will probably not make a habit of compounding your own developer. There are simply too many and too good ready-mixed developers available to you as powders or liquids. All you do is add the necessary amounts of water, mix, check temperatures, and you're in business. But you should, at least once, go through the whole thing so that you will have a better idea of what a developer really is and be able to appreciate the convenience of pre-mixed developers.

Here, for example, is one of Kodak's standard formulas, DK-60a. It is an excellent negative developer.

Kodak Developer DK-60a

Dissolve chemicals in order given.	Avoirdupois	Metric
Water, about 125° F (50° C)	96 ounces	750 cc.
Kodak Elon Developing Agent	145 grains	2.5 grams
Kodak Sodium Sulfite, desiccated	6¾ ounces	50.0 grams
Kodak Hydroquinone	145 grains	2.5 grams
Kodak Balanced Alkali	2 oz. 290 grains	20.0 grams
Kodak Potassium Bromide	30 grains	0.5 gram
Water to make	1 gallon	1.0 liter

(Available, of course, in premixed packages)

This, of course, is only one of several popular formulas. The variety of them serves to give you a broad spectrum of useful developers, each of which has its own particular qualities and capabilities. Some of them have a longer life as solutions than others, some are great for building posterish contrast, some are for soft, delicate results, and some are designed to minimize grain. I suggest that you get to know one of them—DK-60a or D-76, for example—reasonably well, and become adept at using it. After that, branch out. Try other brands. It's all part of getting to know your medium.

Developer at Work

The process of developing invisible latent images into fully realized images involves three distinct steps:

1. Softening and swelling the gelatin so that the developing agents in the solution can get at the exposed crystals of silver bromide.
2. Separating or disassociating the silver and the bromide.
3. Transforming the exposed silver bromide crystals into very minute tangles of extruded silver, commonly referred to as developed "grains."

Because no one chemical can accomplish the whole job, a developer contains several different chemicals. And because there are many chemicals that can achieve the end result, each in its own way, developer formulas are many. All of them, however, contain:

1. A solvent.
2. A reducer.
3. An activator.
4. A preservative.
5. A restrainer.

The *solvent* is water. To perform their tasks the several chemical components must be in solution.

The *reducer's* job is to do the actual breaking up of the exposed silver salts. Kodak Elon Developing Agent is a good reducer: it works swiftly and is little affected by small changes in the developer temperature. But, used alone, it produces images that are low in contrast. So, in several formulas, hydroquinone, another reducing agent, is added. Hydroquinone is a slower worker, but the images it produces have excellent contrast. A formula containing both Elon and hydroquinone tends to work with adequate speed and to produce full-contrast images; it is only moderately affected by changes in temperature.

You may have heard veteran photographers speak of Pyro; some darkroom workers still call any developer "pyro" simply because it was a standard for so long. Pyro is pyrogallic acid, distilled from Chinese gall nuts. It is a brisk and active operator, but it oxidizes rapidly and turns brown. The brown stain, deposited on the negative in proportion to the amount of silver present, produces excellent contrast, but the same stain operates gleefully on fingers, trays, aprons, towels, and everything else within reach. Hence the perpetually brown fingers of old-time darkroom operators. P.S. Pyro is little used today.

The function of the *activator* is a double-barrelled one. First, it renders the developing solution alkaline rather than acid or neutral, thereby facilitating the work of the developing agents. Second, it assists the water in the necessary job of softening the gelatin. Sodium carbonate, borax, Kodalk Balanced Alkali are commonly used activators.

Sodium carbonate has long been used, but it has some built-in problems, one of which is its tendency to produce tiny bubbles of carbon dioxide gas within the emulsion. When the warm, soft emulsion goes from developer into the fixer, those little bubbles formed in the transition from an alkaline to an acid bath, may break and pit the surface of the film.

Kodalk Balanced Alkali is a better, safer activator because it produces no volatile gas bubbles within the emulsion, even at a temperature of 80° F. In fact, it was introduced and first used in special developers designed for high-temperature applications; today, it is used in general-purpose developers.

Borax is another activator. Because it is less active and drastic, it is used principally in fairly fine-grain formulas.

The job of the *preservative* part of a developer is to retard the "rusting" or oxidizing of the reducing agents. Those agents are greedy for oxygen; as they get it, they "rust" themselves away until they become photographically inactive and deposit rust-colored stains on the film. They take oxygen from both the air and water. Sodium sulfite in the developer minimizes this gulping of oxygen. Moreover, when larger proportions of sulfite are used, there is a tendency to dissolve part of the silver, so that somewhat finer-grained images are produced.

Finally, a *restrainer* is incorporated. Its job is to control the action of the developing agents, which, in their chemical zeal, may attack *unexposed* as well as exposed silver grains, thereby creating a kind of overall fogging. Obviously such a fog destroys the crispness and beauty of the negative. Potassium bromide is the classic restrainer; it makes the developer more selective, makes it harder for unexposed grains to get themselves developed and, in general, prevents fog.

This, then, is your developing team—solvent, reducer, activator, preservative, and restrainer. Each has its own very specific role; the extent to which each is called into play has been determined through many years of practical experience plus no-nonsense research. On the basis of this experience and research there have been established exact procedures for every developing formula. It is simple common sense to follow these set procedures faithfully; in so doing you are almost certain to get good results. After long experience and careful study you may be tempted to ad lib a bit; meanwhile, don't be too proud to follow the printed instructions faithfully.

SOME VARIATIONS

Despite the warnings of the paragraph above, experience may suggest some small variations in technique or procedure.

For example, you may find that your picture-making system (which includes camera, printer, enlarger, etc.) consistently gives you negatives that require the additional umph of high-contrast printing procedures. Okay, then you might try increasing the development time a little. With any developer, an increase in time beyond the norm increases contrast. Conversely, contrast can be lowered by shortening the time. But keep the other factors, temperature especially, constant ($68°$ F is standard for most black-and-white processing).

High developer temperature causes undue softening and swelling of the emulsion, making it more easily vulnerable to finger marks and abrasion.

Also, as was mentioned a few paragraphs back, it can promote the formation and popping of carbon dioxide gas bubbles. There is another problem associated with too high developer temperatures: When the soft, swollen emulsion is plunged into the cooler fixing bath, the emulsion shrinks back to its original state. If the temperature contrast is great, the shrinkage is so drastic that the emulsion literally wrinkles. This crinkling and crackling is called *reticulation*. Sometimes it is done deliberately to gain a special effect; otherwise it is simply a picture ruiner.

An increase in either time or temperature is accompanied by additional graininess and a rise in fog level. In fact, anything that increases the general activity of the solution adds to contrast, softens the emulsion, and promotes grain and fog.

AGITATION

To do its work properly during the critical minutes of the developing period, the several components within the developer must have constant and uniform access to the film's emulsion. That is why every developer formula includes in its processing recommendations repeated and specific movement of the film, or agitation.

Without agitation, the by-products of the reduction process can settle balefully on the emulsion and hinder the action of the developing agents. Thus, for example, sodium bromide can—unless literally shaken loose—cling to and veil random areas on the film; the resulting negative has a blotched and totally unprofessional look. Agitation is, therefore, a specific part of the development process.

Usually, agitation involves little more than a gentle rocking of the tray or tank for a few seconds, every minute or so during the development time. In tray development, as we shall see, the necessary agitation is almost automatic as the films are moved about in the solution. Agitation is a small thing, but it can be of real importance in the production of a usable negative.

THE FOLLOW-THROUGH

Developing alone, no matter how carefully done, does not complete the development process. True, the image is duly formed but the film is far from ready for use. If you inspect it at this stage, under a suitable safe light, you will see the developed image unclearly amid a general milky surrounding, and the back of the film will still have its anti-halation coating.

At the end of the prescribed developing time the film should be immediately rinsed, either in clean, fresh water or in a chemical bath specifically designed to make the final processing step, fixation, easier and more effective. This bath is called, reasonably enough, a stop bath; its purpose is to put a firm stop to the chemical processes of development. There is no real need to mix it yourself. Buy a small bottle or package. It also serves to minimize the formation of fog, removes any calcium scums that may have formed in the developer, and otherwise makes the total job of the fixing bath a bit easier, thereby lengthening its life.

A stop bath is, incidentally, more important in making prints or enlargements than in developing film; it is good insurance in either case.

FIXING BATHS

The final chemical step in the development process is the fixing bath. It clarifies, fixes (makes permanent), and generally prepares the negative for a long, useful life.

There are three types of fixing baths—non-hardeners, hardeners, and rapid fixers. The principal ingredients are water and sodium thiosulfate, generally called "hypo" (because its former chemical name was sodium hyposulfate). The hypo does the primary work, although other, specific-purpose ingredients are sometimes used.

1. *Non-hardening fixer*. Except for such processes as color printing, non-hardening fixers are seldom used. They contain sodium bisulfite to help neutralize the alkali of the developer solution, and sodium sulfite to prevent sulfurization.

2. *Acid hardening fixer*. This is the fixing bath almost universally used for both negatives and positives. It has a long life, is easy to prepare, and is more tolerant to varying conditions than most formulations. In addition to hypo and sulfite, it includes acetic acid and a hardening agent, such as potassium alum or potassium chrome alum.

3. *Rapid fixer*. This is used primarily by news photographers and others to whom speedy delivery of printable negatives is important. As dry powders, the fixing agents in this type of fixer are unstable; so it is generally sold in concentrated liquid form. Such a fixer completely fixes a negative in three minutes, a print in half that time.

Like developer, fixing baths can be purchased in package form, ready for dissolving in water. If you prefer to mix your own hypo, here's a standard formula for a gallon of fixing bath, to be used without added dilution. Dissolve the chemicals in the order of their listing.

Kodak Fixing Bath F-5

	Avoirdupois	Metric
Water, about 125° F (50° C)	80 ounces	600 cc
Kodak Sodium Thiosulfate	2 pounds	240 grams
Kodak Sodium Sulfite, desiccated	2 ounces	15 grams
*Kodak Acetic Acid, 28%	6 ounces	48 cc
**Kodak Boric Acid, crystals	1 ounce	7.5 grams
Kodak Potassium Alum	2 ounces	15 grams
Cold water to make	1 gallon	1 liter

*To make approximately 28% acetic acid from glacial acetic acid, add 3 parts glacial acetic acid to 8 parts water.

**Crystalline Boric Acid is specified because of the great difficulty of dissolving powdered Boric Acid.

(This and other fixing solutions are available in packaged form.)

In a fresh fixing bath, films should be fully fixed in ten minutes, or about twice as long as it takes them to be completely cleared (that is, fully freed of milkiness, front or back, and of any of the by-products of development). A fixer that takes twice the usual time should be discarded. Here's a tip; use *two* fixing baths. The first, generally a partially worked-out bath, does most of the work; the second, a much fresher bath, completes the job in fine fashion. (Be sure your solutions are properly marked, not only for fixers but for all the other solutions you use.)

It is entirely natural to want to inspect a film or a print under normal light as soon as it is in the hypo. But *don't*. Give it at least a couple of minutes; and be judicious about it for another minute or so. Give it a quick peek if you must, but make it quick—at least for the first half of the total fixing period.

DEVELOPING YOUR FILM

Let's go back, now, to our talk of darkrooms and their equipment, and get down to cases with this business of film development. There are two basic methods of film development. One involves open *trays* of developer and the other closed *tanks*. Today—and remember, this has to do with negatives, not prints—the tray method is seldom used; it is sloppy, it is sometimes uncertain and possibly incomplete because of the complete darkness required for pan films, and it is wasteful of chemical solutions. Still, you should know about it and practice it; someday, in an emergency, you may need to develop some film right away, without benefit of a tank. (While it is relatively easy to develop plates or sheet film in trays, it is hilariously impossible to develop a 36-exposure roll of 35mm film in a tray. Many a photographer has tried it only to wind up hopelessly snarled in a five-foot length of wet, slippery, splattery film. Take my word: avoid it.)

So, for our first run-through let's pick up where it was assumed that you had a piece of panchromatic sheet film ready to be developed.

The Tray Method

Arrange three trays (large enough to take your film, plus finger room) on a table or bench. The first tray on the left is No. 1; it is for the developer solution. Tray No. 2 is for rinse water or stop bath, and No. 3 is for the fixing bath. Okay, pour enough developing solution into No. 1 so that the film can move around easily in it; less than half an inch of depth should suffice. The rinse water should practically fill No. 2; water is cheap and useful. The amount of hypo in No. 3 should be a bit more generous than is absolutely necessary; live it up.

Okay. Turn off the safelight, close all light-admitting openings, check the position of the film holder exactly so you can find it when the light is out, and douse the white light.

At this point you'll remember that you didn't check the time, or the temperature of the developer. So, make sure the film holder is still closed, turn on the light, use the thermometer, correct the temperature (by floating the tray of developer in another tray filled with hotter or cooler water, as may be required), start your timer or check your watch, and turn off the white light.

This time you're in business. Extract the film from the film holder, touching only the edges, and ease it, right side up, into tray No. 1—the developer. (With sheet film you can be sure, even in black darkness, that the emulsion side is up if your finger finds the notched code cut into the edge of the film *at the right side of the top edge.*)

If the prescribed developing time is, for example, five minutes, don't bother the film very much for the first minute. Just be sure it is fully submerged in the developer solution. Then, rock the tray gently several times during the next few minutes; you will hear the quiet "clink" as the edge of the film hits the side of the tray. Some workers play with the film, lifting it out, turning it over, slapping it around—for the present, restrain any such impulse. Agitate the film by rocking the tray and handle it only if you suspect it may have stuck to the bottom of the tray. (Some development procedures are very explicit about agitation; follow directions for the developer you use.)

Okay, time's up. Lift the film carefully—it's very slippery at this stage—over into tray No. 2—the rinse water or stop bath. Swish it around a bit to make sure that most of the superficial gunk is dissipated, and then slide the film into tray No. 3—the hypo. Give it just about the same degree of agitation in the hypo as you did in the developer. In about five minutes it will be safe to turn on the safelight to inspect the image and to make sure that the creamy veil, front and back, has disappeared. Put it back for another five minutes, and then turn on the white light.

The final phase, washing, is not to be sluffed off. It is important to the life and quality of the negative, for it removes all traces of the chemicals that have been acting on or around the film and assures its long and useful life. Your No. 2 tray, repeatedly filled with fresh, cool water will do, or you may reserve a No. 4 tray for the washing process. Actually, if you have a fairly deep vessel into which a rubber hose from the faucet can be directed, washing will be easier.

If the water is running or constantly replenished, one half-hour washing will be enough. Be sure the film is not subjected to the direct stream of water from the hose; water can abrade the still relatively soft and vulnerable emulsion. A couple of film clips or even pinch-type clothespins suspended from a rod over the washing vessel will hold the film so that the water can swirl usefully around it.

When washing is complete, carefully clean both sides of the film with a wet swab of cotton or fine viscose sponge. Work gently; your object is to find and remove dirt, fluff, and other excess baggage. The clean film is then hung up by a clip or pin so that air can circulate freely around it. In an hour or two it will be dry and ready for use. The emulsion side, you will note, has a dull, almost matte finish; the back is shiny.

As was said a while back, tanks are preferable for roll film and practically essential for miniature camera film. Having performed the sheet film development using trays, you're in a position to assess the tray method, possibly as follows:

1. It is principally for the beginner, or
2. For the experienced worker who has a couple of sheets of film to be developed quickly, wherever he may be.
3. Because it is frustrating to handle films in complete or nearly complete darkness, the tray method makes more sense when you're using films that can tolerate a degree of safe-lighting.
4. The tray method is a tiresome bore when development times of more than five or ten minutes are called for.
5. The tray method should be understood, used once or twice, and then relegated to a once-in-a-while basis. The tank method is generally better.

Roll Film and Trays

Before we leave the subject of tray development, it should be said that roll films of the usual two- or three-foot length can be tray-developed, if necessary. But wear an apron because there is bound to be some splattering of chemicals. Because practically all roll films today are panchromatic, you'll be working in the dark for all of the developing and rinsing procedures and for about half of the fixing operation.

The trick is entirely one of handling or manipulating the film so that it gets the full benefit of the successive solutions. First, in darkness, break the seal on the roll and unwind it, stripping away the paper backing as you unwind. You will find that the film has a tendency to curl in on itself, which means toward the emulsion side. So grasp both ends firmly and, before immersing the film in the developer, run it through a bath of clean water several times; this will relax the curl, and also, if evenly done, will prepare the emulsion for the ensuing development.

Then, having preset the timer, move the operation to the developer tray. With the film emulsion side up, slowly see-saw the film up and down in the developer. You can feel when the bottom end of the "U" formed by the film is within the solution. Control your see-sawing motion so that all of the length of the film gets about the same amount of time in the developer. Because the greater part of the film is automatically exposed to air, oxidation is a bit more rapid and development times can be cut a little; experience and experiment alone can indicate by how much.

At the end of the development period, switch over to the rinsing tray and repeat the "U"-loop, see-sawing motion for one minute. Then do the same thing as you shift to the fixer tray. After a minute or two, however, let the film lie flat in the fixer tray, only making sure that there is enough solution to cover the film fully as you gently fold it within the confines of the tray; never crease the film to make it lie flat.

As was suggested when the subject of tray development first came up, an attempt to tray-develop longer lengths of film can result in maddening, frustrating gyrations and, quite easily, in scratched film. If you attempt it, you'll feel like one of the characters in the famous statue of the Laocoon group.

Tank Development

Tank development reduces the whole process to a simple matter of "time and temperature." It is by far the easiest and the most efficient method.

You will find that there are tanks for sheet film, for roll film, and for miniature film. In some tanks there are adjustable cores that can be made to take either 35mm film or wider roll films. Most tanks are so designed that the film remains inside for the whole developing, rinsing, and fixing cycle.

Most of the roll-film developing tanks are designed so that the film is held in an open spiral coil, wound from the core of the reel outward. Because the film must fit in spiral grooves or between the coils of spirally wound stainless wire, it has to be gently bowed as it is fed into those tracks or coils. This is a bit of a trick, and should be practiced—in full light, then in absolute darkness—until you can do it so gently and deftly that you do not crinkle or crease the film *at all*. Why? Because any small crinkle may result in a little half-moon or crescent of density in the emulsion of the film. And, things being what they are in this imperfect world, those little half-moons usually show up in exactly the right places to spoil your best frames. One of the easiest of all tanks to use is the Kodacraft Roll-Film Tank. No spiral threading of the film is required; you merely roll the exposed film inside a plastic apron, the crimped edges of which assure free access of solutions to the enclosed film.

Sheet tanks are different. Some have lighttight lids and some don't; in either case, they are nothing much more than water-tight boxes made of a material unaffected by photochemical solutions. They assume the use of film hangers, one hanger for each film. In professional work a series of tanks is used, one for each step in the process.

In general, these are the virtues of the tank method:
1. It is economical. There is less spilling and splattering.
2. Hence it is cleaner—for you and for the dark room.
3. It is safer for the negatives because, after they are loaded, they are not handled.
4. Temperatures are much more easily controlled.
5. Using a tank, your hands are less involved with the sometimes toxic chemicals .
6. After the film is loaded and the tank closed, you can have white light on. And that's a comfort.

Fig. 6-2. Two popular makes of film-developing tank. Left, the all-stainless-steel Honeywell Nikor outfit, with two of the several available film reels. Right, the F-R "Special" Adjustable reel and tank, all of hard plastic. Loading film into a spiral reel is a bit tricky but, once the trick is mastered, no sweat.

Push-Processing

As I hope you have noted, there are times and circumstances under which strict adherence to conservative rules of procedure can be relaxed. Nobody blames manufacturers for being conservative in their suggestions for the proper use of their products; their survival depends on the successful use of their stuff. But, once in a while, along comes a situation which, going strictly by the book, is impossible. So you put the book aside.

Suppose you want to or *have* to cover a skating performance. You know you need to shoot fast, at about 1/250 sec., but your meter indicates that, with the film in the camera, the best you can do is 1/125 sec. at $f/2$. What do you do?

You deliberately underexpose by shooting at the needed 1/250 sec. Then, just as deliberately, you overdevelop the negative about 50 per cent. This is push-processing. It amounts, essentially, to equal doses of underexposure and overdevelopment. Inevitably, some shadow detail will be lost and the whole negative may not be up to your normal excellence. But, just the same, it may save the day for you.

Push-processing is primarily a black-and-white salvage technique. But commercial color processors have become so proficient that some of them offer an equivalent service for color reversal (slide) films. But you have to ask, and pay extra, for it.

WHEN IT'S DRY

A well-processed film is a joy. It is clean, firm, and the image is invitingly crisp. But it is vulnerable—vulnerable to finger marks, and dust, and casual abrasion. So protect it. Don't let it sit around in the open, collecting dust and inviting damage. There are negative envelopes for all forms and sizes of film. Establish a stock of them for the kind of films you use, and set up a file. Your file system can be based on anything that seems appropriate—number sequences, names, dates, types of subject, and so on. Without a file, you are almost certain to handle and re-handle negatives. Even if you're careful, damage or loss is easily possible.

7
Contact Printing

A developed film is a fine and fascinating thing, especially if you developed it yourself. But it isn't the real objective of your picture making. (Unless you're making an X-ray analysis in which every recorded subtlety *must* be visible: doctors therefore "read" negatives.) You want a *positive* in which all lights and darks and brightness variations are restored to normal.

So you make a negative *of* the negative. Your new "negative" is made on paper, and you have an enjoyable, sharable, keepable print, or as many of them as you wish. The process, of course, is printing.

Photographic printing begins with the passage of light through a negative onto photographic paper so that a corresponding image is formed in the paper's light-sensitive emulsion. When the negative and the paper are in tight, uniform contact—emulsion to emulsion—during the printing exposure, you have a *contact print*. The image on the paper will be precisely the same size as that of the negative, and every detail of the negative will be recorded on the paper with optimum accuracy. Prints made by projection may be larger or smaller, but their sharpness is not automatic. That depends upon the precision of the enlarger's optical system and the sometimes fallable focusing ability of the operator. (See Chapter 13, devoted to enlarging.)

With the growing emphasis on miniature cameras, fewer and fewer people today bother to make contact prints at all. Still, there will be times when you need to make test or comparison prints of a group of small negatives. Contact printing is the easy answer.

Incidentally, in this chapter we shall be dealing only with monochrome (black-and-white) printing. Color printing is, of course, possible, but it is not for anyone who is not experienced in monochrome printing. Not at the moment, anyway.

The contact printing process involves five basic steps: exposure, development, fixation, washing, and drying. The first two steps are so interesting

81

that the other are sometimes neglected; if you're to have prints worth keeping, give every step its due.

As with developing film, you need a room from which all white light can be excluded. But because printing papers are less light-sensitive than negative films, the room need not be blind-black. You can work safely by the illumination of a Kodak Safelight Filter OA (greenish yellow) or OC (amber) on your 10-watt safelamp; once your eyes are adjusted to it, the level of light is comfortable. The important consideration is, of course, the actual safeness of the safelight.

Test your safelight under normal darkroom conditions, with paper, trays, and so on in their usual positions. With the white light excluded from the room, turn the safelight on. Lay a piece of unexposed printing paper, face up, on a dry spot near your developer tray. Cover all but about a half-inch strip of it with a sheet of black paper. After about one minute slide the black paper back to expose another segment of the test sheet; another minute, another strip uncovered, and so on. So, at the end of five minutes, your test sheet will have been exposed, successively to the safelight for periods of 5, 4, 3, 2, and 1 minute. Okay, now develop the test sheet for normal time and at normal temperature. If the segments exposed for the least times show fogging, your safelight is obviously not safe. So take steps to correct it.

Contact printing exposures are usually on the order of one to five seconds, but during those crucial seconds the paper and the film must be in perfect, unmoving contact. There are various means by which this firm contact can be made and maintained. The simplest is probably the printing frame, which has a clear glass face and a hinged, spring-clamped back. Negative and paper are held tightly against the glass by the spring clamp; the exposure is made with the frame, glass side up, on a table with a 75- or 100-watt light a foot or so directly above it. Switch on, switch off, remove the paper, and the exposure is made. A variant of this method involves a small sheet of plate glass, which simply sits heavily on the film and paper during the exposure. By far the best printing apparatus is the printing box, which has the light for the exposure inside it and a hinged and felt-lined top that clamps down to hold paper and film in perfect contact on a sheet of plate glass. Some such boxes have a ruby lamp of low wattage inside the box, in addition to the exposing light, to facilitate positioning of the paper over the negative. The exposing light may switch on automatically when the hinged top clamps down, or there may be a separate manual switch. There may be such refinements as slits for the interposition of masks above the light and below the glass. In professional work there may be a complex grid of small lights with which any desired pattern of intensity can be obtained. A printing box is fortunately easy to make, because it is not so easy to buy, new or secondhand. One of its virtues, by the way, is the fact that, being lighttight, there is little or no hazard of accidental fogging of any unexposed paper that may be around; this is no made-up hazard, as sheepish-looking photographers all over the world will attest.

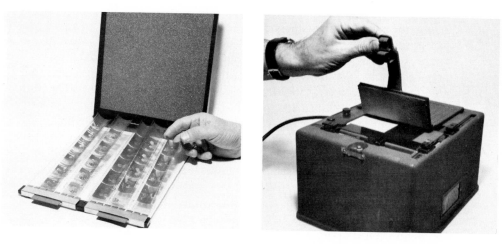

Figs. 7-1a & b. A simple printing frame (left) and contact printing box (right). From **Elementary Developing and Printing,** by Robert Hertzberg.

So, okay. You have some sort of printing device. Now set up three trays— each a little larger than the printing paper you plan to use—on a splash-protected table or bench. The trays are for *developer, stop bath* or *rinse,* and *fixer,* in order of their use. Both developer and fixer can be purchased in pre-pared form (either liquid or powder); the rinse may be either fresh, cold water, or, preferably, a stop bath made from prepared chemicals. You can, of course, formulate your own chemicals for these three steps; the formulas are given at the end of this chapter. Meanwhile, the packaged chemicals are so easy to buy....

In addition to the trays for processing, there should be provision for a good washing tray, deep enough and large enough to take half a dozen or more prints. If it can also accommodate a hose for continuous and gentle flow of water, fine.

With your solutions at 68° F. in trays, your printer ready, the white light off and the safelight on, a splash apron on (developer makes mean, dirty brown stains), and a paper package opened and negative in position in the printer, you are set to begin printing. Extract a piece of paper from its pack-age. One side is slightly shiny, the other matte; the paper tends to curl a little toward the shiny side, which is the emulsion side. Position the paper on the negative, emulsion to emulsion, and you're ready for the exposure.

Once you have established a printing set-up and know what to expect of it, you will probably be able to say, "Well, it's a normal-looking negative, so I'll give it two seconds." Meantime, trial-and-error is in order. So, make your first exposure about two seconds; then slip the paper into the developer solution, making sure that the whole surface is fully immersed. If your solution is at a normal working temperature, the image should begin to come up in five or ten seconds, the strongest blacks first, then the middle tones, and, finally, the highlights. Rock the tray gently or move the print about as the process goes on. When the image appears to be fully realized (usually, it's after about 60 seconds), slip the print out of the developer into the stopbath for a few seconds, and then into the hypo. After about a minute, check on the safety of your unexposed paper supply, and then turn on the white light for a real scrutiny of your print.

Is it *good?* Does it have the richness, the full range of tones from highlights to blacks, that you expected? If it does, all is well—and you are very lucky. Frankly, it seldom happens that you get a really satisfactory print on your first try. More often than not, it will be too dark, or too light, or it may have an overall grayness and lack sparkle and snap.

Before you start corrective procedures, check the data for the developer and the paper you are using. Normal time and temperature for the development process are specified; if you're correct in those respects, then you can consider corrective exposure. If the print is too light, try doubling the exposure; if it came up quickly and became dark all over, try half the time. But if it simply lacks the character you feel it should have, you may need a paper of a different contrast.

Photographic paper manufacturers are realistic; they realize that normal contrast paper, such as Nos. 2 or 3, may not always deliver a perfect print. Some negatives are soft and "flat," and others are hard-as-nails with contrast. So the makers have concocted papers that have abnormal contrast characteristics. Thus you have the means for perking up a dullish, flat negative; print it on a high-contrast paper such as a No. 4 or 5. For an over-contrasty negative, try a No. 0 or 1 paper. This does not mean that you need to maintain supplies of all grades of paper; to your normal stock of No. 2 paper add a relatively smaller stock of No. 1 and No. 4. Occasions on which you may feel that No. 0 or No. 5 are indicated will be, I hope, fairly rare. Meanwhile, you will probably be able to cope very well with minimum worry about emergency measures.

So, either by changes in exposure or in paper, you have a good print. It should stay in the hypo for about ten minutes but not much more, for hypo can, after a long time, degrade the quality of the print. During fixation, prints should be moved around frequently to make sure that the chemical action is uniform.

Then transfer your prints to the wash, which is no slap-happy procedure. Paper, unlike film, absorbs a lot of the chemicals in which it is immersed, and, therefore, washing needs to be thorough. The wash tray should be big and deep enough to permit the prints to move around freely; if they don't swim around by themselves, move them; don't let them cling together. Prints washed in a tray supplied with constantly running room-temperature water (preferably at about 68° F.) should be adequately free of chemical carry-over in three-quarters of an hour; otherwise use ten or a dozen complete changes of water in the course of one hour.

White light, of course, can be on after the last print has been in the hypo for a couple of minutes.

Drying is no slap-dash operation, either. It is a sad thing to see good prints ruined in drying by careless handling. Each print, on removal from the wash, should be lightly gone over with a soft, fine sponge—moistened in clean water—to remove surface water, grit, or any other water-borne impurities. Then put the print face down on a big, clean white blotter, or on a taut frame of clean cheesecloth. Make sure no print overlaps another, that edges do not get curled under, and that wrinkles and creases are smoothed out before drying begins. Drying can be speeded up with heat and forced air circulation; however, too fast drying can result in stiff, curled prints.

A curled print can be uncurled when it is thoroughly dry by drawing it gently but firmly, face-up, over a smooth straight edge. But do be gentle, for the dry emulsion is easily cracked.

In order to produce prints with a high-gloss surface, as most commercial photofinishers do, you need two things: the right kind of glossy surface paper and some ferrotype tins. These tins are mirror smooth. The wet prints are squeegeed or rolled, face down, on the tins and left there to dry. If the tins are clean as well as smooth and the rolling has been properly done, the prints will pop off the tins when dry. Don't hurry them, great as the temptation may be. Commercial shops now use automatic electric dryers, but you're perfectly respectable without one.

Printing is an art. This is simply to say that good printing is not entirely a matter of "going by the book"—this or any book. There is much room in it for the exercise of your personal tastes, for overcoming a negative's short-comings, or for emphasizing some aspect of it.

Obviously, the smaller the negative the more difficult it is to exercise local control in making contact prints. With larger prints, however, consid-erable control can be used during both exposure and development.

With a printing box equipped with slots for a clear glass slide below the film-paper level, it is possible to position small torn bits of tissue paper to hold back the light from a part of the image. Or, conversely, a full-size tissue mask may be used, with a hole torn in it to pass extra light where it can do the most good. In such operations, be sure the tissue is far enough below the image-forming level so that it casts no specifically outlined shadow.

In the developing process you can sometimes, but not always, bring up a stubborn detail or area by rubbing it gently with the tip of your finger; it's the heat created by rubbing that does the trick. This is not suggested as anything but an emergency practice, because it can all-too-easily lead to staining and chemical fog.

Speaking of emergencies. If that stubborn area mentioned above remains stubborn, you might try this. Yank the partially developed print from the developer, rinse it with cold water for a moment (to arrest the general development process), and then "paint" the retarded area with a bit of cotton wet with developer; when and if it shows signs of emerging, drop the print back into the developer for the completion of the process.

While it is good to know that such emergency measures are possible, life is much easier if you get into the habit of producing negatives that require no such drastic doctoring. Lucky you.

PHOTOGRAPHIC PAPER

In the course of producing a print, or many of them, you may become impressed with the fact that you are dunking *paper* into all sorts of chemical solutions and a lot of plain, wet water. And yet the paper stands up.

Ordinary paper wilts when it's wet. But photographic paper can take it. It *has* to, for its very usefulness depends upon its ability to withstand processes that would make useless pulp out of ordinary papers.

Photographic paper is not only tough; it is very much purer than even the best of non-photographic paper. Again, it *has* to be; for if it contained even traces of iron or copper or other chemical impurities, there would be trouble all along the line—from the emulsion coating of the paper in manufacture through the development process in your darkroom.

In addition, photographic paper is given a coating of baryta (barium sulfate and gelatin) before the light-sensitive emulsion goes on. Baryta, which is chemically inert, fills the surface pores of the paper and provides a smoothly uniform white surface as a foundation for the emulsion. Too, the baryta prevents the permeation of the paper fibres by the chemicals in the emulsion, which would produce inevitably uneven results. The matte or gloss finish of the paper depends, for the most part, on the consistency of the baryta coating.

PAPER EMULSIONS

The variety of photographic papers is great, and complex. In the first place, there are three basic types: slow emulsions for contact prints, fast emulsions for easy enlarging, and an in-between type that can be used for either contact or projection printing. They are known, respectively, as chloride, bromide, and chloro-bromide papers.

There is no need for high "speed" in papers for general photography; in fact, it is advantageous to have paper that is slow enough to permit some degree of control during exposure.

Within each of the three general paper types, there are dozens of subtypes distinguished by the character of their surfaces—matte, semi-matte, lustre, glossy—or by the paper tint—natural, white, cream, or ivory. Then there's the "warmth" of the emulsion itself (blue-blacks are cold, brown-blacks are warm). The various contrast grades run to six more variations— 0, 1, 2, 3, 4, 5. Finally, many papers are supplied in both single- and double-weight. So...how would you like to be a conscientious photo-shop dealer, trying to stock all the papers in all the sizes, surfaces, tints, contrasts, and weights your customers might want to try?

The paper situation is further complicated by the fact that there are fashions in paper, just as there are in clothes, dogs, or cars. This year everyone may want novelty surfaces, full of "character" and texture; next year the demand may be for straight, completely "honest" glossy prints.

Avoid the fads and novelties, at least for now. If you expect to do much work for publication, you will need a supply of glossy paper, for photo-engravers like their "copy" to be crisp, with maximum reflectance, but not always ferrotyped. For personal prints, you will probably prefer a semi-matte or a lustre finish. For most usage, single-weight is preferable to double-weight; it is also much less costly.

It is much better to know one or two papers well and to be able to use them consistently than to have a passing (though glib) knowledge of dozens.

8

The Sense of Sensitometry

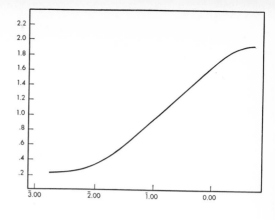

Most of this book is devoted to the achievement of useful photographs. To that end, there is a good deal of talk about specific values and characteristics and interrelations.

Those specifics simply could not exist if there were no science backing them up. In photography, this science is mainly a matter of *sensitometry,* which embraces everything that affects or results from the basic phenomenon that light blackens silver.

Sensitometry is not new. It is the product of centuries of work by thousands of chemists, physicists, metallurgists, optical experts, biologists, electricians, and inspired dreamers. Nor is sensitometry a complete, fully understood thing; for there remain mysteries and unexplored areas. It can, in fact, never be complete; for any newly established fact almost invariably trails behind it a few new puzzlements. So the work goes on in scores of great laboratories all over the world.

The more specialized photography becomes, the greater the demand for more answers from the sensitometric scientists. Color photography, space photography, the exploration of the infinitely small (as with the electron microscope), very high-speed photography, printed circuitry, these and many others are not only the results of sensitometric research but also the reasons why the labs often work nights and weekends.

Inevitably, the lore, the literature of photographic science has grown great in both size and complexity, and is still growing. No attempt will be made here to summarize or to elucidate it. All that can reasonably be undertaken is a definition of some of its terms, plus a sketching of some of the procedures of sensitometry and their applications. Incidentally, this chapter concerns sensitometry as applied to black-and-white photography only; the chapters on color contain a little more of the scientific considerations that have been developed for that aspect of photography.

The language of sensitometry includes many familiar words—words such as *exposure, opacity, transmission, density, speed, latitude,* and *definition.* But they are used in new and specific senses.

The sensitometric application of exposure, for example, is not to be confused with exposure in terms of camera controls. It is, rather, a statement of the amount of radiant energy, or light, which acts on a small, specific area in the photo-sensitive emulsion. In sensitometry, exposure (E) is basic. For exposure results in silver deposits in the emulsion—and at precisely that point the success or failure of the eventual photograph hangs in the balance.

Exposure is the product of the illumination (I) as it reaches the film, and of the time (t) that illumination is allowed to act on the film. It is a convenient coincidence that the fundamental equation of the science of photography reads thus:

$$E = It$$

Exposure is obviously "it" in photography.

Any photographable scene is made up of an infinitude of varying amounts or intensities of light. Without those variations, in fact, there would be no picture. When the shutter opens, the lens takes in all those assorted brightnesses and sends them on to the film as a compact bundle of equally assorted exposures. Sensitometry seeks to determine, as precisely as possible, what happens when, and after, any exposure encounters a specific photo-sensitive material.

One of the tools used in this quest is the *sensitometer,* a device that has a built-in tonal step tablet by means of which the full gamut of exposures is fed to a sample of the film under study. When the film is developed, a grey scale emerges. Each step in the scale (which has a definite relationship to its neighboring steps) can thus be studied.

The light-stopping ability—the density—of an exposed and developed area is measured in another instrument, the *densitometer,* which gives its readings in fractions or percentages. These readings are the indices of *transmittance.* They indicate how much of the light used in making the exposure actually manages to get through any specific area or step in the negative. In subsequent mathematical considerations, transmittance is indicated by T. The opposite of transmittance is *opacity.* Obviously, maximum transmittance turns out to result in minimum opacity, and vice versa.

Opacity, therefore, is a statement of effective density. In creating sensitometric graphs, the logarithm of opacity is used as the equivalent of density. Densitometers, accordingly, are calibrated to read directly in density units.

With these several accurately determinable qualities, it becomes possible to set up, for any given kind of film, a "characteristic curve." This curve graphically describes how the film, developed in a specific developer for specific times, reacts to the whole range of exposure, from none at all right on up to the point where it cannot take any more. In the data books and film data sheets you will invariably find these characteristic curves. They can be called performance profiles.

Typically, a characteristic curve begins with a flat section (the toe) and then curves gracefully up and out until a relatively straight, climbing line is achieved; finally, the curve flattens out again into the "shoulder" section. In all, the curve forms an "S"—a graphic description of the film's response to exposure.

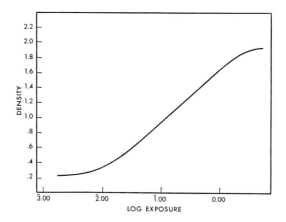

Figs. 8-1a & b. Actual characteristic curve of an emulsion (above); impossible "infinite" density increase (below).

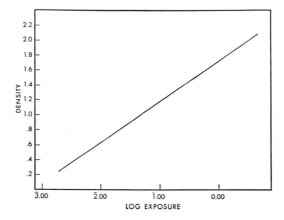

To the layman, the interesting thing about a characteristic curve is that it *is* a curve. One might, reasonably or not, expect the whole line to be straight, with density building up in proportion to exposure. This simply doesn't happen, however, because there is a kind of initial inertia when the film does not respond proportionately to each increment of exposure. Like a plane starting its take-off run, it cannot respond directly to each advance of the throttle. It has to "get going." This gradual start is reflected in the toe section of the curve. As exposure increases, however, the curve does straighten out, matching each increase in exposure with a fairly uniform increase in density. But, eventually, there comes a time when added exposure produces less and less added density; the film is satiated, it cannot take any more. This, of course, is where the curve flattens out into the shoulder section.

To technicians, a characteristic curve on graph paper is eloquent, for it reports with dependable accuracy the film's response, as it is developed, not only to increments of exposure but to a specific developer-time-temperature factor.

The so-called "straight line" segment of the characteristic curve is of major interest; for, to repeat, it is in that segment that the build-up of density corresponds most directly to increments of exposure. It is, so to speak, a constant, and, in any science, a constant is something to cherish and to use.

This "constant" was, for many years, referred to as *gamma* (the Greek letter γ) and used as a kind of cumulative indicator of development time needed to provide optimum density and contrast. Films were developed, for example, to a gamma of such-and-such in an effort to produce negatives that would all print, given uniform processing, on the same contrast grade of paper.

Today, gamma has been replaced by a value called *contrast index*. Its utility is similar to that of gamma, but it is more flexible in that it applies to a wider variety of negatives made on more varied films. Thus, instead of seeking to develop a film to a pre-selected gamma, the technician achieves uniformity by developing his negatives to a point where their contrast indexes are the same—as determined by comparing the characteristic curves of the negative materials.

It is probably wiser for those of us who are neither technicians nor technical-minded to think of gamma and of the contrast index as devices by which a negative can be made to deliver contrasts similar to those in the pictured scene. After all, our prime objective is to reproduce that scene as accurately as possible. In practical work, contrast in the negative need not be precisely the same as in the scene, for the printing process, either by contact or by projection, usually tends to increase contrast. Hence, a negative developed to a point considerably less than 1 : 1 can give you, on printing, an image that is very close to 1 : 1.

Film data sheets and data books that illustrate the characteristic curves of films usually include, as a supplement to each such curve, small graphs in which contrast index is shown as a curve plotted in terms of development times.

PAPER CHARACTERISTICS

A photographic paper emulsion responds to light in essentially the same way that film does; characteristic curves of paper reveal the same kind of relationship between density and log exposure. But paper, compared to film, is less flexible in its response. You know very well that you have wide control over the contrast qualities of a negative; for comparable variations in printing, you use another contrast grade of paper.

Here's the characteristic curve for Kodak Velox Paper No. 3. You'll note that its toe rises slowly but that at higher densities the contrast is much greater. Remember that, in printing, the negative is the "subject." The shadows of a good negative are a bit low in contrast; they transmit considerable printing light to produce the higher print densities in the region where paper contrast is high. Conversely, the highlights in the negative are higher in contrast and are reproduced by the flatter, sweeping toe portion of the paper. In other words, the shapes of film and paper curves have been engineered to complement one another.

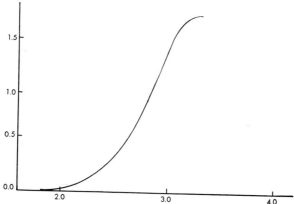

Fig. 8-2. Characteristic curve of Kodak Velox Paper No. 3.

Papers of lower and higher than normal contrast permit compensation for some errors in exposure and processing, in variation in subjects, and in equipment; but they cannot and should not be thought of as cure-alls.

Speed. The American National Standards Institute's system of speed determination is based on the minimum exposure required for an excellent negative. In application of this value, a safety factor is added—and the safety factor depends upon the exposure latitude of the film and on the characteristics of the exposure-determining device involved. The result is put into words on Kodaguide Dials and into numbers called exposure indexes or speed numbers for photoelectric meters.

Speed considerations are important when it comes to determining actual camera exposures. You need to know how fast your film is. Beyond that, however, the importance of speed, as such, diminishes rapidly. Almost all films are fast enough for anything you are apt to undertake. Extreme speed is attained only at the expense of other qualities, fine grain, for example. Ratings in terms of speed are not, alone, clues to quality. Uniformity in manufacture, color sensitivity, graininess, these are, in the long run, far more important to you as a photographer than speed alone.

Latitude. The classic definition of the word latitude has always stated that it was the horizontal extent of the straight-line section of the characteristic curve. However, with the shifting of sensitometry toward practicality, the concept has become what might be called *camera exposure latitude*—or, the difference in camera exposure between the least and the most exposure resulting in negatives capable of affording excellent prints. Here we run afoul of a subjective consideration—what is excellence? Likewise, results are affected by the quality of the camera's optical system. So, latitude is not assigned specific values. It is, instead, incorporated in the determination of a film's speed— along with a safety factor.

Definition. Most of us, looking at a negative, are satisfied if we find it "sharp." Here again, sensitometry delves deeper.

You may have noted that the data sheet for film usually includes an inconspicuous little panel that describes the film's definition characteristics in terms of three or four contributory factors: *graininess, resolving power, sharpness, acutance,* and *enlargability* (or "degree of enlargement allowed"). Because all of those factors are partially dependent on intangibles or immeasurables—such as the cleanness of the lens or the accuracy of the focus— they are not given numerical value. They are described in *words.*

Graininess is the phenomenon you may have observed in light gray areas of a film under considerable magnification. That grainy appearance, remember, is not evidence of individual grains of silver; it is, rather, evidence of irregular distribution or clumping of the grains that make up the image. (It takes very special laboratory microscopes to isolate even finite groups of silver grains.)

We know that graininess tends to increase with film speed, and that some developers are better than others in minimizing grain. But grain is always there. Fortunately, it seldom becomes obvious. Minimal grain, as you'd expect, promotes definition: visible grain defeats it.

The words used in the tabulations to describe graininess range from *coarse* to *moderately coarse, medium, fine, very fine,* and *extremely fine.*

Graininess in a print increases with the density of the negative that fathers it, and with the build-up of contrast in development. Should graininess

The search for standards by which film speeds might be accurately stated goes far back in photographic history. You may very well encounter references to such systems as DIN, BSI, Older Weston, and Scheiner, all of which were and are serious, scientific, and useful. (Kodak publishes a Customer Service Pamphlet [AF-18] that gives the ASA equivalents of those older systems; it's free if you write for it.) The ASA system was evolved through a great deal of cooperative effort, concentrated in the American National Standards Institute, Inc. To date, it appears to be the most generally useful and practical system. The ASA indices assign mathematical values to the response of photo-sensitive materials. In other words, a rating of ASA 200 is twice as fast, or sensitive, as a rating of ASA 100.

The fact that ASA ratings can be assigned to a film is, in itself, a tribute to the film makers. For it means that film making has become a nicely controlled process in which any given film has and holds its ASA rating throughout its effective (and dated) life, from shipment to shipment, all over the world.

Okay. With the sensitivity or speed of a film known and stated mathematically, we are in a position to add it to our exposure calculations. Effective exposure becomes a combination of three known values: aperture, time, and film speed.

There are many kinds and sophistications of exposure meters. All of them sense and evaluate the light as it falls on or is reflected by part or all of a given scene. With that evaluation established, you are equipped to set your lens and shutter controls to make best use of the light, in terms of your picture-making requirements.

The photocell exposure meter is an absolute *must* for the professional; he cannot afford the luxury of even occasional near misses, especially in color work.

But most of us will benefit by working up to exposure meter status by way of two preliminary stages. The first depends upon the printed data sheet that is packed with most non-professional roll films. That little sheet of thin paper is crammed with information. It is by all odds the best source of the latest, the most specific, and accurate dope on that film and its use. For an outdoor film, for example, it states the film's type, its ASA rating, the kind of light for which it is intended, the kind of supplementary flash to use, and, in some cases a set of little sketches describing, graphically, four basic lighting conditions and the recommended exposures for each. One look at those drawings identifies the picture-making situation in which you find yourself. If you then follow the printed exposure suggestions, you'll be on-the-button most of the time.

Having used data-sheet guidance faithfully for a while, you will soon be able to make your own exposure estimates. If you do this intelligently (not merely relying on the charitable nature or the latitude of the film), you will have achieved the stage of exposure sophistication. It is a fine, satisfying status.

But one day you will perpetrate a real boner, misjudging a situation violently. Swallowing what's left of your pride, you will then acquire an exposure meter (or a camera with its own built-in meter) and settle in for a career of less flamboyance—and a consistently higher batting average.

Exposure value numbers. Out of much experience with exposure meters came a logical simplification. In normal use of a meter, first you set it in terms of the film speed (ASA) rating of the film you're using; then you feed in either the diaphragm setting or the shutter speed you want to use. The meter then comes up with the correlative shutter speed or aperture. That's very good. In the exposure value scheme, the meter, primed with the ASA rating and activated by the existing light, comes up with an arbitrary number, any number in the sequence that runs from 2 to 18. A few cameras include these exposure value numbers in the mechanism of the rim settings. The controls are interlocked so that, assuming the meter gives you an exposure value of 12, diaphragm and shutter speed give you the whole gamut of apertures and speeds that, together, afford exposures according to EV 12.

The accompanying tabulation explains things better.

SHUTTER-SPEED AND LENS OPENING EQUIVALENTS OF EXPOSURE VALUE NUMBERS (EVN)										
		f/Numbers								
		2	2.8	4	5.6	8	11	16	22	
	2	1								
	3	1/2	1							
	4	1/4	1/2	1						
	5	1/8	1/4	1/2	1					
	6	1/15	1/8	1/4	1/2	1				
	7	1/30	1/15	1/8	1/4	1/2	1			
Exposure Value Numbers (EVN)	8	1/60	1/30	1/15	1/8	1/4	1/2	1		
	9	1/125	1/60	1/30	1/15	1/8	1/4	1/2	1	
	10	1/250	1/125	1/60	1/30	1/15	1/8	1/4	1/2	
	11	1/500	1/250	1/125	1/60	1/30	1/15	1/8	1/4	
	12		1/500	1/250	1/125	1/60	1/30	1/15	1/8	
	13			1/500	1/250	1/125	1/60	1/30	1/15	
	14				1/500	1/250	1/125	1/60	1/30	
	15					1/500	1/250	1/125	1/60	
	16						1/500	1/250	1/125	
	17							1/500	1/250	
	18								1/500	
		Shutter Speeds								

An EVN of 2 indicates light so low that it takes one second at $f/2$ to provide adequate exposure; while an EVN of 18, at the other extreme, indicates overexposure at anything more generous than 1/500 sec. at $f/22$. Because the EVN is a function of film speed, some meters read in both EVN and in lens and shutter settings.

The value of the EVN system is in the choice it gives you: a whole series of lens and shutter settings that, for the existing conditions and film, assure you the same total exposure.

Still independent? Some of us are very stubborn animals; we cherish the basic human right to make our own mistakes. Or, to put it more positively, we want to run our own affairs so as to avoid making mistakes. Okay, you can be independent of exposure meters if you insist. Here's how.

Every film has an ASA rating. It is printed right on the film carton as well as on its enclosed data sheet. So start with that. Use it as the denominator in a fraction in which the numerator is "1" (1/ASA number). That fraction can then be used as your shutter speed setting at $f/16$ in bright sunlight. Example: Kodak Plus-X Film has a rating of ASA 125. So, on a bright day with the lens at $f/16$, your shutter speed should be on the order of 1/125 sec. Such an exposure would have or provide a normal safety factor of 1.2; to be even safer, you could shoot at $f/11$. With color film and its much more exacting exposure requirements, you have no safety factor. With Kodachrome-X Film, ASA 64, you would shoot at 1/60 sec. and $f/16$ on a bright day, and that would be that. This scheme of getting along without an exposure meter has been referred to as the Guesstamatic System. But it works very well... if you are quite sure what bright sunlight is.

Incidentally, speaking of bright sunlight and getting along without a meter, you have with you at all times a device for judging the clarity of sunlight. Look at the shadow cast by your opened hand on any flat surface from a distance of about one foot. If that shadow is really sharp, the sunlight is correspondingly clear and bright; if there is no distinct shadow at all, you know that the exposure must be increased considerably—at least two stops. In between, you have to use judgement plus experience; but, as you will discover, even with the most exquisite metering techniques, there are times when your judgement is the overriding factor.

EXPOSURE METERS AT WORK

There are, of course, many kinds or makes of exposure meters; some are completely independent bits of hardware, and others are built right into cameras. They are of two basic types: *Selenium cell* meters and *Cadmium Sulfide (CdS)* meters. Both of them are useful because of what *light* does with and to them.

A Selenium cell meter reacts to the impact of light by actually generating a very small, but measurable, amount of electricity. That very tiny amount of power is, fortunately, enough to swing a needle over the face of a dial. The greater the light, the greater the power—and the greater the swing of the needle.

The CdS meter is quite different. In this case, light affects the electrical *conductivity* of the unit. The greater the light, the greater the conductivity or, putting it the other way round, the lower the resistance. Obviously, a CdS meter has to have a flow of electricity going before the effect of light on it becomes measurable; hence a small battery to provide that current must be incorporated in the unit. And the state of that battery should be checked semi-annually.

The makers of the meters—or of the cameras incorporating them—provide specific information as to their best, most effective use. Hence, we won't go into detail here; study your manual. But, in general terms, there are some basic techniques.

Reflected light. The oldest and most widely used metering procedure is by reflected light. And understandably so, for you perceive your picture in terms of reflected light, your camera images it by reflected light, and your film records it as reflected light. It is also the easiest metering technique. From your selected camera viewpoint you read the meter's reaction to the light reflected from the whole scene, and you're in business. A camera with an integral meter generally operates this way, but not always. Some camera meters make a big thing of metering in terms of very selective included angles or in the precise positioning of the meter on or inside the camera.

In general, however, a meter reacts to and reports on an *average* of the light intensities in the scene, whereas a camera dutifully records them individually. Thus a meter's reading can be heavily influenced by the inclusion of a bright sky, by a strong but pictorially unimportant shadow, or by an over-bright foreground. Train yourself, therefore, to look for and to recognize such metering influences; you can compensate for them by carefully aiming the meter, or by arbitrarily discounting its reading. Experience with your own outfit is by far the best learning device.

Meanwhile, here's a small tip. On cloudy or overcast days the sky will, nonetheless, be relatively whiter and brighter than the dark foreground. So, start your reading with the meter aimed at that foreground. Then raise its aim slowly. The needle will rise with corresponding slowness but, as the sky begins to dominate its reading, it will jump. Note the point where that rapid rise begins. The reading at that point will probably work out well for your picture of the whole scene.

It is when you undertake to analyze a scene in terms of its individual parts that metering techniques vary most. Some people make a lot of individual readings and use the average thereof; some stress readings of shadow areas to assure shadow detail; others study highlights. Some meters have such narrow angles of inclusion that they can be used on long-focus lens shots and for detailed metering of small elements in a scene. The techniques suggested by the several meter or metering-camera manufacturers differ in some specific applications. So covet and study your manual.

It is safe, however, to make a couple of suggestions. First, in making reflected-light readings always operate *from the camera's point of view;* everything else is irrelevant. Second, there is a rule of thumb about reading important details in a scene: The meter-to-subject distance should be approximately the same as the longest dimension of the detail itself—as seen from the established camera angle. An adult face, for example, is about ten inches high, so ten inches should be your metering distance. A horse should be metered from about six to seven feet, and so on.

A third generality is nothing but common sense, and probably shouldn't even be mentioned. However, avoid casting your own shadow on the subject from which you are taking a reading. That shadow can result in a considerable metering error.

Incident light. The second major division of metering technique is by incident light. It is the exact opposite of the reflected-light method, for it reads the light falling on the scene, or a part of it, with the meter aimed back toward the camera. There are special incident-light meters, but there is no law against using a conventional meter. (I suppose one *could* use a built-in light meter for incident-light reading, but your results would tend to be suggestive rather than specific.)

For specialized photography, as in professional movie making, this is the almost universally accepted metering principle. In fact, incident-light metering is so easily adapted to various kinds and types of lighting, indoors as well as outdoors, that an understanding of it is important.

Because the incident-light method involves the raw, unmodified light falling on a subject or a scene, the readings are considerably higher than with reflected light. So there is usually a baffle of some sort built into a meter for incident-light reading; this baffle reduces the impact of the light on the photocell so that the readings become more nearly like those of reflected-light meters. However, with a reflectance meter, you can still utilize the advantages of the incident-light method; all you need is some sort of standardized intermediary: a gray card, a sheet of newspaper folded to about quarter size, or the palm of your hand. Whatever it is, it becomes your working standard and readings made from it, by reflectance, can serve you faithfully, day after day after day.

The procedure goes something like this. First, decide on what your intermediary is to be. It should be something you can handily refer to at any time, something not easily lost, something stable in color, matte in texture, and unchanging in shape. Classified-ad pages of newspapers the country over have just about the same quality of grayness; so a folded ad page might be your standard. An 8″ × 10″ medium gray card (a laundry shirt card, for example) is perfect, and your hand is undoubtedly the, um, handiest.

Out in the unobstructed sunlight take a closeup reading of your intermediary, whatever it is, and make a note of it. Then whip out your camera and make a series of exposures right then and there, all of the same scene, making one that is pretty sure to be *under-* and another that is certainly *over-* exposed. Jot down the exposures of all these shots, and hurry off to the darkroom to develop the series. Then study your results. There's bound to be one shot that is just right. Consulting your notes you find that it was made at, say, $f/11$ and 1/25 sec. You know what your meter registered when you "read" your intermediary. Okay, so now you know that next time your intermediary gives you that same reading, you're safely in business at $f/11$ and 1/125 sec.—or any of the equivalents thereof. If a reading from your intermediary shows only half as much light as it did in your original experiment, you know that exposure should be doubled; and, of course, vice versa.

As you become familiar with this incident-light method, you will find that it is particularly useful in photographing interiors by artificial light. In fact, some photographers use it as a means of tailoring their light to meet their exposure desires. On the basis of such readings the lamps can be moved forward or back until the illumination is found to be right in terms of the film and the exposure to be used.

But…incident-light readings or reflected-light readings, there are no perfect answers. They are still, fortunately, very much up to you.

Fig. 9-1. Three more-or-less typical off-camera exposure meters. Left, an incident-light meter; center, a narrow-angle reflected-light meter; and right, a general-purpose reflected-light meter.

Fig. 9-2. Reflected-light reading of a general scene.

Figs. 9-2 to 9-5. Exposure meters at work.

Fig. 9-3. Making a "spot" reading of a part of the whole scene.

Fig. 9-4. Making a close-up reading.

Fig. 9-5. Making an incident-light reading.

10
Filters

The photographic use of the word *filter* is very apt. For a filter absorbs what is not wanted and passes or transmits what *is* wanted. Light filtration is used in many aspects of photography—over the lens in both monochrome and color exposures, between the layers of a color emulsion, in printing, in enlarging, and even in darkroom safelights—and it therefore behooves us to know something about it.

In its commonest form a light filter is a piece of dyed gelatin or glass, held in place in front of the camera lens during an exposure. Rays of light from the subject are either absorbed or transmitted, depending upon their color relationship to the filter. You use a filter to absorb the colors you want to appear darker *in the print,* and to transmit the colors you want relatively brightened.

Because the usefulness of filters depends upon the nature of light, and because it is a short step from filters to color photography, this is a good point to review what we know about light and to delve a little deeper into some of light's characteristics.

Light, like all radiant energy, travels in waves. The length of those waves, from crest to crest, determines the color of the light. Red waves are long, green waves shorter, and blue waves still shorter. Within those general wavelength groups, the shades of red, green, and blue vary with lesser wavelength changes.

If there are no waves, there is no light. If all the waves travel together, with all of the several color groups bouncing along as one, the result is white light—the composite of all colors. A mixture of less but relatively equal parts of red, green, and blue results in gray, in any neutral tone from black to white.

Red and green waves combine to form yellow. A yellow book is one that reflects both red and green *and absorbs blue.* Similarly, all other colors are combinations of the three light primaries, red, green, and blue. Thus:

107

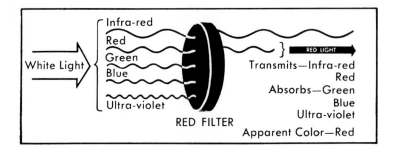

Fig. 10-1. How a filter works. It transmits light of its own color, holds back the the others. Often absorbs part of invisible ultraviolet.

Orange is red plus some green.
Yellow is red and green in equal parts.
Pink is red and blue in equal parts.
Darker pink is less red and less blue.

Because of their ability to absorb certain wavelengths of light, filters appear colored when held in front of a white light. A filter looks green if it transmits green light and absorbs red and blue. Thus, through a green filter, green objects look light and other objects, not containing green, appear dark or even black. Those other colors are absorbed, or filtered out.

A yellow filter absorbs only blue, and allows both green and red light reflected from objects to pass through to the eye or to the film.

There are hundreds of filters, all of different absorptive characteristics and, hence, of different colors. However, only a half dozen or so of them are of real, practical value to unspecialized photographers (us); the others afford exact control over light for specific purposes in film manufacture and in commercial and technical photography.

FILTERS FOR BLACK-AND-WHITE PHOTOGRAPHY

Practically all present-day black-and-white films are panchromatic; they respond, with varying emphases, to all the colors of the spectrum. They can, accordingly, be filtered to produce special effects—haze penetration, darkened skies, softened textures in faces and flowers, and so on. But should you have some orthochromatic film, which is primarily responsive to blue light, it's a case of "signals over." Similarly, infrared film is distinctive and different. In other words, filters must be used in relation to the operative film.

In photographic usage there are three arbitrary words used to describe unfiltered and filtered effects: *correct, undercorrection,* and *overcorrection.* A picture that appears to our eyes (let's assume we are all free of color blindness) as entirely normal, with tones that correspond to the same relative brightnesses we see in the scene, is said to be correct. (Remember, we are talking about black-and-white work, not color.) Correction filters are used to overcome the tendency toward undercorrection on the part of a film that, without a filter, interprets blues as too light and reds as lighter than they appeared to be. And filters that produce exaggerated effects, such as very dramatically dark skies, are called overcorrection filters. Actually, the terminology is unimportant, so long as you understand that selective filtration can normalize or, if you wish, *abnormalize* a film's interpretation of any given scene.

You may have heard something about "contrast filters." Actually, that term refers more to the effect obtained than to any unusual characteristics of the filter itself. The "contrast" effect is a distortion of brightness values so that two colors of about equal visual brightness are interpreted on the film as quite different. The filter absorbs one, and transmits the other.

Almost any filter can emphasize subject contrast when used in the right place with a film capable of properly recording the differences the filter sets up. For example, a red filter is a "contrast" filter when used to photograph blueprints. Maximum contrast between the white lines and the blue background is obtained as the red filter transmits the red component of the white lines and absorbs all the blue from the background. Conversely, if the subject were a red and yellow beach umbrella, the yellow filter would add no contrast at all; the red and yellow would look and photograph the same.

Figs. 10-2a to 10-2d. In making scenic or architectural photographs, you can "tailor" your skies and textures as you please, as these four pictures, all on Pan film, demonstrate. Below, left, without a filter; right, with a K2 (yellow) filter. Next page, left, with a G (orange) filter, and right, with an A (red) filter.

There is a very dramatic revelation of what filters do in the *Kodak Master Photoguide*. Inserted into one of its pages is a series of colored discs that, when held to your eye, give you a very fine preview of what could be expected when you used typical red, yellow, green, and blue filters. Translating those phenomena into words, this is the line-up:

Purpose	Filter	Film
For smooth skin texture and "corrected" skies, lighter foliage	**Yellow** Filter No. 8 (K2)	Any Pan Film
For haze penetration, contrast in marine scenes, sky-cloud contrast	**Orange** Filter No. 15 (G)	Any Pan Film
For exaggerated sky-cloud contrast, storm pictures, etc.	**Red** Filter No. 25 (A)	Any Pan Film
For natural reproduction of blossoms, foliage, outdoor portraits against sky	**Bright Green** Filter No. 11 (X1)	Any Pan Film

Fig. 10-3 (left). In medium close-ups a filter can help to de-emphasize facial contrasts, gaining a general sense of softness. A K2 (yellow) filter was used here.

Fig. 10-4 (right). The X1 (green) filter can help to preserve textures in a delicate subject like this flower.

Wratten filters. Originally of English development and manufacture, Wratten filters are made by Kodak primarily for scientific and advanced amateur use. They are available in dyed gelatin sheets, from which needed segments are cut. The color absorption and transmission characteristics come from organic dyes of great purity. Both the supporting gelatin and the colors are held to extremely fine tolerances, both physical and optical.

Filters supplied in gelatin sheet form are relatively inexpensive but, because they require some handling in the process of being fitted to a camera, there is some chance of scratches or finger prints, neither of which can safely be eradicated.

Some suppliers may be able to provide Wratten filters cemented between glass. This is the more convenient form of filter; the fragile gelatin is protected by the two layers of optically clear glass, and the glass itself can be cleaned— with care. In most instances, the filter is simply a thin disc that can be fitted to a camera by means of a slip-on or a screw-in adapter ring. There is a wide range of sizes or diameters that can be fitted very neatly to any conventional camera lens by means of adapter rings. Thus, with a single adapter ring and several filter discs, you are ready for practically any filtering situation.

There is a third type of camera filter that is quite adequate for most amateur needs. This is a disc of glass into which a filtering dye is dissolved while the glass is still molten. Inspect any filter you buy carefully; the glass should have no evidence of distortion or damage, and the filtering color should be uniform.

Neutral density filters. Neutral density simply means that the filtration effect is even or uniform for all colors. Obviously, such a filter has little use in normal work because its effect is to decrease the total amount of light reaching the lens and the film. However, you *could* be faced with a super-bright situation—brilliant sunlight on a dazzlingly white beach—with nothing but very high-speed film in your kit. Your exposure meter flips over to a reading of something like $f/16$ at 1/1000 sec. or $f/22$ at 1/500 sec. But your camera may have a minimum aperture of $f/16$ and a maximum shutter speed of 1/500 sec. What to do?

You use a neutral density filter to cut down the overall brightness to a level with which your camera can cope. Nothing complex about it. It is simply a brake, a slower-downer. Neutral density filters are identified with "factors" that indicate the extent to which they affect exposure. A neutral density filter is not one you're likely to need every day.

In dire emergencies, people have been known to substitute sunglasses for the filter they lacked. This is very chancey, for you have only the vaguest notion of the transmission and optical characteristics of such "filters" (and the optical quality of a pair of sunglasses is questionable, anyway). In black-and-white photography the sun glass gambit is, at best, a gamble; in color work it is strictly *out,* for it merely distorts the image by adding to it the color of the glass.

The neutral density filter can be used with either color or monochrome film; in neither case is it likely to become the most used tool in your kit. Another dual-medium filter is the....

Polarizing screen. In this instance, the desired filtration—to produce darkened skies, minimize reflections from nonmetallic surfaces, and, to a degree, penetrate haze—is achieved by a sophisticated little gadget that weeds out what might be called the extraneous emanations from light rays that have been polarized (made to vibrate in one plane only) in their encounter with nonmetallic surfaces such as dust, glass, or water.

By selective rotation of the polarizing screen, in place over your camera's lens, you can control the extent of its influence. Use of the polarizing screen involves a considerable (2.5) filter factor, which means an exposure increase of 1⅓ stops, plus whatever further increment the kind and angle of the existing light may necessitate. The techniques are tricky; the optical phenomena are complex. For our present purposes, it is enough to be aware that a tool exists with which many unwanted reflections, among other things, can be

Fig. 10-5. The polarizing screen eliminates distracting reflections and intensifies the blue of the sky.

controlled. Several of Kodak's little Information Books deal with polarization and its use and control; the booklet on filters is probably the most specific.

Filter factors. Because a filter may cut out from one-third to two-thirds of the light available for making a picture, corresponding changes must be made in exposure. The number of times which the proper *un*filtered exposure must be increased when a filter is used is called the filter factor.

The filter factor depends upon the filter itself, the film, and the nature of the light source. And there is a nice interdependence between these three. For example, a red-transmitting filter, used with a red-sensitive film, does not involve as large a filter factor as a filter that inhibits part of the red light.

The filter factor is also dependent upon the light source. Outdoor light is bluish; most artificial light is reddish. A bluish filter used outdoors therefore absorbs little of the existing light, and the exposure need not be increased materially to equal the *un*filtered exposure. Indoors with tungsten light, mostly red, a blue filter cuts out all but a small portion of the light; hence, a bluish filter used indoors necessitates a relatively high filter factor.

In applying a filter factor to the calculation of exposure, you have several options. The indicated exposure for the shot, unfiltered, may be $1/60$ sec. at $f/11$ and the recommended filter factor is 4. You can apply that factor to the shutter speed, coming up with a figure of $1/15$ sec. With the filter, then, your exposure becomes $1/15$ sec. at $f/11$. However, if you need a shutter speed of $1/60$ sec., apply the factor to the lens opening; opening the diaphragm two stops quadruples your light volume, so you shoot at $1/60$ sec. and $f/5.6$, with the filter in place. Or, of course, you can compromise by doubling both time and aperture; that gives you 1/30 sec. at $f/8$.

A final word about filter factors. It has been indicated, even in some technical manuals, that it is okay to take meter readings through the same filter you propose to use for the impending picture. Or, with built-in metering systems, to take your reading with the filter on the lens. Thereby, the man says, you eliminate the need for filter-factoring arithmetic. Well, yes and no. Some meters react to color differently, so there's the chance that the indicated exposure will not be quite the same as with unfiltered metering, appropriately factored. You can make tests, of course. *Then* you'll know.

It is unquestionably true that the current emphasis on small, automatic cameras and, particularly, on color has had a great and depressing effect on the market for filters, filter discs, adapters, and so on. But in black-and-white photography, with which this chapter has been primarily concerned, you may have need for discerning use of filters. You should know about them, and experiment with them. For a filter, wisely used, can save an otherwise dull looking picture.

11
Color Photography

Today, we accept and use color photography as casually as coffee. No one who wasn't around and reasonably aware back in the 1930's can possibly appreciate the excitement caused by the announcement that a good, practical, workable system of color photography had, at long last, been achieved. For photographic scientists had been working toward that goal since before the beginnings of really practical photography in black-and-white.

The basic principles of color were stated and understood (by a few) way back in the first years of the 19th century and fully elucidated, in terms of photography, before the end of that century. But the means of achieving color photography simply did not exist. It took a very long time to develop the necessary chemistry, the physics, the optics, and the understanding of sensitometry. The parallel achievement of the complementary manufacturing methods and processes was nearly as slow, and just as important.

So when Mannes and Godowsky, two brilliant young musician-scientists working with and at the Kodak Research Laboratories, came up with their Kodachrome process in 1935, there was, almost literally, dancing in the streets. As of that point in history, photography was revolutionized, reborn, and revitalized.

If color was, and is, that important, we should know a little something about it.

SENSATIONAL!

Color is a sensation, just as hot and cold are sensations. A hot flatiron radiates energy in the form of heat waves. Touch it—and at once nerves in your fingertips shoot a message to your brain where headquarters decodes it as "HOT!" and activates muscles that snatch your fingers away, fast. Color

115

is, usually, a less violent sensation but the means by which it is perceived are just as fantastic.

Light waves are waves of energy, too, differing only in size from heat waves. Waves of light stimulate the incredibly complex system of receptors in our eyes; the receptors pass the word along to the brain where the decoding is done and, in no time at all, we are able to report that the observed color is red, blue, purple, brown, or whatever.

Whether or not we *like* the color we see is, at the moment, unimportant. But it is worth while to point out that the same output of radiant energy does not always produce exactly the same perception. This is but one of the puzzlements of color photography; there will be more about them a little later on.

The fundamental fact, basic to all color and thus to color photography, is that the visual appearance of any color can be matched by appropriate mixtures of red, green, and blue light (*light,* that is, not paint!). Early researchers into color theory demonstrated this fact by projecting colored light from three lanterns (ancestors of today's slide projectors) mixing red, blue, and green light on a white screen. By changing the proportions of the projected colors, they were able to produce any desired color.

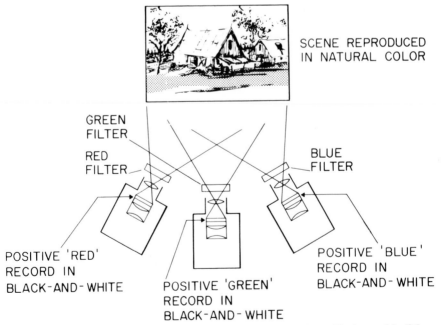

Fig. 11-1. Early method of additive color photography. (From **Photographic Principles and Practices,** by Harry Asher.)

Red, green, and blue emerged, therefore, as the *primary* colors of light; primary because they were and are all that we need to match any known color. This fact is demonstrated in the nearest color TV set; it also seems to support the contention of optical scientists that the receptor system in our eyes is a three-color system, with one receptor group sensitive to red, a second sensitive to green, and the third sensitive to blue. Every color we perceive depends upon the extent to which these three receptor groups are stimulated. If all three primary colors are present in about equal amounts, the sensation we receive is white or gray. If none is present, there is no light. We see no color, so we call it black.

The foregoing may not quite jibe with what you learned with your first grade paint boxes. But it is true in terms of light. As we shall see, light and paint are not the same thing.

Color addition. A demonstration of this fundamental fact of color is shown in Plate 1. Except for the modern projectors shown, it is very much the same arrangement as that used when the principle was first stated, back in 1802. Red, green, and blue light—colored filters on the projection lenses do the trick—are converging on the screen from the three projectors, in equal amounts but not in register. With the displacement or overlapping of the three beams of light, we therefore see not only the three primary colors but four simple combinations: (1) the combined three primaries give us white, (2) red plus green light add up to yellow, (3) red plus blue result in a kind of pink called *magenta,* and (4) blue and green combine in *cyan.*

Okay. But suppose we start varying the amounts of the three light-colors on the screen. We can do this by changing the apertures of the projectors. By controlling the mixture systematically, we can produce any desired color, thereby demonstrating the fundamental fact that the three primaries, suitably controlled, are truly primary.

In so doing, we have been adding colors, as required, to the screen. The starting points were the three primaries; their presence on the screen was controlled by the apertures of the three projectors. The same measure of control could have been accomplished photographically by using, instead of the apertures, black-and-white photographic slides or transparencies. The density of each slide would have determined, in each case, how much of that color of light would have reached the screen.

Whenever color is produced by mixing the three primary colors of light from three separate sources under some sort of control, the color mixing and the color produced are described as *additive color.*

Color subtraction. Refer now to the color graphics of Plate 2. In demonstrating color subtraction we start with the white of the paper. It is white because it reflects red, blue, and green light about equally (assuming your viewing light is reasonably normal). Now let's see what happens when we start overlaying the white paper with various dyes (or pigments or printing inks). If we overlay the paper with an ink having the ability to filter out or to absorb blue light, only the red and green will remain of the white reflected by the paper itself, and this combination of red and green will give us the color we call yellow. Yellow ink or paint appears yellow because it absorbs or subtracts blue light and reflects or transmits the red and green; again, those remaining colors appear together as yellow. If lesser concentrations of yellow ink are used, less blue will be absorbed and the resulting yellow will be weaker, or closer to white.

An ink or dye of different chemical composition will absorb other colors. For example, think about one that absorbs green light. When this happens we see what is left of the primary colors reflected by the white paper, namely, red and blue—or magenta. Thus, magenta ink has that particular color because it absorbs green light.

Similarly, the third printing ink in the graphic absorbs red, allowing only green and blue, or cyan, to be reflected by the paper. Varying the intensity of any of these light absorbers naturally changes the degree of absorption and, hence, the strength of the reflected color.

In this same illustration, we see four combinations where the pigments overlap. Where all three of the inks are present, no light emerges from the sheet, and we have black; for the yellow ink has absorbed the blue light, the magenta has absorbed the green, and the cyan has absorbed the red—so there's nothing left. Where yellow and cyan overlap, they absorb blue and red respectively, and only green remains. Magenta and cyan together absorb or subtract green and red, so that only blue remains. By varying the concentrations of yellow, magenta, and cyan inks, all degrees of blue, green, and red absorption can be accomplished.

Thus, by mixtures of various proportions of those three inks, or dyes or pigments, any desired color can be produced by absorption—which is to say, by *subtraction*. The color wheel (Plate 3) is an example of 12 subtractive mixtures with each color resulting from particular amounts of blue, green, and red having been absorbed by the inks. This is a direct example of the principle of subtractive color mixing.

We have called red, green, and blue the *primary* colors. What, then, are yellow, magenta, and cyan to be called? Some people say they are the *secondary* or even the *complementary* or the *subtractive primary* colors. In view of their obvious function, I prefer to think of them as the basic *control colors*.

Remember your first grade watercolor paint box? You were probably given to understand that the colors included were yellow, red, and blue, and that these were the primary colors; the only trouble with this is that the actual colors in your little tin box were not the primary colors at all. The blue was really blue-green, or cyan, and it was possible to mix it with yellow to get green. Similarly, the other colors were so doctored that you could obtain with them anything your little, uncritical hearts desired. Those colors were really neither primary nor control colors; they were merely convenient colors. Strange, isn't it; science sometimes has to appear to be unscientific.

So, okay. Let's review:

1. All colors can be matched by appropriate mixtures of red, blue, and green light.

2. Red, blue, and green light can be added from separate sources to match any desired color.

3. Red, green, and blue light can be subtracted from white by cyan, magenta, and yellow pigments to produce any desired color.

THE ADDITIVE PROCESS

Probably the best way to learn about any process is to use it. So, consider the following procedure in the making of a projected image in full color by the additive process, exactly as was done 150 years ago.

1. The subject to be pictured is, appropriately enough, a color chart. Three identical cameras, each loaded with a sheet of black-and-white pan film, are lined up close together and all aimed precisely at the chart. Camera A has a red filter over its lens, camera B a green filter, and camera C a blue filter. When exposures are made with the three cameras, each of the films "sees" the chart in terms of the light passed to it by the filter on its own camera lens. Red light comes through the red filter, green through the green, and blue through the blue. Where the color is complex, a mixture, two or even three of the films will share in the recording of it. When developed, the three resulting negatives are silver records on film of the amounts of the primary colors in the subject chart. They are called *separation* negatives, for they separate the primary colors, each of the three onto its own film.

2. The separation negatives are then printed, onto three other pieces of black-and-white film, to produce positive images. The *clear film spaces* in each positive represent the corresponding primary color in the subject. The black, or silver areas indicate an absence of the primary color in those particular areas.

3. Now, with three small projectors all aimed at a white screen, and each provided with its appropriate color filter, we project the three separate images. Individually, each looks like a highly biased version of the chart— and that is precisely what it is. Projector A shows us only those parts of the chart that have red in them, projector B gives us the green version, and projector C the blue.

4. If these three images are carefully merged into one, in perfect register, we are delighted to see a full-color image of the chart. Chances are it is excel-

lent in its reproduction of the original. Red and green, as projected, are combined to form yellow; blue and red are combined to form magenta, and blue and green to form cyan. Varying intensities or saturations of the basic hues have given us an infinite variety of colors, bold or subtle. Yet only the primary colors were used to give us this result; this was possible because, to repeat, those colors can be mixed to give *any* color. They are *added;* hence the technical term, *additive process.*

This example is additive color photography in its simplest, most rudimentary form. Obviously it is limited to a motionless subject, but it requires only black-and-white sensitive materials and produces excellent results. Its inherently good quality has led scientists and researchers and dreamers by the hundreds to try to find a way of making it a convenient system.

And in some applications, they have succeeded. Photoengravers still make and use separation negatives in the course of producing full-color printing plates. The famous old "one shot" camera, with its built-in filtering system, may now be gone, but it is not forgotten; it contributed generously to our knowledge and understanding of color. And dye transfer color printing, of which you probably have heard, depended on the separation process.

THE SUBTRACTIVE PROCESS

Subtractive color processes depend upon the subtraction of unwanted colors from white light to produce the colors of the original. As you'll see, subtraction appears to start out very much like addition.

Speaking schematically:

1. Three separation negatives are made on black-and-white film through filters of the three primary colors—red, green, and blue. As with the additive process, the silver on each film negative represents the presence of the primary color in the subject; clear spaces indicate an absence of that primary.

2. Film positives are made from the separation negatives. Silver in each positive indicates the extent to which the corresponding primary color must be subtracted from white light to produce the color picture.

The trick, then, becomes one of substituting dyes for the silver deposits— dyes that will subtract only the unwanted colors. Cyan (blue-green) dye is substituted for the silver deposits on the positive made from the red-filter negative, and it filters the red from the white viewing light. Similarly, magenta coloring is substituted for the silver on the positive made from the green-filter negative, and yellow for the silver on the positive from the blue-filter negative.

3. Now, suppose that these three colored images are superimposed, matched, or registered, and viewed against a white surface. The white surface, being itself a source of white light, is giving off red, green, and blue. The three

dyes, the basic control colors, which are present in a wide variety of concentrations, combine to subtract red, green, and blue to various degrees to produce a color picture.

The subtractive process may seem to be the long way home but, complex as it is, it is nonetheless the most practical and workable of color processes. It requires manufacturing control and precision undreamed of before the color revolution; and the processing is so exacting that it is best done by fully automatic machines, with precisely programmed controls. But it works, and beautifully.

COLOR PROCESSES

Currently available subtractive color processes can be classified in either or both of two ways. They can be grouped as (1) transparency or (2) print processes, depending on whether they are intended for viewing by transmitted light, as is the case with the familiar color slides or home movies, or by reflected light, as with prints and enlargements. Then, too, they can be divided into reversal or negative-positive processes, depending on the photographic means involved in arriving at the end result.

Reversal Processes

To most of us, the chemical and physical processes by which color images are achieved are so complex that they simply have to be classed as phenomena —and taken on faith. The reversal process, for example, can be described as one in which the negative image is developed in the conventional manner, then, rather than removing the unused emulsion with a fixing bath, it is exposed to light and developed. Then the silver image is removed with a chemical bleach, leaving a positive dye image on the same film used for the camera exposure. Within those few oversimplified lines are compressed the end results of generations of research, experiment, and experience. The literature on the subject is voluminous and, to technical minds, rewarding. The following description of specific processes may, meanwhile, shed a little light.

The Kodachrome Process is by far the best known of all subtractive color reversal processes. Kodachrome film consists of three layers of sensitive emulsion, plus intervening filter layers, all on a single film base or support. Together, they constitute a marvellously complex and precise sandwich. When exposed in a camera, each of the sensitive emulsions makes a negative record of one of the primary colors. When processed, the negative images are developed, reversed to positives, and cyan, magenta, and yellow dyes are substituted for silver in the appropriate layers. The same piece of film you rolled through your camera comes back to you with the same three layers, with the cyan, magenta, and yellow (the basic control colors) subtracting from white light to produce a brilliant, full-color positive transparency.

Kodachrome film for still pictures is available for cameras using 35mm film, 126 (Kodak Instamatic) 110 (Pocket Instamatic) and 828 films. Kodachrome II (daylight type) and Kodachrome-X are intended for use by daylight, blue flash, or electronic flash. Kodachrome II Professional, Type A, is for use by photoflood light or other 3400 K light sources.

Kodak Ektachrome Process

Ektachrome film also is a sandwich with three principal layers or emulsions. But it differs from Kodachrome in that the color formers are incorporated in the individual layers, so that all three colors are formed simultaneously, without recourse to the dye-forming solutions used in the Kodachrome process. Thus, while the "internal" complexity of the process is even greater, the actual processing is so simplified that it can be done at home by competent, careful work with the chemical packs available at well-stocked dealers. In most of the larger centers there are commercial labs qualified for Ektachrome processing.

Kodak Ektachrome-X and Kodak High Speed Ektachrome are supplied in 135 and 126 formats. Other forms of Ektachrome are available in sheet film sizes as well as in rolls and are primarily intended for professional or semi-pro use.

Negative-Positive Color Processes

In general, the negative-positive process, although inherently complex, has a more familiar "feel" for most of us. For, roughly speaking, the film exposed in the camera is developed, fixed, washed, dried, and then printed, by contact or enlargement, on paper. The paper has an emulsion similar to the film itself, and is developed similarly. Thus we are dealing with the familiar negative-positive cycle. The negative, however, is not only negative in terms of light and dark; it is also a negative in terms of its color, and an odd-looking thing it is.

Kodacolor and Kodak Ektacolor Processes

Like Kodachrome and Ektachrome, Kodacolor and Ektacolor films are sandwiches, with several layers of film in which the primary colors are recorded.

Development of Kodacolor and Ektacolor film produces negative silver images in all three layers. As this takes place, by-products of development react with special chemical couplers, incorporated in the several layers during manufacture, to form the three colored dyes.

A color negative looks strange because it is difficult to think in terms of negative color; the fact that the clear areas have a brownish cast adds another exotic touch.

The paper for negative-positive color printing is, unlike the color negative, conventionally white; but the essential three-color layers are there just the same.

Kodacolor film is supplied in a universal form that may be exposed by daylight, by flash, or by flood light. The correct and suitable color balance is obtained by careful use of filters during the printing process, or by highly specialized and flexible printing equipment in commercial photofinishing plants. Available in all principal roll film sizes, plus 110, 126, and 135 formats, Kodacolor film is the best answer yet to the old quest for a generally useful form of photographic color.

Although most users of Kodacolor will rely on the services of adequately equipped processing labs, it is possible for careful darkroom operators to produce their own Kodacolor negatives and prints. The necessary kits of chemicals and paper are generally available in good photo shops.

Kodak Ektacolor film is generally regarded and used as the professional counterpart of Kodacolor. It is available, in addition to the usual rolls and cassettes, in sheet film form. Unlike Kodacolor, Ektacolor is intended for processing by the competent user who understands how to follow established procedures faithfully and to use time and temperature as precise procedural factors.

Printing from Ektacolor negatives, on Ektacolor paper, involves several steps not encountered in black-and-white printing. Again, it should be stressed that the procedures are precise but, after study of the detailed instructions accompanying the materials, far from impossible. For example, proper color balance in the final print may involve the use of color filters; to achieve this balance requires not only technical precision but critical evaluation of an extremely perceptive sort. In short, you can do it but there is nothing slapdash about it.

Although a successfully completed Ektacolor print or enlargement is a beautiful thing, there are times when it is practically useful to produce black-and-white versions thereof. With Kodak Panalure or another of the panchromatic papers, it is easily possible to produce first-quality black-and-white prints from color negatives. For strictly record purposes, ordinary contact or enlarging paper can be used; you'll get prints, but they'll be as unbalanced in correctional rendition as old-fashioned ortho film results.

12
Using Color

Color photography obviously was achieved through the application of color theory. The fact that it is also locked in with psychology was not so obvious until color photography had been successfully achieved.

No doubt about it. It was a tremendous achievement. But almost at once it became apparent that there were strange discrepancies between colors as seen, colors as photographed, and colors as remembered. There were even differences observed on various viewings of the same color photograph. There were, in fact, so many puzzlements associated with the results of color photography that Kodak, with its very serious investment in color, established a new kind of laboratory—a laboratory dedicated to the study of the *psychological* problems of color.

You may have noted that manufacturers of color materials generally avoid claiming complete accuracy or trueness for them. That is simply because, without a lot of qualifications, it is impossible to define accuracy or truth in color. For colors vary in relation to the light by which they are observed or projected, the illumination by which they are photographed, and by the conditions under which the finished color photograph is viewed. There is another and very troublesome factor: the light of memory. With this, you are suddenly fighting your way through a jungle of psychological entanglements.

There are trails through this jungle, and some of them can be located and marked. For the present, however, let's concentrate on those color factors that are relatively tangible and can be controlled at the time color is photographed.

THE COLOR OF LIGHT

Around noon on a bright, sunny day you'll find that sunlight is about as white as it can get—composed of nearly equal parts of red, green, and blue.

Photograph a white house and, assuming you have a correct exposure, your color photograph will show an unmistakably white house.

But on an overcast, cloudy day that same house, exactly as white as it ever was, photographs as bluish. Or, on a fair early morning or late afternoon, it photographs as yellow or reddish. How come?

It is simply because the character of daylight varies. In the course of a single day the color of daylight can change considerably; from one season to another it changes much more. Yet we are hardly aware of these changes; to us it is always the same old white house, despite the fact that if we were to photograph it every day, we would soon have a strange collection of houses that looked blue, pink, red, yellow, and even purple. But because we *know* it is white, we *see* it as white. Color technicians call this *color adaptation.*

Color films cannot and do not adapt as we do; so film makers and, sometimes, film users have to do the adapting for them. That's why there are daylight films and artificial-light films and films marked, for example, for use by light at 3200 K or 3400 K. ("K" stands for Lord Kelvin, the great British physicist, who devised a color temperature scale to indicate specific changes along the way from red-hot to the blue-white incandescence of molten metal. Yellow candlelight turns out to have a color temperature less than 2000 K, while an arc light may register as high as 5000 or 6000 K.) And that is why there are such things as blue flashbulbs and white flashbulbs and color compensating filters, color conversion filters, and so on. The purpose of all these films and light sources and filters is to give us color photographs that, accurate or not so accurate, look right to our eyes. Sometimes, of course, photographers deliberately distort colors to achieve desired effects; that's fine, if they know what they're doing.

Summing up, then, we know that:

1. Daylight varies considerably in its real color.
2. Other sources of light have their own characteristic colors.
3. Our eyes adapt, so that a color seems constant.
4. Color films cannot adapt; they have to be helped.

COLOR TEMPERATURES OF COMMON LIGHT SOURCES

Light Source	Color Temperature
100-watt general-purpose lamp	2850 K
500-watt professional tungsten lamp	3200 K
500-watt amateur photoflood lamp	3400 K
Blue-lacquered flashbulb	6000 K
Electronic flash	6200-6800 K
Morning and afternoon sunlight	5000-5500 K
Noon sun, blue sky, white clouds	6200 K
Light from totally overcast sky	6700-7000 K
Blue skylight only, subject in shade	10,000-12,000 K

Conventional exposure meters are designed to respond to the *brightness* of the light falling on or reflected by an object. There are specialized meters that take the *color* of the light into consideration; their use or value to the unspecialized photographer will not, generally, compensate for their cost or complexity.

HUE, VALUE, AND CHROMA

Color matching is, as everyone knows, difficult business, even under standard or controlled conditions. All reds are not the same, and every other color has an almost infinite number of variations. But, for practical purposes, color can be quite accurately described in terms of three basic qualities or characteristics—*hue, value,* and *chroma.*

Hue is what most of us mean when we say "color." Red, orange, yellow, green, blue, and violet are the major hues, with such in-between hues as yellow-green, green-blue, and red-violet.

Within each hue there is more or less brightness; this is the factor called *value.* A value scale in color corresponds to a gray scale in black and white; it is a matter of lightness or darkness.

Chroma relates to the purity of a color—the extent to which it is unmuddied by gray. The less gray in a color, the purer it is, and the higher its *chroma.*

An astonishing number of businesses need to know and to prescribe specific colors—businesses far removed from photography or printer's inks or paints or dyes. So systems have been devised that specify and identify colors very well, and in terms of hue, value, and chroma. One such system, the Munsell, describes a color as, for example, R 4/14. In Munsell terms, that means that the *hue* is Red, the *value* is 4, and its *chroma* is 14. These numbers refer to patches of stable pigments arranged to form a remarkably vivid, three-dimensional "tree."

Looking straight down on this tree you see that its radiating branches embrace the full circle of hues: the five major or principal hues (red, yellow, green, blue, and purple) with, between them, the five intermediate hues (yellow-red, green-yellow, blue-green, purple-blue, and red-purple). The branches of any one hue represent values, darkest at the bottom and lightest at the top, corresponding to the black-and-white gray scale on the tree "trunk." And patches of pigment on each branch show increasing degrees of freedom from grayness, *i.e.,* chroma.

Several Munsell books are available that translate the three-dimensional-tree concept to two-dimensional pages. With either the tree or one of the books, it is easily possible to identify such a color as R 4/14 and to use it for comparison and matching. An example is shown in color Plate 4.

The point of all this is that scientists and technicians in the National Bureau of Standards, the Optical Society of America, the Kodak Research Laboratories, and many other serious and learned groups all over the world have done a tremendous amount of hard work to produce and standardize a system into which any known color can be fitted and to which any new color can be added. Part of their job has been to specify the nature of the light by which the pigments are studied; and that brings us back to the relatively familiar fact that light itself is variable.

IT'S RELATIVE

In color, in light, and in any area you care to name, good old relativity plays a part. For example, consider what happens when a patch of color, say blue-green 4/5, is surrounded by other colors. Surround it with yellow, and it looks darker; center it in a field of dark green, and it appears lighter. A blue background brings out the green, while the blue jumps up in front of a green background. In black-and-white photography a similar phenomenon makes a gray seem darker on a white background than on a black one. This phenomenon has the name of "simultaneous contrast." It has its uses. You will discover them as you play or experiment with color.

You may discover, too, that an arrangement of colored objects, all of which have approximately the same value, tends to be, as you look at it, a kind of color hash, without the necessary emphasis. But when you photograph it in color, that overall sameness may very well disappear; for color materials have a tendency to exaggerate color differences. Your problem then becomes a matter of controlling or subduing rather than intensifying color contrasts.

You may have grown up with a fear of color. I know I did. Some colors, I was told, were inherently terrible and some *combinations* of colors downright scandalous. So, out of ignorance, I avoided strong color of any kind. But painters, primitives, and decorators went right on, successfully combining those allegedly *verboten* colors. Finally, I realized that this apparent flouting of the "rules" was actually, a sophisticated (or instinctive, or both) use of subtle values and chromas of the forbidden hue combinations. There is no escaping the fact that two colors of similar value and strong chroma do not make good neighbors. Take a strong red and its complement, blue-green; placed side by side they "vibrate" unpleasantly. But, vary the value or the chroma of either, and you can achieve something that does not vibrate and is useful.

Having mentioned complementary colors, let's back up a bit. Consider the color wheel, as shown in color diagrams or as in the radiating branches of the Munsell "tree." Any two colors that are directly opposite one another

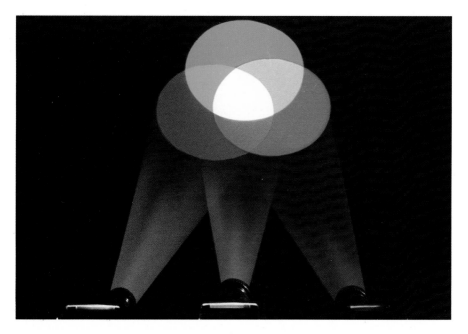

Plate 1 (above). Additive color mixture. Projectors with red, green, and blue filters cast overlapping circles of their respective colors, creating pairs of cyan, magenta, and yellow. Where all three overlap, the result is white.

Plates 2 and 3 (below). In subtractive color mixture (left) cyan, magenta, and yellow filters (which act as pigments) superimposed combine to produce red, green, and blue. Where all three overlap, all color is subtracted, leaving black. The color wheel (right) contains twelve subtractive mixtures. Opposite hues are complementary; hues touched by the triangle, if it is rotated, are harmonious.

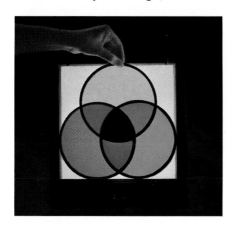

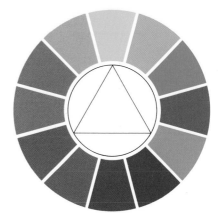

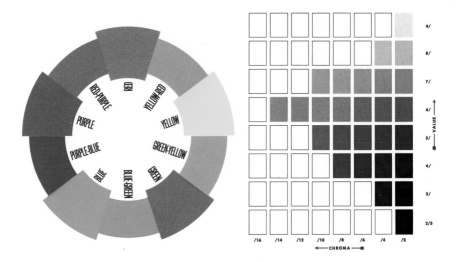

Plate 4. The Munsell System. (Left) Hue circle showing the Major Hues. Each is number 5 of a family of 10 adjoining hues. (Right) Chart showing variations in value and chroma for 2.5 YR. (Below) Color tree showing the three-dimensional relationship of hue, value, and chroma. (Illustrations by Munsell Color Company)

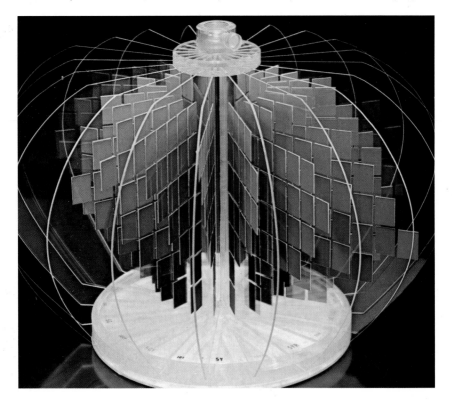

Plate 5. This photograph and the next combine light sources: twilight sky and tungsten light.

Plate 6. A photo such as this requires a long exposure, a tripod, and properly balanced color film.

Plates 7a, b, & c. Fluorescent illumination presents special problems for color photography. With daylight film and no filter (above left) the results will be slightly off. Tungsten film and no filter (above right) create unpleasant bluish effect. Best color is obtained with daylight film and appropriate filter (left), here High Speed Ektachrome (Daylight) with a CC30M filter.

Plates 8a & b (opposite page, below). Where overhead fluorescent lighting is combined with tungsten illumination, as from lamps, daylight film (left) provides the best rendition. The righthand picture was made on tungsten film.

Plates 9a & b (above). Where daylight and tungsten light combine, the color looks best, again, on daylight film (right).

Plates 10a & b (below). Since color film has less latitude than black-and-white, it pays to reduce contrasts, especially in portraits, by filling-in shadow areas with reflectors; here, a large white card is used.

Plate 11. Existing light and a careful exposure, combined with a wide-angle lens, capture both the beauty and the mood of this church interior.

Plate 12. Where flash would be obtrusive, as during a wedding ceremony, an existing-light exposure is necessary. Here, Kodacolor-X Film was exposed at $\frac{1}{2}$ sec. and $f/4$.

Plate 13 (above). Available-light color can be used to stop action, provided you catch it at its peak. High Speed Ektachrome (Tungsten), at ASA 320, 1/25 sec. at $f/2.8$. Plate 14 (below). Spotlights permit the use of daylight film. Here, Gunther Gebel-Williams' famed tiger act was captured on High Speed Ektachrome (Daylight) at ASA 400, 1/125 sec. at $f/5.6$, by John Wolf.

Plate 15 (next page). Another example of low-level light and fast color film. High Speed Ektachrome (Tungsten) at ASA 320.

in those circles are complementary. (They "complete" one another to form an apparently neutral, colorless gray.) At any rate, the complementaries do not get on well together; they vibrate. However, if you choose colors at the points of an isosceles triangle rotated within the color circle, you find that the three indicated colors are harmonious; they do not vibrate, they get along well together.

Furthermore, as you scan a color wheel, the series of neighboring colors embraced by an arc of the circle tend to be key colors, setting the mood of a color composition. Thus, an autumn scene is very reasonably made up of the warm, ripe colors in the neighborhood of red, with the deep blue of the sky and the dark green of pines providing a natural and (according to that inner triangle) harmonious set of contrasts. A "cold" picture, on the other hand, includes an arc of the greens, blue-greens, blues, and so on.

A case can be made for the uses of the colors of nature as guides to successful color combinations. Watch what nature does with colors; the observation can be very instructive.

Some colors, you will find, are natural backgrounds. Outdoors, the blue of the sky is hard to beat. Indoors, for portraits or still-life studies, medium blue or gold will generally work excellently.

Color and mood or emotion is a combination that has its puzzlements. Red, we have been told, is angry, passionate, or war-like. Yet what could be more cheerful than the red of Christmas decorations? Still, even at Christmas, the bright reds are mitigated by blues, greens, silver, and gold. The point is simply that unless you want the effect to be angry and passionate, you introduce other colors, chosen for their ability to relieve and comfort the viewing eye.

In our modern world of color photography it is not enough, as it certainly once was, to introduce into a landscape, for example, a pretty girl in a red coat. Today we should know and understand why that red coat may or may not do well for our picture, or for the girl.

FILTERS FOR COLOR

A few pages back, in summing up the talk about the color of light, it was stated that color film, remarkable as it is, cannot adapt (as the eye does) to the endless variety of light's color characteristics. The film, it was stated, had to be helped.

And that is precisely the function of the many filters now available for color photography—to re-balance the incoming light, to compensate for what it may lack, or to convert it into kinds of light the film is capable of recording.

This is just a bit less troublesome and expensive than trying to provide different kinds of film for every kind and color of light, quite a bit less. Even so, filters involve problems. And using them well is something of an art as well as a science.

Parentheticaly, it should be said that the casual amateur photographer may never own or use a single filter. He may spend a lifetime recording his famliy, his travels, or his hobbies—and never feel that he is deprived because he hasn't a filter to his name. Of course, he may wonder sometimes why his shots look too blue or too red or why he didn't get what he thought he was going to get in a mountain scenic. But he shrugs it all off—just luck.

If this casual amateur were to be just a little less casual he would find that a very simple, inexpensive, easy-to-use filter would give him the kind of mountain scenics he really wanted. Having discovered this, he might venture farther, but at that point he might well be in danger of losing his casual amateur status.

Filters for color work are not all designed for use on the camera lens. Some are expressly, and very precisely, made for color printing and enlarging processes. And still others are designed to be placed between the light source and the subject, thereby changing the character of the light by which the subject is photographed. Quite another kind of filtration is employed in the commercial plants where miles of color prints are turned out every day; in such plants the operators can, by punching a button or two, vary the colors of the printing light so that optimum results can be obtained.

But our concern is expressly with filters for our cameras. There are three general types:

1. *Color compensating filters,* which are designed to compensate for deficiencies in the quality of the light by which color film must sometimes be used. They absorb specific slices of the spectrum and, in so doing, change the overall color balance. You may find your supplier has these filters in several densities of six colors: red, green, blue, cyan, magenta, and yellow.

2. *Light balancing filters,* which change the color quality of the illumination so that you can obtain cooler (bluer) or warmer (yellower) color rendering. Unlike the color compensating (CC) filters they do not absorb parts of the visible spectrum. Rather, they serve to provide an adjustment, a shift, throughout the spectrum—a shift that can amount to a change in the color temperature of the light.

3. *Conversion filters* are actually light balancing filters with a special function. They change the color of the light (as passed by the lens) of various light sources so that they can be used with specific types of color film, or vice versa.

Because there are many color filters, it is suggested that you can best begin to shop for them by consulting with a knowledgeable photographic dealer or studying of one of the excellent Kodak Data Books (there are several) dealing with color photography and filters. Incidentally, the photographic industry has provided the means by which any filter can be accurately fitted to practically any camera lens.

LIGHTING FOR COLOR

Use fairly flat, even illumination and let the colors take care of contrast and emphasis.

This is the basic rule of lighting for color photography. And it makes sense; there is nothing arbitrary about it.

Simple, uniform lighting gives all of the colors in a scene the chance to rise up and be enjoyed. The minute you add an emphasis with special lighting, or throw in a shadow for dramatic effect, you complicate things; for colors do not behave as tones of black-and-white do. The colors take on totally new personalities in terms of value and chroma, and may fall completely out of harmony.

Illumine the shadows; don't let them go empty and black. The colors, of themselves, give you just about all the contrast you need. If you instinctively abhor flat, frontal lighting, as many veteran monochrome photographers do, try working in color on a day when the sun is overcast, when shadows are not at all sharp. You may find the results vastly more pleasing, especially in portraying people.

There are, of course, problems in using full, strong, frontal lighting. People tend to squint, and textures and facial modelling tend to get lost. So, fudge a bit; let the light come in over your left or right shoulder. In so doing, you do not hide colors and you add just enough third dimensional quality to provide character, texture, and depth.

Closeups made under a bright blue sky may require a reflector (or a controlled flash) to throw light into the shadows, but watch the color of that supplementary light. If it isn't a white or neutral gray, it can completely upset your picture. Even nearby foliage or buildings can reflect unwanted colors of light onto your subject.

In photographing groups it is even more important in color work than in black-and-white to be sure that all the members of the group have about the same illumination; otherwise you may find that the people in the shade simply do not show up right.

Backlighted color work is tricky, although it can be very effective and dramatically beautiful. But don't bother with it until you are sure of yourself with ordinary lighting. If and when the time comes for some backlighted shots, you will probably provide some degree of frontal light, either by a flat reflector or with a flash of synchronized light. But, again, be judicious about the color of that added light. The supplementary flash, assuming that you have daylight film in the camera, should be in terms of flashbulbs that are consistent with daylight—M3B or 5B, for example.

EXPOSURE LATITUDE AND COLOR FILM

In black-and-white work you can sometimes over- or underexpose considerably, and make up for it in development or printing. But no such compension is possible in color; when you are off, the colors themselves suffer. You may get an image, but the colors will not be correct or satisfying.

Reversal (slide) color films require the most exact exposures; half a stop one way or the other is generally the limit. Negative-positive color processes have more latitude, provide greater leeway—as much as a full stop on the under side and maybe even a little more on the over side.

Fortunately, correct exposure is usually attainable. The instructions packed with the film are, if you really use them, very specific for a wide variety of picture-making situations. And, of course, intelligent use of an exposure meter can help you be on the button consistently.

TAKE CARE OF COLOR FILMS

All films need and deserve careful storage. Color films and transparencies rate even greater care.

Before exposure, color film has very good keeping qualities, unless you allow it to get too warm or fail to protect it from humidity and moisture. But after exposure, the film should be sent off for processing as soon as possible. If it is impossible to get it away promptly (you *may* be on safari or in the far country of Australia), give your film special care. Be sure it's dry and then seal it up in metal foil or strong plastic, and keep it as cool as possible.

When the processed film is returned to you, see that it gets clean, dry, average temperature storage. Use it and enjoy it, of course, but don't be careless with it; for you're dealing with dyes, not stable silver deposits on film. Dyes are delicate and sensitive to both light and heat. So, if you value your prints or transparencies, protect them. Color negatives should be filed in envelopes, transparencies in covered cases or files, and color prints should be kept in covered albums. Color enlargements should be hung on walls that get no direct sunlight. With reasonable care, your color materials will last as long as you need them.

COLOR SHOWMANSHIP

Comedians and cartoonists love to tee off on people who show their color slides or movies to hapless viewers who cannot gracefully escape. This is because the photographers impose on their audiences. They make a big thing of setting up projector and screen, and then they present a hetero-geneous, miscellaneous collection of slides—poor slides, trivial slides, mean-ingless slides, and a few good ones. No wonder people are bored!

Your first duty to your audience is to weed out your poor and trivial shots; if they happen to have personal, family values, okay, but reserve them for family showing. Second, be sure that your projector is in order, that the lamp is good (keep a spare on hand) and the projection lens clean. Check on the need for and availability of an extension cord. And know where your pro-jection screen is and whether or not it is in good condition. In short, don't put yourself in a position requiring excuses or alibis or apologies. And never, *never* show a slide with the comment, "Uh, this doesn't really show it as it was." In a spot like that, throw the slide away and tell people about what you saw; they'll believe you and imagine a beautiful picture.

Even if you have a tubful of good shots, *don't show them all*. The first rule of showmanship is to leave your audience wanting more, not less.

It is easier to make a presentation of color slides than of color prints. To begin with, the slides are shown brightly on a screen in a darkened room; they are automatically "on stage." Everyone in the room is practically forced to look at them.

Color prints enjoy no such advantage. Ideally, good color prints should be shown individually, each on a mount of a neutral color and large enough to isolate the print from surrounding, distracting, and possibly conflicting colors. Certainly color prints deserve more than being passed around, like a deck of playing cars, to be pawed and viewed in any available light and amid all sorts of visual distractions. A good album with a minimum of prints per page is a reasonable compromise. Furthermore, the light by which the album is viewed should be good and as white as possible. Each print represents an investment of time, care, intelligence, and money. Don't squander it.

BLACK-AND-WHITE PRINTS FROM COLOR

Sometimes you will need or want black-and-white versions of color shots. It is not difficult to get them.

With color transparencies the procedure is direct and simple. From the original you make a print (only it's negative) onto a panchromatic film, preferably one of the slower emulsions. Because transparency materials are largely grain-free, enlargements to considerable size can be safely made. With the negative so obtained you can then make as many prints or enlargements as you wish.

Some workers use their enlargers to make such negatives; others place the originals in the opening of an illuminated box and, with a view camera or with a camera adjusted for extreme closeups, photograph the brightly lighted images (with room light off or greatly subdued). With care, excellent results can be had.

With color print materials there's an even simpler method, if you have access to an enlarger. You simply use the color negative as you would a black-and-white negative. But you don't use conventional enlarging paper. You use a panchromatic paper, such as Kodak's Panalure paper, which not only shortens the printing times required by conventional enlarging papers but affords prints of far better color sensitivity. Eyes, lips, skies, skin textures, and so on come through looking right. With Panalure you can filter the enlarger light to achieve emphasized skies or any other desired effect. Because Panalure is more sensitive than normal papers, it must be used with little or no safelight. But that's not exactly an insurmountable problem.

In sum, color materials emerge today as being as useful under as many varying conditions as black-and-white materials. And, they can be immensely satisfying.

13
Enlarging

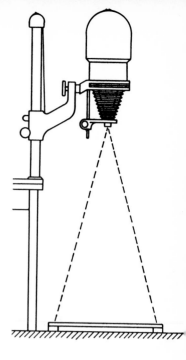

An enlargement is, photographically speaking, the proof of the pudding.

For in an enlargement, your picture, which may have looked pretty good as a negative or even as a contact print, becomes a big, fully revealed image. It reflects and magnifies the care with which the original was shot; conversely, it makes any mistakes stick out like sunburnt noses. Enlarging is a delightful, satisfying, and rewarding process—or a frustrating, sometimes humiliating experience.

There is more to enlarging than simple magnification. It offers you a variety of controls by which you can (1) realize the full potential of your photograph, (2) correct shortcomings in composition or emphasis, (3) subdue unwanted features, (4) emphasize an element or a part of the image, and (5) add the finishing touches that separate exhibition prints from mere blowups.

Theoretically, of course, item 1 is all that should really be necessary. You did your study of the composition in the camera viewfinder, you assured a perfect negative by your choice of exposure, and by your careful selection of angle, lighting, and all the rest created a work of art. Sure, theoretically.

In practice, none but the top masters of our art produce negatives that enlarge perfectly, unaltered in any way except size. Most of us are grateful that enlarging offers us one more chance to make a fine picture out of the scene we enjoyed and, in high hope, photographed.

A good enlargement is a pleasure because it transmutes what may have started out as a postage-stamp-size negative into a fine, big, frameable picture. But there is an even more important reason. In a small print you cannot achieve the proper sense of perspective unless you hold the print abnormally close to your eyes; in an enlargement the perspective appears to be normal and right at ordinary viewing ranges.

135

A CAMERA IN REVERSE

Enlarging is, essentially, just a variant of the photographic printing process. But it differs from contact printing in that the image of the negative is projected, much as a color slide or a movie scene is projected. Enlargements are often called, in fact, projection prints. The projected image is focused on a piece of light-sensitive paper rather than onto a viewing screen.

Thus an enlarger is a camera in reverse. Instead of receiving an image, it projects one. There is a strong light source, rays from which pass through the negative to a lens that transmits them, in an expanding cone, to the paper. Obviously, the greater the distance from lens to paper, the more the light cone expands, and the larger the projected image.

In some respects an enlarger has a simpler job than a camera, for the enlarger seeks only to transmit rays of light from one flat plane (the negative) to another and parallel flat plane (the paper). Depth of field is, generally, no problem at all. Stopping down the lens becomes only a matter of adapting the brilliance of the projected image to the sensitivity of the paper and to your convenience, or to an exposure time that is neither so long that it invites trouble from vibration nor so short that it inhibits your use of some of the controls we shall be talking about shortly.

The primary function of the enlarger is to project as uniform an image as possible, with full detail out to the corners. Negative and paper must remain perfectly still and parallel during the exposure, hence any wobble, shake, or vibration cannot be tolerated.

In professional studios you can find enlargers that are big, beautiful, motorized, and computerized mechanisms, costing very large amounts of money. For most of us, enlargers entirely adequate for our requirements fall within the $75 to $250 bracket.

They vary in light sources, optical systems, sizes of negatives accommodated, negative carriers, lenses, mechanical adjustments, rigidity, and precision of design and operation. Let's consider some of those variables.

Light sources. Real old-timers can remember enlargers with carbon-arc or Cooper-Hewitt illuminants. Today, the sources are considerably more convenient—and more varied. You'll find ordinary domestic frosted light bulbs, projection lamps, and special, high-intensity halogen lamps. For each type of light source there is an appropriate kind of optical system, the purpose of which is to get the maximum of the available light organized and directed to the negative as uniformly as possible.

Some enlargers, the condenser types, are close relatives of the classic lantern slide projector. The light source is a high-powered light, rays from which are collected and lined up by a pair of big glass condensers. From the condensers the light goes to and through the negative, on to the lens and thence, ultimately, to the paper. Pure condenser enlargers tend to be high in contrast and, because they *are* pure, also tell the truth and the whole truth about the negative—and any dust, dirt, finger marks, or scratches that may be present.

At the other end of the enlarging illuminant spectrum are the straight *diffusion* enlargers. They have no condensers at all, depending upon the shape of the lamp house to scramble the light and to direct it down toward the negative. As could be expected, diffusion enlargers are less precise in the quality of the projected image, less contrasty, and much more willing to overlook dust and fingermarks.

A compromise between the condenser-type and the diffusion-type enlarger would seem to be reasonable and desirable. It is, and most of the enlargers available today embody it. The light source and/or the lamp housing diffuses the light so that the condensers pass on a broad column of light rather than rays from a single point or clump of points. The image received down on the paper is of medium contrast, adequately sharp, and not too revealing of superficial flaws on the negative.

In any enlarger, whatever its price or type, the most important characteristic to look for is its ability to project onto the paper board an image that is uniform in illumination, sharp clear out to the edges, and free of optical distortion. To do this, it must have a well-designed optical system that is married to a suitable lens.

Fig. 13-1. The four types of enlarger.

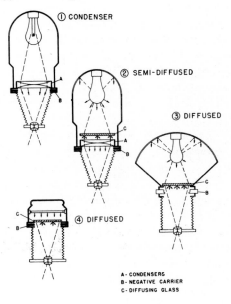

Lenses. Assuming that the camera in which the negative to be enlarged was exposed has a demountable lens, there is no good reason why that lens should not also be used in the enlarger. On the other hand, there are advantages in using a good projection lens in the enlarger; usually such a lens will have click stops that facilitate its setting without the visual inspection an ordinary lens requires (and visual inspection is not always easy in the safe-lighted darkroom). A good lens costs money, but not excessive amounts of it. The general rule for projection lenses, as for camera lenses, is that the focal length should be a little longer than the diagonal of the largest negative to be enlarged.

No integral shutter is required, because normal enlarging exposures are several seconds long. Hand switching the lamp off and on is sufficiently accurate for all but the most exacting work. Make sure, therefore, that clicking the switch does not involve shaking the whole apparatus; a switch in the electric line rather than on the enlarger itself makes good sense.

Negative Carriers. The gadget that holds the negative in place in the enlarger has one prime function—to hold that piece of film firmly and flatly. Most such carriers, today, are simple metal masks with openings in them the exact size of a frame of the film you use. Masks, plus film, should slide in and out without "wrestling" or wracking the whole enlarger. Almost every manufacturer of enlargers has his own pet form of negative carrier, varying from individual masking plates to hinged masks to plates with spring steel fingers that hold the film—to simple glass sandwiches. Ease of placing the film, ease of inserting or withdrawing the carrier, and the firm security of the film, once in place, are the criteria for judging carriers. You will require separate carriers for each size of film you normally use.

Controls. Good enlargers have three major controls; one for changing and holding the distance between the negative plane and the condensers, one for making the big shifts in the "throw" from enlarger head to paper board, and one for final and fine focus. All controls should work smoothly; the final-focus control should, particularly, work without backlash in its geared mechanism and, once set, should stay put.

Filters. A red or safety filter is incorporated in most enlargers, above or below the lens. It is designed to be swung or slid into and out of position. Its purpose is to give you a dim red image on the paper board while you position the paper for an enlargement. It is not intended to be used during focusing operations; it is merely a safe convenience. For most enlarging papers it is reasonably safe *but* if and when you start using Panalure or color print papers it isn't safe at all. The data provided for those papers will give you full information on safe and unsafe filters.

A totally different kind of filter is built into some enlargers. It's a sheet of heat-absorbing glass the purpose of which is to protect the negative if or when long exposures (as for a very dense negative or an unusually large blowup) are necessary. Heat from the lamp can buckle or warp a negative—and there is no unbuckling process I know of.

In making color enlargements you will have to use a variety of special filters. Some of them, the color printing (CP) filters, are intended for use up between the lamp and the negative and should not be used within the image-forming system below the negative. Kodak color compensating (CC) filters are optically much finer and *can* be used below the lens. At any rate, your enlarger for color work should have adequate provision for the special filtration color requires.

The paper board should be and remain unwarped, and husky enough to support the enlarger without strain. It should be large enough to take $14'' \times 16''$ sheets of paper, preferably even larger. Because photographic papers tend to curl in on their emulsion sides, you will need something to hold them firmly flat on the paper board. The simplest "system" is a pair of heavy hardwood sticks, manually positioned along the long edges of the paper just before the exposure. The best and most convenient device is a printing frame or easel, usually so designed as to be adjustable for various sizes of prints and margins. The paper board itself should have a non-skid surface; to reduce ambient reflections it is usually painted matte black.

Rigidity. As already indicated, steadiness is a basic necessity in enlarging. To begin with, make sure that the bench or table on which the enlarger is mounted is rock-steady and built like a battleship. Its top, of course, should be perfectly level. With your enlarger set up on the table, run the head as far up as it can go, as for a maximum size enlargement. Then knuckle-tap it anywhere on the whole mechanism. If there is the slightest shiver of vibration, check all the hold-down bolts and screws. At its fullest extension, the post or girder on which the enlarger head rides is under considerable stress, so make doubly sure of the firmness of its anchorage in the paper board. Sometimes it may be necessary to carpenter a top-side anchor, connecting the top of the enlarger post to the wall; it need not be elaborate but it does need to be solid.

Darkroom safelighting for enlarging is more critical than for contact printing. Enlarging papers are more sensitive and, accordingly, more easily fogged. Generally a safelight filter, Series OA, will be adequate, but you will feel much more secure if you repeat, with a sheet of the appropriate paper, the safelight test outlined in the chapter on contact printing. When using special papers—Panalure or color print papers—special safe lighting will be necessary; the data accompanying the paper will clue you in.

ENLARGING PAPERS

As has been indicated, enlarging papers have to be considerably faster than contact papers because of the relatively greater distance between the negative image and the paper on which it is imposed.

Enlarging paper emulsions are usually combines of silver chloride and silver bromide, and are commonly referred to as chloro-bromides. In manufacture, the proportions and characteristics of these two light-sensitive salts are controlled and balanced to obtain a wide range of photographic qualities, including speed and contrast. The size of the developed silver grains imparts a characteristic tone or color to the image; finely divided silver grains give the print a warm or brownish tone, while larger grains afford a colder, blue-black tone.

Like contact papers, enlarging papers come in great variety, ranging all the way from glossy, super-smooth papers intended for ferrotyping to extremely coarse-surfaced papers whose use is limited (or should be) to those subjects that can justify it. In addition to variations in surface, there are variations in color, in weight and, of course, in contrast.

To describe all the papers available from all the manufacturers here and abroad would require a book in itself. Kodak alone offers nine basic types of enlarging papers (not counting papers designed for special, technical use) and most of those nine come in various contrasts and colors as well as in single- or double-weight. I suggest you get a current Kodak Paper Data Book from your dealer; it will give the latest information on the papers available and on the characteristics of each, together with a recap of appropriate uses, exposures, developers, safelights, and all the rest.

To begin with, it seems reasonable to me to invest in a single kind of paper, in two contrasts; for example, try Kodabromide "N" (smooth but not glossy) single weight, in contrast grades Nos. 2 and 4. You will find it a generously responsive paper that will satisfy your requirements until, having perfected your enlarging technique, you are ready to explore the possibilities of other papers. (After which, you may very well return to old faithful.)

Because enlarging papers cost more than contact papers, you will be even more careful and precise in using and storing them. Waste and spoilage can run into money.

Speaking of economy, there are savings to be effected in using variable-contrast enlarging paper. It is also fun to use, because you can achieve a remarkable degree of contrast control by using a set of simple filters, positioned beneath the enlarger lens. So, while I still favor Kodabromide, I must admit that variable-contrast paper has some real advantages.

THE ENLARGING PROCESS

The preparations for enlarging are much like those for contact printing. Developer, stop-bath, hypo, and rinse are all prepared and brought to the proper temperature. The trays should be large enough to accommodate the largest prints you contemplate making at this session; a little extra room for finger freedom is advisable.

Be sure the enlarger lens, the negative, and the negative carrier (especially if it is of the "glass sandwich" type) are all clean. Remember, in enlarging you enlarge a speck of dust on the negative just as much as the negative itself. Check the safelight for the paper you're about to use, and have the paper itself readily available so that you can extract a sheet without fumbling or exposing it to harmful light. Some workers keep their paper in a lighttight drawer beneath the enlarger; that's fine, if you remember to close that drawer regularly after taking out a sheet.

Procedure. Put a pencil in back of your ear, don your apron, and....

1. Place the negative to be enlarged into the negative carrier and slide it into position, emulsion side down (toward the lens). Because the image on the paper board will be inverted, you'll probably feel more comfortable if, when positioning the negative in the enlarger, you make it upside-down to begin with.

2. Put a sheet of plain white *non*-photographic paper in position on the paper board. Preferably, it should be the same size and thickness as the paper you plan to enlarge on.

3. Open the enlarger lens to its maximum. Turn white light off and darkroom safelight on. Then turn on the projector. Down there on the paper you will see that there's an image, but probably neither sharp nor the size you want. So with the major up-down control, get the image to the approximate right size and then, with the fine-focus adjustment, move the lens mount up or down until the image is in sharp, really sharp, focus. (An enlarging focus-finder is a gadget you may want some day; meanwhile you simply can't be too critical with your unaided eyes. Test focus, of course, on a sharp, clean line in the negative image.) If the white focusing paper is the size of your enlarging paper, move it around on the paper board until you have the composition you want, with horizontal lines horizontal.

4. Very well, switch off the enlarger lamp and place a test strip of the enlarging paper on the paper board. (A $1'' \times 10''$ slice cut from an $8'' \times 10''$ sheet should be big enough, if you position it so that it cuts across the face of the image so as to include the fullest possible range of the densities of the negative.)

5. Close down the lens a little to what seems to be a good working aperture and make a series of test exposures of, for example, 4, 6, 8, and 12 sec. You can do this easily by progressive masking of the test strip with a sheet of black paper. Pencil the exposure steps on the back of the test strip.

6. Develop the test strips for the recommended time. If one section of the strip, the 8-sec. exposure for example, appears to be about right, expose all of another test strip for 8 seconds and process it. If the first test shows either under- or overexposure throughout, discard it and try another test with a new

Fig. 13-2. A typical enlarging exposure test strip. Each of the four sections shows the difference three seconds make. First segment, left, received twelve seconds exposure while the others received, successively, nine, six, and three seconds. The nine-second segment was obviously the most nearly right.

set of exposure times, longer or shorter, as seems to be indicated. When you have achieved a test strip that looks promising, fix it for a moment.

7. Then, turn on the white light for a real inspection. Check the strip for focus, of course, but concentrate on its density and contrast. Blacks should be truly black and the highlights should be clear. If they're not, maybe you need to use a contrastier paper. Use test strips freely; you'll save paper and money in the long run.

The test strip method of determining correct exposure and contrast-grade paper is a little slow, but it gives you practice and sharpens your discriminating eye. Another and very neat means to exposure determination is the Kodak Projection Print Scale. Laid over the paper during a fixed time of exposure, it gives you a wide range of results from which to choose.

This business of exposure determination is a bit tricky for beginners for two reasons. First, a print in the developing solution under safelight looks darker and contrastier than it really is and, accordingly, tempts you to rinse and fix it prematurely. Second, a hurriedly fixed print lacks the full contrast and brilliance of a fully fixed image. Try to avoid the dull flatness of tonal quality that typifies so much amateur enlarging. So, okay, you have determined the correct exposure.

8. With a full sheet of enlarging paper, make your first full-size enlargement. Develop, rinse, and fix it carefully, and drop it in the wash bath for at least half an hour.

9. Clean the face of the washed print with a tuft of wet cotton or a very soft sponge and place the print on either a big white blotter or a cheesecloth rack, face down. It will be dry in an hour or so, depending upon the circulation of air around it.

And there you have it—a "straight" enlargement. It may live up to all your hopes and expectations. Fine! Or, it may not, but do not despair; for there are several corrective measures you can take.

CORRECTIVE MANIPULATION

It is not suggested here that your first full enlargement can be doctored to produce the kind of print you want (although, as we shall see, some superficial improvements *can* be made). But there are several things you can do in making other prints from the same negative to make the results more to your liking.

Cropping
Cropping can help you to reframe the image on the paper board to produce better composition, better emphasis. Indeed, you may decide after studying the full print to crop out everything but some one single feature or area. This may also mean changing the degree of enlargement, but—no problem. Usually a relatively minor amount of cropping will be found adequate.

Dodging
Dodging (shading) parts of the image during exposure naturally reduces exposure in those areas shaded and, accordingly, lightens them in the print. You can make a simple, adequate dodging tool in half a minute with a length of stiff wire with a half-dollar size piece of black paper taped to its end. For areas near the picture margin, a black card may be preferable. The trick in using any dodging tool is to keep it in constant, gentle motion over the area to be lightened; otherwise you'll get hard lines around the dodged area, dead give aways of your corrective measures. Incidentally, be sure the dodged area gets enough initial exposure to assure some degree of image detail.

Burning-in
Burning-in is the exact opposite of dodging. It is the local addition of exposure to areas in the "straight" print that appear to be inadequately exposed. The whole sky may need a darker tone, or one highlight area may lack the detail you know is in the negative. What's needed, therefore, is a device that will protect the rest of the exposed image while a part of it gets more. A sky can be burned-in with the aid of a piece of cardboard torn in two along a line that corresponds roughly with the pictured horizon line. The card, kept in motion a few inches above the paper and in the general neighborhood of the horizon line, protects the foreground from additional exposure while the sky gets the extra exposure it seems to need. If the underexposed area is

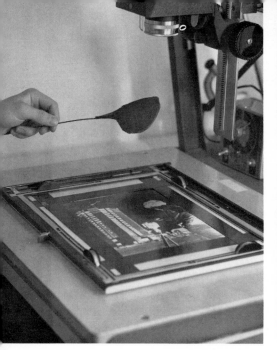
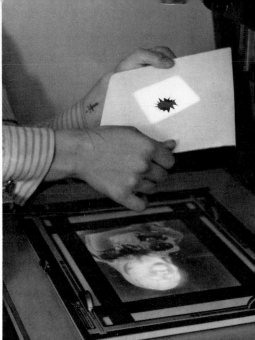

Figs. 13-3a & b. In enlarging, there are two basic special-area controls—dodging and burning-in. In dodging (left), you shield an area of the image which otherwise would come up as too dark, or without detail. Burning-in (right) is just the reverse; you add exposure to an area to bring up highlight detail. In both cases, the tool must be kept in constant motion to preclude the casting of hard shadows.

small and central, tear an appropriate hole in a sheet of cardboard (shirt cards from the laundry are both useful and expendable). With the card held in the enlarger beam to protect the rest of the image, after normal exposure, feed light through the hole to the needful area, while moving the card up, down, and around gently and smoothly. Only trial and error plus practice can make you adept at this. As in dodging, constant motion is a must. If the technique is obvious, it is no good.

Vignetting

Vignetting is a combination of manipulations—cropping, dodging, and burning-in. It is used to single out some feature in the image area—typically, one face among several in a group—and to do so without sharp, hard marginal delineation. The usual procedure involves a card with a hole torn in it, approximately the size and shape of the area to be featured. The edges of the hole should be uneven or saw-toothed. Kept in gentle motion as the projected image pours through the opening, the card keeps the rest of the image from getting any exposure at all. The desired feature will thus emerge, fully exposed, with everything around it fading off to pure white.

Figs. 13-4a & b. Vertical distortion results from camera tilt. Parallel lines converge (left). It **should** be corrected in the camera (right), but...

Flashing

Flashing is a variant of burning-in. It deepens tones but does not add detail because the light used is separate—usually a small flashlight with its beam slimmed down by a cone of black paper. It can be used for darkening corners (as some pictorialists love to do), for relieving contrast in specific areas, or for subduing highlights. The extraneous light is played over the paper during the exposure—deftly and judiciously, of course. Total exposure time is not increased.

There are a couple of other procedures that can be used; however, they are not suggested here as standard practice.

Combination Printing

Combination printing is a sort of nature-faking. Suppose you have an excellent landscape negative, excellent, that is, except for its sky. Suppose, further, that you have also a fine skyscape negative, with an indifferent or nonexistent foreground. Okay, use them *both* to produce one beautiful picture. This is the drill. Project your landscape negative to the size and proportion desired on the paper board. Then make two masks by cutting apart a white card along the line of the horizon—cutting around any foreground objects that may be above the horizon line. The upper one of these two masks will protect the sky area while the foreground is being printed, and the lower one vice versa.

Sure, this can get complicated; it can even get absurd—as when the clouds in the sky are lighted from the left and the foreground is lighted from the right. It can also look artificial. Still, it is a technique to know about and to be reasonably adept with, just in case....

Distortion Correction

There is one enlarging gambit that can help you rescue otherwise perfectly good pictures—*distortion correction.* In photographing tall buildings you may have noticed that you sometimes get a pyramidal effect, with the sides of the building off vertical, leaning to the center. This is nothing but perfectly normal perspective, but it still doesn't look right. In all but the most wildly distorted instances, you can restore verticality by deliberately raising one end of the enlarging easel; usually an inch or two will be sufficient. Focus on a point halfway up the image of the structure and then stop down the lens to achieve greatest depth of field. This is one of the few instances in which stopping down a lens has real optical, functional value in enlarging.

Skill in the techniques of enlarging is useful and admirable; still more admirable is the exercise of skill in producing a negative that needs little or no doctoring when it is enlarged.

Fig. 13-5. Vertical distortion in a negative can be minimized—or emphasized—by deliberate angling of the enlarger easel.

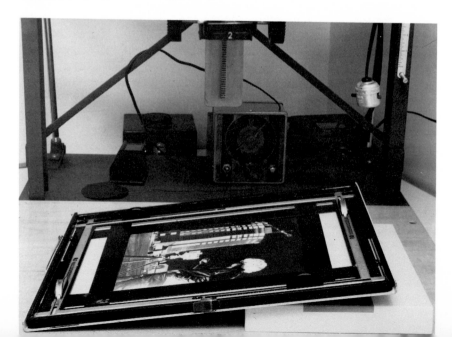

Diffusion

Diffusion is another sometime thing. Perhaps you have a negative that is so sharp and brilliant that it produces almost commercial-looking enlargements. Generally, that's fine, but maybe, from a purely pictorial point of view, you prefer a little less hardness. A diffusion disk—flat glass with slightly raised concentric rings pressed into it—positioned just below the projection lens for a part of the total exposure may give you exactly what you want. All sorts of things have been used to obtain special, novel, bizarre, or "artistic" effects. Please note the quotes around that word.

Texture Screens

Similarly, there are *texture screens* that can be used, flat over the paper, to induce special effects. Generally (and personally) speaking, anything that gets between the viewer and a really good picture doesn't make very much sense.

CHECKING UP

To repeat, an enlargement is, photographically, the proof of the pudding. Check it, as objectively as possible, against this list of questions:

1. "Have I used the right contrast grade of paper?"

   You have, if your print shows the full tonal range of which the paper is capable, with detail in both highlights and shadows.

2. "Is the paper surface right for the subject?"

   Yes, if you are practically unaware of it. A surface that calls attention to itself rather than to the image is not right.

3. "Have I exposed and developed it properly?"

   You have, if it came up to its full potential in the recommended time. And if it is completely free of streaks, strains, and the mottling that is evidence of inadequate immersion and agitation in all solutions.

4. "Is my print sharp?"

   Certainly, if you took time to focus accurately and to protect the enlarger from vibration during the enlarging exposure.

5. "Will I or anyone else be able to enjoy this enlargement a few years from now?"

   Yes, speaking of it strictly as a photograph, if fixation and washing were carried out according to both the letter and the spirit of the laws governing these processes. And yes, too, speaking of the enlargement as a picture, if it is the result of perception, appreciation, and skill—and not merely a novelty for novelty's sake.

14
Talking Pictures

In these days when a smear of house paint across the face of a newspaper can be proclaimed as "Art," it is a little chancey to talk about what makes a picture.

Chancey or not, here goes.

We aren't going to get involved in that dreary old argument about *What Is Art?* But I think I know what Art is not. First, it is not accidental. True, accidents can achieve results that are interesting, picturesque, or even beautiful, but they are not the results of any conscious effort to make a statement—to say something. They are essentially doodles without intent, content, or meaning.

Second, Art is not the product of unskilled *nudniks* who have nothing to say, and flaunt their dumbness.

Third, Art is not the product of earnest souls who may be full of ideas but are devoid of any ability to express them in painting, photography, music, or whatever.

All this, of course, is a rather sneaky way of getting around to my belief that art, with a capital A or not, is the result of an idea, a desire to say something, worked out by someone who knows how to do it. It does not follow that the greater the technician, the greater the artist; but it does follow that an idea, a statement, has a much greater chance of being read, loud and clear, if the perpetrator of that message is skilled in the medium he uses to express it.

To be skilled in the uses and the materials of photography is the first step toward creativity in photography. And, to know how to arrange, present, and emphasize the elements of a picture is the second.

This brings us right down to such old-fashioned concepts as composition, arrangement, emphasis, and unity. They are old because they represent the cumulative experience of the human animal trying to express himself. But they are not old-fashioned, really. They have never been replaced by something better. They are, in fact, so basic that even the most far-out innovators keep coming back to them.

149

THE PHOTOGRAPHER-ARTIST

In some schools of photography, there are prerequisite or parallel courses in the theory and even the history of art. This seems sound, for the more familiar you are with the language and the tools of graphic representation, the better you are equipped to use a camera as a vehicle for pictorial ideas.

Some of the principles can be suggested here. But, more important than written words are the examples of fine, effective picture-making you'll find in museums, art galleries, art books, and some current periodicals. Get the habit of scanning pictures to determine whether or not they are as effective as they might be, and whether or not you'd truly call the persons who signed those pictures artists.

COMPOSITION

Composition can be defined as the arrangement of the elements of a picture so that they make sense, the intended sense. The tools of composition are not elaborate. You begin with the assumption of an arbitrary picture area —square, oblong, round, or whatever. Obviously this is a kind of restriction, but so is the foundation of a house. It's a restriction that keeps things from falling apart.

The important thing is what you do with the elements of your picture within that frame. First, there is bound to be one thing, one pictorial element, more important (to you) than the others. So, you position it so that the beholder's eye goes to it naturally, almost automatically. But position alone is not enough. In terms of light and shade or in terms of color, you make sure that the thing you want to show most clearly is not—cannot be—overlooked. And you make equally sure that nothing else in your picture steals the show.

This brings us to the notion of *emphasis*.

The position of your principal subject involves a choice that isn't obvious. You have to decide whether it is to be portrayed as static, inactive, and formal, or full of life and action, real or implied. If you want to suggest quiet, or formality, or lack of action, it may be perfectly in order to position your principal subject squarely in the center of your picture area. That's the place for a subject that isn't about to jump up and run away. But if your subject is a lively one, actually or potentially, you give it room to move. You place it one side or the other of the vertical and horizontal center lines of your space; in so doing you unleash the action so that it can flow as freely as possible within the picture area.

To repeat, no compositional "rule" is really a rule; it is merely a good idea that is backed up by many generations of experience. Some ideas have

Figs. 14-1a & b. A simple little action shot like this is more "comfortable" when the subject has room to move in. A margin close to an on-coming linear motion suggests a crack-up.

been formalized into formulas. For example, we mentioned something about avoiding center lines for your punch points. Well, this has been developed into an easy and practical working plan. You divide your picture area into thirds, vertically and horizontally, and use any of the intersections of those lines as appropriate places for your principal subject. Whether it be placed at the lower left intersection rather than at one of the other three will depend entirely on how you feel about it, and how you want to show it. Is action present or implied? In what direction? Okay, give your subject room to move, or maybe merely to look, in that direction. Does a shadow or a reflection set up a contrasting directional theme? Fine! Make use of it.

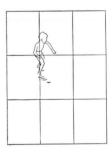

Fig. 14-2. The "rule of thirds" in practice. Try composing some of your own pictures this way.

The point of these considerations is not whether they are in accord with any rule or convention. It is simply a matter of whether or not they help your picture say what you want it to say, and clearly.

Closely allied to the concept of emphasis is *unity*. This means merely that you haven't tried to say half a dozen things at once. Double talk can be a lot of fun, but it doesn't say anything worth saying. So, unity means the elimination of things that distract or confuse or dilute your major theme.

If the general idea of composition interests you, there are many books on the subject, and some of them are pretty sternly dogmatic about it, too. Look especially for a treatise on the subject of Dynamic Symmetry. It's really not a theory; it is a cult, with many and fanatically serious adherents. But its principles can be helpful. Matter of fact, the idea of using the intersections of the thirds, as above, comes fairly close to a tenet of Dynamic Symmetry.

To achieve emphasis, then, you must decide upon what your major subject is. You place it to the best possible advantage. And, to preserve unity, you protect it from distracting or conflicting pictorial elements.

In black-and-white photography, you achieve emphasis in terms of strongly contrasting brightness—white against black, black against white. In color work, in which the colors themselves provide the contrast, it is usually wise to avoid using complementary colors to surround your principal subject. For complementary colors, remember, tend to set up an unpleasant sense of vibration or conflict, which is not contrast! It is conflict, and it can destroy the very effect you hope to achieve.

Believe it or not, one of the oldest and simplest aids to composition is the good old alphabet. You've heard of "S" curves, of course, curves that are similar to the serpentine flow of a capital S. It happens that the "S" curve is a very good and useful device; it is closely related to one of the most famous of compositional concepts—the "line of beauty" that William Hogarth made so much of (having swiped it from Michelangelo). It is an "S" curve, somewhat flattened or condensed, with one of the reversing arcs of the S a little longer than the other. Still and all, it is an S.

If you analyze a variety of good paintings or photographs, you will find that many of them have their elements or lines of force so arranged that they form lines pretty much like letters of the alphabet. You will find compositional As, Cs, Ds, Ls, Ts, and Xes, and probably a few more. This does not mean that any artist ever consciously said to himself, "I shall now compose in terms of the letter K." That would be nonsense. It merely means that the flow, or the rigidity, of a letter can help you in arranging pictorial elements. Something graceful and feminine may work itself out in terms that resemble a C or an O or an S. Where strength and stability are indicated, look for an A form, or an M. Where conflict is implied, look for the sharp angles, the abrupt changes of direction typical of a K or a Z or a P. And what could be more forthrightly masculine than an I? The alphabet is not a batch of recipes for concocting compositions; it is full of suggestions, not answers.

Artists and art critics and art teachers have, over the centuries, spent a lot of time and talk on the subject of composition. Sometimes they got very serious about it. Pictures would be ruled failures or successes simply because they did or did not conform to somebody's arbitrary set of rules. I have seen camera-club print critics throw out beautiful landscapes because "the horizon line cuts the picture in half." Most of the time, true enough, the picture might have been improved a little by cropping it so that the horizon line avoided the midway line. *But not always.* It depended upon what the artist wanted to say. If he wanted to show us a static, totally serene world, his midway horizon may have helped him to do so. In any event, I think the artist should always be given the benefit of the doubt. If the critic can indicate how he might have done a better, more eloquent job, fair enough, but don't let any critic hijack any job you ever do.

We are back where we started. A picture is a way of saying something. As photographers we use the tools at our disposal to help make our statements clearly. How we use those tools is strictly our own business.

There is only one "rule" that, to me, is completely defensible. And that rule is: The more simply you make your statement, the better. People understand simple statements. Whether they like them, or agree with the artist, is another matter.

TO GRAB OR TO PLAN

In commercial work a photographer usually works from a prepared script, a statement of the idea to be expressed, plus a sketch by the client's art director. The job is to come up with a photograph that realizes and, possibly, glorifies the client's idea or objective.

If you are so inclined, you can certainly operate that way in your own personal, noncommercial picture-making. You start with an idea, making a few rough sketches. Then you scout around, looking for the best location or materials with which to produce the desired result. In outdoor work this may involve determining the right time of day or sun angle, as well as selecting the right camera, lens, film, and, possibly, filter. It is an orderly way of working; everything is planned. Moreover, it is excellent training, no matter what your instinctive approach to photography may be.

On the other hand, you may prefer to operate in terms of spontaneous reaction to a visual situation. The French photographer, Henri Cartier-Bresson, wrote a classic book called *The Decisive Moment,* which summed up and illustrated his concept that in any situation there comes one moment that is most significant, most arresting, or most eloquent. His purpose was to capture that moment on film. In somewhat less self-conscious terms, every news or sports photographer does exactly the same thing. It takes a bright sense of observation, enough experience to know what to expect, and enough sense to recognize that "decisive moment" when it comes along.

Nobody is perfect, not even Cartier-Bresson. So, in any picture-making situation you make several shots at each of several moments that may seem to be significant. Then you study the results. One of them, more than the others, will have captured the sense of the event.

Few of us are geniuses or even masters of either the planned or the spontaneous kind of photography. We are a bit of both. The only real stipulation, the only criterion, is whether we recognize it when we really *have* a picture.

CROP AND CONCENTRATE

One of the simplest and most helpful compositional tools is a set of croppers—"L"-shaped and about a foot long, cut out of cardboard. With two of these croppers you can study any rough print, or the image projected on your enlarging easel. Move the "L"s around, trying different framings, different eliminations. Sometimes the picture you took will emerge as quite different, and possibly better. Anyway, mark the margins of the best result obtained with the croppers, and make your enlargements accordingly. Incidentally, you may find that there are several possible pictures in your negative; your croppers help you discover those extra dividends. (Of course, if one of them turns out to be conspicuously superior, don't let on that it wasn't exactly what you composed in your viewfinder; that's your secret.)

Fig. 14-3. With a pair of home-made croppers it's easy (and instructive) to analyze a print or a projected image on the enlarger easel.

SUMMING UP

In any picture, composition refers to the way the pictorial elements are used or distributed so that the result says what you want it to say. The arrangement can be pleasing or displeasing to the eye of the beholder; that doesn't matter so long as he gets the message.

Remember the "rule" of the thirds; it may be a little arbitrary, but it is honestly helpful.

Never take any part of your picture for granted. Backgrounds that your eye may ignore can rise up in the finished picture to plague you. Telephone poles, TV aerials, trees, and the wash out on Mrs. Whoozis' laundry line have a way, unless you are alert, of appearing to sprout from people's heads. They can look pretty funny, too.

The sky is one of the finest of backgrounds, infinitely varied and usually beautiful. Too, when you use the sky for a portrait background you automatically use a low camera angle—and that gives your subject the psychological advantage of looking down at you. (And a nonprofessional model needs all the advantage you can give him.)

Allow more space for your subjects to look or move into than out of. Think of the sides of your picture area as walls. People usually prefer to stand with their backs to a wall.

Aside from these fairly free "rules," together with the overriding one about keeping things simple, there is another that is really important. And that is—keep your camera busy. Make lots of pictures. Try anything and everything. And then *study* your results. Are they pleasing? Are they displeasing? All very fine, but there is, after all, only one thing that is important. Does the picture say, clearly and unmistakably, what you want it to say?

15
Land, Sea, and Sky Scapes

The Grand Canyon, Niagara Falls, the skyline of Manhattan, Big Ben, the Taj Mahal, the Eiffel Tower—these and dozens of other great spectacles, the world over, pack a punch that no one can avoid. Millions of picture postcards have been proclaiming their glories for many generations. A bright weekend at any famous scenic center leaves a terminal moraine of empty film cartons (never, of course, any of yours), testifying to the fact that thousands of snapshooters have made the pilgrimage and paused, dutifully, to make the necessary shots. Like the postcards, those snaps serve primarily as evidence that "you were there"—important, of course, but in no way related to perceptive photography.

Your enjoyment, your appreciation of a scene is a personal thing. You see and respond to it in your own individual way. As a photographer, you try to convey graphically something of your emotional response. And you know that even the most familiar and over-publicized scene has aspects that casual viewers overlook. Your pleasure comes from finding and exploiting those aspects. That's not always easy.

There is a fine kind of one-upmanship in perceiving and recording the essence of a scene that others, less perceptive, have failed to notice. This is especially satisfying when you are able to glorify pictorially some nearby, unpublicized scene. Among the sweetest words a photographer can hear are, "Whaddaya know! I've seen that a thousand times, but I never saw a picture in it."

But wherever you are, near home or far, far away, remember that you are your camera's boss. Your eyes, your intelligence, your perception control it completely, thereby keeping it away from shots that are hackneyed, trivial, and a waste of perfectly good film.

157

THE GRAND VIEW

Consider, first, the spectacular spectacle of natural grandeur, mountain scenery, for example. Faced with such scenic lavishness, the problem is to select the most meaningful, most pictorial fractions of the whole thing. You eliminate and exclude because you know you cannot possibly get it *all* in. And in so doing, you're right back to the first principles of composition; finding something to emphasize.

Scan the spectacle with your eye glued to your camera's viewfinder, thereby excluding everything outside the finder frame. Find some aspects of the total scene you like better than others, and zero in on them. You may prefer to select your views with your hands, used "art director fashion," or with a rectangular hole cut in a gray card; the device doesn't matter. What *is* important is that the device should permit you to concentrate on picture possibilities, thereby eliminating such psychological considerations as the pleasant company you have, or that wonderful breakfast at the inn, or the fact that you've picked up a rotten cold.

Fig. 15-1. A "picture finder" can sometimes help you find the heart of a pictorial situation. Held close to your eyes, it gives you a broad view; held farther off, it narrows the included view.

The point of all this is simply that unless you are selective, you can wind up with routine shots that look almost exactly like the thousands of amateurish shots made at the same place yesterday. Or, and even worse, you may find yourself apologizing for it. "This really doesn't give you any idea of the place. You simply can't get it in a picture. It's wonderful, honestly it is." Too bad.

The grand view contains, as does any long shot, a good deal of haze. It may be imperceptible to your eyes, but your film—color or monochrome—may pick it up. So, you have a decision. You may want or need that haze to separate the various receding planes of your picture. Or, you may prefer a scenic that is as clear and sharp, all the way, as you can possibly get it. If you want the haze, your problem is one of exposure and the characteristics of the film being used; if you don't want the haze, use filters. With black-and-white film you can use a yellow or an orange filter to sweep that blue haze away, even out to the far horizon; with color film use a skylight filter, which reduces the bluishness out toward the horizon.

On a bright day in the mountains you have another factor to deal with—the presence of a great deal of very powerful light. *Actinic* is the word for it. Your exposure meter can generally be counted on to recognize it.

Fig. 15-2. "The Grand View"—getting the most out of your mountains.

The angle of the light is another thing to watch. In black-and-white work you'll find that quartering light does more for the scene than full, frontal lighting. So select the time of day when the lighting is favorable. Even working with color you may find that quartering light gives you better results, even if the shadows tend to go blind or off color. I have seen some beautiful shots of Grand Canyon, for example, in which the shadows were coal-black; the total effect was posterish and not very subtle but very striking....The Grand Canyon, after all, *is* striking and dramatic.

In any big, spectacular scene you have distance, usually lots of distance. It's one of the essentials of grandeur. Lighting plus mist plus the change in tones toward the horizon combine to spell distance, of course, but you can emphasize distance by including some foreground material that is in sharp contrast to the far reaches of your picture. A tree, a jutting rock, a group of people, or even one person, back to the camera and sharing the camera's point of view, gives the picture's viewer a guide, a measuring stick, by which the true depth of the scene can be sensed.

THE INTIMATE VIEW

The intimate scenic differs from the grand view primarily in scale. You shift from miles to yards. If the distant horizon is included, it generally serves only to give your picture a sense of naturalness. Most of the scenics in this category contain more than "scenery"; roads, boats, buildings, and animals share the stage. The scenes that most of us find near home are intimate rather than grand, and they are generally more fun to make. They are less austere, less impersonal.

Special filters are seldom needed; exposures are as nearly normal as exposures ever are.

Included in this fairly arbitrary category are pictures made along lakes and ponds. Sometimes the waters are so perfectly calm that they mirror the surrounding trees, buildings, and landscape. And, the more perfect the mirror the more you may be tempted to compose your picture so that it may be viewed either way up. This, it seems to me, is a stunt, not a picture. You can report on the glassy waters quite as effectively if you introduce something that spoils the perfection of the reflections—a stone tossed into the water will create charming ripples without destroying the reflected image. The inclusion of a foreground object, something that is not part of the water reflections, will give your viewers the necessary knowledge of which way is up, and won't mar the picture at all. Usually, this problem is resolved automatically for you; the water absorbs part of the light it receives thereby reducing exposure so that it registers as darker. Even so, the choice is up to you—a tricky mirror shot or a straight-forward, right-side-up picture.

Plate 16. A pattern of similar shapes can be enlivened by introducing a strongly contrasting element. The balloon man's hat contrasts very nicely with the balloons, despite the fact that it has very nearly the same shape.

Plate 17. A perfect illustration of the old "rule" that rainy nights are better than dry nights for city scenics. Thanks to the rain, we see an infinitude of colored reflections.

Plate 18. Getting closer to the wet reflection creates a different effect—an abstraction.

Plate 19. One of the easiest "tricks" is to create patterns of light streaks by means of long exposures. Here, Ektachrome-X was exposed on a tripod for 20 seconds at $f/22$. The traffic did the rest.

Plate 20. To convey a vivid sense of speed and strain as you picture an athlete in action, you can sometimes combine the "panning" technique with a slow shutter. Conversely, to depict niceties of form and technique a high shutter speed may be necessary. By John Paul Murphy; at 1/15 sec., while panning, on Ektachrome-X.

Plate 21. Because it was passing at close range, a good shot of this speeding car required (and got) both a fast shuter speed (1/500 sec. at $f/4$) and smooth, perfectly-timed panning on Ektachrome-X.

Plate 22. Though daylight color films are balanced to get "true" colors at mid-day, dawn and sunset photographs have a quiet beauty of their own.

Plate 23. The gulls on the piles in the foreground are sharp; the groping steamboat is almost hidden. This fuzzy-sharp combination perfectly conveys the sense of the harbor mist; it becomes pictorially real, almost tangible.

Plate 24. To capture the spontaniety and grace of this little girl practicing her ballet lessons, only window-light was used.

Filters can, of course, be used to help any scene that includes clouds. In black-and-white work something like the No. 8 (K2) filter will preserve cloud-sky contrasts without darkening the foliage too much. In color photography, favor the underexposure side to achieve the same results.

For truly drastic and dramatic effects you might try infrared film, together with its complement, a deep red filter. Such a combination reveals distance as no other does or can. But it also does strange things to the familiar landscape. The sky is rendered very dark, almost black, and clouds are white as paper; trees and grass, generally, are white, and fair complexions come through as chalky. The general effect is unreal and fantastic; nonetheless, there are times when infrared can give you precisely the off-beat results you want.

Fig. 15-3. Infrared film with a red filter puts strong tonal values in any landscape.

Theoretically, by the way, the greater length of infrared rays is enough to throw focus off just a little—about a quarter of a per cent. No problem. Adjust your exposures to use the smallest practical diaphragm opening, and good old depth of field will take care of the discrepancy.

In infrared work as well as in landscapes, you may prefer to use long exposures coupled with small diaphragm openings. Good enough. But for any exposure longer than 1/30 sec., use a tripod. It's just good sense to do so.

SUNSETS

Everybody enjoys good sunsets, and for very good reasons. They can be extravagantly flamboyant, filling the western sky with spectacular shapes and colors, or they can be calm, serene, and very subtly colored. Inevitably, they invite photography.

In black-and-white, there is little about a quiet, unsensational sunset that photographs significantly. True, everything between the camera and the sun is in various degrees of silhouette and darkness, but the sky itself comes through as nothing to get excited about. It is only when the sunset is alive with strong shapes and colors that the black-and-white photographer can produce striking results. Even so, it's chancey. For the panchromatic film we use these days is remarkably "level" in its response to the various colors; we really need, oddly enough, an emulsion that's not so even—something like the old ortho films that rendered the warm colors dark and the blues very light. You can certainly use filters, and you can certainly underexpose. Try it, anyway.

With color, all is made relatively easy for us. A little underexposure usually is beneficial. And with color you can even portray those quiet, subtly colored sunsets that baffle the black-and-white filmer.

PANORAMAS

Sometimes a scenic seems almost to defy you to pick out any part of it as "best"; it's all great. You need the equivalent of the movies' eye-boggling wide-screen.

There's a way, known as the panorama technique. It is simply a matter of making a series of overlapping shots from a fixed position. Ideally, you pivot the camera on a point directly below the lens; actually, pivoting on the usual tripod socket works perfectly well. And, *in extremis,* you *can* make a series of hand-held shots, taking care that you maintain a constant camera level. Each shot in such a series should overlap its neighbor by one-fourth or even one-third.

When the prints are finished, all uniform in tone, line them up in sequence, mark the points in the overlapped areas where the joins will be least obvious (usually a tree or a post or something of the sort), and then cut them very cleanly and accurately so that when the prints are butted together, you get a smooth, even join. Mount the cut prints on mounting board, touch up any obvious errors, and then copy the whole business. From the resulting negative you can make as many prints or enlargements as you please.

Fig. 15-4. A city panorama, made with three overlapping exposures, all from exactly the same spot. Much the same technique is used in aerial surveys; for the sake of maximum accuracy, much greater overlapping is required.

There are problems, of course. If your series of shots embraces a very wide arc, you may find exposure differences at the extreme ends. Usually, it is possible to compensate in printing; to do so in terms of diaphragm and shutter becomes a bit tricky.

All the foregoing applies primarily to monochrome work. If you can do it successfully in color, fine! And ... my compliments.

SEASCAPES

Marine scenes are challenging. Consider a vast expanse of sea and sky. It's tremendous, but—where's the picture? The problem is to find or to establish a center of interest or to utilize any of the tried-and-true principles or schemes of composition. Marine painters use either of two gambits; they either conjure up a large foreground wave or some white caps to provide the necessary nubbin of interest or they introduce a boat or birds or spectacular clouds—anything to break up the sameness of the setting.

The photographer has, within limits, much the same freedom; only, instead of inventing or creating his centers of interest, he must find them. The more familiar you are with the infinite variety of sea and sky, the more you'll find to give your picture what it needs.

In one respect, marine scenics have pictorial potentials that landscapes cannot offer. There's the sparkle of sunlight on water, for instance. To get it photographically, use backlighting; shoot against the light. With the light coming toward you over the water, you can pick up a multitude of sparkling lights, each the reflection of the sun. Such a picture can be very exciting, very beautiful. If you expose for all those playful glints of light, you will automatically underexpose anything between you and them. Nearby boats or docks or rocks become silhouettes, and that may be all to the good, pictorially speaking.

But beware. Light coming into your lens from either the sun or a watery reflection of it can create flare and dazzle within your lens. At least try to protect the lens with a lens hood or shade the lens with your hand held above the included angle of the lens. An alternative, if you cannot escape including the low sun in your picture, is to stop down as far as your lens will go—$f/22$, $f/32$, or whatever it may be—and hold to a fairly high shutter speed. This way, you will come up with a pseudo-moonlight shot that can, with luck, be strikingly beautiful.

Speaking of the moon, you may be tempted to try a few shots by the "brilliant" light of the full moon. I say *"brilliant"* because it really isn't bright; it is all reflected light and really pretty dim. You'll need time exposures and a tripod.

Fig. 15-5. The sparkle of light on water is revealed by back-lighting, coupled with a very lean exposure, something like 1/250 sec. at $f/16$. Obviously, foreground subjects are silhouetted.

Shooting the moon itself is a different matter, because the moon is an object in full sunshine. So it can be photographed with an ordinary daylight kind of exposure. Include some foreground material—trees or a house or some such—which will be rendered in silhouette. But it will help make a picture.

Without suitable filter protection do not attempt shots of the sun. The hazard to your eyes, as you go about making a sun shot, is real and not to be trifled with.

GIVE NATURE A CHANCE

Only a few generations ago scenery, in all its great variety, was the favorite preoccupation of photographers. In some places it still is but, generally, we have become so intent on realistic interpretations of our sophisticated and often unlovely world that anything pastoral seems hopelessly old-fashioned. This is a false assumption, for nature will remain nature. It can teach us, comfort us, and satisfy us as few other things in this world can do. Try it.

Fig. 15-6. The progress of a partial lunar eclipse, pictured in a series of ten exposures on one film. All but the three central exposures, made during maximum occlusion, are overexposed. Remember, the moon is an object in full sunlight; over-exposure is all too easy.

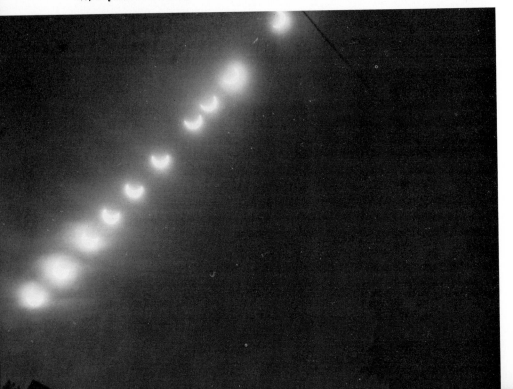

16
Speed – Action – Sport

Speed has always been one of photography's most appealing aspects. A century ago, people marvelled that a portrait could be made in a matter of minutes or seconds, for they still thought in terms of portrait painters and the weeks and months a painting involved. And when snapshots, with their shutter speeds of about 1/40 sec. came along...well, the age of speed was truly here.

Today, of course, we take for granted the much greater speeds of modern shutters, coupled to "faster" lenses and films. Even the cheapest, simplest camera works at something like 1/60 sec. And our better cameras operate at shutter speeds of 1/250 sec. or 1/500 sec. without raising an eyebrow. When electronic flashes of light are used instead of relatively cumbersome shutters (as in stroboscopic work), speeds become astronomical.

But speed, as I believe a Mr. Einstein pointed out, is relative. Even in picturing action you may not often need the top speed of which your camera's shutter is capable.

The fascination of picturing fast action is real. No small boy with a simple camera can resist the temptation to photograph a low-flying plane, or a fast car, or a freight train thundering through town. Often as not, the small boy gets passable pictures despite the slow speed of his camera shutter. And the shade of Mr. Einstein smiles benignly.

It is in the photography of straight-line action—a moving car, a train, a race—that relativity becomes most important (to us, that is). When you stand close beside a highway watching the cars (assuming, of course, that they're moving at the usual five miles above the legal limit pace) you will observe a phenomenon. While the cars are still a hundred yards or so way, they give you no strong impression of speed; they merely grow larger. As they come nearer, they grow larger faster. And as they whiz past, you have to swivel your head quickly to see them at all. As they recede from you, the process goes into reverse; they grow smaller, quickly at first and then more slowly.

167

Camera-wise, this phenomenon means merely that it takes much higher shutter speed to "stop" action as it crosses in front of you than when it is either coming or going.

Back to the highway again. This time, stand back about a hundred feet from the nearest lane. Now the angle between you and the oncoming cars is less acute; their speed, at a distance, is a little more apparent but, oddly enough, not at the instant of passing in front of you. You can almost pick out details. You don't have to swivel your head quite as violently to follow the action. Thus, for such a situation you may need a little more shutter speed for the approach and not quite as much, relatively, for the pass-by.

Figs. 16-1a to 16-1d. Everything is relative. In all four following shots, car speed was 35 mph, shutter speed was 1/125 sec. Below (a), at 100 feet, a car approaching at an acute angle is adequately "stopped." Opposite, top (b). At 20 feet, a car approaching at an acute angle isn't "stopped."

Fig. 16-1c. Similarly, passing at 90°, the nearer the car the greater the blur.

Fig. 16-1d. Seen close-up, the car becomes a blur.

Fig. 16-2. The relativity of action-stopping. Taped to the rim of the bike wheel were 18 little barber poles. As the wheel turned, at moderate speed, an exposure was made at 1/60 sec. The little poles advancing directly toward the camera are rendered with fair sharpness; ditto those retreating. Those on the far side of the wheel are barely distinguishable, and those passing nearest the camera are nothing but blurs. Moral: Angle and distance are the controlling factors.

FUZZ VS. SHARP

There are two different and opposite schools of thought about the best way to picture speed. One demands the *stop-it-cold* technique and the other favors the *whoosh*.

The best possible illustration of the stop-it-cold concept is the classic picture of a speeding bullet. Made by the light of an electronic flash, automatically triggered, the bullet is pictured sitting serenely in space, going nowhere in particular and threatening no one. It is "stopped," right enough, *so* stopped that there is no more sense of speed in it than in a still-life portrait of a banana.

The opposite of this is a shot that is so *un*-stopped that it is nothing but a fuzzy blur. It's speed, but it is speed without meaning.

Obviously, the photographic answer—a picture that both identifies the subject and gives us a sense of speed—must lie somewhere between *stop-it-cold* and *whoosh*.

Recently, there has been a great fad of unstopped action, particularly in sports shots in color. Such pictures glorify blur, showing us just enough significant shape or outline to hint at the subject. They're interesting and sometimes effective, but their very novelty forces photographers to seek more revealing answers.

Figs. 16-3a & b. When "panning" is beautiful. The effort to capture a passing motor-cyclist with an ordinary exposure produced only an indifferent landscape and a ter-rible blur (previous page). But, by using the "panning" technique, the cyclist was very clearly and cleanly revealed, with the blurred landscape providing an extra sense of speed.

There are at least two answers. One is an oblique or nearly head-on shot of action in which there is enough contributory evidence of action—flying dust, straining muscles, feet off the ground—to convince the picture viewer that things are happening, fast. The subject of the picture may be truly "stopped," but the circumstances spell speed and action.

The other answer is to panoram with the action so that the camera, as it swings, gets a good look at the subject but registers everything else as a blur of horizontal streaks. Actually, a good pan shot recreates your optical ex-perience as a car goes by; your eye follows the car and disregards all else.

ACTION-STOPPING FORMULA

Here's a simple statement of photographic relativity to aid you in exposure calculations for picturing straight-line movement.

For Subjects Such As	Distance From Camera	Shutter Speeds for Subjects Moving:		
		HEAD-ON	ABOUT 45°	ABOUT 90°
Pedestrians, general work,	25 feet	1/125	1/250	1/500
most ordinary activities	50 feet	1/60	1/125	1/250
	100 feet	1/30	1/60	1/125
"People" sports and other	25 feet	1/250	1/500	1/1000
energetic activities	50 feet	1/125	1/250	1/500
	100 feet	1/60	1/125	1/250
Moving cars, trains, planes,	25 feet	1/500	1/1000	. . . . . .
and other swift motion	50 feet	1/250	1/500	1/1000
	100 feet	1/125	1/250	1/500

Now!

So far, we have been talking about continuous, more or less straight-line action. But much of the action, in ball sports particularly, is anything but continuous or uniform. Part of baseball's charm, for example, is the way exciting action erupts, often without warning.

Good sports shots are based as much on the photographer's knowledge of the sport and his intuition as on his mastery of his equipment. He knows that there are moments of seemingly suspended animation in sport and that those moments are, fortunately, just as pictorial as any others. Sometimes, they're better. Consider a baseball pitcher; in the middle of his delivery he appears to have a broken arm and is awkward to boot. But when he r'ars back, ready to uncoil, he looks great; similarly, he is 100 per cent pictorial when, fully extended, he releases the ball. And at both of those points you can stop the action with considerable ease.

Much depends on your reaction time. It doesn't matter whether it's fast or slow; the important thing is that you need to be aware of it so that your action pictures can be tailored accordingly. Somewhere around, there's a big clock with a sweep second hand. Okay, try a series of shots from about five feet, catching the second hand *exactly* as it points to the ten-second mark. After a few such experiments, you'll know fairly well what your reaction time is; obviously, it can be improved with practice, but don't assume it's very good until you have proved it.

Veteran sports photographers know their sports and also know their reaction times. In boxing, for example, they shoot for the impact of a blow, not for its travel. Speaking of boxing, there is a story about one of Joe Louis' fights that is pertinent here. Two press photographers covering the fight were on directly opposite sides of the ring. As the bout neared its climax, both men sensed what was about to happen. They saw a heavy blow launched, and both shot for the impact. Both cameras worked in the same split second, but the flash on one of them failed. One man, accordingly, got a fully lighted picture, while the other came up with a dramatic and vivid silhouette—made by the light of his rival's flash.

The only moral to this small tale is that there are right instants for any shot; in this case both men sensed the knockout punch and got it, at precisely the same instant.

In his *genre* photographs in France and all over the world, Cartier-Bresson looked for the "decisive moment" in making each picture; in sports or action shots, look for the *"NOW!"*—and train yourself to take advantage of it.

Fig. 16-4. Because the action is frozen at the farthest swing of the rope, emphasis falls on the threat of the water below. An unfrozen or panned shot, under these circumstances, would have missed the suspense, the potential hazard of the moment.

Fig. 16-5. Full out. Action stopped at the end of the pendulum swing. Those horizontal bars are really in the background, but they make it appear that the swinger will be bent double on the downswing.

POISE VS. POSE

This is a small admonition, mentioned only because every once in a while —especially in school yearbooks—we see unhappy examples. Simulated or imitation action looks silly. Usually, it is evident at a glance. And it is silly because it is not necessary. With high shutter speeds, with fast flash and, most of all, with an understanding of what's going on, no pretension is needed.

I do not include in that category the standard head-on shots of football players in the signal-calling crouch. That's classic. Moreover, it's a matter of poise rather than pose. Poise makes sense; pose doesn't.

PANORAMS (NOT PANORAMAS)

A page or two back, mention was made of the panoram technique for capturing passing action, a fast car, for example. It's a simple trick, but it justifies a little experiment and practice.

First, set your focus for the distance at which the car will pass directly in front of you. Then, with shutter cocked, pick up the car as it approaches in your viewfinder. Keep your eye glued to it, pivoting your head and shoulders as the car comes nearer. Swing with it. And make the exposure when the car is squarely in front of you, but don't stop there. Follow through, as in golf. The smoother your swing, the straighter the blurred lines in your picture will be, and the better those blurs will suggest speed.

Try it at several shutter speeds, beginning at about 1/25 sec. The higher the shutter speed, of course, the less blur. On studying your results, you can decide which of the effects you like best, and try it on other subjects.

FOCAL-PLANE PHENOMENON

Many sports cameras as well as a majority of the SLRs now in use have focal-plane shutters, shutters that travel across the face of the film. At, say, 1/500 sec. all parts of the film get their allotted 1/500 sec. of exposure, but they do not all get it at exactly the same time. The slit in the shutter has to travel across the film, and that takes a little time. So the first exposed parts of the film record their parts of the image just a whisker before the last exposed parts.

If the shutter travels in the same direction as a fast-passing subject, there will be some pictorial elongation thereof; if the direction of shutter travel is opposed to that of the subject, you can get a compressed effect. In neither case, especially with miniature cameras, is it likely to be a serious problem, but you should know about it.

SPEED, BUT ...

To get a good record of fast action is fine and well worth doing. But, once you have mastered the basics of speed shooting, check over your work. Have you gained speed and lost pictures?

For pictures, good pictures, are the ends of photography. So, do not succumb to the temptation to accept any reasonably successful action shot as good enough. You're after pictures, not good enoughs.

Figs. 16-6a & b. Distortion by focal-plane shutter. The slit in a focal-plane shutter takes a little time in its trip across the film plane, and a fast-moving object changes its position slightly during that time. The result is distortion. When the shutter moves top-to-bottom, you get a general cant or slant; when it moves sideways you get either compression or elongation, depending on the relative movements of the shutter and the subject.

17
Where There's Light...

Back in the not-so-good old days, when really fast lenses and fast film were rarities and when push-processing was a hit-or-miss thing, people only snickered hopelessly over the thought of picturing "a black cat in a coal hole at midnight." Today, the cat's a sitting duck.

For we have the lenses, the fast film, and standardized push-processing *plus* a bundle of artificial light sources. Even without those lights we have reached the point at which we can say, almost truthfully, that if you can see it you can picture it. This, of course, is no snapshot matter; it takes know-how, a little patience, and even ingenuity.

EXISTING LIGHT PHOTOGRAPHY

Call it existing light, or available light, or ambient light; doesn't much matter. The point is that there's an infinity of photographic possibilities in 24 hours of every day, so long as your camera has a reasonably fast lens—$f/2.8$ or faster—and is loaded with fast film, either color or black-and-white. To that basic equipment you can add a flexible shutter-release cable, a monopod or a tripod, and know that each such addition extends your photographic reach. And grasp.

Even if you are the most ardent photographic adventurer, avid for unusual shots, you are unlikely to run out of exciting pictorial material, armed with nothing more than your good, fast-lensed camera and fast, modern film. For every time you achieve a successful shot under limited or even adverse lighting conditions, your notion of what you can do next time out is stretched. Very stimulating.

All photography, of course, is done by existing light of some sort or quantity, but the term existing light has come to imply photography by relatively

179

subnormal light—at twilight, at night on city streets, at ice shows, at artificially lighted athletic or sporting events, at theatres, at concerts, in the lighted rooms of your home, or in the dim vastness of a cathedral. The possibilities are endless, and none of them could be classed as a snapshot.

Existing light work can be either black-and-white or full color. Sometimes, in using color, it may be a little difficult to decide which film, daylight or tungsten, should be used; for the available light may be a mixture of several kinds and colors of light—candlelight, pyrotechnics, twilight, incandescent light, fluorescent light, arc light, or even moonlight. All you can do is to go ahead in the knowledge that scenes recorded on daylight film will tend to be on the yellowish, reddish side; on tungsten-type film the same scene will tend to be colder, bluer. Obviously, when you know what the basic color of the light is, you use the appropriate film. For hopeless mixtures, daylight film is probably preferable, although considerations of mood and taste may sway you the other way.

I suggest that you make your first existing light pictures without accessories of any sort; concentrate on getting the most from your faithful camera, loaded with good fast film. Handhold every shot, using shutter speeds of 1/30 sec. or faster. Later on, you'll be using a camera support of some sort for exposures longer than 1/30 sec. Kodak's little Information Book, *Adventures in Existing Light Photography,* offers some very useful hints on exposures appropriate to a variety of situations. Obviously, those suggestions have to be generalized because few situations offer you specific, standardized quantities and qualities of light. Still, Kodak's suggestions are based on a lot of experience.

Fig. 17-1. The watchful women waited for the wash. A not particularly pictorial aspect of modern living, but an excellent example of low-level-light pictorial communication.

Can you use your exposure meter? Certainly, if there's enough light to budge the needle at all. Otherwise, you're on your own. The usual procedure is to make a reasonable guesstimate and expose your first shot accordingly. Then, in the manner of the field artillery, bracket that shot with one taken at a full stop over and another one at a full stop under. Chances are you'll get your picture and add materially to your know-how.

Outdoors at night you'll encounter situations in which the light is extremely uneven, with blobs of lightness as islands in a sea of darkness. Don't worry about the darkness; your camera will discern practically nothing in it anyway; concentrate on those lighter areas where there's detail to be seen and recorded. Because such scenes produce little or no response from your meter, move in close—if you can—and take a reading from one or more of the lighted areas.

For any shot requiring longer than 1/30 sec., some sort of camera support is indicated, although I have friends who insist that they can hand-hold an exposure of one second. Hmm. True, it is possible to hug your camera against a pole or up against the side of a building for a second or two, but a camera clamp or a tripod is a much more reasonable solution. A flexible shutter-release cable will minimize the chances for camera shake in an iffy situation. For really long exposures, as in making a record of star trails, a rock-steady camera support is a prime necessity.

Once the existing light virus has bitten you, you may be tempted to forego supplementary lighting of any sort—flash, flood, or whatever. Existing light pictures look so natural, so unforced. Things just look right. True, but resist that temptation. For one thing, you hardly rate as a photographic sophisticate if you don't know how to use lights, on or off camera. More importantly, there are so many situations that simply cannot be pictured without some sort of supplementary light. So, use and enjoy the freedom of existing light. But don't pass up the opportunities and rewards of camera-related artificial light.

LIGHT SOURCES

For the first third of this century, amateurs had very slim resources in the way of accessory light. They had ordinary or even medium-high-wattage electric light, but their film was slow. So they needed either very long exposures or light that was really punchy; and the only available source of that kind of light was flash powder. Oh me, oh my—flash powder! An epic could very well be written on the drama, the pyrotechnics, the flames and smoke and thunder, the singed anatomy, the hurry-up ambulance calls, the frustrations, and the occasional triumphs of flash powder photography. Despite earnest efforts to make the use of flash powder simple, safe, and effective, most amateurs used it very seldom; even then it was more a demonstration of high spirits than of photography.

Kodak knows no dark days

With its allies, the Kodak flash sheets and a Kodak flash sheet holder, your Kodak camera is ready for every picture opportunity.

Ask your dealer or write us for our little booklet "By Flashlight." There's no charge.

EASTMAN KODAK COMPANY, ROCHESTER, N. Y., *The Kodak City.*

Fig. 17-2. Once upon a time there was flash powder for "informal" portraits. A technical refinement, the flash sheet, was hailed as the liberator of indoor photography, but it was still an instrument of torture, terror, and pyrotechnics.

The situation today is materially improved, thanks primarily to two quite different developments that came along in the 1930's and '40's. First, somebody discovered that an ordinary, heavy-duty electric light bulb, the 60-volt lamp normally used in railway service, produced a great flood of brilliant, photographically useful light when subjected to the 110-115 volts of ordinary domestic current. True, the over-stimulated lamps burned out after a few hours' use, but they lived their short lives so brilliantly that they provided picture-making light for dozens and scores of exposures. Re-named "photoflood light," the little old 60-volters gave out with the equivalent of hundreds of watts. The heat output was high, too, but nobody minded, for the brilliance was there. Today, there are No. 1 and No. 2 photofloods (roughly equivalent to 250- and 500-W lights), there are photofloods incorporated in "sealed beam" formats, and there are spot floods with narrow, concentrated beams. Because all of these lights are inexpensive, compared to professional studio equipment, most of us can afford a variety of them, with plenty of spares.

The second big change was in flash photography. It was no happy-coincidence kind of development, and, in the long run it was very significant. It began with a Dutch discovery that an electric element that burned or fused at the impact of even a few volts of electricity could ignite metal foil (magnesium or aluminum) contained within the same oxygen-charged bulb. On ignition, the "bonfire-in-a-bulb" emitted a swift and intense flash of light. True, the bulb died in doing it, but the light of its demise was bright enough for picture-making. It soon became possible to synchronize such a flash with normal camera shutter speeds, incorporating just enough delay (in milliseconds) to assure full shutter opening with the peak intensity of the flash. Today's flashbulbs are very much smaller and more efficient than the originals; they are so consistent and reliable that a formalized technique for using them has been evolved. There are many kinds of flashbulbs, varying in color, in shape, in size, in potency, and in methods of detonation.

Most flashbulbs, fitted with conventional reflectors, are effective only at normal "group picture" range; beyond 20 or 30 feet they contribute very little (aside from the snickers evoked from those who know better). Greater depth of illumination usually involves extra-big bulbs or multiple units and electric or electronic hitches or existing light procedures.

Speaking of electronics brings us to the second general class of photo flash sources, the electronic flash or the electronic discharge lamp.

It had long been known that an electric discharge—a "spark"—was very fast and, depending upon the current involved, very bright. Back in the middle of the 19th century the great photo pioneer, Fox Talbot, made a shot in which he "stopped" a whirling newspaper by the light of a discharge from an awesome array of generators and accumulators. But nothing much came out of Fox Talbot's experiment until about 1930 when Dr. Harold Edgerton and his associates at M.I.T. discovered that when a massive jolt of electricity was delivered to a closed tube filled with Xenon gas, the resulting flash was not only fast but ample for photography.

The setup was complex because it required either cumbersome, high-voltage batteries *or* electronic gear that converted and rectified ordinary AC current so that the resulting high-voltage direct current could be stored in a condenser, ready for release when the flash was needed. This, of course, was no one-shot flash; after a few seconds of recovery, the unit was ready to go again. The first studio outfits that evolved out of the Edgerton research were big and cumbersome; the smaller versions were *alleged* to be portable. But the idea was great, for the light was intense, it was fast, and it could be shutter-synchronized. Today, of course, there are still big, heavy, studio outfits but there are also many compact and truly portable electronic flash units; some of them are smaller than a pack of long cigarettes and not much heavier.

Figs. 17-3a & b. Flash cubes (left) offer copious light, integral reflectors, and four shots per cube. Most of them operate from in-camera batteries; Magicubes require no batteries but must be used with suitable in-camera mechanism. Small electronic flash outfits, of which there are many, provide high-speed flashes, and many of them can be recharged from the nearest AC outlet.

Anything that emits light can be used in photography. Some of it is inconvenient and some of it introduces problems in color. But there is nothing to stop you from using ordinary electric or fluorescent light, lamplight, automobile headlight brilliance, or candlelight. It's a rare amateur, indeed, who can permanently resist the temptation to make a few shots of or by candlelight.

Figs. 17-4 & 17-5. And so, goodnight. Any campus offers endless variations on this scene. Offhand, I'd say that these particular scenes are just a bit **too** well lighted.

REFLECTORS

Put a pie pan back of a lighted candle, and the illumination out front is increased considerably. Conversely, if you try to drive at night by your car's headlights without their complementary reflectors, it would be like driving by Braille.

In other words, a reflector organizes and directs the radiant energy of a light source. How well or how much it does this depends upon its shape, size, and the skill of its design; a simple white collar flared around the neck of a lamp helps a little, a coffee can sliced in half can do better, and a scientifically determined, silvered-and-polished parabola plus a light-columnating lens (your car's sealed-beam headlight, for example) can do a great deal better. Any well-stocked photo shop will be pleased to bewilder you with a variety of large and small, flat and curved, cylindrical and parabolic, matte and polished reflectors. Whatever you choose, be sure that there is some means—a spring clamp or a fixture of some sort—that will hold the reflector and its contained light source wherever and however you want it.

All of the foregoing reflectors are *source reflectors*. To supplement them you may need, once in a while, some *subject reflectors*. The commonest of these is simply a largish (maybe three feet square) sheet of white or silvered cardboard, the purpose of which is to bounce otherwise wasted light into parts of your picture setup that may be underillumined. Subject reflectors can be any shape, and can be plain white, matte aluminum, crinkled aluminum, polished aluminum, or even a light gray card. Too much or too hot reflectance can give your photograph the same kind of artificiality you get with excessive supplementary flash in outdoor work. But discreetly used reflectors can give your photographs a subtle, definitely professional look. Using them, obviously, is an art and the skill is seldom acquired in a mere day or two. The key to the art is developing the habit of scrutinizing your lighting setup *from the camera's point of view*.

USING LIGHTS

First, let us consider flood lighting, or lighting with steady artificial light sources, such as photoflood.

It is usually suggested that the camera be mounted on a tripod for exposures longer than 1/30 sec. on the very sound assumption that few people can hold a camera steady for any longer exposure. Check, and okay. But there is another reason for establishing camera stability; unless your camera is firmly fixed in position, you cannot freely roam your set, adjusting a light here, resetting a reflector there, and generally checking and rechecking the whole business through your viewfinder. A firmly established camera simply increases your capacity for command of the situation.

Figs. 17-6 to 17-8. Using Photofloods. Top, a sealed-beam photoflood (reflectorflood) in a spring clamp holder. Center, a bare photoflood in a parabolic reflector, plus clamp. Bottom, the same combination in an adjustable floor stand.

In Chapter 18, Humane Portraiture, a basic lighting scheme, using two or three lights, is described. It suggests a main light, a fill-in light, and—if needed or desirable—a top or backlight. The same basic considerations apply in non-portrait shooting, for your objective is not only to *reveal* your subject but to present it as interestingly as possible. You will find that the Kodak Master Photoguide deals with photoflood lighting very well and specifically but, like all such guides, it cannot possibly cover all contingencies.

So, use your own judgment, backed up, if possible, with an exposure meter; take both reflected-light and incident-light readings. Out of simple consideration for economy of both time and money, it is suggested that you concentrate for a while on black-and-white photography, familiarizing yourself with basic procedures. Then, on moving over to color, you will be better prepared to meet its special opportunities and problems.

Check your outlets

Before you undertake anything at all ambitious by electric light, make sure that there are adequate and convenient electrical outlets. While you may think it looks professional to have long yardages of wire snaking all over the floor, it is much better to use simple, direct connections, avoiding overloading any outlet. No one circuit, for that matter, should have to supply electricity to more than two or three photofloods. So, before you start on actual picture-making, be sure that you have access to the outlets you need, that you have adequate extension cords, and that the circuit will safely take the load you impose on it. Otherwise... panic.

The Family

The members of a family at home are comfortably at ease, so try to picture them that way. Don't line them up and demand cheese-y smiles. Select a situation that is typical, reasonably amiable, and so concentrated that the camera can encompass it. Watching TV, gathered around the piano, at the bridge table, at dinner—any such grouping is much to be preferred to a tin soldier line-up.

Your lighting should avoid overall harshness. Typically, the home lighting scheme involves uneven lighting; don't try to even it out too much, because you want a natural-looking photograph. If you look for them you will find that there are built-in subject reflectors in most homes—light-colored or white walls, mirrors, tablecloths, and so on. Substitute a photoflood for an ordinary bulb in a reading lamp if you wish *(caution:* a photoflood can and will singe paper or cloth in contact with it) or even in a ceiling fixture. The fewer special lamps and lamp stands scattered around, the better.

From your camera angle check carefully for reflections of light in mirrors, windows, and polished surfaces of any kind. Many an otherwise good shot has been spoiled by the glare of a light reflected from a window in the background.

Fig. 17-9. For "comfortable" group pictures, create a comfortable situation, with everyone at ease, doing something that's natural and unforced. Note use of a light, high at left, to add highlights and luster.

Groups

When your picture involves a half dozen or more people, you are forced to rely on a higher general level of light. Concentrate your subjects as naturally as possible—on and around a davenport, at a table, clustered at a doorway, or something of the sort—and give them something to do other than watching you. Sometimes, it may be necessary to add a little extra punch to the lighting; the easiest way to do this is with a flash at the camera. But *aim it at the ceiling,* halfway between the camera and the subjects, rather than at the people. Such bounced light is soft and so widely scattered that it can add a lot to the picture, very unobtrusively.

If your group is very large, with a dozen or more members, it is probable that your best bet is not flood lighting but flash, and multiple flash at that. This will be dealt with in a little while.

Interiors

A really good picture of the interior of a home is a rarity, partly because some of us have the notion that our livingroom should look as much as possible like the rooms pictured in *House Beautiful* or *Interiors*. This is nonsense, because any room good enough to be enjoyed and lived in deserves sympathetic picturing. The trick in photographing any room is to select vistas and angles that emphasize its spirit. It is really a good deal like portraiture, for you're dealing with the personality of the place.

Photography of an interior by daylight illumination alone can be tough. In fact, the sunnier the day, the greater your potential problems with excessive contrast—overbright windows, sunny patches on the floor, uncontrollable reflections, and pools or corners of darkness. You need a fairly even level of light, and the brighter the day the more artificial light you need to balance it. The more lights you use, the greater the chance for unwanted reflections and for a crazy multiplicity of shadows around the legs of tables and chairs. One approach to the problem is to use a double exposure; a short one to register any bright, visible windows, and a longer one with the window shades down and your special lighting full up. But this is both a difficult and a chancy technique.

Another approach is to wait until dusk or an overcast day, when the outdoor light can be more easily balanced by your indoor lighting. Because there are so many variables, no valid "rules" can be set up. The easiest method is to work after dark, when *all* of the light is at your command. You may discover that the room's normal lighting gives you the "feel" you want but is uneven. So you bounce light off the ceiling—either flood or flash—to even things up.

There's another technique that can be both useful and fun. Set up your lights and adjust the camera for a *very* long exposure at minimum aperture. When ready, start the exposure and then walk into the set, carrying an extra light source in its reflector. So equipped, you can "paint" with light into dark corners or other neglected areas and then, just before time's up, move back to the camera and close the shutter. Caution: Wear dark clothes and be sure that the light you carry *never* aims back toward the camera. Obviously, this takes practice—but it has been done thousands of times, and with success.

For very large rooms—auditorium, churches, halls, and so forth, you need great amounts of light, maximum depth of field, and a lot of patience. No one set of lights near the camera can possibly give you the result you want. So hook up as many lights as possible, positioning them so that they light up the whole place, but keep them hidden from the camera. Remember, your camera records a steadily broadening vista; the greater the distance the more care is needed to hide your supplementary lights. Try to avoid criss-crossing streaks of light; they are dead give-aways of your technique. Flood lights are fine for this kind of work because they give you a chance to check every thing you do, from the camera's point of view. The necessary exposure may be longish, but, compared to the time taken in setting up, it is unimportant. If any persons or action are included in your picture, you can—with an ample budget—substitute larger flashbulbs (with standard screw-in bases) for the photofloods and, when ready, bang them all off together. Expensive and showy, but useful.

The alternative to the foregoing may be the use of existing light procedures. It is certainly far less trouble, but sometimes even the longest exposure and push-processing can't give you the result you want. It's up to you.

Outdoors with lights

There is undeniable fascination in photographs made outdoors at night, by whatever light is present or available. Usually, time exposures are necessary and a tripod is therefore indicated; but many a good shot has been made with the camera set up on a balustrade or snugged tight against a wall for the necessary period. Usually it's a matter of only a second or two; Broadway at its brightest can be recorded with Verichrome Pan or Plus-X with an exposure of about ½ sec. at $f/16$, and with Tri-X you need only $1/20$ sec. at $f/16$. Or, if the camera is hand-held, you need only $1/30$ sec. at $f/5.6$.

Night scenes are enhanced if the streets are wet; you get the advantage of the lights reflected in the pavement and, in addition, you get a fine sense of sparkle. Most exposure meters register little or nothing under night lighting, so you're on your own—and that's a good idea.

There are a few "rules" for night photography.

1. Avoid including strong foreground lights, if you're interested in photographing what's beyond them.

2. If automobile headlights threaten to point your way during an exposure, cover the lens until the car is past. (Unless, of course, you want to record a stream of headlights.)

3. Compose your shot as carefully as you would for a daytime scenic. Remember, every light the camera "sees" will register on the film.

4. During a long exposure, ten seconds or more, pedestrians will disappear, and passing cars will become merely streaks of light; in order for a figure to be visible in the finished picture, it must be stationary.

Under very strong commercial flood lighting, as at a ball park, all you need is a fast film (Tri-X Pan, for example) and an exposure on the order of $1/60$ sec. at $f/6.3$.

USING FLASH

When photo flash was new, there was a technique that avoided the necessity for synchronization with the camera shutter. It is still used, and useful. All it amounts to is setting the shutter on *time* or *bulb* for a count of 1—2—3;

Figs. 17-10a to 17-10c. Photographically, every room is a problem. Here are three attempts at a solution of one such problem—a room with full-length doors at both ends. In a, nothing but daylight was used, and the sunny end of the room came through as a massive density of sunlight. In b, the draperies were closed and ordinary room lights turned on. In c, a couple of photofloods, plus the room lights, were used to battle the sunlight. But look at those big double shadows cast by the piano wing. None of these is **the** answer, but b probably comes close.

at "1" open the shutter, at "2" flash the flash, and at "3" close the shutter—mission accomplished. Because the flash is generally fast, you may not even need a tripod—especially if the situation is so dark that nothing registers on the film before and after that crucial "2." And that's the story on "open flash."

Obviously, nothing that simple could long endure. Today's synchronized flash techniques stem from open flash, in the sense that they seek to set off the flash while the shutter is wide open; but the procedures have been tightened up, speeded up, and made far more effective. With the old open flash, everything was on the basis of faith, hope, and luck; today, luck and hope are taken for granted, leaving well-justified faith in charge.

GUIDE NUMBERS

As flashbulbs increased in number and kind, as film speeds climbed higher and higher, and as reflectors of various types and shapes came on the market, the need for a reasonably exact method of determining exposures with flash became all too obvious. There were just too many variables: distance, reflector shapes and efficiencies, the output of the flashes themselves, film speed, diaphragm setting, and shutter speed. So scientists and photo technicians went into a huddle and emerged with a very useful concept—the *guide number*. It was perfectly named; for it did guide, and it was nothing but a number.

This is the gist of it. For any or each combination of film speed, kind of flash source, and type of reflector a number was assigned, and not arbitrarily, as shall be seen. With an assumed shutter setting of $1/30$ sec., optimum diaphragm opening (f/number) for any flash shot could be determined. Simply divide the guide number by the distance (in feet) between the camera-flash and the primary object. For example: Your Film is Kodachrome-X and your flash source is a flashcube with its built-in reflector. The guide number for this combination is 80. Okay. Your flash-to-subject distance is 10 feet. 80 divided by 10 is 8. So, $1/30$ sec. at $f/8$ is your basic exposure. As you know, there is a series of exposures equivalent to $1/30$ sec. at $f/8$–$1/60$ sec. at $f/6.3$, $1/15$ sec. at $f/11$, and so on. But avoid high shutter speeds; you might miss all or part of the flash.

Try again, now, with a faster film and another source, say, Plus-X Pan and an all-glass (AG-1B) flashbulb in a well-designed reflector. The indicated guide number becomes 160. Our flash-to-subject distance is still 10 feet. So, 160 divided by 10 is 16, and $f/16$ therefore becomes the optimum aperture at $1/30$ sec. And that exposure has many equivalents: $f/22$ at $1/15$ sec., $f/11$ at $1/60$ sec., and so on.

Or you can work it the other way around. Suppose, with Plus-X Pan and a well-reflectored AG-1B flashbulb, you need or want to use an exposure of 1/30 sec. at a minimal aperture, something like $f/22$. How far away can or should the subject be? Using that 160 guide number, you divide it by 22. 160 divided by 22 comes out at 7.2, plus. So, your flash-subject distance had best be about seven feet.

In the many published guides and data books, as well as in the instructions often packed with flashbulbs, flash units, and films you will find guide numbers listed for just about all the possible combinations of film, flash source, and type of reflector.

Despite the fact that these published data specify half a dozen or more kinds of reflectors, usually illustrated to permit you to identify and classify the outfit you're using, there remains an area of uncertainty: Is your outfit typical and efficient? You can find out, specifically, at the cost of a half-dozen or so test exposures, on either color or monochrome film.

Here's how. Pose a subject at exactly ten (measured) feet from the fixed-camera position. Your subject should be an amiably cooperative friend; for one thing, he provides a constant skin tone criterion and, second, can hold a card on which you have boldly lettered the f/number or aperture used in each of the test shots.

Okay. Camera ready. Flash outfit all set with fresh batteries or, if it's an electronic flash, fully charged. If you are using Plus-X Film (ASA 125) for your test, with a flashcube and a shutter speed of 1/30 sec., your suggested guide number is 110. 110 divided by the distance (10 feet) comes out 11; so you make your first test at 1/30 sec. at $f/11$.

Maintaining the same shutter speed, make your next shot with the aperture increased one-half stop, to $f/9.5$. Change the card held by your model accordingly. Make another shot at $f/6.7$. Now make a few more, closing down beyond $f/11$ for shots at $f/13$, $f/16$, and $f/19$.

Thus you have a half-dozen test exposures which, when developed, tell you graphically whether or not the suggested guide number is right for your outfit. For example, should the best of the series turn out to be the one made at $f/9.5$, you multiply that number by 10, and come up with the tailor-made guide number of 95. But remember, that guide number applies only to that one type and kind of light source and to the other conditions that you standardized in making the test.

Perhaps you have been wondering why guide-numbers are predicated on shutter speeds of 1/30 or 1/25 sec. The flash itself is, in most cases, considerably faster than that. It is simply a matter of making sure that the flash occurs while the shutter is fully open.

The various types of flashbulbs have their own distinctive reaction times and durations. The M-2 and AG-1 lamps are intermediate-peaking; they reach their top output about 15ms (milliseconds) after current hits them and have a total effective duration of about 20ms, or 1/50 sec. Obviously, then, efficient use of a flash requires that the shutter be open long enough to make optimum use of those 20ms of brilliance. A shutter speed of 1/30 sec. is 33ms, and that's just about right. With a faster shutter speed you gain nothing and may lose much.

Class M lamps (this class includes many of the most popular flashbulbs) are medium-peak, reaching full brilliance about 18-20ms—a bit more or less, depending upon the potency of the battery—after the button is pressed. So, cameras equipped with Class M synchronization incorporate a delaying mechanism that gives the flashbulb a tiny headstart; but in about 20ms, shutter and lamp are in full synch, and the flash is fully effective.

Type X synchronization is for electronic flash that is so fast, so nearly instantaneous, that the built-in delay controls the flash rather than the shutter. With electronic flash, shutter speed is really unimportant, for the flash determines not only the brilliance but the actual speed of the exposure. Provided, of course, that the flash unit is set off while the shutter is open.

Class S flash lamps are intended for open-flash work in studios; they are not dependent on close synchronization with shutter action. They are useful primarily because of their power, an output rated at something like 100,000 lumen seconds (lumens $\times$ milliseconds), which is about five times the punch of a Class M lamp.

Class FP flash lamps are designed for use with focal-plane shutters (many of the popular single-lens reflex cameras have such shutters.) A focal-plane shutter is a curtain with a slit in it that whips across the face of the film; the narrower the adjustment of the slit, the less any part of the film is exposed and, hence, the higher the effective speed. But no matter what the width of the slit, the whole curtain has to travel fully across the film, and that takes time, even if it's only milliseconds. So, a flashbulb for a focal-plane shutter must have fairly long duration with a relatively long period of full brilliance, or a "flat peak." The Class FP flashbulbs, Nos. 6 and 26, have a total duration of some 40ms, and for more than half that time they maintain a remarkably level plateau of brilliance. Hence, effective speeds ranging from snapshot to 1/1000 sec.—achieved by adjustment of the slit in the curtain—are entirely within reason.

The Color of Flash

All light has color, and flash is no exception. Similarly, color films have their specific color balances. It is only sensible, therefore, to use flash and film combinations that are or can be made compatible.

Daylight-type color film, for example, can be used with electronic flash, flashcubes, magicubes, blue flashbulbs, or daylight. But when daylight color films are used with clear flash or with photoflood, a light-balancing lens filter is required to "de-red" the reddish color of the light. Usually, this filter would be one of the blue filters such as 80C or 80D.

Artificial light films need no color-balancing filters when used with photo-flood light; but with clear flashbulbs one of the light-yellow filters (81A or 81C) is recommended.

There is a great deal of detailed information available in this area (the Kodak Master Photoguide is full of it), but for general purposes the statement printed on the end of the film carton is your basic guide. It states the kind of light for which that particular film is intended. It is only when you use a kind of light for which your film is *not* balanced that you run into puzzlements. The information in the Photoguides resolves these questions neatly and specifically.

Multiple Flash

A few pages back, it was suggested that standard screw-base flashbulbs could be substituted for photofloods in the lighting of large interiors. True, but there is another technique you should know about; the use of "master" and "slave" flash units to accomplish the same kind of coverage-in-depth.

In this system the master unit is on the camera and the slave unit to the side and, usually, a bit higher. It actually becomes the main light for the shot, with the master unit serving as the fill-in.

No wires connect the two (or more) units. Instead, the slave unit picks up the light from the flash at the camera and uses it, electronically, to trigger its own flash. It all happens in thousandths of a second (milliseconds); if your camera shutter is working at 1/30 sec. it (and you) will be unaware of anything but a single, simultaneous burst of light. Obviously, the slave unit must be positioned so that (1) it is not visible in the resulting picture, and (2) the peeled eye of the slave unit has an unobstructed view of the master unit.

The same result can, of course, be obtained with direct, inter-unit wiring, but the wireless method is generally easier and just as reliable. In either case, the distances at which slave and master illuminate the subject will determine the lighting ratio of your picture; less contrasty, more pleasing pictures will generally result when the main light (actually, the slave) is only a few feet closer to the subject than the fill (actually, the master).

FLASH FLUFFS

Probably the most common and disconcerting fluff in flash photography is using a light setup that creates a sharp shadow behind or beside your subject. You have certainly seen such shots. They are the result, first, of posing your subject too close to a wall or background and, second, of a flash position on or close to the camera. Where you have strong light, you have strong shadows. To eliminate the possibility of a shadow frame, move your subject well away from the wall so that the shadows can fly away, with little or nothing to indicate their flight.

A second difficulty—specifically in color work—is what is called "red eye." It is a tiny speck of reddish light visible in the very center of your subject's eyes as he looks at you and your camera. It is simply a reflection of your on-camera flash. It can be eliminated by using your flash off its usual camera perch. Any displacement that effectively separates the axis of the light beam from the optical axis of the camera lens will suffice. "Extenders" are available for many cameras and for various kinds of flash, including the very useful little Magicubes.

The third easy flash boner—and incredibly easy it is—is to aim the flash so that your picture picks up an all-too-obvious reflection of the flash in a window, a mirror, a shiny wall, or the polished surface of a piano. You may have thought you eliminated the possibilities of any such reflections, but the finished picture may include some unnoticed source of glare. The only guarantee of a no-glare picture is to carefully check and double-check the picture situation from the point of view of the camera.

All of us, of course, have experienced flash failure; it is a dismal, frustrating experience. The reason for the failure may be weak or deteriorated batteries. The only way to be sure they're okay (lacking a volt meter of your own) is to test them at the nearest hardware shop or drugstore. Or, there may be corrosion on the battery terminals, the contacts, or the bulb base; clean those terminals with an eraser or a cotton swab. Some people have a habit of licking the bulb base just before use; okay, but that moisture can actually promote corrosion in the internal contacts. The fact that flash outfits often remain idle and unused for long periods probably accounts for most flash failures.

Speaking of fluffs, never drop a hot flashbulb into your pocket where there are several unused bulbs; the retained heat can detonate the fresh bulbs and scorch your pocket. And never toss a used bulb into a glowing fireplace; you're almost certain to have a glass grenade on your hands—or face.

Flash shields are not old maidish, because flashbulbs do sometimes shatter. No fun.

Take care with a strange or cold flash unit as you insert a bulb; should the contact be on, you run the chance of burning your fingers and blinding your eyes.

Figs. 17-11a & b. Harsh background shadows in flash work look (and are) amateurish. With a removable flash unit, you can change its angle so as to eliminate those shadows.

18
Humane Portraiture

People are the most interesting things in the world, especially to other people—photographers included.

A photographer may think of himself as very far out. He may spend his time picturing details of the town dump or faded posters peeling from old walls—or the third pore from the left on a model's nude nose. But let this same liberated soul have a new baby in his family, and he starts making baby pictures by the gross. He emerges as human after all; he is one of us.

More pictures are made of people than of anything else. *But* if you were to review a weekend's crop of new pictures, fresh from the photo-finishing plants, you would be shocked. For the evidence is that, in our picturing of one-another, we are an unkind, unperceptive, and almost sadistic lot. We chop off heads, we blind our victims with light, we stick telephone poles down the backs of their necks, and so on and on.

Actually, of course, our purpose in making a picture of someone is to perpetuate a glimpse of him as a friend, as someone we enjoy, as someone others might like, too. But carelessness, plus a failure to use our eyes, all too often defeats our purpose.

It is not necessary to become a professional portrait photographer in order to produce humane pictures of people. But we should understand some of the basics of the art.

These are the basic factors involved:
1. Existing mood
2. Setting or environment
3. Light
4. Colors involved
5. Camera angle and range
6. Film
7. Processing and printing

201

You have undoubtedly laughed at someone's passport picture, possibly your own. Passport pictures don't *have* to be horrible, but most of them are. It is primarily because the photographers who make them completely ignore any consideration of the humane basics.

MOOD

To begin with, consider *mood*. The bored passport photographer usually plunks his equally bored subject down on a hard chair in a bare room and fires a volley of light at him, simultaneously making the exposure. A photograph results, but it is hardly understanding, sympathetic, or perceptive. Mostly because the mood killed it.

Mood has nothing whatever to do with the luxury of the situation or the fancy quality of the equipment. It is primarily the result of the photographer's attitude. If you, as the photographer, are hurried, harried, unsure of your equipment, bored, or impatient, how in the world can your subject be at ease? He probably does not enjoy having his picture taken anyway, and is anxious to get the whole thing over with as quickly as possible. Infected by your mood, he displays the same symptoms. No miracle can, under such conditions, produce a humane picture.

You can consciously control *your* mood. It is materially helped if you are using equipment—camera, film, lights, filters, and accessories—with which you are so familiar that you have no mechanical or technical worries and are free to concentrate on your subject.

Your subject's mood is more complex. To repeat, he is bound to reflect your own mood. If you are uptight, it is next to impossible for him to be at ease, to be himself. So it is up to you to so humanize the situation that your subject relaxes and becomes the sort of person you enjoy and whose portrait others can enjoy.

Your subject will be most at ease if he is doing something other than having his picture taken. With modern equipment there is seldom need for him to "hold it"; you can picture him in action—fussing with a dog, tinkering with a car, reading a book, bird-watching, whittling, or doing anything else, within reason, in which he is sufficiently interested to bring animation into his expressions. Your job is to be ready with the camera, ready to take advantage of characteristic gestures, facial expressions, attitudes, and all the rest.

SETTING

Under this heading are included several factors that affect the picture-making situation—the place itself and its environment and surroundings. A straight chair and a blank wall may be what the passport photographer needs and wants, but it is not exactly a humane setup. On the other hand, the setting itself is less important than the degree to which your subject is at home or at ease in it. Your patrician Aunt Sophia is unlikely to be at ease in a situation involving a chain saw and a pile of logs; by the same token, rough-and-ready Butch will feel ridiculous seated in a high-style garden chair. The key word for settings, therefore, is *appropriate*. Whatever it may be, try to keep it simple, for a complex, confused setting automatically draws attention away from the subject and, accordingly, dilutes the emphasis.

LIGHT

Your people-pictures can be glorified or ruined by light. Harsh, midday sun, for example, throws heavy shadows under eyebrows, nose, and mouth; even with the mitigation provided by reflectors it is not ideal, especially for pictures of women and children. And low-angle sun (within an hour or two of sunrise or sunset) throws long, disfiguring, horizontal shadows. People facing such light cannot keep from squinting. In general, such light is not really favorable. Midmorning and midafternoon are the best times for general people-picturing; the sun doesn't make them uncomfortable, and the shadows are not grotesque.

"Open shade" is one of the best lightings for outdoor portraiture. This is the kind of light you find on the shadow side of buildings or trees, with unobstructed sky overhead. There are no hard shadows, yet the light is good, especially if there are a few fleecy clouds in the sky. While open shade portraiture requires somewhat more exposure than direct sun, the increase presents no problem.

It is common practice among many commercial photographers to use a supplementary or fill-in flash for almost all their shots, even in full sunlight. But unless it is used with care, it tends to produce pictures that have a hard, commercial look. You may have seen publicity shots, as of some Miss Contour being crowned queen at a convention of geodetic surveyors, in which fill-in flash, used willy-nilly, battles natural sunlight and produces a completely unnatural-looking picture. It may be bright and fully detailed, and the publicity people may love it. But as a humane portrait of a blameless girl, it is a failure.

Supplementary flash, used sensibly, serves to illuminate and soften shadows, not to eliminate them entirely. You can control the brilliance of the flash by using it on an extension cord at a greater subject-distance than the camera itself, by bouncing the flash off a nearby wall, or (most commonly) by draping a diffuser over the flash. One or two thicknesses of a handkerchief will materially tone down the exuberance of almost any flash.

The central fact of outdoor daylight portraiture is that the sun is at your service; it may be clear, diffuse, high, or low—it doesn't matter so long as you are aware of it and work accordingly. Learn to look at shadows; by their sharpness, their softness, or their near invisibility you can accurately judge the kind of exposure you should use.

BACKGROUNDS

Although consideration of backgrounds was not specified in the list of portrait basics, it relates to several of those basics—setting and lighting particularly. Never take a background for granted, because it can rise up to smite you. Make it a habit to scrutinize the background of any setting *through your camera's viewfinder*. Particularly, watch for background elements that can disrupt your picture, such as isolated trees, poles, or TV antennae. Such things have a way of intruding and absorbing a disproportionate amount of attention. They can also be downright ridiculous.

If you simply have to put up with a bad background, you can control, minimize, or even eliminate it by making use of the depth-of-field phenomenon. An unwanted picket fence even ten feet behind your subject can be reduced to an inoffensive blur simply by using your lens wide open—assuming, of course, that your lens is faster than $f/8$ to begin with. The closer you are to your subject or the longer the focal length of your lens, the easier it is to fuzz-out unwanted backgrounds.

The finest, most trouble-free of all backgrounds is the sky. Whether it is clear or clouded, the sky is appropriate, it needs no explaining, is usually beautiful, and stays where it belongs—in the background.

ANGLE AND RANGE

Camera ang'e and camera-subject distance are so easily controlled that they are sometimes disregarded as factors in portraiture. Just as a too-high camera angle tends to diminish your subject, a too-low angle presents him as a looming monster. A "conversational," eye-level angle is the simplest and probably the most logical of angles, but sometimes you may need to use an angle in which the camera is aimed upward a few degrees from the horizontal. This is really a psychological gambit, for it gives your subject the advantage of looking down on the camera. It's a small point and possibly no one, especially your sitter, will grant its validity—but it can be useful.

The general topic of angle includes consideration of both camera angle and light angle. When both camera and light are aimed head-on at your subject, there is a lack of revealing facial feature shadows. While this is acceptable (or even approved) in color work, it is seldom the answer in black-and-white. Generally, a quartering light coming in from over your shoulder produces a more pleasing, less arbitrary kind of illumination. Incidentally, one of the hazards of direct, head-on lighting is that, unless you watch for it, your own shadow may appear in the foreground of your picture. And that is a sin not easily forgiven.

Range or subject-to-camera distance is another factor to be considered. Ordinarily, a portrait almost presumes a normal, conversational range, something between five and ten feet. For how can you achieve a "speaking" likeness if your subject is so far away that shouting seems more appropriate? Conversely, an extreme closeup suggests whispering.

It is entirely possible to use a long-focus, zoom, or telephoto lens to bring a distant subject close. (Actually, a moderate long-focus lens can be used effectively for portraiture, even at normal range.) For candid shots, for pictures of timid or overly self-conscious subjects, long-shot procedures may be necessary. You should remember, however, that some people resent being taken, literally, unaware. They consider it an invasion of privacy, and, as such, it becomes a mood factor. True, such a reaction is an after-the-fact mood and may not detract from the picture itself. But it will affect your subject's subsequent feelings about you.

Enlargements can be used, too, to overcome the handicap of distance. Carried to extremes, of course, enlarging can involve you in excessive graininess.

Film and processing are included as the last two items in the list of portrait basics simply as reminders that both give you additional control. Even the paper you select for the final prints can be a factor. For example, you would hardly pick a coarse-textured paper for a portrait of a beautiful girl.

To sum up the foregoing generalities, it must be emphasized that they *are* generalities. In a widely circulated publication I once wrote that black dogs were best pictured against light or neutral backgrounds. Seemed reasonable, I thought. But shortly thereafter a reader sent me a really excellent picture of a very black Scottie against an equally black background.

In other words, any generality, any "rule" can be successfully violated, if you are skilled enough and not simply breaking rules for the fun of breaking rules.

OUTDOOR COLOR PORTRAITS

In black-and-white work the colors of your setting or of the prevailing light are minor concerns. But in color portraiture, those colors have to be considered carefully, for they become elements in your pictures.

For example, your subject or model may be standing beside a sunny wall. In black-and-white, the light reflected from that wall may provide exactly what you need to balance strong daylight. In color work, however, the color of that wall becomes a big factor. If the wall is red, your subject will be ruddy. If the wall is green, your subject will look sick; if it is blue—but you get the idea.

Similarly, the coloration of other surroundings—foliage, fences, lawn chairs, cars, or any other props—can influence your picture. Sometimes a relatively minor element, something you would tolerate without quibble in a monochrome, will jump out of the picture and, because of its jarring or dissonant color, spoil the general harmony of a color composition. You, as well as your film, must be color-sensitive.

The light by which you work has its own color. Clear daylight, with a blue sky liberally laced with fleecy white clouds, is just about ideal. If the sky is a clear deep blue, you will probably benefit by using a haze filter that warms up all that blueness.

Sunrise or sunset light, on the other hand, is very red and suffuses everything with red light. Because sunset pictures are almost always obviously sunset pictures, you may accept the rosy glow, using it as it is, for what it is. If, however, you prefer to mitigate it, you can use a filter that absorbs red light and gives you a more normal-looking result.

INDOOR PORTRAITS IN MONOCHROME

When you move your portrait making indoors, you will discover that your job is both easier and more complex. It is easier because all the picture-making factors—light, particularly—are under your full and absolute control. And it is more complex because, with everything under your control, it is easy to overlook something.

You will need a camera tripod, preferably one that is just a little sturdier than you feel is necessary. That's simply a safety factor.

You will need convenient access to at least two electrical outlets. (If you go in for many and powerful lights, don't hook them all in on any one circuit.) You should have room enough for an uncramped setting and the placing of lights all around your subject; give yourself easy access to all lights and reflectors.

Now, about lights. Unless you are using an old-fashioned sky-lighted studio, you will need several good lights. They should either be mounted on folding telescoping metal stands or should be in reflector-holders equipped with padded spring clamps so that they can be attached to the edges of tables, backs of chairs, tops of doors, and so on. They should be easily moved but, once in position, should stay put.

The available illuminants for indoor portraiture are many. They come in a great variety of types, sizes, shapes, and powers. Any well-stocked photo dealer will be delighted to sell you all sorts of specialized lighting equipment —pin spots, baby spots, barn-door fixures, baffles, matte reflectors, polished reflectors—all sorts of fascinating gadgetry.

The point is that the available lighting tools are many and varied. In normal work, fortunately, you need only a few simple light sources.

A SETTING-UP EXERCISE

Because this exercise can be very dull for a live sitter, it is suggested that you use a sit-in—an inanimate object that is roughly the shape and size of the human head. Of course, an old mannequin or dummy would make a fine one, but few of them are readily available. So settle for something else, a football, for example. Embellish it with putty eyebrows, a nose, mouth, and ears; your "sculpture" need not be realistic; it need only cast more or less normal shadows. Set it up head-high, level with your camera (which should be loaded with a normal pan film) and six or seven feet distant. This camera-subject relationship will remain constant throughout this exercise; ditto exposure.

Start the exercise using a single No. 2 photoflood or reflector flood clamp-held or on a stand. All other light in the room should be so subdued that it makes no difference in your portrait lighting.

Shot 1. The light is aimed squarely at the subject from a point as near as possible to the camera, preferably beside rather than above or below.

Shot 2. Maintaining the same light-to-subject distance, move the light to one side or the other so that the line from light to subject is at a 45-degree angle to the camera-subject line.

Shot 3. Now raise the light, without changing its lateral position, so that it beams down on the model at about a 20-degree angle.

Shot 4. Lower the light from the same position so that it aims *up* at the model.

Shot 5. This time, move and raise the light so that it aims directly down over the forehead of your model from a height of three or four feet.

Shot 6. Finally, move the light, level it, and aim it so that it hits only the *back* of your model, taking care to keep the lamp and its direct rays out of the ken of the camera.

Having made these six shots, develop them at once and make prints as soon as possible. Spread them out on a bench and study them. Remember, you're after good portraits, not passport pictures. Be critical in your scrutiny.

Number 1 will probably be a fair likeness, but flat, lacking in roundness. Number 2 will almost certainly seem contrasty, with prominent shadows beside the nose and mouth. Number 3 will look better, although the nose shadow may, depending upon the architecture of your model, seem unduly prominent. Number 4 will look odd because the shadows "fall" upward in an abnormal-looking way. Number 5 will have deep shadows under eyebrows, nose, and mouth. Its opposite, with the light coming from directly below, would be nothing but grotesque. And Number 6 will be mostly a silhouette, with little or no illumination on your subject's face, depending upon the extent to which the walls and ceiling of the room bounce the backlight around.

The moral of all this seems to be that a single light, without reflectors or supplements is a stark thing, with unrelieved shadows and hard highlights.

Now try using a sheet of cardboard—matte-white and at least 20 by 30 inches—as a reflector, repeating shots numbers 2 and 3. If the light is aimed in from the right of the camera, the reflector is propped up at the left, near the model, so that it bounces light back into the model's facial shadows. Watch those shadows as you move the card around, seeking the best placement and angle. When you have obtained optimum reflection, make a couple of shots. It is probable that the results will now be better but still not as good as they should be. For maximum reflection you may find that the card has to be so close to the subject that it shows up in the picture. That, of course, cannot be tolerated.

So you take the next step. You introduce a second light, keeping your main light in approximately the position of Shot 2 or 3 in our setting-up exercise. The purpose of the second light is to soften the shadows created by the main light—soften, not eliminate. You need some shadows to reveal facial topography.

This second light will be, classically, less powerful than the main light. After you've experimented with it for a while, it may very well end up close to the camera, serving as a frontal light.

Now, your results should be getting better. You almost have the makings of portrait lighting, but not quite. Something is still missing. Something is needed to relieve the bread-and-butter, strictly-functional look, something to add a bit of lightness and animation. For a starter, see what happens when you use a small spotlight, aimed down from well above and a little behind your model, and to the left or right. You will get highlights in the hair, a touch of light along the shoulders, and a distinct increase in liveliness.

Nobody pretends that the formula of the three lights will meet any and all situations perfectly. But, until the use of the formula is so familiar to you that it's practically a habit, resist the temptation to add more lights, more reflectors, more gadgets.

There is a law of light that should be part of your understanding as you use artificial light for portraits, interiors, or whatever. The intensity or brilliance of a light falls off rapidly as the distance between light source and subject is increased. Mathematically stated, it falls off *as the square of the distance*. Double the distance and the light becomes one-fourth as effective.

You will almost certainly be using a light meter in your indoor work; so check the validity of the foregoing law. And, as you meter the various places in your setting—the subject's face, his clothes, the visible furniture, the background, and the deepest areas of shadow—you will not only be able to arrive at a reasonable overall exposure but also to note the existing subject and lighting contrasts.

In monochrome those contrasts can run fairly high and still be tolerable; only experience with repeated experiments will give you the answers that will determine what you like and what is best for your subjects.

Figs. 18-1a to 18-1i. Here's a setting-up exercise for you. Scrutinize these nine different lighting setups and decide, in each case, how many lights were used, where they were placed (relative to both camera and model), and what they did to or for the model.

COLOR PORTRAITS INDOORS

I have a friend, a highly respected color portraitist, who periodically explodes, "Damn color! I wish it had never been invented!"

What he is really saying is that color raises a lot of puzzlements of which the monochrome photographer is blissfully unaware. In spite of its imponderables, however, color portraiture can be immensely and uniquely satisfying. My color-portrait friend is still in business and, in spite of everything, enjoying it.

Much of the difficulty with color lies in the fact that color film sees so much and so selectively. Good old black-and-white film sees things in terms of the gray scale. But color film responds not only in terms of its own color balance but also in terms of the colors in the pictured scene *and* the color of the light or lights by which that scene is illuminated.

Light Sensitivity of Kodak Color Films

Film	Balance	Daylight ASA Rating	3400 K ASA Rating	3200 K ASA Rating
Kodachrome II, Daylight Type	Daylight	25	8*	6*
Kodachrome-X, Daylight Type	Daylight	64	20*	16*
Kodak Ektachrome-X	Daylight	64	20*	16*
Kodak High Speed Ektachrome (Daylight)	Daylight	160	50*	40*
Kodachrome II Professional, Type A	3400 K	25*	40	32*
Kodak High Speed Ektachrome (Tungsten)	3200 K	80*	100*	125

*With proper filtration.

The color of the illumination provided by various commonly-used lights is indicated in the table on p. 126. It can help you select the light sources best suited to the kind of work you contemplate. For further, much more detailed information on matters of light sources, on color-balancing, color-correcting, and color-converting filters, and on the uses of subject and lighting contrasts, it is suggested that you consult a specialized publication such as Kodak's data book *Color As Seen and Photographed;* it is under constant revision so that it can be up-to-the-minute about films, lights, filters, and so on. The Kodak Master Photoguide, the data books put out by Kodak, and the publications of other film manufacturers are also very useful, especially in the sense that they give you a specific background for the scrutiny of the data sheets that are packed with the film; those data sheets have and are the last word on the characteristics of a film. So check them carefully; it's a good idea to have one on hand for each of the films you are currently using. Also, check their publication dates.

To get back to our consideration of lighting. Without being technical about it, it is suggested you try to avoid extremes of lighting contrast. Because the inherent colors of a scene provide the contrasts color film appreciates, don't go overboard in the matter of lighting contrasts. Generally speaking, illuminate your subject so that no part of him receives more than three or four times as much light as any other part of him.

Lighting is a science. Its components are voltages, watts, lumens, specific distances, color temperatures, reflectance characteristics, and filters, all arrayed on one side of the equation, and with the color film in your camera on the other side. Fortunately, it is one of those sciences that turn out to be less fearsome in application than in theory.

Lighting is also an art. It deals with a lot of variables—variables you introduce in your handling of the lights, the effects you seek, the things you want to soft-pedal or to emphasize, and the character of your subject. Too, your perception of color harmonies and dissonances is a personal, non-technical thing, and therefore a matter of art.

It is in your control of the science and the art of lighting that you demonstrate your status as a color portraitist. My feeling is that a really successful portrait in color is 60 per cent a matter of art, 30 per cent science, and at least 10 per cent bulldog determination not to be frustrated by the unpredictables.

Precisely because color films are so single-minded about their function—recording color—don't tempt them. Like the legendary chameleon that knocked itself out trying to adapt its coloration to a Scotch plaid, color film attempts to respond to every color in sight. And the more nearly it succeeds, the more likely you are to achieve a picture that is a mishmash of color, unless you control the situation. Simplicity in setting and lighting can well be your salvation.

Some of the finest color portraits ever made are so subtle in their coloration that, at first, they do not appear to be in full color. The color is there, but under beautiful control. Obviously, such subtlety is not appropriate for all people and all settings. But keep it in the back of your mind. In color, as in so many aspects of living, too much is much too much.

In portraiture it is very easy to become obsessed with technique, with systems and devices. It is therefore a good idea to stop every so often and contemplate the fact that the end of portraiture is to depict a person, not to display your cleverness. It's the old business about ends and means. The experienced photographer commands his means, driving them expertly to an explicit end.

19
First Aids

Way back in the beginning of this book it was suggested that the well-equipped photographer has some appreciation of art, a little understanding of what is meant by composition, and a sense of the magic in the interplay of lights and shades—good old *chiaroscuro*.

All true. But now it should be added that our well-equipped photographer possesses, as well, a few other, less glamorous skills. He knows, for example, what to do and how to do it if a negative is spotted or scratched, or too thin, or too heavy. He knows how to keep a print from looking amateurish or ordinary. Our man, it appears, has a practical side, which is probably the understatement of this or any year.

SPOTTING

The commonest of flaws in prints or enlargements are little white specks, usually faithful reproductions of dust on the negative. Sometimes, too, you will find dark spots, whose ancestry is more remote and uncertain. Both kinds of spots can be remedied with a little care, plus some sharply pointed re-touching pencils, a card of retouching inks or paints, a few fine brushes, and a well-lighted work space.

Remember this basic rule about all superficial work on a print or nega-tive: *If it is obvious, it is no good.* So, take time to learn how to do it well—so well that it becomes, in the best sense, invisible.

Case 1: White specks in the surface of a print on matte or semi-matte surface. With a sharply pointed retouching pencil (which, unlike an ordinary pencil, leaves no shiny, glinting trail) make a series of small, closely-spaced dots over the white spot area until you have built up a tone that blends with the photographic surroundings. What you will have, actually, is an approxi-mation of a tone of gray as achieved by the half-tone process. And it may be

213

exactly right. If it needs a bit of smoothing, use the tip of a finger or a tuft of cotton, but always gently. Resist the temptation to noodle, to overdo; understatement is generally preferable anyway.

Case 2: White specks on glossy or ferrotyped paper. Because any pencil tends to emboss rather than to mark such a surface, use a fine brush, lightly moistened and carrying a bit of the ink or paint from one of the patches on a retouching card. *Build up* to the desired tone; don't start with a tone that is dark enough. Retouching paints or inks are hard to erase, so avoid the need to do so.

Case 3: Dark or black spots on prints, regardless of surface. Because your objective is to lighten a small area, you use a retouching brush carrying a tiny bit of light-toned paint. No problem.

Obviously, spotting or touching-up a print cannot correct *any* photographic shortcoming. But it can help to make a print look clean and professional; indeed, you will probably not show any print to anyone until you have given it a professional once-over.

RETOUCHING

Because retouching is applied to a negative rather than to a print, it must be done with the sober realization that whatever you do will be registered in all future prints or enlargements from that negative. Retouching is a much more critical process than spotting, and should be practiced carefully. It is also an exacting, eye-straining business; so make your retouching setup as efficient and comfortable as possible.

The classic arrangement is an illuminator—a sheet of heavy glass propped up over a white, evenly-lighted background. The negative lies on the glass, emulsion-side up. If you rig a low-power magnifying glass over the negative (thereby freeing your hands) you will be able to see what you're doing clearly—maybe too clearly.

Your tools are the usual needle-pointed pencils, fine brushes, retouching inks or paints, and tufts of cotton, *plus* a bottle of retouching fluid to put pencil-receptive "tooth" on the surface of the emulsion, and a couple of very fine, very sharp etching knives.

Case 1: A "hole" or clear spot in the negative, resulting in a black speck in a print or enlargement. The object is to add just enough "density" to blend the hole into its surroundings. With either pencil or brush, work up a conglomerate of dots until the "hole" is gone and the area appears normal. Overdoing here will give you a white or light speck in the finished print; so be judicious.

Case 2: A flaw or blemish in which there is excessive metallic silver deposited on the film. (We are not talking about overall densities here; merely limited and very local.) This is serious. Surgery is indicated. With your small, sharp knives try to shave away enough of the silver so that the afflicted spot ceases to be bothersome or conspicuous. This is really finicky work, for a slip of the knife can do great and almost fatal damage. In a normal, non-professional photographic career you may never need to perform a single such surgical operation; but you should know that it can be done.

Superficial treatment of color transparencies or color prints is, like negative surgery, highly specialized. In all probability, you will not become involved. If you do become involved, however, you will have graduated to a level of photographic competence beyond the ken of this book. Selah.

PAPER NEGATIVES

The paper-negative idea or process is an extension of the concept that you can improve on (1) the scene you photographed or (2) the way it was recorded in the poor, dumb negative. It is, indeed, a hangover from the days when photographic pictorialists were more concerned with what they deemed to be "art" than with discernment in the photographer's eye or integrity in the photograph.

The paper negative is mentioned here because it is a kind of extension of the touch-up and retouching techniques we have been talking about. These five steps are basic:

Step 1. A straight enlargement, to the full size of the final picture, made on single-weight, smooth-surface paper; it is printed deeper and darker than normal.

Step 2. When this print is dry, put it face-down on your illuminator and study it, deciding what areas or details need to be changed, darkened, lightened or even removed entirely. Okay. The thing to remember in this process is that you *add* density, at any stage of the game, to achieve *less* density in the next. You make your changes and emphases on the backs of the prints so that they supplement densities on the face of the paper.

Step 3. Make a contact print from (right through, that is) the retouched print of Step 2. This gives you a negative image on the paper.

Step 4. This is your last chance to improve on nature. Go to it, remembering that any tone added now becomes correspondingly lighter in the next and final stage.

Step 5. A contact print from Step 4 may be on any kind or surface of paper you wish, for transparency now ceases to be a factor.

Obviously, the paper-negative process is fine when drastic changes must be made, as when telephone poles or wires have to be eliminated, inappropriate or unsightly buildings erased, or clouds and distant hills added. The freedom this process gives you in correcting the landscape is great; it also involves you in several stages of exposure *through* paper, the fibre of which is bound to show up and dull the rendering of detail.

Some of the relatively new photographic media made for use in the graphic arts, Kodalith Sheet Film, for example, offer the paper-negative enthusiast even greater freedom, plus detail. I cling, however, to my original contention that a lot of time and trouble and misdirected "creativity" can be saved if a little extra care is devoted to the making of a good photograph to begin with.

While we are into this, the neighborhood of hand-made photographs, you should know that there was once a photo-pictorial process called *Bromoil*. Bromoil was intoxicatingly arty, for it involved brushes and pigments and masses of "creativity," all of which bolstered the *amour propre* of some photographers who hadn't quite made the grade as paint-and-canvas artists. Bromoil was neither easy nor simple, and the relatively few people who mastered it deserved the applause they got. You may find a few out-of-print books on Bromoil in your library; an evening with one of them might give you an unexpectedly vivid glimpse of what it meant to be a pictorial photographer 70 or 80 years ago.

TONING

A really good black-and-white enlargement is a fine accomplishment. But sometimes a bit of appropriate overall toning may make it even better, more realistic, more natural—or more fantastic. Toning simply involves changing the customary silver grays and blacks to tones of color—blue, brown, red, yellow, or green. It depends upon the subject, the lighting, and the effect you seek. Normally, subjects and tones would line up like this:

Indoor Portraits ....brown
Snow Scenes ....blue
Fall Landscapes ....brown
Sunlighted Summer Landscapes ....green
Marine Views ....blue

But perhaps you have a sunrise effect on snow, and you know that the light was reddish. Red snow? Fantastic! Yes, and if not overdone, capable of being very effective.

Toning techniques are of two major types:

First, the gray or black silver forming the image may be wholly or partially replaced by other metals or their compounds, including sulphur, iron, gold, or selenium. These are generally the brown and blue toners. Because some intensification of the photographic image takes place during the toning process, it is best to begin with prints that are a shade on the light side.

Second, under the influence of the toning bath, the silver image of the print may attract dye in the toner and hold it in an insoluble form. This type of toning process affords more variety, but the colors tends to be less stable than in the first group and the highlights tend to color up rather than to remain clear.

Toning, especially in the first of the two groups, is not difficult. But only repeated experience can guide you in the matter of when to yank the print from the toner. Overtoning can look muddy, and undertoning may seem to be some sort of processing accident. You will find many excellent toners readily available, all made up and ready for use. Kodak Rapid Selenium Toner is fine for warmish tones; Kodak Blue Toner is self-explanatory.

INTENSIFICATION

It is unlikely, but someday you may find that you have an obviously anemic negative from which even No. 5 paper isn't going to give you a full-bodied print. A re-take is impossible. What to do?

It is just possible that chemical treatment—*intensification*—may save the day, *if* the lack of density is the result of underdevelopment; if the overall weakness of the negative is the result of *underexposure* . . . sorry.

Every formulary lists several intensifiers. Get to know one of them and what to expect of it. Keep it in your photographic bag of tricks, and hope you never have to haul it out.

REDUCTION

Should you have a negative too dense to print on even No. 0 paper, there are several possible remedies, each with its own set of variables and imponderables. The *reduction* of silver in the developed image is accomplished in a physical sense: There is simply less of it there when the process is complete. As used here, *reduction* should not be confused with the chemical reduction of exposed silver bromide during the original development.

Reducers fall into these three general groups:

Subtractive reducers take equal amounts of silver from all densities. They are generally used to correct for overexposure or fog.

Proportional reducers take from each density an amount proportional to that density; they are used to correct high contrast.

Super-proportional are precisely that—unusually active proportional reducers.

Reducers are standard items in every photographic formulary. As with intensifiers, know how to use one of them, and reserve it for emergencies.

20
A Few
Special Techniques

A FEW SPECIAL TECHNIQUES

In the course of growing up, photographically, it is wholly in order to experiment, to try a few things that are beyond the range of normal photographic activity. Some of those special techniques may not appeal to you at all; some you will try—and forget; and a few will become permanent parts of your standard operating procedure.

MULTIPLE EXPOSURE

This involves two or more separate images on a single frame of film. You have undoubtedly seen what happens in an accidental double exposure; two separate images are scrambled together, inextricably and meaninglessly.

In a deliberate multiple exposure there is no scrambling at all; everything is reasonably clean and sharp and realistic, save that, if you can believe the evidence before you, something abnormal and contrary to nature is going on. One character may appear two or more times in the same picture, or there may be a ghost wandering around. Or Barbara may appear to have got herself inside a milk bottle...

(Because many modern cameras have built-in double exposure prevention devices, be sure that your camera has a mechanical over-ride so that, when you really want to, you *can* make multiple exposures on a single frame.)

This kind of nonsense is about as old as photography itself, and fun to perpetrate.

Suppose you'd like to make a picture of Bill playing table tennis doubles with himself as his own partner. No sweat. The camera is set up on its tripod at the far end of the pingpong table; you check to make sure that the lens angle is wide enough to include both courts at the other end. Okay, black out the background completely; it should show no detail, even with a flash at camera. Next pose Bill in the right-hand court, in the act of delivering his favorite explosive serve—and make the shot. Without advancing the film or changing camera position, move Bill over to the other court and pose him again, this time registering awe, admiration, ridicule, or complete apathy over his "partner's" service. Another flash, another exposure, and that's that.

The "ghost" business is similar, of course, except that this time you want the background to show very clearly and right *through* your ghost. The variations and permutations of this sort of thing are practically endless; for most of us, one or two experiments are usually adequate. (Of course, two negatives can be printed together, if you'd rather work that way.)

The third double-exposure type is considerably more difficult; Barbara-inside-a-bottle obviously involves a close-up of the bottle and a medium-long shot of Barbara. As in much other trick work, view cameras with ground-glass focusing screens can help you materially; you can actually grease-pencil the outline of the bottle on the ground glass, thereby assuring a perfect fit for Barbara. The exposure dealing with Barbara obviously has to be one in which there is little, if any, other detail.

If you have considerable interest in the nature-faking antics of photography, why not work up a local exhibit or competition devoted exclusively to demonstrations that, contrary to legend, photographs not only lie, but do a good job of it?

Fig. 20-1. All from one—by means of multiple exposure.

PHOTOGRAMS

Photograms, or photographs made without benefit of a camera, have a basic integrity of their own. They do not pretend to involve anything more than shadows made permanent. And nothing could be easier to make.

Arrange an object or a group of small objects on a sheet of photographic paper, with a fixed and undiffused light source about two feet overhead. When the arrangement suits you, turn on the light for a few seconds, then develop the print. It will show the arranged objects as sharp, clean, white silhouettes against a jet-black background.

Easy as it is, the photogram offers tremendous scope for imagination, for play with light. The bold black-and-white patterns have decorative qualities, as the illustration of a photogram-covered dinette wall indicates.

Fig. 20-2. Photograms, or shadowgraphs, of kitchen and dining ware make a reasonably appropriate decoration for a wall such as this between kitchen and dinette. No camera was used. The strong blacks and whites of the photograms are set off nicely by the dividers.

Technically, photograms are completely casual and non-critical. If you have a supply of out-dated or questionable paper, make yourself some photograms. If you're not careful, you may find yourself dipping into supplies of brand *new* paper. . . .

LINE DRAWINGS FROM PRINTS

There are two methods by which you can obtain useful and vivid line drawings from photographs. And the easier, more obvious method is generally the better. Put a print of the object to be translated into a line drawing on the glass of your illuminator, tape a piece of bond paper over it, and then, with pen or pencil, simply trace in the significant lines. If you use tracing cloth instead of bond paper, you can use the tracing as a negative and make as many prints or enlargements as you require.

The second method involves drawing directly on the surface of the print with drafting ink. When you are sure you have inked in everything that should be inked in, dunk the print into a bleaching solution that eradicates the silver image, leaving only the inked lines. Chances are that when the bleaching process is complete, you will find a couple of details you forgot to ink in. So, back to the old drawing board.

COPYING

Today there is much less of the laborious old business of camera-copying documents, charts, printed pages, and such; the automated copying machine to be found in most libraries, offices, and schools has very kindly taken over. This is not to say, however, that the technique of photographic copying is either a lost or a dying art. It has, rather, been freed to concentrate on the kinds of work it does supremely well.

Symmetry is basic to good copying. The camera (on a tripod) is accurately centered on the material to be copied (the "copy"), and the illumination, left and right, is nicely balanced to provide uniform, glareless, and shadowless lighting. The strict centering of the camera and the precise paralleling of film plane and copy are not mere suggestions—they are fundamental.

Because individual reflectors and lamps vary a little, it is a good idea to build up the lighting for each copying job methodically. Illuminate the copy with *one* of the two lights, changing the vertical as well as the horizontal angle until the copy is as perfectly lighted as it ever can be with one light. Turn the light off and repeat the process with the other light. Then, with both lights on, lighting should be right.

If you plan to do a lot of copying, it may pay you to build a permanent copying stand. But otherwise, the basic scheme of copying is so simple that you can get along very well with a drawing board (to thumb-tack the copy to), a camera tripod, and two reflector floods in separate, free-standing holders.

Just as it is important that the copying setup be geometrically and optically accurate, it is also important that exposure and development be on the

SUGGESTED CAMERA SETTINGS FOR PICTURES OF TELEVISION IMAGES

KODAK Film	Black-and-White Television Set		Color Television Set	
	Leaf-Type Shutter	Focal-Plane Shutter	Leaf-Type Shutter	Focal-Plane Shutter
VERICHROME Pan PLUS-X Pan	$1/30$ sec f/4	$1/8$ sec f/8	$1/30$ sec f/2.8	$1/8$ sec f/5.6
TRI-X Pan	$1/30$ sec f/5.6 ↓ 8	$1/8$ sec f/11 ↓ 16	$1/30$ sec f/4 ↓ 5.6	$1/8$ sec f/8 ↓ 11
KODACHROME-X* EKTACHROME-X* KODACOLOR-X*	$1/8$ sec f/2.8 or $1/15$ sec f/2	$1/8$ sec f/2.8	$1/4$ sec f/2.8 or $1/8$ sec f/2	$1/4$ sec f/2.8 or $1/8$ sec f/2
High Speed EKTACHROME (Daylight)*—with Normal Processing	$1/15$ sec f/2.8 ↓ 4	$1/8$ sec f/4 ↓ 5.6	$1/8$ sec f/2.8 ↓ 4	$1/8$ sec f/2.8 ↓ 4
High Speed EKTACHROME (Daylight)*—with ESP-1 Processing for a Speed of ASA 400	$1/30$ sec f/4	$1/8$ sec f/8	$1/30$ sec f/2.8	$1/8$ sec f/5.6

Important: With leaf-type shutters, use a shutter speed of $1/30$ second or slower. With focal-plane shutters, use a shutter speed of $1/8$ second or slower to avoid dark streaks in your pictures.

*Pictures of color television taken without a filter will look blue-green. With the color films in the table you can use a KODAK Color Compensating Filter CC40R over your camera lens to help bring out the reds in your pictures. Increase the exposure suggested in the table by 1 stop.

Note: The ↓ symbol indicates the lens opening halfway between the two f-numbers.

LEGALITIES OF COPYING

The copyright laws are designed to protect us all from the raids of operators whose joy is to capitalize on somebody else's work. The respectability of automatic copiers in hushed libraries is no guarantee against hanky-panky. So protect yourself. Do not get involved in copying someone else's work, if you expect to use the copied material for other than your own personal use. If you do plan extra-personal use of the copy, get permission; otherwise, you can be in serious trouble.

TV images, money, bonds, citizenship papers, and a lot of other things are surrounded by a variety of copying restrictions. Because they vary—and also because they get pretty complicated—I suggest you consult the nearest federal officer if or when you bump into a copying problem involving official documents.

COPIES FROM TRANSPARENCIES

Here's an odd situation. While it is perfectly possible to make black-and-white copies of color transparencies, it is much easier and probably less expensive to have color duplicates made by your regular color processing lab.

If home-grown black-and-white copies of transparencies are really important to you, you can:

1. Use your enlarger to produce a moderate enlargement of the transparency, maybe something like $3'' \times 4''$, on a piece of slow fine-grain pan film. From the resulting negative, you can make as many prints or enlargements as you wish. (This enlarger technique is one of the very few in which exposures will be short enough to justify fitting a shuttered lens to your enlarger.)

2. Set up your transparency in a light box and photograph it, same size, with a camera loaded with the slow fine-grain pan film. One-to-one setups require special lens extenders and modified exposure. (There are, as your dealer will be pleased to tell you, neat little contraptions called duplicators which, fitted to your camera in place of the usual lens, afford one-to-one copying almost, but not quite, automatically. And, if you have a view camera with a long bellows extension, you can actually enlarge as you copy.)

3. Apply the technique of the paper negative (see p. 215). With the transparency mounted in the negative carrier of your enlarger, make a paper negative of the desired size, touch it up as you may wish, and then make as many prints as you want. Minimum sweat.

Sometimes, teachers, salesmen, preachers, students, politicians, almost all of us—need to make a slide presentation of some sort. Usually we must include both new and old material. Well, the cheapest and easiest way to go about it is to shoot everything, color or not, on color slide film with your regular 35mm camera, and send the exposed film off for ordinary processing. In a day or so, your material will be back with each shot neatly mounted and ready to be put in sequence for your presentation.

In only the rarest of cases will you be justified in setting up a copying technique efficient enough to compete economically with that of a professional processing station. Just because you *can,* don't feel that you have to do everything.

21
Applied Photography

The term "applied photography" used to be a euphemism for commercial photography. But today it covers more and more of the total function of photography. For very few of us regard photography as an end in itself; our real concern is what we get *by means of* photography. We apply photography in order to attain some desired end.

If all the highly specialized technical applications of photography were included, a yard-long list of uses could be compiled. But the length of that list is less important than the fact that on it, every now and then, we encounter applications that have meaning and utility for us.

Only a very few general areas of applied photography are indicated here. More are not needed; because you, with your expanding understanding and appreciation of photography, will undoubtedly add and interpolate freely, creating your own list or catalog.

Therefore the following categories are presented as a kind of "sampler." Some of the applications require, as has been indicated, special equipment; most of them can be undertaken on the basis of your present capability and equipment.

ADVERTISING

Advertising is really the father of applied photography. Inevitably, some advertising art is junk but the level of technical excellence and creativity is, in general, high. Now and then, indeed, real masterpieces emerge. Some mail-order catalogs involve photography of a very high order.

The photographer who seeks to serve advertising's purposes must be more than competent; he must be ingenious, versatile, and imaginative. He must,

229

most importantly, be able to take an idea sketched by an art director and—in photographic terms—make it sing.

If photography has been inspired by advertising, as it has, it is equally true that advertising has been benefited and elevated by photography. It has been, and is, a unique kind of team work. To make the team, you'd better be good.

AERIAL PHOTOGRAPHY

The science of photogrammetry is a field apart. Most of us do not and cannot command the resources of specially-equipped planes, cameras, and lab techniques that are necessary for precise aerial mapping or even for ecological analysis.

But most of us *can* make aerial views of our home, our town, our schools, or our parks, that can be useful in community planning, in real estate development, in school board planning, in farm operations, and so on.

You will need the cooperation of a pilot with a small plane, preferably a high-wing monoplane that offers full visibility from the cockpit. The pilot should be briefed on the pattern you wish to fly, and on the most desirable altitudes and orientation. It will usually be possible to open a door or a window so that you (properly safe-belted) and your camera will have vision unimpeded by glass or plexiglass.

Use a camera with which you are completely familiar, preferably one that can be reloaded very easily. A direct viewfinder or a SLR is desirable. *Never* expose your camera to the slipstream just outside the cockpit; it can tear a bellows camera apart and subject even a solid camera to severe buffeting.

Most of your aerials will be obliques, *i.e.,* angled rather than vertical shots. For maximum detail, however, shoot as nearly vertical as possible. The altitude you choose will be an almost direct function of the area to be included in your picture. Small area = relatively low altitude.

Shutter speed should be as high as possible, compatible with adequate exposure, not because of the plane's flying speed but because of the vibration. A shutter speed of 1/250 sec. will be about the slowest you can tolerate. A filter will almost always be needed—a haze filter for color and a K2 for panchromatic film.

ARCHITECTURAL PHOTOGRAPHY

This is, or can be, interesting because it involves so many considerations: time of day for best sun angle, detail revelation, vertical or horizontal distortion, color (of the building, its surroundings, or the prevailing light), and most advantageous viewpoint.

A view camera, with its ground-glass screen for accurate composition of the scene and its distortion-correcting adjustments, is fine for architectural work, but far from necessary. Any good camera, with a lens of appropriate focal length, can handle the job, if *you* can.

Keep in mind the needs of your client. The architect, for example, regards his building as a work of art; to the owner it is something to use or perhaps to sell as profitably as possible. To its neighborhood it is an asset or a liability, depending upon its relationship to local history or to the current and future needs of the community.

Good architectural "portraits" almost always demand good sky, embellished with impressive clouds. You know how to take care of that.

ASTRONOMICAL PHOTOGRAPHY

Here is another area in which most of us simply have to admit that we are limited. For the biggest, the most expensive, the most complex of optical telescopes are all, essentially, highly specialized cameras. You cannot compete with Palomar.

However, there is much you *can* do, even with very simple equipment. For example, one of the most charming of photographs is a portrait of star-trails, or star tracks. In it you sense the roll of Earth as the stars wheel by. If your chosen view includes the Pole Star, Polaris, and a bit of a tree or some other early detail, your star-trail picture will relate understandably in terms of direction and location. The technique is simply to position your camera, on a firm tripod, and to make a long time exposure—five minutes, half an hour, five hours or whatever you want. Time doesn't matter as long as extraneous light doesn't get into the lens.

Photographs of the moon are even simpler, for the moon, as we see it, is nothing more than an object in full sunlight. Conventional snapshot exposures will do the trick. But the moon will look much less impressive than it did to your eye, for its diameter will be only about 1/50 or 1/25 inch on the negative; in our present state of sophistication in lunar matters, such tiny images carry very little wallop.

Photographs by moonlight aren't simple, for our moonlight is nothing but watered-down sunlight reflected from a small and distant sphere. Maybe you can "read a newspaper" by the light of the moon, but your camera finds it tough going; time exposures become very much in order.

Eclipses are good picture material. With ordinary equipment you can record succeeding stages of both lunar and solar eclipses and produce interesting conversation pieces; for scientifically significant photographs *extra-ordinary* equipment is needed. What you can do is photograph the progress of an eclipse by a series of exposures, all on the same film, and at fixed intervals, say five minutes. The camera must be absolutely stationary and aimed to include the arc of the eclipse, from its beginning to its climax at or near totality. Exposure will increase in proportion to the increasing obscurement.

Solar eclipses are, of course, more exciting than eclipses of the moon. But they are also more difficult, for you must deal with an incredible range of brilliance; for all but the final, most nearly obscured shots you will need a neutral density filter. And there are real hazards even in aiming your camera; even a hasty squint, directly or through the viewfinder, can literally be blinding. You can make a pretty good eye protector out of *two* thicknesses of exposed (off camera) and fully developed black-and-white film. Color film makes an unsafe viewing medium; also avoid reliance on sunglasses or "smoked" glass. Protect your eyes, always!

There are many devices made for coupling cameras to spotting scopes or telescopes or binoculars. Obviously, the less precise the coupling, the more make-shift the photography. Some of the better semi-pro telescopes (the Questar, for example) provide accessory means for smooth, accurate positioning of the camera without deranging the scope.

MACRO- AND MICROPHOTOGRAPHY

At the other end of the line from astronomical work is the photography of the extremely small—macrophotography (low power magnification) and microphotography (high power magnification.) In some respects this kind of work is easier, for you have control of both the subject and its illumination. On the other hand, precision is a must. There is standardized equipment, as well as procedure, for adapting cameras to microscopes. Incidentally, microscopy in color can be downright beautiful.

As for macroscopy, check with your dealer on the matter of extreme-closeup lenses. You can use supplementary lenses, of course, but I think you'll find more satisfaction in replacing your regular lens with a special closeup unit.

BUSINESS OR INDUSTRIAL PHOTOGRAPHY

There's a broad field, if there ever was one. Look over recent issues of *Fortune* for some hint of its broadness; then check the library for some of the hundreds of specialized industrial journals. Every business, every industry, has its own photographic needs; and some of them can be very far removed from the old-fashioned picture of "our plant," "our product," or "the founder." Incidentally, an up-and-coming young business man can use his ordinary 35mm camera to make slides that can supplement his written reports and make his contributions to conferences stand out brilliantly.

Fig. 21-1. A fine example of single-light-source photography. The man is at work, and at ease. The strong shadows make the type stand out in sharp relief.

CLUB PROJECT PHOTOGRAPHY

Photography, intelligently used, can bring new value and meaning to members of all of the thousands of big and little clubs, all over this club-happy land.

Travel clubs, for example, exist primarily to give members the chance to show the latest slides they made during their latest vacation trips. You, as a knowledgeable photographer, have a tremendous advantage in such groups, for your slides of even an unpretentious trip can make the average traveler's work look feeble. For you eschew the obvious, the postcard-type shots, and concentrate on those experiences that made your trip unique.

Applied photography can and does serve 4-H and Future Farmer members by providing visual records and proof-of-project progress; advancement and prestige depend on such records.

Some club activities, such as scuba diving, spelunking, and surfing, may need specialized photographic equipment. But the majority of club activities can be adequately illustrated by means of standard equipment in reasonably skilled hands. Yours.

HISTORY-RELATED PHOTOGRAPHY

With his camera, a teacher, a city planner, a politician, a minister, or a student can make vivid the course of history in any community. With the help of aerial photography he may even build a pictorial bridge between the past and the future. All it takes, really, is a little thinking and a little imagination. Plus the application of both thought and imagination to camera use.

In all areas of applied photography your mastery of the camera has to be assumed; you cannot afford to waste time worrying about photographic techniques. You have a job to do.

HOME PHOTOGRAPHY

Every new home, whether it's one in a row or one in a million, is a story full of vivid, eloquent pictures—from the first noodling of floor plans to the triumphant moving-in. And thereafter there are stories in its decoration, its remodeling, its repainting, landscaping, and all the rest, including, of course, its changing inhabitants. And these illustrated stories can be of considerably more importance than any superficially impressive pictures of merely "pretty" places. They can be useful.

Construction pictures—before, during, and after—can report on the way the place was built; as such they tell much better stories than blueprints and specifications.

Interiors, with and without furniture, can serve as guides to decorators, amateur or professional. Too, they constitute records, in case of fire or other disaster, to show proof of the quantity and quality of furnishings, thereby substantiating insurance claims.

Speaking of insurance, it is sound policy to photograph a house, room by room, including closets and work shops. Such pictures are visible proof, if proof is ever needed, that your standard of living was thus-and-so. Insurance companies find them more truly descriptive than general lists of claims. A set of these pictures, dated, belongs in the home-owner's safety-deposit box.

HOBBY PICTURES

It is useless to try to go into any particulars at all, as far as hobbies are concerned. All that can be said is that there isn't a hobby of any kind that cannot be made more interesting, and more fun by the application of photography.

With the hobbyist providing the specialized knowledge, the perception, and the interest, the photographs cannot easily be dull. Not, at least, to the hobbyist and his fellow hobbyists. The photographs enhance one of the finest aspects of any hobby, the sharing of your findings and experiences with others who understand your enthusiasm .

SCHOOL-RELATED PHOTOGRAPHY

This is another enormous, almost unlimited field for applied photography. It includes practically everything from acrobatics to zoology. Faculty, students, and administrators all need it; and, today, more and more of them are using it. Academic reports, papers, and surveys need it; teachers' lectures need it; yearbooks and school journals need it; even the Board needs it.

Providing the pictures a school needs could be a life work. There are worse ones.

STILL-LIFE AND TABLE-TOP PHOTOGRAPHY

This is a phase of applied photography that needs some firm-handed overhaul. For it has suffered, generation after generation, from a bad case of cuteness. It's a disease that seems to afflict workers in other miniature media. Did you ever look at the miniature "sculpture," the figurines, the little animals in a second-rate gift shop? They are atrocious as art and impossible in terms of taste. And the more they attempt to be realistic, to tell a little story, the worse they get.

Table-top photography is, simply, the photography of small objects, lighted and arranged to imitate a full-scale scene of some sort. I once encouraged a group of Boy Scouts to try their hands at table-toppery using my equipment. They got the idea fast, and came up with fascinating and tremendous scenes they proposed to create in photography. Train crashes (involving small-gauge model trains, of course), aerial dog fights, ocean liners on stormy seas, and so on. But their enthusiasm went into decline when their painted backgrounds began to look phony (out-of-scale, to be exact), when they found that tin soldiers somehow looked wrong alongside a miniature diesel, or a diving Spad looked just plain ridiculous, with its shadow plastered all over the background "sky." Very sensibly, they gave up the whole idea and went out to play ball.

The trouble with many table-top photographers is that they didn't go out to play ball. They kept right on and produced vapid little scenes of shiny little shepherdesses or of crudely cast deer drinking at poorly concealed mirror pools.

Table-toppery can be fun—and imaginative and creative and all the rest—but unless it is done with great skill and taste...anyone for a quick game?

Figs. 21-2 to 21-6. Table Toppery. On the next few pages is a group of table-top photographs exploring some of the possibilities and problems of the "art." Fig. 21-2. Is it a gigantic knife or a subminiature locomotive? Obviously, objects do not belong together merely because they are small. **Scale** is the important thing. Fig. 21-3. As a picture of a caboose, this is fine, but it is spoiled by the obvious casting seams in the figure of the brakeman. Fig. 21-4. An effort to produce a scene in the railway yards at night failed because the crushed rock (coffee grounds) between the tracks is very much too rocky, and because the highlights on the embossed metal of the cars are unrealistically bright. Fig. 21-5. By eliminating all attempts to be cute about atmosphere and landscaping, this depiction of passing trains comes off much better. Fig. 21-6. Here's "atmosphere" gone hog wild. The little model of the hospital ship sits unconvincingly on a sea of crinkled aluminum, and the dramatic backdrop of painted clouds, sky, and lightning is merely silly.

Fig. 21-2 (above). Fig. 21-3 (below).

Fig. 21-4 (above). Fig. 21-5 (below).

Fig. 21-6.

22
So What?

Millions of curling prints are stored forlornly away on closet shelves or in bureau drawers. Hundreds of thousands of enlargements, mounted and unmounted, lie in forgotten clumps of dusty envelopes. And the negatives for all those prints—well, no one really knows where they are.

At best, this is a stupid state of affairs; at worst, it is a colossal waste of perfectly good time, energy, material, and money. Should everything be kept? Not at all. Take inventory of your accumulated photographs now and then. You will find many that have no present or possible use. Throw them out. You will find others that reflect unkindly on your ability as a photographer. If they cannot be redeemed by additional cropping, by new enlarging, and if they have no personal, sentimental, historical, or potential significance, throw them out.

In your inventory, you may very well come across forgotten treasure— material that your new knowledge and ability can transform into things of beauty or undreamed-of utility.

Some sort of file for your negatives, transparencies, and prints is necessary. And the sooner it is set up, the better.

WHAT KIND OF FILE?

One man's file, of course, may be another man's Miscellaneous Department. It all depends upon how you use photography. If portraiture is your specialty, your file will be mostly a matter of names and dates; if you travel a lot, classification may well be in terms of place-names and dates. Unless you are operating an extensive picture agency, there is no need for an elaborate Dewey-decimal-type system. The good old alphabet is still our basic tool, for it easily classifies people as well as places and things and categories.

241

The physical form of your file will be determined by the size and format of your equipment. If you make color slides exclusively, you have many good, covered, compartmentalized files from which to choose. But if you also use your 35mm camera for negative color or for black-and-white work, you'll need a file that will take strips of 35mm film, four or five frames to each strip. Larger negatives or transparencies should have individual paper envelopes. Remember, dust, handling, and heat are the enemies.

Like black-and-white negatives, color transparencies are *originals;* prints, duplicates, and enlargements can be easily made from them but not *vice versa.* So protect them.

Identify everything! It may seem silly, now, to record the *Who, What, Where,* and *When* for each shot; you think you'll remember. I hope you do, but don't depend on it. Whether or not you also record the photographic data —film, lens, filter, and exposure—depends on the kind of photographer you are. If you are naturally systematic, you'll do it automatically; if you would only *like* to be systematic, you'll start out bravely and then slide into a permanent lapse.

But a file of some sort for your negatives, color or black-and-white, and for your transparencies is a basic need. Establish a simple, workable file early, and keep it up.

WHAT ABOUT PRINTS?

Because prints and enlargements can be replaced (if you know where to put your hand on the negatives), the need for print files is not so vital. Still, bundles of assorted prints serve no purpose at all; they cannot be enjoyed. And the print you'd like to show someone is always the print that got out of the bundle. Even the old-fashioned, black-paged photo album, with its scratchy white-ink captions and clumsy mountings was better than that. It was seldom a thing of beauty, but it had the virtue of preserving a lot of record pictures so that they could be found and enjoyed. The closest modern parallel to the old-style album has white pages and overlays of clear plastic designed to keep the prints in position. And it works pretty well, especially with standard-size color prints. You will find several variations on this theme in the shops.

The albums favored today are essentially yearbooks, one book per year. Thus a basic kind of classification is established, and some sort of organization is better than none. The best such books I have seen combine both prints and small enlargements. In putting together such a book, you have a chance to exercise editorial control, to emphasize and to "feature" people, places, or events.

Some photographers paste a print on the envelope containing the appropriate negative; thus, the negative file is also a print file. It's a workable plan.

And that's the nub of all photo-filing systems. If your system doesn't work, it's almost worse than no file at all.

One thing is certain: If you establish and maintain an adequate photo file, you become a member of the photographic aristocracy. In addition, if you set up a plan so that your pictures can actually be enjoyed, you become elite among the aristocrats.

PICTURES AT WORK

Prints have uses beyond files, or albums, or letter enclosures. The simple, almost automatic record-keeping capacity of photographs has never been used as it might. For example, you probably have some sort of household insurance, which covers the contents of your home against assorted risks and hazards. But do you have a photographic record of your home, room by room, to back up your claim that you had such-and-such, or were equipped to do thus-and-so?

Another kind of record is, surprisingly, often missed: the before-and-after pictorial recording of changes in a home's decoration, of additions to the house, or of changes in the landscaping. Seems obvious and rudimentary, but most people anxiously await the *completion* of any remodelling project before a camera is unleashed; by that time, it's too late to get a comparable "before" shot.

The building of a home or of any structure that is important to you deserves its own photo-recording, from the ground up. Incidentally, the fact that many individuals, school boards, and even corporations overlook the documentation value of photography may offer both amateurs and young professionals certain opportunities; give it a thought.

Photographs have been and are being used in a tremendous variety of specialized ways—business cards, book plates, place cards, change-of-address notices, calendar decorations, and so on and on. Probably the single greatest use of personal pictures is in holiday greeting cards. Sometimes the greetings are mass-produced by commercial photofinishers, using negatives supplied by the individual customer. And sometimes they are made in the individual's own darkroom, where the project becomes a production-line lark for several members of the family. Photographic greeting cards need not be self-conscious or "clever"; they need only be reasonably appropriate and reflect your personality and your photographic standards.

Line the underside of a glass-bottomed tray with a mosaic of prints, make lamp shades of big enlargements, plaster your walls with prints, but remember, too much of even a very good thing is . . . too much.

This brings us to the use of enlargements in home decoration. It's a great idea, but a challenging one. The challenge is in the ability of a photograph to face up to familiarity. If a picture grows on you, acquiring new interest and meaning, day after day, it certainly rates a place on the wall in your home, along with your old-favorite watercolors, etchings, and prints from the work of the masters. If your fine, big enlargement cannot meet such competition, take it down and try another. Your satisfaction will be all the greater when, finally, one of your prints survives the competition and makes the grade.

Fig. 22-1. Before you go to the trouble and expense of putting up a framed enlargement in your home, make sure the picture is live-with-able. Some—and maybe some very good—photographs may have uncomfortable connotations for you; others, such as this old portrait of Mt. Vernon, turned out to be loaded with amiable nostalgia.

In some rooms—playrooms and family rooms especially—you can go wild with your pictures. Use whole panels of them; make a frieze of them, if you like, all around the room.

For any "permanent" exhibition, prints should be mounted on sheets of thick, stiff cardboard, ⅛-inch thick or thicker. Otherwise, they will tend to curl out of shape. Dry mounting tissue—fine glue in tissue-thin sheets—is much the most satisfactory adhesive. The actual mounting is the product of heat and pressure, both applied with a dry (non-steaming) iron. Big studios have great, heavy, automatic presses; for most of us the family iron, used with discretion and according to the directions, will achieve a smooth, clean, non-buckling bond.

Traditionally (and officially, in some groups), exhibition prints are displayed on $16'' \times 20''$ mounts. It happens that this is a size that shows off an $11'' \times 14''$ enlargement very nicely, if the print is centered laterally and given just a little more room at the bottom than at the top. Speaking of prints and mounts, resist the temptation to "fancify" things with elaborate or multi-color borders and underlays. Usually, a single thin black line around the print will suffice; it will not call attention to itself and will keep the emphasis where it belongs.

VACATION OR VOCATION?

For most amateur photographers, photography is a vacation, a change of pace, a recreation; as such, it is hard to beat. Its rewards and satisfactions grow, gamma-like, with each increment in skill and understanding.

But there are others to whom photography is sure to appeal as a *vocation,* a career, a profession. If the smell of hypo, the promise of a fine negative, or the sparkle of a beautiful print—your own or in an ad or magazine—makes you sit up and say "That's for me!" you may be on your professional way.

But it takes more than appreciation and enthusiasm. Exactly *what* it takes depends on the aspect of photography that interests you most: technical lab work, portraiture, photojournalism, scientific applications, sports, travel, commercial studio work, or whatever.

It is certain that you cannot excel in *all* of these areas of photographic specialization. To be really good in any one of them takes a lot of doing. But here's a kind of checklist of fundamentals for all but the purely technical aspects of the art:

1. Know your photography. Books, I hope, help, and there are many excellent ones. But actual practice is vital. There are a number of good schools of photography (Kodak has a printed list [#T-17] of them available free on request to Dept. 641, 343 State Street, Rochester, N.Y. 14650), some of which lead to special certificates and some to undergraduate degrees.

2. Get the habit of perception, recognition, and appreciation of the visible world. Study photographs of all sorts, from snapshots to salon prints and from

lucky news shots to the most carefully contrived studio shot for an expensive advertisement. Study all the art you encounter. Haunt the art galleries. And, if you possibly can, take a course in sketching or watercolor.

3. Develop the knack of improvisation, for you may have to extemporize props, costumes, settings, and lighting. Know something about basic electrical hook-ups and hazards.

4. Remain flexible, for today's standard procedures and ideas may be outdated by tomorrow afternoon.

5. Be willing to pitch in and get your hands dirty, for studio photography or location work can be rough and tough.

6. Develop, if you can, a sound sense of business. Competition is neither kind nor forgiving; for survival's sake, operate on a strictly business basis.

OVER TO YOU

Way back at the start of this book it was said that you are the most important part of any camera you may ever own. It's still true. Furthermore, you are the essential ingredient in every good negative, every revealing picture you'll ever make. May your negatives sparkle, and may your finished work speak well of you.

Index

Index